THE EXPERIENCE OF
ECONOMIC GROWTH:

Case Studies in Economic History

THE
EXPERIENCE
OF
ECONOMIC
GROWTH

Case Studies in Economic History

Edited by

BARRY E. SUPPLE

Random House   New York

TO

Caroline, David, and Timothy

Preface

Of all the problems with which economists have wrestled over the last two hundred years, that of the economic development of nations is undoubtedly the most susceptible to historical analysis. But, of course, it is not only economists who have sought growth patterns in the past. Historians, urged on by intellectual curiosity, and the new-found interests of the social sciences as a whole, have also produced a large and growing body of empirical studies of the growth process. It is the modest object of this book to bring together some of these essays for the convenience of students of economic history and economic growth.

There are already in print various collections of readings in the theory of economic growth, as well as of studies of twentieth-century economies. (Some of these are listed in the Selected Bibliography of this work.) But as far as I know there is no previous book of essays in the economic history of development which ranges over a suitable time-span and touches on the past experience of economies which are now industrialized. As far as its use by university students is concerned, it is hoped that this collection will satisfy part of the needs of courses in economic growth which demand some historical perspective and courses in history which are oriented toward development or modern industrialization.

Compiling such a work is a frustrating task. The potential candidates for inclusion are multitudinous with respect to the countries studied, the topics considered, and the level of sophistication attained. The solution adopted here has been to exercise an eclectic choice. In Part II, "International Comparisons and the Lessons of History," will be found comparative studies which attempt to establish overall patterns of economic development—patterns which both delineate and, hopefully, explain the course and structure of historical growth. Parts III and IV are logically concerned with the experience of the pioneer of industrialization, Great Britain, and of the most successful nineteenth-century economy, that of the United States. Unfortunately, space would not permit a comparably detailed treatment of other examples of successful development, and a virtue was therefore made of a necessity by a highly selective choice of countries and topics for inclusion. In Part V, for example, France is represented by two articles on the possible causes of its relatively poor economic performance in the nineteenth century, and Italy by a discussion which relates it to the problems of modern "dual economies." Since space, and the shortage of available material, did not allow a satisfactory treatment of Germany it was reluctantly decided to omit consideration of that economy entirely. No such collection would be satisfactory, however, without some analysis of the two "latecomers," Russia and Japan (Part VI).

Since comprehensiveness was obviously impossible, the principal aim was to provide examples of historical essays on a limited number of economies, written at various levels of theoretical and historical sophistication. Economists, on reading this book, will therefore find themselves on familiar as well as new ground, while it is hoped that the language of even the most technical study will not be too technical for historians. With the exception of the general essays, the time period is in most cases confined to the generations before 1914—the epoch in which modern industrialization became not only a possibility but an irreversible fact.

Some apology for the length of the editorial introduction (Part I) may be appropriate here. Its object is to provide a broader and more comprehensive framework for the specialist studies which follow. It was felt necessary to discuss the nature of economic history and its relationships with theory, to outline some of the problems which theorists encounter when they study the process of development, and to offer a general survey of economic history and growth as a background to the more detailed essays. Undoubtedly, many students will be able to dispense with a reading of one or more of these sections. In any case, in deference to instructors whose students may use this book, I have avoided as far as possible giving any note of finality to the discussion. This particularly applies to the section on the theoretical approach, which is largely confined to a presentation of some of the topics normally discussed by economists. As a further aid to students, I have prefaced each Part with a brief introduction, and have included a Selected Bibliography of further readings.

My thanks are due to Professor William Letwin of the Massachusetts Institute of Technology, Consulting Editor in Economics for Random House, for his editorial patience, and to my wife and children for their domestic forbearance.

BARRY E. SUPPLE

Contents

PART
· I ·

INTRODUCTION

ECONOMIC HISTORY, ECONOMIC THEORY, AND ECONOMIC GROWTH

In the relatively short space of the last fifteen years the discussion of economic development[1] has provoked an outpouring of analytical and empirical literature which probably exceeds the quantity of writing devoted to any other economic problem in the course of the last two centuries. The principal explanation for this must surely lie in the urgency of the problem under consideration—an urgency reflected in the fact that for the first time an important field of economic theory is receiving international attention. And the near-universality of the discussion has led to its extension not only across national borders, but also across the boundaries dividing such disciplines as history, economics, sociology, anthropology, psychology, political science, and geography. This book is primarily concerned with the first of these, with the historical approach to economic growth, as illustrated in a variety of empirical studies. First, however, it may prove useful to examine, from a more general viewpoint, the nature of economic history's possible contribution

---

[1] In this introduction the words "development," "growth," "expansion," and "progress" will be used interchangeably. This is for stylistic variety, although it loses something in analytical precision.

to our knowledge of the phenomenon of economic growth—an examination which will also entail some appraisal of economic theory.

In this introduction, the following topics will be briefly considered in turn: the traditional subject matter of economic history; its relations to economic theory; the relevance of the historical experience to the apparently new economic problems of the twentieth century; the various approaches to the study of growth illustrated by the work of economists and historians; and the historical course of economic development up to the twentieth century.

A. THE NATURE AND USES OF ECONOMIC HISTORY

Economic history, considered as a systematic discipline, is relatively young. For, although men have been writing about particular historical aspects of commerce or industry or agriculture for many centuries, it is really only during the last one hundred years that such studies have transcended the mere collection of a limited range of facts. In this period a definite body of knowledge has been brought forth, systematically organized, and subjected to detailed research and analytical testing. As with other disciplines, different topics have engaged the attention of different generations of historians, and old theories and explanations have been constantly replaced by new ones on the basis of fresh information or improved methods of analysis. But the field as a whole has been linked by a general, albeit loose, unity of its subject matter—if not of the methodologies employed in its study.

Defined at its most general level, economic history is the historical study of man's efforts to provide himself with goods and services, of the institutions and relationships which resulted from those efforts, of the changing techniques and outlooks associated with his economic endeavor, and of the results (in social as well as economic terms) of his strivings, or his failure to strive. Clearly, phrased in such a loose manner, the definition includes far more than economic growth as that process is generally understood. It encompasses the study of the medieval manorial system, the nature of changing trade routes, trade union activity, the evolution of economic thought and policy, technology, demography, seasonal fluctuations, marketing, guild organization, income distribution, etc. For, basically, economic history has been concerned with the totality of economic experience, including the degree to which that experience has influenced or been influenced by non-economic phenomena. A consideration of the advantages and disadvantages of what at first sight appears to be a state of advanced academic anarchy will provide some insight into the role of the historical study of growth. But first it should be appreciated that the subject matter of economic history has not been quite so haphazard as the foregoing definition suggests.

It has been said that each new generation rewrites its own history. And this is as true of economics as of other varieties of history. One striking feature of the progress of economic history (as of theoretical economics) over the last few generations is the extent to which each generation has tended to be preoccupied with specific topics, and the extent to which such topics, although considered in their historical context, have been derived from contemporary problems. In the late nineteenth century, for example, free trade and protectionism, or laissez-faire and state control, stood foremost; as, in the United States, did the discussion of the westward movement once the frontier appeared finally closed. In the early twentieth century, with the rise of a politically conscious working class, much attention was devoted to the economic history of labor and trade unions, and to the social costs and consequences for average living standards of the industrial revolution in Great Britain. (This last topic has been revived since 1945 in the light of the new interest in the process of industrialization.) And in the interwar years, particularly during the troubled decade of the 1930's, economic difficulties on both sides of the Atlantic helped turn many historians' minds to the history of price movements, to the study of the performance of particular industries in the past, and, especially, to the history of economic fluctuations and business cycles. This tendency to reorient historical studies has, of course, been even more evident in the years since 1945. For the present generation of economic historians the principal, although by no means the only, topic of intensive study has been the processes and implications of economic development. And, significantly, this is true irrespective of whether their specific field of investigation is medieval Europe, the sixteenth and seventeenth centuries, or particular societies in the last two hundred years.

Of the varying fashions in historical writings, each of which has served as a partial focus of the otherwise bewildering variety of subject matter involved in "economic history," this most recent one is in many ways potentially the most fruitful, because it is, as well, the most inclusive. This is because it serves, or should serve, not so much as a means to limit or restrict the historian's interests, but as a way of posing research questions to, and consequently of ordering and organizing, the enormous mass of facts and topics with which the student has to deal. And, in the historical perspective, there are relatively few topics which do not bear some relation, albeit remote, to growth. For in the last resort economic history, even in its consideration of apparently static economic and social institutions, has always been directly or indirectly concerned with the economic performance of men and societies.

In the light of the modern interest in economic progress, this situation has both advantages and disadvantages. The advantages derive from the fact that economic history, by virtue of its broad range of interests, has never been restricted to merely one aspect of growth or to one interpretation of what growth is. In the very process of covering an indiscriminate number of particular topics it has investigated a host of economic, technological, demographic, political, social, and ideological subjects, and has thereby ranged over many interrelated areas, all of which may be relevant (in differing degrees) to economic expansion, or to its absence. Moreover, taking a long view of human activity, it has been able to investigate not only the sharp institutional and technological changes and the rapid acceleration of rates of national-income growth and industrialization which the twentieth century identifies with economic development, but also the slow-moving and longer-lasting surges of economic prosperity which individual countries or regions experienced before modern industrialization became a familiar fact. In a sense, therefore, given the modern definitions of the words, historians have been accustomed to dealing with the implications of underdevelopment as well as development.

Yet if these are the advantageous aspects of the variety to be found in the corpus of writing in economic history, they must be set against some serious drawbacks. Notwithstanding the fact that the varying subject matter of the discipline has been *potentially* unified by the interest in the economic performance of different societies, in reality this unity has hardly ever been usefully achieved: historians in the past have often undertaken research of a specialist nature with very little coördination, and without always agreeing on points of reference which should be common to them all. The result has been that many prewar studies in economic history, while individually valuable, do not bear any useful relationship to each other because they were not based upon comparable interests. More specifically, research into subjects which in theory are closely bound up with economic growth (e.g., the nature of business enterprise or agricultural systems) has not always been approached with an explicit regard to the question of growth. And, inevitably, the products of the historian's work are not always relevant to our modern interest in economic progress. This irrelevance is largely due to two reasons: first, historians, quite justifiably, may have been interested in other aspects of economic processes; second, when they *were* interested in growth the methodology and techniques of research which they used sometimes lacked the precision and the consistent orientation which must accompany any systematic investigation of such an area.

B. ECONOMIC HISTORY AND ECONOMIC THEORY

As it is closely related to the problem of defining economic history, so the question of the proper relationship between theory and history is too complex to be exhaustively considered here. Nevertheless, some of its aspects must necessarily be mentioned. It must be noted that, with shining exceptions, both historians and theorists have frequently been skeptical about the validity of the relationship between their respective disciplines. Some historians have complained that much of theoretical economics is too remote and artificial to be of much use in the study of economic society in the past; that, on the whole, its hypotheses and its analytical concepts are abstractions which bear little resemblance to the real world, or which are too restricted in scope to be used in historical investigations without distorting facts to fit them into preconceived theoretical "models"; and that, by adhering so strictly to *economic* factors and forces, it ignores the varied elements which comprise any "economic" situation, and fails properly to take account of unique and individual cases. Theorists, on the other hand, have not been slow to respond that historians have too often been mere anti-quarians, gatherers of miscellaneous facts for their own sakes; that they have been too enamored of special cases and too preoccupied with the apparent uniqueness of events; that they are doomed to produce pedestrian narratives unless they approach their subject matter in a consciously systematic way, asking pertinent questions, excluding ex-traneous material, and looking for consistent answers; and that, in general, as long as historians do not commence with a theoretical frame-work history will never be anything more than an interesting but largely useless hobby.

It is tempting to conclude, as we do in so many instances of sharp controversy, that "the truth lies somewhere between the two." Un-fortunately, however, the resolution of the argument is not so simple. In fact, *both* sides can be right—and *both* sides can be wrong! This is so because neither all historians nor all theorists have had the same ap-proach to their respective studies. Some theorists have been too fond of clever abstractions and too dependent on arbitrary concepts and models which are void of empirical content and bear little if any rela-tionship to the mutability of historical reality. Equally culpable, some historians have allowed their prejudices against theory to sway their research and writing to the point where they have become mere ac-cumulators of facts and tellers of pointless stories. The real cause of misunderstanding does not lie in the nature of the subjects themselves, but in a confusion (on both sides) between a "theoretical approach" and particular theories and concepts. The latter can be good or bad, useful or useless; the former is an essential step toward the compre- hension even of historical reality. But historians have been too ready to condemn all theory because some theories are patently almost useless in the investigation of the real world; and theorists have been too eager to consider that the particular hypotheses and models with which they are familiar are the only possible theoretical means of undertaking a systematic study of economic phenomena.

   The point is that real history does not deal with the discovery and presentation of facts, but with the relationships between particular collections of facts. It may, of course, be concerned with a special case, although even here it will have to rely upon explanation and hypothesis. But it can also be argued that "all history and particularly economic history has to deal mainly not with the special case, but with events and situations which recur, and, recurring, exhibit some similarity of feature —instances which can be grouped together, given a collective label, and treated as a whole."[2] In such cases a theoretical framework, whether unconsciously or (preferably) consciously employed, is essential. Such a framework should not be an intellectual straitjacket, nor need it necessarily be taken uncritically from the writings of economists. But the historian must have some concepts which will enable him to sort out an otherwise undifferentiated mass of data, must seek some uni- formities, and must aim to produce some hypotheses, logically relating various facts and trends, which establish a coherent order among those facts. And if he is dissatisfied with the tools which some economists proffer, then he must amend them or seek others—if necessary of his own making, although it is unlikely that he can ignore all the many fruit- ful analytical devices already available.

   In summary, it would appear that economic history must use *good* economic theory. And, of course, economic theory should strive to seek in history both the basis for and the test of its hypotheses. Unless the historian has some general ideas concerning economic processes he will not even know how to *begin* his researches, for he will not know what he is looking for. And it is a concomitant of this argument that theory and history have the best chance of profitable coöperation when they are both keenly interested in the same problems. There are, therefore, grounds for optimism that in the study of the phenomenon of economic growth, precisely because of the interest it has aroused, both the less abstract theorists and the more systematic historians will benefit by

---

   [2] Werner Sombart, "Economic Theory and Economic History," *Economic History Review*, II (January, 1929), 18.

a tolerant as well as skeptical borrowing from each other in order to alleviate their respective deficiencies.

C. ECONOMIC HISTORY AND THE
TWENTIETH CENTURY

But even if the relationship between economic history and some parts of economic theory were joyously harmonious, that would still not answer important questions concerning the relevance of economic history to modern reality. To what extent can we contribute to our knowledge of present-day economic problems on the basis of our study of the past? How far does history teach really useful lessons? And, particularly, in what respect will understanding the process of economic growth over the last two hundred years equip us to meet and comprehend the problems of development which are unfolding in the second half of the twentieth century? The last question is a sobering one, for it has been argued by some writers that the nature of underdeveloped economies today is so dissimilar from that of the preindustrial stages of the developed lands that the history of the latter's growth can contribute very little to an understanding of the former.

The essence of this particular argument is that the economic and social characteristics of modern backward areas place them in a far worse situation, vis-a-vis potential development, than were nations like the United Kingdom, the United States, France, Germany, or Sweden in the late eighteenth or early nineteenth centuries. At its most pessimistic the argument might run something like the following: With one or two exceptions (Japan and, possibly, Russia), the nations which experienced a significant degree of economic development before the First World War enjoyed important advantages in this respect which are to some extent denied to poor countries today. They were part of a "Western culture," combining an empirical and scientific frame of mind with an ideology which accepted innovation and change, and encouraged both hard work for material ends and the voluntary postponement of present consumption in favor of capital accumulation. Their social and political structures were also favorable to development in that they provided the stability and, to varying extents, the social mobility which encouraged a myriad of voluntary actions tending toward an increased output of goods and services. They had indeed *already* experienced generations or even centuries of slow but significant expansion which—in terms of capital accumulation, the diffusion of productive techniques, the exploitation of sources of supply and markets, and the rise of a skilled class of entrepreneurs and a temperamentally qualified class of laborers—had effectively prepared them for the tasks and strains of

sustained economic growth. In addition, their ratios of population to
resources and their demographic patterns were such that overpopulation
was not a real problem; nor was there any great likelihood that the gains
of an initial increase in per capita income would be almost automatically
dissipated by a consequent population explosion. Finally, and as an
outcome of the foregoing factors, they had already attained a level of
average income and wealth which exceeded that of many, and possibly
most, twentieth-century underdeveloped lands. Now, if all this is true,
and *if there are no countervailing considerations,* then not only will the
poor economies of today find it altogether more difficult to achieve a
rapid rate of growth than did the "poor" economies of the eighteenth
and nineteenth centuries, but that achievement (if it comes) is likely
to be so different from the historical experience as to make it extremely
difficult to compare the two.

Fortunately, however, this does not seem to be the case. For one
thing, in Japan and to some extent pre-1914 Russia we do have two
significant examples of nations which were devoid of many of the
characteristics outlined in the previous paragraph, but which nevertheless achieved a most respectable rate of economic change and development.[3] To this extent at least, economic history may be able to outline
the processes by which past societies, directly comparable to many
which today aspire to material progress, underwent economic revolution. Secondly, the argument of the foregoing paragraph undoubtedly
exaggerates the advantages of countries which developed between 1800
and 1914. Growth, superficially, always looks easy in retrospect; but in
fact the advanced countries of today had their own severe problems—
and the fact that their difficulties (or advantages) varied from country
to country raises the possibility of establishing a scale of backwardness
on which modern poor societies would assume a place differing in degree, rather than kind, from say, France, Germany, and Italy 150 years
ago. But in any case the relevance of economic history to modern
problems does not, and in fact should not, hinge upon the precise degree
to which such problems, and their solutions, reproduce the experience
of the past. History never exactly repeats itself, and to study it in the
hope that the future will in some significant way *duplicate* the past is
to engage in a vain and oversimplified exercise. History provides us with
a pattern of past experience, establishes certain uniformities in the
relationships between facts, and illustrates (sometimes obliquely)
reasonably familiar problems which existed on different planes of intensity in the past. It therefore expands the range of human experience
and suggests not so much answers to present and future problems, as

---

[3] See Selections 19–22.

ways in which they can be approached and questions which might be put in our study of the world around us.[4]

How, then, does all this apply to the historical study of economic growth? First, since there is never an exact duplication of historical experience, our investigations of growth in the past, although not irrelevant, do need to be undertaken with an eye to identifying and making allowance for dissimilarities both within the historical examples as a whole and between them and the modern world. Any generalizations which emerge will naturally take account of the peculiarities of the cases dealt with, and we shall be part way toward understanding what *differences* such peculiarities might make. Second, by being aware of these peculiarities we may well be in a better position to understand the nature of present-day underdevelopment and growth problems, even if only by contrast. Third, it is important to remember that, even though from one viewpoint each developed country presents a special case, they have all been through a common process, which apparently entails important structural and technological changes which all of them experienced in differing degrees. Hence it should be possible to propound useful patterns of economic change and data which can be related to the process of development. As long as economic history remains one part of a diverse approach, and as long as its limitations are borne in mind, there can be little doubt that it provides a useful and even an essential perspective for the consideration of modern problems of economic change and development.

D. THE THEORETICAL APPROACH TO ECONOMIC GROWTH

Thus far we have really skirted the central problems involved in the theoretical and historical study of economic growth. It is therefore the purpose of this and the next section to define more precisely what is to be understood by "economic growth" and to appraise, however superficially, the ways by which its study has been approached.

The most commonly accepted definition of economic growth (for any particular economy) identifies it with a sustained and reasonably fast increase in per capita income. On the other hand, the phrase can and has been somewhat loosely used to describe three historically and conceptually quite distinct phenomena:

1. an expansion of activity and production in any preindustrial economy not accompanied by any far-reaching technological or structural changes;

---

[4] For these justifications of historical study, see Alexander Gerschenkron, "Economic Backwardness in Historical Perspective," in Bert F. Hoselitz (ed.), *The Progress of Underdeveloped Areas* (Chicago, Ill., 1952).

2. a sharp acceleration in production accompanied by dramatic technological and structural changes which transform an economy from
a relatively underdeveloped to at least a "developing" status;

3. a sustained expansion of production in an *already* advanced industrial economy by means of economic, social, and technical
changes of a type *already* familiar to it.

Some students have suggested that the word "development" be reserved for the second of these, on the grounds that in the first (and to
some extent the third) the economy does not radically change, it merely
grows in an extensive manner; whereas, with the advance from relative
backwardness, the economy not only grows, it also changes, or develops,
assuming a new technology, new forms of enterprise, new patterns of
economic and social behavior, new relationships between factors of
production and between social groups, and so forth. Nevertheless, each
of these three examples of "growth," although they are sometimes
confused, illustrates an important economic process. Yet since each
presents a somewhat different problem of theoretical and historical
analysis, and since what has just been called "development" is the
process to which the poor nations of the twentieth century really aspire,
the reprinted studies in this book will be primarily, although not exclusively, concerned with examples of countries proceeding from a state
of relative underdevelopment to one of sustained expansion. As a
setting for the history of these various aspects of economic growth,
however, it may prove useful to trace, in this section, some theoretical
approaches to the more general problem.[5]

As is frequently pointed out, in the history of economic thought over
the last two hundred years there have been only two periods in which the
process of growth has been in the forefront of analytical discussion.
The first came with Adam Smith and the subsequent members of the
British classical school (including Karl Marx), the most active period
of discussion occurring in the first half of the nineteenth century. This,
significantly, coincided with the initial stages of industrialization in
Great Britain. The second period commenced in the 1940's and coincided with a heightened contrast between rich and poor nations, and
the liberation of forces in the latter sufficiently powerful and even
threatening to overcome the traditional insularity of Western economists. The long hiatus, from roughly the middle of the nineteenth
century (although Marx lived into the 1880's and the first volume of
Das Kapital was published in 1867) to the middle of the twentieth

---

[5] For comprehensive introductions to the theory of growth and the twentieth-century problem, see Benjamin Higgins, *Economic Development: Principles, Problems
and Policies* (New York, 1959); and Gerald M. Meier and Robert E. Baldwin,
Economic Development: Theory, History, Policy (New York, 1957).

century, was probably due to the fact that in the eyes of most theorists, who were primarily concerned with the economics of advanced not backward countries, economic progress in much of Western Europe and the "new lands" of North America and Australasia appeared to be virtually automatic.

Indeed, the assumption that growth presented no real problems, that it was an inevitable outcome of the operation of economic mechanisms, characterized most of the classical discussion of the evolution of a capitalist economy.[6] Living as they did in an epoch of unprecedented technological innovation, the classical economists could not resist the temptation to consider technical progress and increasing productivity as an automatic factor—at least in the type of economy with which they were familiar. And, confining their studies largely to the advancing lands, and particularly to Great Britain, they had no anxiety about (even while they acknowledged the great importance of) social and political institutions favorable to economic progress. Thus when Adam Smith, to take an early example, undertook "an enquiry into the nature and causes of the wealth of nations," he was able, in the identification of the prime movers of growth, to concentrate on more or less purely economic considerations—on the skill and quantity of the labor supply, on the accumulation of capital, which increased the number and efficiency of workers engaged in "productive" occupations, and on the extension of the market, which (together with the increasing supply of capital) facilitated and stimulated the division of labor, or specialization, which in turn was responsible for higher productivity.

Thus classical writers, from Smith through Malthus, Ricardo, and John Stuart Mill to Marx, approached the topic of economic growth as an illuminating exercise in the interplay of the factors of production, land, labor, and capital. For all of them the crux of sustained growth lay in the area of profits, capital accumulation, and investment. The desire on the part of capitalists to save and to invest savings profitably was taken for granted. Population, it is true, was judged to be sensitive to real wages (though Marx was an exception here), so that any rise in average living standards would sooner or later be restrained by an increase in numbers imposing a brake on wages; but such a population rise, at least over in the long period of initial growth, would not check the course of expansion by using up resources which would otherwise have gone into investment. In the short run some writers, like Malthus and Marx, envisaged temporary crises arising from failures of effective

---

[6] This is true even though classical economists, for technical reasons, anticipated a cessation of growth in the long run. To Ricardo and others this took the form of an ultimate stationary state. To Marx it was an apocalyptic vision of an ultimate collapse.

demand. And, for differing reasons, most of them prophesied a far more chronic check to growth in the long run, arising through the effects either of excessive capital accumulation in lowering profits or of a secular increase in population ultimately encountering diminishing returns in agriculture and thereby raising wage costs. Nevertheless, the classical economists generally assumed that for their own age and for some time to come, growth, even though it was not frictionless, would continue through the effects of market forces on the combination and productivity of the various factors of production.

The fact that much of this appears to bear little relationship to the situation in underdeveloped economies today should not be allowed to detract from its authors' analytical insight into economic processes. The reason for the apparent inappropriateness of their theories to some modern problems lies largely in the fact that so many of these problems relate to the inception of development, to the difficulties of transforming a backward into a growing economy. By contrast, the classical economists, writing in nineteenth-century England, were concerned to explain the nature and mechanisms of growth once that process was already under way.

With the exception of Karl Marx, and one or two individual theorists, for almost a century after 1850 there was no fresh, systematic discussion of the nature of economic development. Economists, instead, turned to a consideration of the implications of progress in an advanced economy —to an analysis of prices, wages, interest, competition, and the like. Even when, at the end of this period, the appearance of widespread dislocation and depression undermined academic complacency, the new attempts at analytical originality and synthesis were largely concerned with the explanation of economic fluctuations. Nevertheless, some writers clearly recognized that in advanced economies the two phenomena—fluctuations and growth—might well be intimately related. Hence, although they were fashioned primarily as elements in the theory of fluctuations, a small number of the additions to economic literature were very significant contributions to growth theory. The two principal examples are the writings of J. A. Schumpeter and what has come to be known as the Harrod-Domar theory.

Schumpeter first put forward his views early in the century,[7] and brought them forward (in conjunction with a good deal of empirical data) for reconsideration in 1939, with his book *Business Cycles*. He hinged his theory of fluctuations and growth almost exclusively on the activities of the innovating entrepreneur (thereby making up one of the classical economists' most serious deficiencies). Economic expansion

---

[7] J. A. Schumpeter, *The Theory of Economic Development* (published in German in 1911; translated into English in 1934; reprinted in 1961).

in a capitalist economy, on this view, is above all the responsibility of
the entrepreneur who recognizes a profit opportunity—in a new commodity, a new technique, a new market, a new source of supply, or a
new organization of production—and takes the lead in exploiting it and
so lowering costs and increasing output. Three other cornerstones of
the theory should also be mentioned. First, the financing of development is not a function of voluntary savings and capital formation, but
is effected by means of credit creation (whereby entrepreneurs borrow
from financial institutions) and, therefore, through the forced savings
of inflationary pressure, which reduces the consumption of people with
relatively fixed incomes. Second, in sharp contrast to most classical and
neoclassical writers, although not to Marx, Schumpeter held that growth,
far from being a harmonious process, was *necessarily* discontinuous,
carried forward by the alternation of hectic spurts of expansion and
periods of relative economic decline. These fluctuations occur because
innovations have a tendency to appear in bunches or clusters and thereby
create a varying relationship between capacity and effective demand.
Third, the theory has a strong sociological content. This flows from
Schumpeter's vision of the entrepreneur, who, by definition, is a particular social type, whose activities can be sustained only by a particular
social milieu, and whose existence could be endangered by not unlikely
social developments. It should be clear from all this that, for economic
historians, Schumpeter occupies a somewhat special place among theoretical economists. This is so not only because his theories are less
forbidding and more easily grasped than most, but also precisely because,
by placing the entrepreneur firmly at the center of the process of growth,
he seems to provide almost unlimited scope for what historians sometimes consider their particular skill and contribution: an examination of
the individual instances which comprise social and economic activity,
and of the "human" side of the historical course of economic expansion.

By contrast, the theories of Roy Harrod and Evsey Domar[8] have
not (whether justifiably or not) stimulated much historical work, partly
because of the apparent technical complexity of their statements, and
partly because they do not provide the historian with a sufficient
diversity of concepts into which to fit his data. Both theories, it should
be pointed out, were derived from the discussions of macro-economics,
of investment, consumption, income, and employment, which had been
aroused by the cyclical fluctuations of the interwar years, and which
had to a large extent been crystallized in Keynesian economics. It was,

---

[8] R. F. Harrod, "An Essay in Dynamic Theory," *Economic Journal*, XLIX (March,
1939), and *Towards a Dynamic Economics* (London, 1948); Evsey D. Domar,
"Expansion and Employment," *American Economic Review*, XXXVII (March,
1947), and *Essays in the Theory of Economic Growth* (New York, 1957).

therefore, to be expected that such post-Keynesian approaches to economic growth, rather than attempting to deal exhaustively with the mechanisms of expansion, should stress its relationship to the possibility of full employment, and attempt to indicate the conditions which would ensure the latter. Once again, capital formation is central to the approach, but this time because it both generates income and creates productive capacity; and given the need to achieve and maintain a full employment equilibrium, these two effects must balance and must do so by a sustained increase in the amount of investment—which requires in turn, a continuous growth in national income. The resulting models of growth were designed to identify the rate of growth which would ensure long-run full employment.

As was the case with Schumpeter's theory, the relevance of such analyses was designedly limited to the case of an advanced capitalist economy. Even here the precision which their authors sought tends to restrict the explanatory powers of their analyses (though not their use as tools for further analysis). But, what is more important from our present viewpoint, they were not designed to explain the processes by which a backward country is launched into a phase of economic development. Hence, although their appraisal of income, employment, and the equilibrium of demand and supply differ markedly from that of the classical school mainstream, they are in one respect close to the Smith-Ricardo-Mill approach, as well as to Schumpeter's: their field of analysis is largely confined to the growth of a developed, not the development of a backward, economy.

Of course, all this is not to say that the various tools of analysis perfected in economics in general or in the study of growth in particular from the late eighteenth to the mid-twentieth century cannot help in the understanding of modern development problems. On the contrary, although there is a lively debate as to the precise degree of their utility, there can be no doubt that some grasp of them and their implications is essential to a better understanding of all aspects of economic development. Yet the fact remains that the intractable economic problem of our time has proved to be the existence of economies which appear *chronically* underdeveloped; and the relatively new task which economists and other students have set themselves is an explanation of why this is so—that is, what factors or mechanisms keep backward countries backward—and, concomitantly, under what conditions and by what mechanisms they could begin to move forward into a phase of structural and technological change and therefore rising per capita income.

By phrasing the problem in this way it is easy to see why so many economists have recently approached the problem of development looking for "barriers" or "obstacles" or "bottlenecks"—specific features or mechanisms in backward economies which, unless eradicated or over-come, might well inhibit their growth. Moreover, given the particular approach, together with the nature of backward countries, it is hardly surprising that some students should conclude that the real roots of underdevelopment, and therefore the most effective means to secure growth, lie in non-economic factors—that the problem is only in small part an economic one. Hence the modern approach is widely, although not universally, characterized by an interdisciplinary analysis, in which such factors as the legal and political frameworks, social psychology, ideological outlook, social structures, and even climate and culture are all held worthy of the most serious attention.

Such non-economic appraisals generally fall into two (related) cate-gories. On the one hand there are hypotheses which attribute relative backwardness to elements in the social and cultural environment which fail to provide a sufficient incentive to enterprise and other related activities. Examples might be: a system of land tenure which keeps land out of the hands of progressive farmers or does not provide them with sufficient security of possession; an arbitrary and inefficient gov-ernment or an unstable political environment which inhibits long-run entrepreneurial activity; the survival of feudal or traditional institutions which absorb existing resources and deny economic opportunity to qualified men and women; a rigid and backward-looking social structure which has the same effect; an "extended family" system which places the responsibility of providing an income for remote relations on the wealthiest member of the family, whose income is consequently diverted from potential investment to current consumption. On the other hand there are hypotheses which, by an extension of this type of argument, suggest that the inhibiting factors are to a large extent intrinsic to the *individual* members of the economy. Thus the prevailing, and accepted, ideology in a society may place material achievement low on its scale of values and may consider active entrepreneurship, or any work above the effort needed to secure a traditional income, to be at best a waste of time; cultural evolution may have restricted acceptable enterprise to only a few occupations (e.g., estate management); the weight of tradition and custom may be so great as to prevent the introduction of new techniques and to make men wary of any violent change such as normally accompanies development; in terms of education or tempera-ment, potential managers, technicians, and workers may simply not be qualified to overhaul the economy; and mores and outlook may have the effect of channeling the little saving that exists into unproductive uses (luxury consumption, impressive houses, real estate, commodity speculation, moneylending).

This is not the place to pass judgment on the significance of such non-economic aspects of growth problems. Certainly they can play an important role in the economic performance of any society, and their presence explains why so many students of the backward lands have emphasized the need for political and social reforms and for education and training as prerequisites for economic development. Yet, although they must necessarily be taken into consideration, the influence of cultural and sociological factors, at least of the second variety described above, may well have been exaggerated.[9] And since, in any case, their manifestations (e.g., a shortage of capital, underemployment, maldistribution of income, regressive taxes, undersupply of skilled labor) are often susceptible to economic analysis, the latter must probably still play the leading part in any appreciation of underdevelopment and any explanation of growth.

As did their classical predecessors, modern economists frequently adopt an initial factor-of-production approach to the question of development. More than this, many of them also place a good deal of weight on the nature of, and the difficulties inherent in, capital accumulation, although they also go on to consider in far greater detail the mechanisms as well as the actual sources of savings and uses of investment. To many economists the supreme problem of economic growth is to break the vicious circle which makes countries poor because they save very little, and makes them save very little because they remain poor. Apart from the possibility that capital accumulation might be substantially helped by the loan or grant of capital from wealthier countries, a backward economy must clearly rely on its own potentialities. And since, contrary to many sanguine expectations, no economy can realistically expect to grow solely on the basis of other people's assistance, these potentialities under any conceivable circumstances are going to be of crucial significance.

For a given underdeveloped country, there can be a variety of reasons why savings are not forthcoming for productive investment. The economy may be so poor throughout its income range that the overwhelming bulk of its product has to be consumed, leaving only a negligible amount of resources for investment. Alternatively, the surplus of resources above minimum needs, while not negligible, may be hoarded or dissipated— for example, by expenditure on luxury commodities, imports, or land speculation. Another possibility is that the savings are there but are not flowing into productive uses because the calculus of profit and risk does not offer a sufficient incentive, because of such factors as restricted markets or political insecurity or poor communications. Finally,

---

[9] See Barry E. Supple, "Economic History and Economic Underdevelopment," *Canadian Journal of Economics and Political Science*, XXVII, 4 (November, 1961), 460–78.

the incentives may be large enough, but the savings remain untapped because there is no effective system of financial or other institutions for collecting and directing them into productive uses. Depending, therefore, on the particular situation, growth will necessitate an attack on one or more of these problems. In the first instance (which is very rarely found in practice), while the need for capital imports is the most urgent, consumption may have to be still further restricted—although this cruelty may be somewhat alleviated, depending on the employment situation, by turning idle hands to the labor-intensive construction of capital. In the second and third cases steps must be taken either to skim off surplus resources into community savings or to offer greater incentives to growth-inducing investments by market guarantees, reforms, the provision of services, or even subsidies; and even here *rapid* growth may depend on the availability of potential savings above current levels of luxury consumption or hoarding so that further measures may be needed to boost the percentage of national income saved (i.e., to lower the rate of consumption) to the desired level. And in the final example, again with this last-mentioned proviso, a financial network for the gathering of savings must be created or extended—a step which is in any case probably helpful in all the examples.

The foregoing paragraph gives only a superficial glimpse of the difficulties involved in just one aspect of development: securing a sufficiently high level of savings to undertake capital accumulation. Yet even in these bald generalizations a further range of important problems is implied. One concerns the role of planning and the extent of state action. Others concern the relative merits of voluntary as against forced savings. And as regards the latter there are controversies as to means (taxation, or wage control, or inflation, or regulated prices for certain sectors), and repercussions, in terms of the incentives to private economic activity and social peace. Moreover, economic policies tailored to fit particular savings needs might well have to encompass specific commercial policies, such as those directed to maximizing export earnings while diverting them from luxury imports to the import of necessary capital goods. Clearly no one aspect of economic growth can be analyzed in complete isolation.

This is also clear from a study of other aspects of capital accumulation. For assuming that this approach is valid, we have still only dealt with one half of the main problem. We have yet to mention the relationship between particular types of actual investment and growth. On an aggregate view capital formation raises output and productivity, and is therefore obviously associated with economic expansion (although the association clearly works in both directions). But capital accumulation alone is not the most effective stimulant to rising productivity. For product per worker to increase, it is most advisable to utilize capital of a better "quality"—i.e., to introduce advanced techniques. One characteristic of economic development in the past, as it must be in the future, has therefore been technological innovation and adaptation. And a large part of the discussion of the economics of underdevelopment has correspondingly been devoted to the processes of improving technology, the social and economic prerequisites of successful innovation and imitation, and the proper relationship between the available techniques of the most advanced lands and the needs of the most backward.[10] This question of technological improvement and productivity is also part of the much broader question of capital investment. For "capital" is not a homogeneous product, and, depending on the particular location and nature and timing of the investment, its effect on growth may well vary enormously. Some economists, for example, place considerable importance on the absence or presence of social overhead capital (e.g., a transportation and communications network), viewing its large-scale and intensive construction as an historic and theoretical prerequisite of economic development, since it lowers real costs for primary production and for a wide range of manufacturing industries. Yet the most important characteristic of social overhead capital is precisely the huge amounts of investment needed—amounts which, for many poor lands, are beyond the means of private enterprise alone. And even apart from the question of this sort of investment, there is the theoretical problem of which types of investment in the production of commodities most facilitate the process of economic development.

One of the crucial questions in this respect concerns the allocation of capital as between primary production and manufacturing industry. Concentration on either has potential disadvantages as well as advantages. Thus, high and readily perceptible growth rates may be secured in the early stages of development by concentrating investment in industrial uses, although industrialization redistributes labor into the manufacturing sector and increases the demand for raw materials, so that if primary production is neglected, serious bottlenecks in the supply of food and industrial materials may well develop. In the alternative case, however, if scarce resources are devoted to the raising of agricultural productivity, then there is a danger that capital will replace labor in the primary sector, while the lack of attention to manufacturing will limit both the supply of jobs necessary to absorb the displaced agricultural workers and the supply of manufactured commodities which the rising incomes of the primary sector will demand. Thus, in any particular example, the course of economic development (or the most efficient plan, if economic decisions are centralized) will depend upon the such variable factors as the existing level and distribution of popula-

[10] See below, pp. 22, 27–30, 38–40, 60–63, 73, 116–117, 427–428.

tion, the state of employment, the relative efficiency of labor and capital in the two sectors, and the respective markets for food, raw materials, and manufactures. Correspondingly, therefore, while theory can feasibly set out the considerations which have to be taken into account, it cannot propose an "answer" which is applicable to all instances. Nor, in any case, can there be any final decision concerning the long-run structure of the economy. For the allocation of capital is really a choice about a chronological sequence, about means rather than ends, for the working out of the development process implies and necessitates that productivity and output in *both* primary and secondary sectors should ultimately be raised.

The foregoing discussion implicitly assumed a "closed" economy. But one particularly important example of the general controversy concerns the "balance" of an underdeveloped or developing country with respect to international trade. Many poor countries have an apparent advantage for the production of a limited range of primary commodities and it has been widely advocated that they maximize economic benefits by specializing in such production (using the proceeds to buy manufactures, and capital goods in particular). But it has also been argued that the international market for food and raw materials is now too inelastic and too unstable to be the basis for sustained growth, and that primary production itself has "linkages" (with other domestic economic activity) which are too tenuous to induce a broad-based development through its demand for and supply of goods and services. The concomitant of the second argument, therefore, is that resources should be purposefully directed into manufacturing enterprises—by which means the dependence on primary exports and secondary imports will be reduced.

The idea of "balance" is also relevant to the question of the allocation of capital between industrial sectors of the economy. The problem here is whether it is necessary or desirable for one or two industries (or types of industries) to spurt forward at a much faster rate than others and, so to speak, to take up the running for growth. Arguments in favor of the beneficial effect of "leading sectors" rest on an appeal to history, on the potentially greater gains in productivity and the generation of skills and technological advances, and on the possible strong inducement effects of rapid development if the relevant industry (through its supply of goods to other industries and its demand for their products) has substantial "linkages." On the other hand, as in the case of agriculture versus industry, some economists advocate a more rounded "balanced growth," in which a reasonably large number of industries advance more or less in step, so that the inter-industry demand for and supply of goods and services can be roughly coördinated, and development on a broad front can take place relatively smoothly.

Besides implying a choice between sectoral uses, the investment decision for underdeveloped lands also entails a choice of techniques—between different levels of technology. In particular there is a lively controversy as to whether capital should be devoted to large-scale units using advanced and expensive technology or to smaller-scale enterprises which, using simple tools, employ relatively more workers. The former, capital-intensive enterprises clearly use up scarce capital in the employment of relatively few people, but at the same time they use a highly efficient technology and maximize production per worker (and so may be expected to yield greater surpluses for reinvestment). The latter, labor-intensive enterprises, while they do not transform productivity per worker, have the advantages of absorbing a good deal of labor which might otherwise be underemployed, and possibly increasing capital productivity (i.e., lowering the capital-output ratio), so that a given quantity of scarce capital can be spread over more output and employment. Moreover, each, in its turn, may be expected to have different effects in the long-run process of generating further growth—although there is as yet no systematic knowledge of how these effects (operating through the accumulation of capital, the level of wages, the distribution and increase of population, the training of managers and workers, "linkages," and so forth) will in fact work themselves out.

By this time it must surely be clear that any discussion of the relationship between capital formation and economic growth necessarily entails the appraisal of a host of other issues. And these, in their turn, lead to the conclusion that the accumulation of capital is in itself by no means *the* central aspect of the process of economic growth.[11] Moreover, quite apart from the topics already mentioned, there are other very important considerations to be borne in mind. Among them is the well-known population problem.

Contrary to popular opinion, not *all* poor lands are overpopulated; but most of the important ones are, and nearly all of them (simply in the nature of their poverty) face some sort of population problem. As a result of this, the typical underdeveloped economy is frequently in the precarious situation which classical economists like Ricardo only envisaged as a long-run prospect for developed countries. In effect a two-fold difficulty faces them. Largely owing to the ease with which advances in medical knowledge can be applied even in backward countries, most of the poorer regions of the world are already experiencing a sustained rise in population. (Between 1935 and 1955, for example, the poor

---

[11] Even in the area of investment some economists would criticize the production oriented nature of the discussion in the text. Their complaint would be that it ignores investment in "human capital"—that is, social investment which raises levels of education and skills and thereby widens one of the most serious economic bottlenecks of poor societies.

countries of the world increased their populations on the average by almost 40 per cent, as against about 12 per cent for Europe.[12]) And this implies that a moderate rate of increase in gross national product will not be equivalent to economic growth because, if it fails to exceed the rate of population growth, per capita income will remain at best stable and may even decline. Equally or more serious, the response to a spurt of output may well be a further rise in population, sharp enough not only to restrain the anticipated rise in real wages and per capita product, but to retard or prevent (by its increased consumption needs) the sustained growth of investment necessary for the sustained growth of the economy. In view of the real dangers involved, therefore, it is not surprising that many observers view the possibility of modern economic development as depending on a race between the growth of population and capital—a race in which the former often has the advantage. In these circumstances, a good deal of modern growth analysis concentrates on the direct means of restraining population growth, on the forms of growth which would indirectly produce a check on birth rates, and on the need to secure a sufficient momentum in the initial stage of development to outstrip the potential expansion of numbers in a decisive way.[13]

This last point has also been further elaborated in much recent writing on the subject of development. The hypothesis, to which many historians subscribe,[14] is that the transition from backwardness to development cannot be a gradual one, that there is at least an initial discontinuity when rates of growth and the tempo of change suddenly experience a sharp forward thrust. This is the theory of the "critical minimum effort," the "big push" or the "take-off." It rests on a variety of assumptions. One is that gradual expansion would simply not be strong enough to overcome the obstacles and barriers which seem to be built into poor economies. Instead, some measure of rapid achievement is needed to outpace both population and consumption, to energize people who might otherwise feel reluctant to undergo the necessary hardships of growth, to overcome by sheer momentum the inertia of traditional attitudes and institutions, to secure economies of scale speedily, and generally to usher the economy quickly through a period in which the as yet uncertain growth process may meet counteracting forces. Economists and historians who take this view generally assume that after

---

[12] Meier and Baldwin, *Economic Development*, p. 288.

[13] While modern underdeveloped countries with increasing populations rarely enjoy significantly higher standards of living, it is not uncommon for the average expectation of life to increase. Our definition of economic progress (rising per capita incomes) should not blind us to the fact that the prospect of a longer life is itself far from a negligible contribution to progress.

[14] For historical analyses, see Selections 3, 13, and 22.

successfully negotiating the primary "take-off," an economy settles down to a phase of "self-sustained" growth, in which the forces making for expansion experience a cumulative strengthening and the obstacles become far less important than the favorable elements. In addition, of course, the long-run pattern and course of expansion are topics of no small interest. Whether and to what extent actual industrialization is a necessary concomitant of growth; the changing distribution of output and employment between primary production, secondary manufacture, and the service "industries"; the tendency of long-run growth rates to decline in specific industries and, possibly, in the economy as a whole; the apparently universal appearance of long-term fluctuations or trends in economic variables: all these, and more, would find an integral place in the ideal theory of economic development.

As the patient reader must by now have gathered, this ideal theory is still a very remote possibility! While the analysis of some topics has been effectively systematized, no one has yet managed (indeed, hardly anyone has tried) to integrate the component elements into a satisfactory whole. Some measure of the difficulties involved is that even the jumble of "factors" and "topics" and "questions" already mentioned by no means exhausts the potential list. The investigation and elaboration of the entrepreneurial function, for example, has been extended well beyond the Schumpeterian level—particularly as it applies to the inception of economic growth. For economists, however much the subject is not susceptible to their familiar techniques, have been obliged to examine the complex mechanisms and incentives of the multitudinous human decisions which in the last resort are synonymous with economic growth. Indeed it may well be that the factor most strategic to growth is not capital or skilled labor or resources, so much as the entrepreneurial ability to make productive investment decisions.[15] For whatever the social and political framework within which countries attempt to grow, and however far strategic aspects of savings and population and aggregate investment policies are centralized, the pace and path and outcome of expansion will depend upon the choices and actions of many men. It is this fact, as much as the "nationalization" of the developmental problems, which makes economic growth a social phenomenon.

E. THE HISTORICAL APPROACH TO ECONOMIC GROWTH

As is only to be expected, historians over the last sixty years or more have shifted the basis of their discussion of economic growth (insofar

---

[15] See Albert O. Hirschman, *The Strategy of Economic Development* (New Haven, Conn., 1958).

as they *did* discuss it) to a far greater extent than economists. In fact, at times their approach has been so oblique as to be almost irrelevant. And yet, as was implied in Section A, no matter how oblique the approach, and no matter how imperfect the conceptual devices, economic history has traditionally been concerned with topics of at least potential relevance to growth or to underdevelopment. Even before men began to worry about economic growth in the sense in which that term is now used, some of the most important writings in economic history were in fact devoted to the content or implications of expansion. This was true of the detailed stage analyses of economic systems, undertaken in Germany in the second half of the nineteenth century; of the scholarly investigations of the medieval origins of capitalism and capitalist, which came at the end of the nineteenth and early in the twentieth centuries; of the controversy on the causal relationship between the Protestant Reformation and the rise of capitalism; of the deep interest, among British historians, in the processes of their own industrial revolution; of the far-ranging studies of the economic consequences of the discoveries of the sixteenth century; of the detailed analysis of medieval trends in population, prices, production, and trade; and, it need hardly be said, of the host of Marxist historians.

Yet it is only in the last decade or two that economic historians have realigned their approach to the topic of development so that it is parallel to at least part of the approach which theorists have also recently come to use. And as a result they have been able to shed at least a partial light on some of the significant questions referred to in the previous section—as well as on some of their own creation.

Since he is naturally attracted by the dramatic and the spectacular, the historian has been most sympathetic to the new-found interest in the process of development from backwardness, as against the expansion of an already industrialized society. Moreover, even more than the economist, the historian identifies this process with the rise of manufacturing and the idea of a spurt. And, as a consequence, a large part of the real historical treatment of growth centers on the concept of a revolutionary economic transformation; in other words, of an industrial revolution —either in its original manifestation, in the British economy, or in the subsequent examples (all to some extent conditioned by the British pioneering effort) in other parts of the Western world and, ultimately, in such a country as Japan. To the historian questions of timing and precedence are of considerable significance, and in the study of industrial revolutions economic history is bound to ask and attempt to answer such questions as: Why did the industrial revolution occur first in Great Britain? Why did it happen in the late eighteenth and early nineteenth centuries? What was the process by which industrialization spread from country to country? What explains, in the case of specific countries, the timing and the nature of bursts of development?

When the actual mechanisms of growth and industrialization are being discussed, the historical approach, although its language is somewhat different, does not stray too far from the "theoretical" topics referred to in the previous section. Thus the financing of economic growth —the role of voluntary as against forced savings, the contrast between borrowing and internal financing by the plowing back of profits, and the role of private enterprise as against the state—preëmpts a large part of the historical writing on industrial revolutions and inevitably leads to some consideration of banking, profits, prices, real wages, and the extent to which exports generated national purchasing power. On the investment side of capital accumulation, historians are naturally interested in the relationship between agricultural and industrial improvement and in the fact that particular industrial sectors did indeed appear to take the lead in a growing economy. Moreover, stemming in large part from the impact of more modern problems, the economic role of government policy and (even more) the relationships between demographic and economic trends are receiving a great amount of attention.

It would be very possible to continue such a listing of the subjects which historians of economic growth are accustomed to consider, albeit in a far more generalized manner than students of theory. Yet the result would be equally or more frustrating than such a listing was in the previous section. The point is that in history, as in theory, the time is not yet ripe for an all-embracing set of related hypotheses which would systematize the subject of economic growth and allocate a functional role within it to the various factors which we have so far briefly mentioned. Indeed, historians and economists have only recently begun the crucial task of *measuring* economic trends over long periods so that we can have some more precise idea of the dimensions of progress and the nature of its characteristics (e.g., capital accumulation, the changing importance of different industrial sectors, trends in output and growth rate).[16] The only comprehensive, and the most ambitious attempt so far to delineate the *process* of economic growth is that by Professor Rostow (see Selection 3). But even here the descriptive aspects of his approach are clearly more illuminating and searching than

---

[16] There is currently an organized international effort to extend the range of our statistical knowledge of many countries. Although the extreme paucity of materials before about 1860 or 1870, and the not insignificant gaps thereafter, render this a most difficult task, a great deal of very useful information is emerging. The most comprehensive summary, on a comparable basis, of these data and their implications is to be found in a series of studies by Simon Kuznets with the general title of "Quantitative Aspects of the Economic Growth of Nations." See *Economic Development and Cultural Change*, 1956, 1957, 1958, 1960, 1961.

the explanatory or analytical parts. All generalizations about the inner workings of the growth process are obviously going to be no more than tentative for some time to come.

In spite of all this, economic history has undoubtedly succeeded in extending our comprehension of many aspects of the growth process in the past. It is, of course, the function of the studies which follow this introduction to display some of these achievements. And it is hoped that they will make explicit the extent to which the analytical problems presented in the foregoing pages have received satisfactory historical answers. Since, however, they are largely confined to the economic experience after 1800, and since in any case most of them are devoted to an analysis of particular countries or specific topics, it may be advantageous to devote the rest of this introduction to a general historical survey, in order to provide some overall background material for the individual chapters. This will be done, first, by proposing a useful viewpoint from which to study man's economic efforts and by appraising the evolution of the ancient world; next, by considering the medieval European economy, and the processes of change which occurred before the late eighteenth century; third, by examining the nature of economic development between the late eighteenth century and 1914; and, finally, by some mention of twentieth-century problems.

A. *Techniques, Economic Growth, and the Ancient World*

As has already been implied, one of the most significant contributions which the study of history can make to modern knowledge is to relate contemporary problems which, from a limited viewpoint, seem at first to be specific or even unique, to themes which have been playing themselves out since the birth of human society. In this sense to go back five or ten thousand years, or even more, need not be an irrelevant, and may well be a most illuminating, exercise in the study of economic progress. In economic history one of the principal themes which is most consistently exemplified by such a very long view is the extent to which man's strivings after material progress, his economic activities, have been expressed in the use of techniques designed to control the forces and exploit the potentialities of nature. Techniques in this sense can mean "technology" in its traditional usage, or ways of organizing economic activity in institutions, or even man's social outlook on the importance and intensity of his own efforts. But, however they express themselves, in the last resort they are all directed, with more or less efficiency, toward mastering man's physical environment, toward transforming natural resources into usable commodities and services, or toward overcoming natural obstacles (distance, weather, harvest fluctuations, poor soils, floods) to these ends. To this extent economic history is the story of man's effort to control his own destiny. Left alone with no incentive to effort, he would starve, go naked, freeze, have no remedy against a thousand dangers and natural occurrences. Organizing his efforts coöperatively and systematically, and evolving techniques to improve his efficiency, he can feed, clothe, house, and protect himself. And at each level of his efforts, they are directed toward raising the productivity of labor. From the invention of fire and the wheel to the achievement of flight and atomic power, from the communal irrigation systems of 4000 B.C. to the continental marketing networks of the twentieth century, economic activity has been directed by first the need and then the desire to secure growing amounts of material comforts by the manipulation of nature. And the obvious facts that improvements have been discontinuous, that centuries have passed with no significant increase in production and productivity or with actual regressions, or that the techniques man has shaped have sometimes been used as much for destruction as for production, do not really weaken the basic argument.

Two further points should be noted about the evolution of the means of controlling and exploiting nature. One is that, nothwithstanding the periods of decline and technical regression, man's knowledge (the fundamental basis of his economic efficiency) has a *tendency* to be cumulative: the achievements of one generation are built on its inheritance from its predecessors and, unless a historical tragedy intervenes, are handed on as the potential basis for further advances by those that follow. Moreover, their cumulative process is both *social* and *cultural*: men have to work together to perfect and use their techniques; and the knowledge and use of such techniques are transmitted by means of an essentially cultural process, by man's ability not only to translate his particular discoveries into concepts and general principles, but to transmit his discoveries in writing and the spoken word. (It is for these reasons that technological development is an integral part of cultural history, and is normally associated with particular societies and cultures rather than solely with individuals.) Largely owing to these facts, the acquisition of technical knowledge, of means of environmental control, has had a tendency to accelerate, so that technological or organizational or ideological revolutions take place at shorter and shorter intervals. It is only necessary to compare the events of the one hundred years after 1800 with those of the two hundred years before that date, or the last fifty with the previous one hundred years, to establish the truth of this observation.

The second noteworthy feature of such changes in the techniques of economic activity concerns their relationship to production and efficiency. As has already been indicated,[17] two types of growth are important in this respect. One refers to economic expansion within, and up to the limits of, an existing framework of technology and economic institutions. In this case the basic structure and appearance of the economy probably does not change, but grows, either by extending the use of already popular techniques or by the tapping of new markets or the acquisition of new sources of supply, or new lands. In the other type, by contrast, the techniques and structures of the economy do change, and growth—spurred on by cumulative increases in productivity —can proceed virtually indefinitely as long as they continue to be perfected.

These very general remarks about the social, cultural, and cumulative nature of improvements in economic techniques, and about their relationship with development, provide a useful means of generalizing about very long periods of human history. For it is clear that from the beginning of his existence Homo sapiens was engaged in a painful and slow struggle to master his environment, and shape his own destiny, by the perfection of relevant techniques, and this struggle was inextricably bound up with the evolution of primitive society and its cultural attributes. Thus while standards of living in the most primitive stage of society no doubt varied solely with the access to abundant or meager hunting grounds, or with climatic and weather changes, real progress in terms of economic activity had to await the convergence of some critical technological and organizational innovations. Such a "spurt" (very long-drawn-out by modern criteria, but nonetheless distinct in the context of prehistory) came in two stages: with the perfection of neolithic techniques roughly ten thousand years ago, and the rise of urban civilizations in the Middle East some six thousand years ago. Each in its own way was accompanied by significant advances in productivity, and their combination represents relatively the most significant advance until the technological, scientific, and economic developments of the last three hundred years or so. The first stage witnessed the extension of the previously invented instrumentality of fire (for warmth, cooking, and defense against wild animals), the perfection of stone tools and weapons by grinding and polishing techniques; and the domestication of animals and the establishment of settled agriculture, which increased food supplies and thereby facilitated the concentration and specialization of labor and the rudimentary accumulation of capital. The second stage extended these techniques, particularly those relating to agriculture and water control, and augmented them with the use of copper and bronze, the spreading application of the wheel in pottery manufacture and

---

[17] Above, pp. 11–12.

transportation, the development of advanced building techniques, the development of a more articulated hierarchy of specialist occupations (including administrators), the invention of writing, and the outlook and organizational devices which could sustain complex urban and even imperial societies.

The revolution which all this implied culminated in the flowering of the civilizations of the Tigris-Euphrates and Nile river valleys; and —although its beneficial consequences were somewhat dissipated by population growth, war, and luxurious waste—it represented real and intensive economic development. For the first time on a large scale, man had employed an array of techniques which facilitated a partial mastery of natural forces and an important augmentation of his output of goods and services. And on such bases he was able to take the giant step of creating an urban society. That there was, in relative terms, no comparable advance until more recent times does not, of course, mean that there was no economic growth between, say, 2000 B.C. and A.D. 1600 or 1700. There was, indeed, a considerable degree of progress, occasioned either by new techniques (the production of cheap iron toward the end of the second millennium B.C. is a case in point) or the extension of existing economic systems. But throughout this period there was no forward surge quite as impressive as that which has just been mentioned. Certainly, in terms of the development of new techniques neither the accomplishments of the Greek city states nor those of ancient Rome were of the same order of magnitude. And yet it is necessary to bear in mind that each attained a higher level of development than any previous major civilization.[18] For while the technology of both was essentially derivative, they *did* make some advances in the way of agricultural, commercial, financial, and industrial organization and institutions, and (perhaps more significantly) extended their economic systems, in the case of the Greek cities through a colonial and trading system embracing much of the Mediterranean and the Black Sea, and in the case of Rome through a unified imperial system which ultimately drew together most of the regions west and south of the Rhine, the Danube, and the Black Sea, and north of the Sahara.

Considerable as were the relative economic achievements of, say, the Roman Empire in the first two centuries of the Christian era, its wealth was still (by modern standards) meager and was, moreover, dependent to some extent on the exploitation of dependent provinces and in very large part on the efforts of slave labor. Roman "prosperity," in other other words, was partially parasitical and was firmly based on, and

---

[18] A possible exception to this rash generalization was the Minoan civilization which flourished (principally with the aid of commerce) in the island of Crete in the first half of the second millennium B.C.

therefore limited by, the potentialities of muscle power. Ideologically, too, Rome—or, rather, the upper class of Roman society—was less than wholehearted in its commitment to material progress, and the consequent diversion of capital and entrepreneurial ability from production and trade to colonial exploitation and to administrative occupations acted as a distinct brake on economic expansion.

B. The Medieval Economy and the Beginnings of Change

The collapse of the Roman political and social system, which was completed in the second half of the fifth century A.D., ushered in a period of chronic economic dislocation in Western Europe. The causes of this collapse need not concern us here, except to note that the barbarian invasions were only part of the story: an internal loss of direction, an inability to maintain an efficient administration over so vast an area, and severe economic disturbances in the last generations of the Empire, must all bear some responsibility for the weakness which was the prelude to the shattering of Roman unity. Thenceforth, although sophisticated economic activity never entirely ceased, the so-called "Dark Ages" (roughly from the late fifth to the ninth century), under the impact of invasions and external pressures by barbarians, Moslems, Scandinavians, and Hungarians, witnessed an extended epoch of political disintegration and economic regression.[19]

When economic expansion began once again in the tenth and eleventh centuries its constituent elements were far more extensive than intensive, for it was based upon the geographical extension of trade and agriculture, the growth of population and the settlement of relatively abundant free land, the spread of inherited techniques, and the rise of progressive institutional arrangements like towns and international finance. Innovation and enhanced productivity were also to some degree responsible for the rising economic trends, and some historians detect the origins of capitalism (i.e., capitalist institutions) in contemporary financial and commercial practices. But compared with the economic transformation of the prehistoric Middle East, or with the more recent process of industrialization, the medieval economy underwent hardly any significant structural or technological changes. And, significantly, the same is broadly true of the downturn of aggregate production and trade in the fourteenth and fifteenth centuries: the trend was not a catastrophic collapse, but rather a downward drift of population, prices, and output

---

[19] From the world (as distinct from the West European) viewpoint the relatively gloomy picture was brightened by the prosperity and economic sophistication of the Arab and the Byzantine Empire—the latter centered on Constantinople and the vestigial survivor of the Roman political system.

—in which the first and third elements combined to alleviate the pressure on the average standard of living. Thus in the downsweep, as in the earlier upsurge, the medieval economy of Europe presented an institutionally stable appearance. Its attributes were in many respects those which today we are inclined to label "traditional" or underdeveloped: low levels of productivity, a very high proportion of the labor force engaged in agriculture, widespread reliance on manual methods of production, a semi-feudal and static social system, antipathy to experiment and a clinging to traditional technology and ways of thought, localization of markets, and a restricted division of labor.

The relative stability of the foregoing economic and social system was not effectively disturbed until the sixteenth, seventeenth, and early eighteenth centuries. This epoch, aptly called the early modern period by historians, witnessed a variety of changes (many of them not strictly speaking economic) which, while not comprising development in the modern sense, nevertheless established an essential bridge between the medieval economy and modern industrialism in Western Europe. First, and perhaps most important, the inherited ideological outlook was decisively overhauled under the influence of the Renaissance, the Scientific Revolution, and the Reformation. Each of these indirectly provided the basis for ultimate economic advance: the first by emphasizing, among other things, the worth of the individual and the creative excitement of man's new striving to control his own destiny; the second by propounding new empirical, pragmatic, and experimental ways of enlarging and using the field of knowledge; and the third (although there is some controversy on this point) by weakening the overt and the psychological restraints which medieval theology had imposed upon economic activity in general and profit-seeking in particular. As a consequence, therefore, intellectual developments converged to loosen the hold of tradition, to facilitate individual action and systematic experiment, to encourage the use of man-made techniques to control man's environment, and to provide new and powerful incentives to the application of effort to secular ends. Competition, change, and economic appetite emerged as the embryonic hallmarks of Western society.

The early modern period also witnessed economic developments which, even if they were not as significant as the ideological changes of the time, were still of great importance in laying the basis for ultimate economic growth. It was in these years for example, that the commercial horizons of Europe were vastly extended and economic relationships which had formerly been confined to the European land mass and parts of the Mediterranean were pushed thousands of miles across the oceans to Africa, Asia, and North and South America. The great geographical discoveries (facilitated by navigational innovations) and the new oceanic trade routes and colonies to which they led were basically economic phenomena: they extended the markets for European commodities and capital, enlarged the supply of foodstuffs, raw materials, precious metals, and textile fabrics, and fashioned a rudimentary intercontinental economy of which Western Europe was the center, the coördinator, and the beneficiary. This was not a sudden economic transformation, for it took generations and even centuries to accomplish. But its long-run economic consequences were revolutionary—for the world as well as for Europe. Yet not all European nations secured equal benefits from world trade and colonial systems. The reorientation of Europe's trade routes was inevitably accompanied by a shift in its economic center of gravity, and regions like Italy and Germany, which had formerly benefited by their central geographical positions, lost ground to regions on the Atlantic shores, at the termini of the new trade routes. First Portugal and Spain, then (after their late sixteenth-century eclipse) Holland, England, and, to a lesser extent, France, staked claims to commercial supremacy. In a "mercantilist" age, when trade was the principal basis for economic power, it was the seafaring nations which progressed the most.

All this should not be taken to imply either that agriculture had declined in relative significance or that production and trade *within* the European economy had sunk to a position of secondary importance. The foundation of Europe's wealth and income still lay in its own natural resources and the efficiency with which they were exploited. And here too, at least in some countries, the period between 1500 and 1750 witnessed developments which reflected the gradual breakup of the medieval economic system, and presaged even more dramatic changes to come. Particularly in England, in which the preconditions for growth evolved most effectively, gradual agricultural reorganization introduced a greater measure of flexibility and productivity into the supply of food and raw material (e.g., wool); the conservative influence of the guilds was considerably reduced by direct assaults on their exclusive powers and by the growth of industry in the countryside, away from their urban influence; specialization, both of geographic regions and economic functions, was extended; a small core of mining and other "heavy" industries was added to the existing consumer goods manufacturers; and significant improvements were made in transportation, financial, and marketing techniques and systems. All such developments, it should be emphasized, appear in retrospect as hardly more than the first stirrings of an economy which was still rudimentary in organization and poor in income. But from the viewpoint of the age, they comprised a spectacular, if long-drawn-out, surge of economic expansion. It is true that the revolutionary transformation of techniques and the accompanying *intensive* development of the economy were only to come in England during the century after about 1760. But the roots of the subsequent dynamism were firmly embedded in the changes which steadily gathered momentum in the two hundred or more years before that date.

C. Economic Development in the Modern Period

If the "preconditions" of economic growth, to use Professor Rostow's terminology,[20] were established in Britain, and to a somewhat lesser degree in some other West European economies, before the late eighteenth century, then the "take-off" came in the course of the late eighteenth century (for Great Britain) and the nineteenth century (for the United States, France, Germany, Sweden, Russia, etc.). But the process of economic development and industrialization, as has already been emphasized, was neither automatic nor inevitable. Why only certain countries experienced it and what the mechanisms were which produced it are topics about which no definitive conclusions are yet possible. Nevertheless, on the basis of comparative studies (some of which are illustrated in the selections which follow) it is possible to make some useful generalizations.

Any overall view of the phenomenon of modern industrialism must start with the experience of the British industrial revolution for a reason already touched on: the British case was the pioneer example and consequently had a significant and continuing influence on all subsequent spurts of industrialization throughout the Western world. Henceforth, for most of the nineteenth century, the British economy provides the best touchstone for the degree of backwardness or development in other countries.

Britain's economic, social, and political experience before the late eighteenth century explains with relatively little difficulty why she should have been an industrial pioneer. For better than any of her contemporaries Great Britain exemplified a combination of potentially growth-inducing characteristics. The development of enterprise, her access to rich sources of supply and large overseas markets within the framework of a dominant trading system, the accumulation of capital, the core of industrial techniques, her geographical position and the relative ease of transportation in an island economy with abundant rivers, a scientific and pragmatic heritage, a stable political and relatively flexible social system, an ideology favorable to business and innovation—all bore witness to the historical trends of two hundred years and more, and provided much easier access to economic change

---

[20] Selection 3.

in Britain than in any other European country. It is, however, far more difficult to explain why development came when it did, for economic change did not experience a steady acceleration; rather there was a more or less precise point (which most historians place in the 1780's) after which innovation, investment, output, trade, and so forth all seemed to leap forward. It may be, of course, that there was no single "cause" of the industrial revolution, but rather that a set of varied economic and social conditions attained a rare balance sufficient to initiate a process vastly different in kind from what had gone before. In this respect the availability of markets, the cumulative process of innovation, and investment and savings habits would all play an important role. Alternatively, attention might be focused on specific "proximate" causes. Some historians have concentrated on innovating and enterprising elements by studying the pioneer inventors and businessmen. Others have seen in market changes, or a combination of inflation and lagging wages, the cause of rising profits and capital accumulation. And, at a more sophisticated level, it has been argued that given the favorable convergence of other factors, the industrial revolution was basically a successful response to an economic challenge—either the slowing down of the previous rate of agricultural expansion or the exigencies of population growth.[21] What is certain is that the older interpretation of the British industrial revolution, which saw it as the outcome of an almost spontaneous wave of heroic inventions, is no longer fully tenable.

Whatever the precise causal mechanism of British industrialization, the hindsight which history offers to the economist throws into sharp relief a few necessary enabling conditions. Thus, apart from the general "prerequisites" already mentioned, development entailed those vast increases in productivity which only technological innovations could bring. The industrial revolution may not have been "caused" by, but it was certainly carried forward by, the application of machinery and power to textile production, by advances in the technology of iron manufacture, by the invention of the steam engine and the birth of engineering and the machine tool industry, and by the overhauling of methods in a host of other industries. Industrial growth, moreover, could only be sustained on the basis of improved agricultural productivity: in eighteenth-century Britain an agricultural revolution was a logical concomitant of an industrial revolution. For, while the rise of manufacturing industry was a means of paying for increased imports of food, it could not pay for all the food that the expanding economy needed. And only the reorganization of agriculture and the introduction

---

[21] See A. H. John, "The Course of Agricultural Change, 1660–1760," and J. D. Chambers, "Population Change in a Provincial Town: Nottingham, 1700–1800," both in L. S. Pressnell (ed.), *Studies in the Industrial Revolution* (London, 1960).

of advanced techniques of cultivation could help feed a growing population while at the same time providing for the growing *proportion* of that population which had to leave the farm for the factory and the town: labor as well as nourishment had to be supplied to the expanding industrial sector. A further point concerns the supply of savings to match the growing investment needs. The British "problem" in this regard was far less severe than that of many poor countries today. An unequal distribution of income (which reform movements were as yet too weak to alter) together with a beneficial tradition of saving for productive investment facilitated capital accumulation. And although the corporation as a widespread technique of impersonal finance was still far in the future, there were abundant connections between savers and investors. But perhaps the most striking feature of industrial finance was the extent to which investment was undertaken directly from profits by entrepreneurial abstention from consumption and the plowing back of profits. The classical economists' lack of anxiety about the savings-investment process was clearly derived from and justified by the world around them.

The expansion of the nineteenth-century British economy was attended by structural changes of a type which had never before occurred. The growth of factories and towns entailed not only a massive redistribution in the occupation and place of residence of the people, but an entirely new balance in Britain's output of goods and services. Urbanization and the rise of an industrial sector were further accompanied by the modernization of commercial, transportation and financial techniques, and ultimately by the spread of large-scale enterprises and their inevitable concomitant: the corporation. With the emergence of new and powerful social groupings, primarily factory laborers and industrial capitalists, the balance of political forces was shifted in directions which ultimately favored social and political reforms, the consolidation of trade unions, significant welfare measures, and dramatic departures in economic policy, of which the most important was the advent of free trade at mid-century. Increasingly, the machine and mechanical power (rather than the harvest and the weather) began to dominate the rhythm of much of British life. This was true in a larger sense as well, for expansion was not a smooth process: it proceeded in more or less regular fluctuations of a few years' duration, with deep crises punctuating the cycles. And overlaying these fluctuations there were longer-term trends in rates of growth.

While the long-term trends, which seem to characterize the growth of all capitalist economies,[22] have not yet been satisfactorily explained,

---

[22] See Selections 1, 2, 9, 11, 15.

one of their most important components seems to have been the variations in the rates of growth of particular industries. For aggregate economic development was composed of surges by "leading sectors" which, over long periods of time, replaced each other in economic primacy. Thus in the initial decades of the British industrial revolution it was the cotton textile industry which experienced the most spectacular expansion. Subsequently, after 1840, railroad investment and the spread of a transportation network seemed to dominate the economy, and in the third quarter of the century the steel industry and steamship construction leaped ahead. This is not to deny, of course, the continued significance of engineering, coal, iron, and the like. But there can be little doubt that the pace of growth was frequently set by a limited number of industries which attracted large amounts of capital and which (through their demand for and supply of goods and services) had direct and far-reaching consequences for other sectors of the economy. Indeed, the slowing down of British economic expansion, which came toward the end of the nineteenth century, is generally associated with a failure to participate fully in the new economic possibilities then being opened up by further developments in steel and machine tools, in electrical engineering and other utilties, in chemicals, and so forth. This deceleration of the British economy, which was one element in the aforementioned trends, has been explained in a variety of ways: as the result of a failure of entrepreneurial and innovating drive after decades of too easy success, as an outcome of labor's restrictive practices, and as a consequence of the exhaustion of investment opportunities in metals and steam power.[23]

Whatever the explanation, Britain had lost its industrial supremacy by the end of the century. But the implications of her competitive failure in the contest with American and German industrialism were to some extent hidden (at least until two world wars in the twentieth century had had their debilitating effect) by the supremacy which she had attained earlier in the field of international trade and finance. For, to go back somewhat in time, the industrial revolution had transformed both Britain's trading relationships and her economic role in the newly emerging international economy. On the first point, in the old phrase, Britain became the "workshop of the world": her industrial lead and success (in 1870 she produced almost one-third of the world's manufactures) made for a supreme dominance and expansion of the total trade in manufactured goods, and a concomitant demand for and dependence upon the import of food and raw materials. As for Britain's economic role, her previous commercial success together with the

---

[23] See Selection 10.

advantages of pioneering in economic development placed her in a strategic position to control, and profit from, much of the rest of the world's carrying trade and financial needs: British national income was therefore considerably augmented by the efficiency with which she supplied trading, insurance, banking, and exchange services to other countries. And, more than this, the newly industrializing economy, through its rapid accumulation of capital, became a giant international creditor, and capital exports in the course of the century flowed particularly to (and returned income from) those lands which supplied primary produce to the industrial metropolitan economy: the United States, Australasia, Canada, India, and Africa.

The first three of these areas also bore witness to the energizing consequences of the new international economy. The increased supplies of manufactures and demand for primary products, the flow of capital from advanced lands, and the freedom of movement of large-scale international migrations all combined to stimulate economic expansion in what had been relatively empty lands. For it was the availability of markets, men, and capital which laid the basis of development in areas of white settlement, while they also benefited tremendously not only by a derived technology (e.g., the railroad), but also by the presence of political, social, and ideological systems which, like Britain's, were extraordinarily favorable to expansion. Yet if the international economy can be usefully considered as an "engine of growth," the significance of indigenous factors should by no means be underestimated. They were particularly important, for example, in the case of the United States, the most spectacular instance of nineteenth-century economic development.

In the course of the nineteenth century the United States grew from a nation of 5,300,000 to one of 76,100,000, and from a small, if reasonably prosperous, primary producer to a position of economic and industrial supremacy: by 1900 it was producing 30 per cent of the world's manufacturing output (as against Britain's 19.5 per cent). Besides the general factors already mentioned, it enjoyed the great advantage of enormous supplies of untapped but accessible natural resources, and a good part of the story of its growth can be told in terms of the expansion of the economy, of people and transportation, westward over the mountains for the commercial production of cotton, wheat, corn, hogs, cattle, timber, iron ore, coal, and a host of other products. But while the international demand for such products was a potent incentive to their production, so was the emergence of a domestic market (with the growth of population and industry), the supply of native savings and capital, and the application of indigenously developed entrepreneurship and technique. The same was true of the rise of American manufacturing—of a textile industry, grain and meat processing, iron and steel manufacture, the utilities industries—and of the emergence of articulated financial and distributive systems. Thus the railroads and manufacturing industry brought to the United States its own industrial revolution, although it is significant that so great were its natural resources and fertility that manufacturing output did not overtake agricultural production until the 1880's—by which time the absolute quantity of each was such that America had replaced Great Britain as the world's leading industrial nation. It was in the last decades of the century that the country began decisively to assume the familiar characteristics of modern industrialism: urbanization, the appearance of new economic and social classes, and the growth of large-scale enterprises. Indeed, in this last development—the emergence of big business—productive activity underwent the reorganization which made the United States rather than the United Kingdom the model of organizational progress. The giant corporation came to be associated not with inefficiency or inflexibility, as some had feared, but with a sustained drive for productivity and a systematization of economic processes. The cumulative economies of large-scale production were brought about both by the widespread application of labor-saving machinery (such as had always characterized the labor-short American economy) and by the rational organization of men and machines. By 1900 it was clear that, for sustained economic growth, mass production, as well as its concomitants, mass marketing and consumption, were to be essential ingredients.

All this is to some extent an anticipation of the world-wide process of industrialization. For well before 1900, the widening circle of economic development had transmuted the economies of other important countries. Once again, in any explanation of the advent of expansion (this time on the European continent) we must at least start with the influence of Great Britain. For the generative repercussions of British growth and the emergence of an international economy were not confined to new lands: countries like Belgium, France, Sweden, and Germany were influenced by the expansion of Britain's supply of and demand for goods and services, by the import of British capital and expertise (e.g., in railroad construction or early textile factories), by the availability of a developed technology and proven institutions, by the growth of international flows of men and capital, and, perhaps above all, by the potent example of success which the British experience offered.[24] In addition, of course, they also drew heavily on their

---

[24] It would be wrong to imagine that British development was the sole external influence on the development of other economies. Like technological innovation, economic growth tended to be cumulative, and the example of, say, French expansion together with the direct flow of French capital and enterprise, affected the industrialization of other lands. See Rondo E. Cameron, *France and the Economic Development of Europe, 1800–1914* (Princeton, N.J., 1961). Also see Selection 16.

own resources and assets—not only raw materials, but in the advance of enterprise, the perfection of technology, and the accumulation of capital. Yet, intrinsically, none of the continental nations had the innate advantages enjoyed by Britain or America on the eve of real economic development. And starting from a position of relative backwardness, even while their general aim was to imitate Britain's industrial success, they were each obliged (with varying success) to seek individual answers to individual problems.

One of the most stimulating and searching studies of the consequences of relative backwardness in nineteenth-century industrializations[25] enables us to conclude that the degree of backwardness (measured against British potentialities and achievements) in any particular country was a powerful determining factor in the pace and nature of its industrial development. For the elements of backwardness itself induced underdeveloped countries to undertake growth by means of institutional changes and actions (e.g., the use of large-scale bank credit and control, or the extensive wielding of state power and entrepreneurship) which had not been needed in the original industrial revolution. More than this, both necessary general reforms, such as political unification or the dismantling of serfdom, and the pressure for industrialization were in large part a function of the degree of contrast between existing underdevelopment and the possibilities inherent in advanced technology. The release of this pressure, often sustained by a powerful ideology, was characterized by the utilization in certain lines of the most modern techniques then available—and this, in turn, was normally accompanied by an emphasis on large-scale plant, and the realization of faster rates of growth than had been possible with the less advanced techniques of previous years in other countries.

In effect, then, many of the individual problems of underdeveloped economies seemed to center on the shortage of entrepreneurial skills and investment capital for crucial growth-inducing sectors of the economy. To some extent the retarding aspects of their backwardness were counterbalanced by the advantages of their very underdevelopment—in particular by the availability of relatively advanced technology and techniques (already perfected by richer lands) which offered the possibility of even more spectacular increases in productivity than were enjoyed by, say, Britain at the beginning of her industrial spurt. In addition, each country adapted its institutional response to satisfy its

---

25 Alexander Gerschenkron, "Economic Backwardness in Historical Perspective," in Bert F. Hoselitz (ed.), *The Progress of Underdeveloped Areas* (Chicago, Ill., 1952), pp. 3–29. Professor Gerschenkron is currently collecting and publishing his own studies in economic history, which develop and apply his theories. For a summary statement, see his essay on Russia (Selection 22).

particular needs. But, although a nation such as Germany achieved a spectacular degree of industrial success, such factors could not always compensate for other elements in backwardness. Correspondingly, therefore, some nations (France and Italy, for example) enjoyed only a partial process of economic development when compared with the experience of the pioneers of industrialization. In sum, for a variety of reasons, social and political as well as economic, the timing and extent, as well as the pace, of economic development varied widely as between the individual countries which experienced the spread of industrialism.

In spite of such considerations, in the context of history and the world around them most of the countries of Western Europe, together with their offshoots in North America and Australasia, underwent a process of growth in the generations before 1914 which gave them a measure of material wealth and power which was not only historically unprecedented but unrivaled among the rest of mankind. In the nineteenth century the already existing economic gap between the Western peoples and the rest of the world, between the rich and the poor lands, began to widen to an accelerating, and ultimately dangerous, extent.

Thus, before 1914, the West enjoyed an overwhelming dominance of industrialization, and its control of world politics was based upon that dominance until the mid-twentieth century. But it did not even then have a complete monopoly of economic modernity. One Asian country, Japan, and one country which spanned Asia and Europe, Russia, had begun the process of industrial transformation at an impressive pace. Of the two Japan was perhaps the more impressive, since it emerged from a situation of feudal backwardness which had formerly been hardly touched by Western influences. Yet, as a consequence of political and social revolutions in the 1860's it was able to break through the insular crust of tradition, a process which was based in large part upon direct technological and institutional imitation of the West, upon an ideological upsurge which identified national interest and independence with conscious modernization and entrepreneurship, upon tax and social systems which placed the burden of forced savings on the agricultural sector; and upon massive state action to create a favorable climate for growth and (where necessary) to initiate strategic enterprises in transportation and heavy industry. As a consequence, Japan between the late 1870's and the First World War (as well as after that date) achieved a growth rate, of aggregate and per capita national product, which was among the very highest in the world. Russia provides a comparable if not precisely equivalent example, one in which, although West European influence had always been stronger, a monolithic social and economic backwardness had still to be attacked before development could begin. Once again, therefore, reforms set the stage, and were followed by state entrepreneurship and guidance, by the exploitation of the peasant economy for investment purposes (although capital imports played a more important role in Russia than Japan), and by the beginnings of industrialization and the factory system. Between 1870 and 1914 the Russian economy grew at a rate which was slightly greater than Great Britain's.

In pre-1914 Russia and even more in Japan we have examples of economic development and industrialization set against an initial context of backwardness far more severe than any which the other developing nations had known. And the success of their experiments provides at least some historical justification for the belief that economic growth is not the monopoly of a particular type of culture and society. Nevertheless, in both cases there were strong Western elements. First, as is the case even with mid-twentieth-century communist regimes, recent economic development in most technological and some organizational senses, is a Western phenomenon, for the West was the first to experience (and has been the principal model for) the advent of the machine and power technology and the accompanying institutions which characterize any modern economic system. Second, even though Russia and Japan relied more directly on the state than most other nineteenth-century developing nations, the use of economic policy and government action for the indirect and direct stimulus of development was by no means an innovation. A large part of the American transportation network, for example, was to a significant degree dependent upon public action. Moreover, the extent and significance of state enterprise in these two economies were not such as to overshadow private economic activity. On the contrary, neither Japanese nor Russian development is explicable without an appreciation of the abundant supplies of imaginative and skilled entrepreneurs present in apparently traditionalistic societies. All this is not to imply that there were *no* differences between, say, Japan and Russia on the one hand and Great Britain and the United States on the other. But such differences lay not in the nature of overall economic processes, but rather in the speed with which the prerequisites for growth were established, in the ideological fervor which attended expansion, in the balance between the component forces of development, and in the precise loci of crucial sources of savings and enterprise and productive technology.

D. *The Twentieth Century*

Since we are here principally concerned with the initial stages of economic development, it will not be necessary to describe in any detail the evolution of relatively advanced lands in the twentieth century. Nevertheless, modern problems of growth can best be seen in the light of the 160 years which have just elapsed. To this extent, therefore, some long-term developments are undoubtedly relevant.[26]

Apart from the trends in the rate of growth of advanced lands (which suggest a perceptible but by no means catastrophic long-run decline), perhaps the most significant aspect of the pace of expansion of the last five or six generations has been its effects on the world distribution of income. Thus, while the economies which we now call "advanced" were obviously wealthier (on a per capita basis) than other countries in the early nineteenth century, the very high rates of economic growth which the former group thenceforth enjoyed served to widen, and are *still* widening, the gap in wealth and income between them and the rest of the world. By 1949, for example, the less than 20 per cent of the world's population living in North America, Western Europe, and Australasia received just over two-thirds (67 per cent) of the world's income. At the other end of the spectrum the situation was reversed: the 67 per cent of total world population which inhabited very poor countries received a mere 15 per cent of total income.[27] In 1955–57 there were fifty-two noncommunist countries with a total population of 838 million which "enjoyed" annual per capita incomes of under $100. A further twenty-three (208 million) had between $100 and $199.[28] The implications of this situation for the second half of the twentieth century derive from its two main aspects: the obvious presence of a yawning gulf between wealth and abject poverty, and the dynamic element which is introduced by the fact that the disparity between standards of living appears to be in a state of constant aggravation. It is only in this setting that one can begin to understand the dominant psychological fact of the international relationships of our time: namely, the joining of a tempestuous yearning for economic growth with a latent resentment toward those fortunate few who have already achieved it, on the part of the poor countries of the world.

Yet this is only the beginning of comprehension, for a significant gap in income has existed and has been growing for many generations already. Why did the now familiar political and economic consequences only become apparent after the 1940's? The answer to this question necessarily carries us beyond the strict limits of economic history. The determined aspiration for economic growth on the part of inhabitants of a relatively poor region is not and cannot be a function of economic

---

[26] See Selection 2.
[27] Meier and Baldwin, p. 9.
[28] Paul G. Hoffman, *One Hundred Countries: One and one Quarter Billion People* (Washington, D.C., 1960), p. 18.

appetite alone: it is in fact found in conjunction with a pervasive and powerful ideology, and the ideology which historically in many instances (e.g., in Japan) and almost invariably today is most strongly associated with the desire for expansion is some version of nationalism. It is a yearning for an increase in the income and power and prestige of a *particular* country which (even in the extreme case of communist lands) goes far to explain the current concentration of effort on the tasks of development. Consequently, therefore, we must acknowledge the emergence of a national consciousness as the driving force behind the apparently universal movement for growth. And this in itself sheds a good deal of light upon the timing of that movement—for nowhere is such national consciousness more virulent than among newly independent and ex-colonial nations, and at no time in history has there been a period of "decolonization" to match that which followed the disruptions of two world wars. From 1945 to 1961 more than one billion people and over fifty countries secured their national independence. But the eradication of the political tensions which accompanied a colonial status left behind not only a residue of political prejudice and resentment but other, more powerful, tensions which can perhaps only be relieved by an increase in national incomes. With their dissatisfactions intensified and their appetites whetted by the recent enormous improvements in means of international communication, significant groups within virtually every poor nation in the world can think of few things other than economic development and the strengthening of their own country.

As has already been implied, this is not an entirely new phenomenon in world history. The real novelty and the real danger lie in its universality and its intensity, and (perhaps most of all) in the changed economic and historical situation which underdeveloped nations now face. It is true, for example, that some of them have economic systems not too dissimilar from those of Western nations on the eve of their industrial take-off; but it is also clear that a considerable number of really backward lands which wish to develop rapidly will have to telescope into one generation the preparatory changes (the establishment of the preconditions) which already developed countries sometimes took two centuries to effect. And while the Japanese case may be a partial illustration of its feasibility, the enormous difficulties of such a rapid transformation should not be underestimated.

Quite apart from the creation of a suitable set of prerequisites, however, development itself presents large problems. Thus, the very popularity of the idea of growth is inevitably associated with a keen and widespread desire to enjoy its fruits: it is the American standard of living rather than American statistical growth rates that the poor lands wish to emulate. And this, in turn, poses problems for capital accumulation which most nineteenth-century economies did not have to face. The mass of any poor country's population is anxious to benefit from, that is to *consume*, the products of an expanding economy, and in many circumstances may be in a political position to secure such a benefit. Consequently, the very aspiration for growth may have a built-in brake upon the accumulation of capital and therefore upon productive investment. Hence, in measure as very rapid growth rates may entail some form of "exploitation" the temptation to set up authoritarian regimes (to enforce a high rate of forced savings) may prove difficult to resist.

Another potential stumbling block to capital accumulation and growth, which has already been mentioned, lies in population trends. Many poor countries (India is a good example) find it sufficiently difficult to increase their total output so as to keep pace with rising populations, without having to secure a pace of advancement fast enough to overcome the retarding effects of their actual or threatened population explosion. And to this problem, some sorts of authoritarian regimes are not necessarily effective solutions. Communism, for example, at least in its Chinese version, is ideologically so hostile to Malthusian doctrine that it is reluctant on principle to propound policies designed to check the birth rate, and has even been known to *encourage* population growth.

Moreover, quite apart from such intrinsic factors as the supply of entrepreneurship and capital and the allocation of scarce investment capital,[29] the nature of the economic environment external to the backward lands is such as to cast doubt upon the value of too facile a comparison with historical experience. Thus, it would appear that some of the international mechanisms for the transmission of development which worked so well in the nineteenth century are now seriously (although not irreparably) weakened. The strongest one is probably the continued existence of examples of high national incomes which stimulate emulation; and, as we have already seen, this may prove to be self-defeating—while, on the other hand, the international trading and financial systems no longer justify complete optimism that they can exert the right sort of diversified demand or channel sufficient amounts of private risk capital to produce a broad-gauged growth process in presently backward areas.

Of course, the picture is by no means uniformly gloomy. Poor countries have at their disposal an advanced technology which is productive beyond the wildest expectations of any nineteenth-century entrepreneur.

---

[29] The inefficiencies of communist regimes in their efforts to raise agricultural productivity demonstrate that no "simple" solution can be found to some of these problems.

And, while they clearly lack for private capital imports, the very fact that growth is now considered an *international* problem means that the rich countries are transferring large, although still inadequate, supplies of (public) capital and expertise in an effort to promote their growth. Finally, it is surely a hopeful sign that economic development is now the subject of widespread and systematic thought and effort—and that its advent will no longer depend upon the fortuitous interplay of economic and social forces. To be conscious of a problem is, after all, to be already some way toward its solution. And the full sweep of history demonstrates that man *is* inherently capable of so organizing his society as to produce and apply the techniques necessary for controlling his economic destiny. Notwithstanding the great difficulties and the disheartening disappointments which still face the majority of mankind in their search for an escape from poverty, it is important to remember that some societies have already achieved this aim. With due allowance for the changing needs of changing circumstances, and with patience and the sustained search for wisdom, it is surely not impossible that what some men have done others can do again. With these reservations and this conclusion in mind, the following studies in the economic history of economic growth, which show where man has already been in his quest for wealth, may be of far more use than an unnecessarily pessimistic analysis of current problems would suggest.

PART
· II ·

INTERNATIONAL
COMPARISONS
AND THE
LESSONS OF HISTORY

INTRODUCTION

The five essays which follow present differing (although, of course, not necessarily conflicting) interpretations of the process of growth from a general viewpoint. To this extent, therefore, they contrast with the rest of this book, which is composed of more specific studies, limited in each case to a particular country. Like all such comparative studies, those reprinted in this Part have as their principal aim the formulation of general hypotheses based on comparison of the experiences of a group of countries. It is, perhaps, significant that only two of the five are professional economic historians. In large part this is because the amount of historical information available is not yet sufficiently abundant to permit more than a limited number of generalizations to be made concerning economic growth. That the necessary accumulation of data need not be the task of historians alone is illustrated by Selections 1 and 2, written by economists: Professor Simon Kuznets of Harvard University and Mr. Surendra J. Patel of the United Nations Economic Commission for Europe. Their essays, both based upon detailed measurements of the economic development of many countries, are included here to give the reader some idea of the general framework for any analysis of growth. In addition, each of them goes beyond mere measurement in order to explain some of the processes which lie behind their statistics. Much of Professor Kuznets' academic life has been devoted to the quantitative as well as the analytical study of many aspects of economic growth—and as a result historians as well as economists are deeply in his debt. In the essay reproduced here (which is taken from his book, *Six Lectures on Economic Growth*) he discusses the nature of economic development in different countries, provides statistical data on some of its principal characteristics, and suggests some hypotheses to explain these characteristics. Mr. Patel, on the other hand, is more concerned with the process of industrialization, rather than with the overall progress of the economy— although it is obvious that industrialization and economic growth are closely related. His study is primarily concerned with the rates of industrial growth in various countries, the behavior of these rates (both over time and as between different groups of countries), and the implications of such topics for poor countries which wish to launch themselves into the process of industrialization.

Selections 3 and 4 are far less quantitative in their emphasis than the first two. Probably the best known of all the essays in this book is that by Walt W. Rostow, who taught at the Massachusetts Institute of Technology before joining President Kennedy's administration (at the moment of writing he is Assistant Secretary of State in charge of Policy Planning). Professor Rostow began his extensive studies of economic history with research into the British economy of the nineteenth century (see Selection 9), and subsequently broadened his approach to encompass the whole field of development. Selection 3 is drawn from his *The Stages of Economic Growth*—a work which aroused considerable and widespread discussion (its views were sharply attacked in the Soviet press, for example). Professor Rostow's study is a most ambitious and stimulating attempt to systematize our knowledge of the significant trends and changing institutions which are to be found in the history of economically advanced or advancing countries. (For a discussion of some of Professor Rostow's theories, see the essay on Russia by Professor Gerschenkron in Selection 22.) In Selection 4, Professor H. J. Habakkuk of Oxford University employs another type of approach to the history of economic development. He examines the various mechanisms which induced or were associated with economic expansion in the past, referring to the experience of countries which underwent a significant measure of economic transformation before 1914. Taking some of the topics which economists normally consider in relation to the development of backward lands in the twentieth century, he provides a most valuable exercise in historical perspective.

Finally, Selection 5, an article by the late Professor Ragnar Nurkse, is concerned with a question very relevant to the problems of many underdeveloped (and primary-producing) countries today: the role of the international economy of the nineteenth century in stimulating economic growth throughout the world. Professor Nurkse was an outstanding economist in the field of international trade and investment and economic development, and his essay is included here not only for the light it sheds on problems of economic history, but also as an excellent example of how an economist who is sympathetic to the study of history can use it to advance our knowledge of theory as well.

1

The Meaning and Measurement
of Economic Growth

by

SIMON KUZNETS

‏᎐᎐᎐᎐᎐᎐᎐᎐᎐᎐᎐᎐᎐᎐᎐᎐᎐᎐᎐᎐᎐᎐᎐᎐᎐᎐᎐᎐᎐᎐᎐᎐᎐᎐᎐᎐‎

I. THE NATURE OF ECONOMIC GROWTH

Economic activity is concerned with the provision of goods needed to satisfy human wants, individual and collective. Hence, economic growth of a firm, an industry, a nation, a region, means (whatever else it may imply) a sustained increase in the output of such goods. It must be an increase, if it is to represent growth rather than stagnation or decay. And the increase must be in the volume of product, the provision of which is, from the standpoint of society, the rationale for economic activity. Finally, the increase must be sustained over a period long enough to reflect more than a cyclical expansion, an unusually large harvest, a post-calamity recovery, or some other transient rise.

This definition is quite general: it covers the economic growth of Periclean Athens, Augustan Rome, medieval France, modern United States, and even India and Egypt in some centuries. Being so general, it is hardly useful as a preliminary guide to the topic of central interest to us here—the economic growth of nations in modern times, i.e., during the last one and one-half to two centuries. Modern economic growth of nations has two distinctive features: in *all* cases it involves a sustained and substantial rise in product per capita, and in *almost all cases* it involves a sustained and substantial rise in population. In the more distant past, economic growth meant in many cases a sustained rise in total population and in total product, but not in per capita product; moreover, the rates of rise were far more moderate than those of modern times. When there was a substantial rise in per capita product, it was usually a result of reduced population pressures following drastic declines in numbers. To repeat, the distinctive feature of modern economic growth is the frequent combination of high rates of growth of the total population and of per capita product, implying even higher rates of growth of total product.

The emphasis on a sustained and substantial rise in *per capita* product is particularly important because of its implications for the structure and conditions of modern economic growth. Given the structure of human wants, a cumulatively large rise in a country's per capita product necessarily means a shift in relative proportions of various goods demanded and used—and hence major changes in combinations of productive factors, in patterns of life, and in international relations. Furthermore, a rise in per capita product usually means an even larger rise in product per unit of labor input—since some of the extra product is ordinarily exchanged for more leisure, a concomitant of a higher standard of living. However, marked rises in product per labor unit, when population and therefore labor force are increasing, are usually possible only through major innovations, i.e., applications of new bodies of tested knowledge to the processes of economic production. Indeed, modern economic growth is, in substance, an application of the industrial system, i.e., a system of production based on increasing use of modern scientific knowledge. But this also means structural change as new industries appear and old industries recede in importance—which, in turn, calls for the capacity of society to absorb such changes; society must be able to accommodate itself to and adopt the successive innovations that raise per capita productivity. Thus the rise in per capita product is emphasized because of its implications—the structural changes that necessarily accompany it, and all that these changes imply because of their origin in technological innovations and because of their requirements in the way of society's adaptability to change.

The difficulties in measuring economic growth, supply of empirical data apart, lie precisely in this point: modern economic growth implies major structural changes and correspondingly large modifications in social and institutional conditions under which the greatly increased product per capita is attained. Yet for purposes of measurement, the changing components of the structure must be reduced to a common denominator; otherwise it would be impossible to compare the product of the economy of the United States with that of China, or the product of an advanced country today with its output a century ago before many of the goods and industries that loom so large today were known.

The numerous problems that arise in an attempt to reduce national products of differing composition, originating under different social conditions, to comparable aggregates that are divisible into additive parts, can scarcely be mentioned here, let alone discussed. I shall have to assume familiarity with the questions of scope (inclusion and exclusion), netness and grossness, and basis of valuation, that are usually treated in discussing conceptual problems in measurement of national product; and with the subdivisions by industry of origin, factor and type of income, type of use, domestic and foreign origin, etc., that yield the component classifications usually distinguished. It is important, however, to point out the major assumptions on the basis of which these thorny, and essentially insoluble, problems are usually resolved in actual measurement.

The basic assumption is the community of human nature in that the weights attached to various outputs, or productive factors, although taken from one or a few societies, have meaning for all or at least most of them. This is clearly a prerequisite for all comparisons over space or time. If we assumed that people today are radically different from their forebears of fifty to a hundred years ago, no meaningful comparisons over time could be made. Or if we assumed that the inhabitants of the United States and those of the U.S.S.R. are so different that food, clothing, etc., or labor and capital goods, mean quite different things to them, comparison of the national product of the two countries would be impossible—unless it referred to some exogenous base of valuation with no specified meaning in either country.

Secondly, in actual application, the sets of concepts and weights employed are those of one or a few economies, or of one or a few points in time. And the weights chosen are usually those of the more developed rather than the less developed economies, of the more recent point of time rather than the earlier. Thus, the translation in the international comparison made by the United Nations (used in some of the tables below) is to the purchasing power of the United States dollar, and the same was true of Colin Clark's "international unit" (until the third edition in 1957, when the "Oriental unit" was introduced). Likewise, in the measurement of changes over time, product is usually expressed in constant prices of recent years, not in prices of the past. There is a rationale for these choices, over and above the practical convenience of the greater availability of data for the advanced economies and for recent years. We evaluate economic growth from the vantage point of the higher levels already attained—both in looking back in time and in looking at the lower levels of less advanced economies: we live today and not in the past, and the less advanced economies aspire to the levels of the more advanced, not vice versa. In other words, the more advanced economies and the more recent times yield the *criteria* of economic growth.

Thirdly, it has generally been emphasized that the use of weights and concepts typical of advanced economies, or of recent decades, introduces a bias into comparisons that favors these more advanced units or more recent periods. This upward bias has been ascribed to the obvious danger of excluding from the measures non-market-bound activities that are proportionately much greater in less than in more advanced economies, and in earlier than in more recent decades; and to the fact that our measures do not make full allowance for the costs of the higher levels of output—greater costs of urban life, of accommodation to the job, etc.—which may be proportionately greater for advanced economies and for the more recent decades. There are also factors making for an opposite bias. Thus the use of recent price weights tends to yield a lower rate of growth, in so far as the goods that grow most rapidly are also those whose prices usually decline most. Likewise, the use of the price weights of the advanced countries tends to give many raw materials and simpler goods in the underdeveloped countries *higher* standing (relative to the complex manufacturing products) than they in fact have, and since the proportion of such goods is larger in these countries, there is an upward bias in valuation relative to that in the more advanced economies. One should not, therefore, jump to the conclusion that the common basis of valuation and treatment in international and intertemporal comparisons produces a bias that favors *uniformly* the more advanced economy or the more recent period. Indeed, from the standpoint of the less advanced economy or the earlier decade, the present procedures may *underestimate* the differences across space or the rate of growth over time.

Whatever the case, the conceptual and other difficulties of measurement do not justify the refusal to measure and the substitution of a cavalier treatment of uncontrolled impressions (even if embodied in apparently precise mathematical models) for the strenuous task of empirical corroboration and testing. Despite the limitations resulting from a scarcity of basic, underlying data and from concepts that are outmoded because of a serious cultural lag, much can be learned by a determined scrutiny of the data—provided that one looks at them with significant questions in mind and is sufficiently familiar with the characteristics of both the data and the underlying processes. Whatever mistakes one may make in the process—and they will be many—can at least be corrected by others; cumulative improvement and learning are possible so long as the data are mobilized to serve as a basis of one set of generalizations and as a check on another.

The High Rates of Modern Economic Growth

Table 1 brings together the rates of growth of population, per capita product, and total product (both in constant prices) for nineteen countries. These are all the countries, with population of no less than a million in recent years, for which the records cover a long period—at least four decades, and in most countries extending over half a century. . . .

The first point to be noted is that the records reflect the growth of countries, of national units. In theory, other units could be used—other area divisions, industries, groups of producers distinguished by their organizational characteristics (households, corporations, etc.), down to the individual firm. Indeed, since growth is an aspect of economic activity at large, the primary units engaged in such activity could be combined in various ways, and growth could be observed and analyzed for a wide variety of larger composite units. It is no accident that we begin with the nation-state as the unit for observing economic growth, nor is it to be explained merely by the way the data are most easily available. Nations are the foci of differences and decisions: the historical past of each is a distinctive complex and sets specific conditions for its economic growth, and the organization of each into a political community is of major importance in permitting secular decisions conducive (or inimical) to economic growth. This does not mean that we should not distinguish industries, or regions, or groups of economic organizations, within each nation; or combine nations into larger and more comprehensive complexes. Yet the nation is the dominant unit of observation and analysis, and has been such in much of the history of economics as an intellectual discipline (*vide* its original name of *political* economy). However, like any other limiting choice, the emphasis on the nation-state as the unit of observation and analysis has its limiting consequences which we shall have to bear in mind when we look at the results.

The sample in Table 1 is confined largely to what we now designate economically developed countries, with a few exceptions such as Spain, Ireland, and Hungary, and the intermediate case of Italy. Whatever generalizations we derive from it are thus based on observations relating to a small part of the world—a sample of roughly twenty states out of more than eighty; of less than 700 million people out of a world population of over 2.5 billion. More important, Table 1 includes all the developed countries of the world with few exceptions (e.g., Belgium), and its scope, already somewhat exaggerated by the inclusion of units that cannot be considered economically advanced, indicates the limits of the spread of the industrial system. The fact of the matter is that in the well over one and one-half centuries since the industrial revolution in Great Britain, the industrial system has spread to only a limited part of the world and includes only about a quarter of the world population. The technological and social changes resulting from the emergence and evolution of the industrial system did, of course, have a wider impact, but that impact did not advance the economic performance of the rest of the world to levels anywhere near those for most of the countries in Table 1.

The one outstanding characteristic of modern economic growth, where we can observe it, is the high rate of increase. For population, except in Ireland and France, the rate of increase ranges from 6 to over 20 per cent per decade. For per capita income, except in Spain and Hungary, the rate ranges from close to 10 to well over 20 per cent per decade. As a result, the rate of increase in total product is even higher— never falling below 10 per cent per decade and ranging in most cases from 15 to over 40 per cent.

The rates of increase, particularly in per capita income, are . . . high in that, judging by a variety of evidence, they could not have prevailed over many decades in most of the world, nor could they have prevailed over a very long period in any country no matter how highly developed it is today. The first part of this inference can be easily corroborated if we recognize that in much of the world, as indicated by a variety of international comparisons, *present* levels of per capita income are relatively low. If we use per capita national product estimates for 1952–54 (or some earlier year in a few cases) prepared by the United Nations, and set the maximum income for underdeveloped countries at roughly $100 (in purchasing power of 1952–54), most of the populous countries of Asia (China, India, Pakistan, Indonesia, Burma, South Korea, Thailand) and many in Africa—close to half of the world population— would fall within this group. In these countries, and the many others with per capita incomes only slightly above $100, growth in per capita income over past decades could not have been substantial. Extrapolation backward of rates of increase like those in Table 1 would yield impossible levels in earlier times, impossible because life could not have been maintained at such low levels. Then, too, we have some direct evidence on the presently underdeveloped countries, e.g., India and Egypt, showing that over the last five decades, indeed since the beginning of the century, there was scarcely any rise in real per capita income.

The second part of the inference, viz., that the rates of rise in per

TABLE 1

RECENT LEVELS AND PAST RATES OF GROWTH: POPULATION, PRODUCT PER CAPITA, AND TOTAL PRODUCT; SELECTED COUNTRIES (WITH LONG PERIOD OF COVERAGE)

COUNTRY	RECENT YEARS		RATES OF GROWTH			PER CENT CHANGE PER DECADE		
	Population Mid-1953 (millions) (1)	Product Per Capita 1952–54 (U.S. dollars) (2)	Initial Period (3)	Terminal Period (4)	Decades in Interval (5)	Population (6)	Product Per Capita (7)	Total Product (8)
1. United Kingdom[a]	50.6	780	1860–69	1949–53	8.65	8.0	12.5	21.5
2. Ireland and Eire[b]	2.9	410	1860–69	1949–53	8.65	-3.5	16.8	12.8
3. France	42.9	740	1841–50	1949–53	10.55	1.3	13.8	15.3
4. Germany[c]	49.0	510	1860–69	1950–54	8.75	10.1	15.1	27.4
5. Switzerland	4.9	1,010	1890–99	1949–53	5.65	7.7	15.3	24.4
6. Netherlands	10.5	500	1900–1908	1950–54	4.8	14.3	9.0	24.6
7. Denmark[d]	4.4	750	1870–78	1950–54	7.8	10.9	16.7	29.4
8. Norway[e]	3.4	740	1900–1908	1950–54	4.8	8.2	23.4	33.5
9. Sweden[f]	7.2	950	1861–68	1950–54	8.75	6.6	27.6	36.0
10. Italy	47.6	310	1862–68	1950–54	8.7	6.9	10.4	18.0
11. Spain	28.5[h]	250[h]	1906–13	1949–53	4.15	8.8	5.6	14.9
12. Hungary	9.2[i]	269[i]	1899–1901	1949	4.9	6.2	8.7	15.5
13. Russia and U.S.S.R.[g]	207.0[j]	500[j]	1870	1954	8.4	13.4	15.4	31.0
14. United States	159.6	1,870	1869–78	1950–54	7.85	17.4	20.3	41.2
15. Canada[k]	14.8	1,310	1870–79	1950–54	7.75	18.3	19.3	41.3
16. Union of South Africa	13.2	300	1911/12	1949/50–1952/53	3.95	20.9	23.8	49.7
17. Japan	86.7	190	1878–87	1950–54	6.95	12.7	26.3	42.3
18. Australia	8.8	950	1898–1903	1949/50–1953/54	5.1	17.2	9.5	28.4
19. New Zealand	2.0	1,000	1901	1949/50–1953/54	5.025	18.7	11.8	32.7

Unless otherwise indicated, the entries in Columns 1 and 2 are from "Per Capita National Product of Fifty-Five Countries: 1952–1954," United Nations, *Statistical Papers, Series E*, No. 4 (New York, 1957); and the entries in columns 3–8, from Simon

Kuznets, "Quantitative Aspects of the Economic Growth of Nations: I. Levels and Variability of Rates of Growth," *Economic Development and Cultural Change*, Vol. V, No. 1 (October, 1956), particularly Tables 1 and 2.

The interval in column 5 is calculated from the mid-point of the initial period to the mid-point of the terminal period. All rates of growth in columns 7 and 8 are for net national product in constant prices, unless otherwise indicated.

[a] Excluding southern Ireland.

[b] The entries for 1952–54 are for Eire. The rates of change in columns 6–8 are weighted averages of the rates for 1860–69 to 1904–13 (weight 4.4) and for Eire for 1911 to 1949–53 (weight 4).

[c] The entries for 1952–54 are for West Germany. The rates of change in columns 6–8 are weighted averages of the rates for the pre-World War I territory for 1860–69 to 1905–14 (weight 4.5); for the 1925 territory for 1913 to 1935–41 (weight 2.5); and for West Germany for 1936 to 1950–54 (weight 1.6).

[d] The rates in columns 7 and 8 are for net domestic product. A correction of about 5 per cent was made for inclusion of the area of North Schleswig in 1920 and later years.

[e] The rates in columns 7 and 8 are for gross national product.

[f] The rates in columns 7 and 8 are for gross domestic product.

[g] The rates in columns 6–8 are weighted averages of the rates for European Russia for 1870–1913 (weight 4.3) and for the U.S.S.R. for 1913–54 (weight 4.1). The national product in columns 7 and 8 excludes personal and government services.

[h] The population total is from the United Nations *Demographic Yearbook*, 1954; per capita product is a crude estimate based on the relation in 1948 to the comparable figure for Italy, given in W. S. and E. S. Woytinsky, *World Population and Production* (Twentieth Century Fund, 1953), Table 186, pp. 392–93, and applied to the figure for Italy in column 2.

[i] The entry is for 1949; from "National and Per Capita Incomes, Seventy Countries—1949," United Nations, *Statistical Papers*, Series E, No. 1 (New York, 1950).

[j] The population total is from Colin Clark, *Conditions of Economic Progress* (3rd ed.; London, 1957), Table XXVI, p. 250. Figures in that table yield a per capita net national product (in I.U.'s) of about 300, compared with 1,128 for the United States for 1952 (*ibid.*, Table XI, p. 193). This suggests a figure of roughly 500 United States dollars.

[k] The rates in columns 7 and 8 are for gross national product.

capita income for the developed countries could not have prevailed over very long periods, can be demonstrated by extrapolating the rates in Table 1 back and observing that low levels are reached too rapidly to be historically true. . . . If we assume that a per capita income of $100 in 1952–54 prices (about half the level for Japan) is about rock bottom for the northern and western countries, extrapolation would bring us to this level in most of the presently developed countries (except Australia and New Zealand) by the late eighteenth, early nineteenth, or even the middle of the nineteenth century. . . . Certainly per capita income in the United Kingdom in 1779 and in the United States in 1795 was not that low; and certainly growth in per capita income in both countries had been substantial before these dates. It follows that the rates of growth shown in Table 1 . . . are exceptionally high in the sense that they could not have persisted over really long periods in the past. Regardless of whether we can envisage continuation of such rates in the future, the records of the past tell us that against the perspective of many centuries of human history, the rates of growth of both population and per capita income (and hence of total income) in the recent past were unusually high.

The extremely high rate of modern growth in population, suggesting what demographers often refer to as a "population explosion," has been observed and known for some time; nor is there anything new about the conspicuously high rate of modern growth in income per capita. While these facts have become increasingly known and accepted, some of their implications are not so well recognized. It is to these implications that we now turn.

II. THE NECESSARY CONDITION

As already noted, sustained high rates of growth of per capita income meant, in the decades covered by our estimates, even higher rates of growth in product per man-hour; when population also grew rapidly, this meant major changes in the production functions that could not have occurred except for continuous innovations—particularly for countries where extensive expansion was impossible. Innovation is a new application of either old or new knowledge to production processes (production defined broadly); since old knowledge, in a form ready for extensive application, is limited, a continuous and large rise in product per unit of labor is possible only with major additions of *new* technological and related knowledge. Continuous technological progress and, underlying it, a series of new scientific discoveries are the necessary conditions for the high rate of modern growth in per capita income combined with a substantial rate of growth in population. As evidence, we need only note the industries that loom large in an advanced economy: many in the electrical, internal combustion, and chemical fields were entirely unknown a hundred years ago, and even the older industries are permeated by processes whose origin lies in relatively recent scientific discoveries.

In these days it is hardly necessary to emphasize that science is the base of modern technology, and that modern technology is in turn the base of modern economic growth. Without the emergence and development of modern science and science-based technology, neither economic production nor population could have grown at the high rates indicated for the last century to century and a half in the developed countries. True, growth of tested knowledge, both scientific generalization and empirical information, and of modern technology based on it, were necessary, not sufficient conditions: knowledge in itself does not suffice, for reasons some of which will be noted below. Yet the growth of science and technological knowledge has distinct patterns of its own; difficult as it is to discern them (particularly for a mere economist), some attempt should be made to do so, for they are relevant to the pattern, intra- or international, that modern economic growth exhibits.

In attempting to trace these patterns we may distinguish the following: a scientific discovery—an addition to knowledge, ranging from a minor item like the formula for a new organic compound to a major principle like that relating matter and energy; an invention—a tested combination of already existing knowledge to a useful end; an innovation—an initial and significant application of an invention, whether technological or social, to economic production; an improvement—a minor beneficial change in a known invention or process in the course of its application; and finally, the spread of an innovation, usually accompanied by improvements, either through extensive imitation or internal growth. While these can be seen as successive phases—from discovery to invention to innovation to improvement to spread—there is also a feed-back effect. The spread of innovations may favor further inventions, and the latter may stimulate further discovery.

Within this complex, two characteristics relevant to the problem of economic growth may be suggested. First, there is a bottleneck relationship between the successive phases—from the scientific discovery to the spread of an innovation. Each scientific discovery is potentially a base for a wide variety of inventions (which is one major reason why discoveries are not patentable), but not all these possible inventions are produced. Each invention is a candidate for an innovation, but only a small proportion of inventions is adopted. Each innovation is a candidate for widespread use, but only a limited proportion is extensively used and can then be characterized as major innovations. The factors that determine the choice of inventions made, among those possible with the given stock of scientific discoveries; of innovations made, among all the inventions that clamor for application; and among those, of major innovations, are diverse and still little known. But at the link where innovations transform new technological knowledge into production reality, three factors are obviously important: (a) Many major inventions, if they are to become successful innovations, demand heavy capital investment—both in material goods and in the training of the labor force. Material capital is necessary to channel properly the new power in its application to intricate ends, and an educated and skilled labor force is indispensable in operating complex machinery and production processes. (b) Innovations, by definition, represent something new and require entrepreneurial talents and skills to overcome a series of unexpected obstacles. (c) Much depends upon the responsiveness of the would-be users of the new products or processes who are the final judges of the potential technological changes to be adopted for widespread use and hence for mass production. All these requirements combined with the *necessary* condition of increased technological knowledge constitute the *sufficient* condition for modern economic growth.

Second, there is a tendency for scientific discovery, invention, and innovation to be concentrated at any given time in a few fields—rather than be evenly distributed among all. In the late eighteenth and early nineteenth centuries, it was the iron, stationary steam, and the cotton textile industries that constituted the focus of much invention and innovation. In the late nineteenth century emphasis was put upon electric power and communication, and then the internal combustion engine. In the mid-twentieth century emphasis is being put upon atomic energy, with the steam era well in the past and the electricity era coming to an end as a field for major discovery, invention, or innovation. There are two reasons for such shifts in the focus of discovery, invention, and innovation. First, the available intellectual and material resources are never sufficient for the pursuit of new knowledge, invention, or innovation in all possible fields with equal vigor; some choice, conscious or unconscious, of the more promising areas must be made. Second, at any given time only a few areas are *most* promising: the potential of further invention and innovation in the older areas is limited by earlier progress and growth, and some very new areas may not yet be ready for successful invention and innovation.

An important consequence for the pattern of economic growth follows. This shift of emphasis from one area within the productive system to another in addition to knowledge, new technology, and innovation means changes in the identity of the new and rapidly growing industries. By the same token, there is a tendency toward retardation in the rate of growth of older industries, as the economic effects of technical progress and innovation within them slacken and as they feel increasingly the competition of the newer industries for limited resources. To put it differently, a sustained high rate of growth depends upon a continuous emergence of new inventions and innovations, providing the bases for new industries whose high rates of growth compensate for the inevitable slowing down in the rate of invention and innovation, and upon the economic effects of both, which retard the rates of growth of the older industries. A high rate of over-all growth in an economy is thus necessarily accompanied by considerable shifting in relative importance among industries, as the old decline and the new increase in relative weight in the nation's output.

Another aspect of the interrelation of science, technology, and economic growth may be noted. In the late eighteenth and early nineteenth centuries, before some of the wide potentialities of scientific discovery and science-based technology became evident, there was a general tendency to assume a fairly narrow limit to the effects of technological change in offsetting increasing scarcity of irreproducible natural resources. One inference based on this view was that as a country develops economically, it must rely increasingly upon the natural resources of the less advanced countries. It would thus help spread the beneficial effects of modern economic growth elsewhere, since reliance upon supplies from the outside naturally means a *quid pro quo* in the way of industrial goods, capital, etc. The emphasis above on the availability of a much greater stock of knowledge than is in fact utilized in innovations, implies a fatal qualification upon this view, which connected the limited effects of technological change with the export of modern economic growth to the rest of the world. While economic growth in developed countries does lead to greater demand for raw materials from the rest of the world, it seems unlikely that investment opportunities for domestic savings in developed countries will be limited by the extreme costliness caused by scarcity of land or other natural resources under conditions of limited technological change. On the contrary, it may well be that the continuous growth in the rate of scientific discovery and potential technological change will provide *increasing* opportunities for domestic investment of the capital funds of the developed countries—leaving only enough capital exports to assure the supply of raw materials for the capital-exporters' domestic economy. To put it differently, the change in the rate of scientific discovery and potentially new technological development should lead to a careful and critical reconsideration of the nineteenth century notion that the limitations of natural resources in the more advanced countries automatically make for the spread of the industrial system to the rest of the world

—as an inevitable sequence from raw materials to industrial products; from capital import by the less developed countries for the expansion of raw material production, to capital import for industrialization.

The Time Pattern of Growth

Do science-based technology and invention, as a necessary condition of modern economic growth, operating within the limitations indicated above, set a time pattern of growth, once a nation enters upon modern economic development? By time pattern of growth we mean some order in the sequence of rates of increase. Do the rates rise, are they constant, or do they decline? And are there any reasons to expect a systematic pattern?

The answer may well differ for various components of a nation's economy, e.g., for population and for per capita product; or for nations with different antecedents, e.g., for old and settled countries like Great Britain and Germany, and for young and "empty" countries with room for expansion like the United States. Nevertheless, some elements of general order can be suggested, and these are important for our interpretation of secular trends in those measures of economic growth that we have.

One element of order is clearly indicated by what has already been said. The spread of the industrial system, based on the additions to useful knowledge made since the eighteenth century, meant much higher rates of growth of population, per capita product, and total product, than before. At some period in the transition from pre-modern conditions to modern economic growth, therefore, there must have been a shift from lower to higher rates of growth. Since such shifts are rarely, if ever, sudden, there must have been a substantial period, extending over several decades, during which the rate of growth was accelerated, i.e., the rate of increase was rising.

. . . . .

The intriguing question is whether we should expect the rate of growth in per capita income to fall after a while, from whatever high levels it may have reached at the end of the acceleration phase. Difficult as it is to imagine unlimited growth in any social process, there are no inherently *compelling* reasons for the rate of growth of per capita product to decline. In the light of our earlier discussion, technological and other limitations on the *supply* side can hardly be viewed as an important factor. The major reason would therefore lie on the demand side. A long-term rise in real income per capita would make leisure an increasingly preferred good, as is clearly evidenced by the marked reduction in the working week in freely organized, non-authoritarian advanced countries. One could argue that after a high level of per capita income is attained, the pressure on the demand side for further increases is likely to slacken. If so, there would eventually be retardation in the rate of growth of per capita income, but it would come much later than that in the rate of growth of population.

The time pattern of growth in total product is obviously a compound of those in growth of population and per capita product. Acceleration in the rate of growth of population, provided the rate of growth of per capita product does not decline, would necessarily produce acceleration in the rate of growth of total product; and the latter would be further accelerated when the growth in per capita product quickens. When both population and per capita product stabilize at a constant rate of growth, total product will also grow at a constant rate. When retardation in the rate of population growth begins, the growth of total product will be retarded, *unless* the rate of growth of per capita product begins at that point to accelerate—which is highly unlikely. Thus one may expect a long secular swing in the rate of growth of total product, its phases of acceleration, constancy, and retardation falling, with respect to timing, between those for population and per capita product.

Before we consider the general implication of these time patterns, the evidence in Table 2 should be noted. Here we distinguish two sub-periods for those countries with relatively long records. Unfortunately, there are only eleven such countries, and even for some of these the value of the evidence is reduced by breaks in historical continuity and by the wide margins of error in the estimates for the early decades. In regard to population, if we exclude Ireland as the exceptional case, we find a retardation in the rate of growth, i.e., a lower rate in the second than in the first sub-period. The finding for Canada can be explained largely in terms of immigration, and that for Japan may not be significant because of deficiencies in population statistics for the early period. Regarding per capita product, we also find evidence of slowing down in the rate of growth, with the conspicuous exception of the U.S.S.R. and Italy whose industrialization occurs rather late, and of Sweden which managed to maintain its exceedingly high rate of growth of per capita income. The rates of growth in total product naturally reflect those just noted: in the majority of countries retardation is observed. Thus the evidence, on the whole, supports the notion of the time pattern suggested above—although it covers primarily the constant and downward phases of the pattern and does not reach sufficiently far

TABLE 2

RATES OF GROWTH OF POPULATION, PRODUCT PER CAPITA, AND TOTAL PRODUCT; TWO INTERVALS WITHIN THE LONG PERIOD; SELECTED COUNTRIES

COUNTRY	MIDDLE PERIOD	NUMBER OF DECADES		PER CENT CHANGE PER DECADE					
				Population		Product Per Capita		Total Product	
		Interval I	Interval II	Interval I	Interval II	Interval I	Interval II	Interval I	Interval II
	(1)	(2)	(3)	(4)	(5)	(6)	(7)	(8)	(9)
1. United Kingdom	1905–14	4.5	4.15	11.1	4.8	12.5	12.5	25.0	17.9
2. Ireland and Eire[a]	1904–13	4.4	4.0	−5.4	−1.4	17.9	15.7	11.6	14.2
3. France	1901–10	6.0	4.55	1.9	0.6	16.3	10.4	18.6	11.1
4. Germany[b]	1905–14	4.5	3.9	11.5	8.6	21.6	8.4	35.6	18.9
5. Denmark	1904–13	3.45	4.35	11.3	11.0	19.3	14.7	32.7	27.3
6. Sweden	1904–13	4.4	4.35	6.8	6.4	26.2	28.9	34.8	37.2
7. Italy	1904–13	4.35	4.35	7.0	6.7	8.1	12.7	15.7	20.3
8. Russia and U.S.S.R.[c]	1913	4.3	4.1	15.7	11.1	10.4	21.0	27.7	34.4
9. United States	1904–13	3.5	4.35	22.3	13.7	27.5	14.7	56.0	30.4
10. Canada	1905–14	3.5	4.25	17.8	18.8	24.7	15.0	47.1	36.6
11. Japan	1908–17	3.0	3.95	12.0	13.3	32.2	22.0	47.9	38.2
11a. Japan[d]	1908–17	3.0	3.0	12.0	12.8	32.2	37.2	47.9	54.7

The data are from the source cited for Table 1, columns 6–8. . . . In general, the aim was to divide the long period fairly equally, but in most cases the division line is just before World War I. The period given in column 1 is the terminal period of the first interval and the initial period of the second interval. The entries in column 1, together with those in Table 1, columns 3 and 4, give the distribution of the total time span into the two intervals. For other notes on the series for the various countries, see Table 1.

[a] The first interval runs from 1860–69 to 1904–13, and relates to all Ireland. The second interval runs from 1911 to 1949–53, and relates to Eire proper.

[b] The first interval runs from 1860–69 to 1905–14 and relates to the territory of the Reich before 1913. The rates for the second interval are weighted averages of the rates for 1913 to 1935–41 for the post-Versailles territory (weight 2.5); and for 1936 to 1950–54 for West Germany (weight 1.6).

[c] The first interval is for the period 1870–1913, and relates to pre-World War I European Russia. The second interval is for the period 1913–1954, and relates to the U.S.S.R. (interwar territory).

[d] In the second grouping of intervals for Japan, the first interval runs from 1878–87 to 1908–17; the second interval runs from 1903–12 to 1933–42. The 1933–42 decade shows the highest per capita income for the period from 1878–87 to 1950–54.

back (except for the U.S.S.R and Italy) to cover the acceleration phase.

The general implication of such a pattern can be clearly perceived if we assume that countries do not enter upon modern economic growth simultaneously. On this premise, their phases of acceleration, of constant high rates, and of retardation all occur at different times. The result of such differences in timing, combined with the nature of the pattern, can be seen most clearly if we assume as an initial simplification that the rates, duration of phases, and extent of acceleration and retardation are identical for all countries. On this assumption, differences in timing of entry of the various countries upon modern economic growth mean correlative differences in the rates of growth of population, per capita, and total product. Countries that start later than others soon shift from a position lagging behind the early entrants into a position where their rates of growth are distinctly higher than those of the early entrants which meanwhile may have entered the retardation phase. Such shifts among countries in relative rates of growth of population and product are pregnant with political shifts and strains. Obviously, greater knowledge about the time patterns of economic growth, the duration of the phases, and the rates involved, would shed light on the effects that different times of entry into modern economic growth have on the relative economic position of nations; hence also, on the stresses and strains that shifts in economic position may engender.

2

Rates of Industrial Growth
in the Last Century, 1860-1958

by

SURENDRA J. PATEL[1]

Nearly two centuries have elapsed since the start of the industrial revolution. But in the first of these two centuries the revolution was essentially an experimental and small-scale affair. Although many inventions had been made by the middle of the nineteenth century, the adoption of advanced technique was limited to Great Britain and even there, except for the textile industry, only on a small scale. The world of the first quarter of the nineteenth century had little experience with the steam locomotive and the railways which were to revolutionize transportation; even by 1850 the total length of the railway network in the three most developed countries—the United Kingdom, France and

Reprinted from *Economic Development and Cultural Change*, IX, 3 (April, 1961), (pp. 316–30, with omissions), by permission of The University of Chicago Press. Copyright 1961 by The University of Chicago.

[1] The author is a member of the Secretariat of the United Nations Economic Commission for Europe at Geneva. The views expressed herein, however, are his personal views and should not be interpreted as those of the Organization. He is indebted to Mrs. A. Brandt and Miss L. Danieli and a large number of his colleagues in the Economic Commission for the basic statistical work and for extensive discussions on the substance of the main arguments in this study.

Germany—was not quite 20,000 kilometres, i.e., less than a sixth of the network that these countries had by the end of the century. The output of pig iron in the whole world was only 4.6 million tons in 1850, half of which was in Great Britain. The technique of producing steel had hardly gone beyond the handicraft stage. Even the most advanced countries in the world were still in the last days of the iron age. Cast iron could be used in rails, pillars, bridges, engine cylinders and even wheels, but it had its limits; it was not suited for the working parts of engines and machines. The steel age was about to begin. The Bessemer converter was invented in 1856 and even with the advance made by the Martin-Siemens process (1864–67) the total output of steel in the world was no more than 700,000 tons in 1870, or less than one-half of India's output in 1958.

Hence only the last hundred years can be regarded as a century of the machine age and industrial expansion. This study attempts to measure the scale and the speed of this growth and the relationship between the major sectors of industrial output in various countries; it also sets out to indicate the rates of growth at which the gaps in the volume of industrial output among the major industrial countries were closed in the past in order to suggest the rates of growth that may be necessary to close the present gap between the industrial and the pre-industrial countries.

The limitations of index number series stretching over a hundred years should not be overlooked. The availability and accuracy of the figures cannot be expected to be uniform over so long a period of such rapid change. Moreover, since they were prepared in part by different individuals or institutions, linking the various series introduces a number of distortions in the continuity. In consequence, and in order to avoid repeating words of caution every time these figures are mentioned, it should be emphasized right at the beginning that they represent no more than an order of magnitude—adequate for indicating the broad sweep of movement over the century, but not precise enough to measure accurately each succeeding stage.

I. THE RATES OF GROWTH OF INDUSTRIAL OUTPUT

Over the last century industrial output[2] in the world as a whole rose some thirty-to-forty fold (see Table 1). World population, on the other hand, slightly more than doubled. Hence industrial output per capita is now some 15 to 20 times higher than a hundred years ago. The absolute growth in per capita industrial output in the last 100 years

---

[2] Throughout the study, industrial output refers to the production in factories and excludes that of the handicraft and cottage industries sector.

was thus a number of times higher than that attained in the entire preceding period of man's existence; and the per capita rate of growth (2.6 percent per year in contrast to less than 0.1 percent in preceding centuries) was much higher still.

Considerable interest attaches to an analysis of the rates of growth

TABLE 1

GROWTH OF INDUSTRIAL OUTPUT AND POPULATION IN WORLD AND SELECTED COUNTRIES, 1860–1958

Period	World[a]	United King- dom	France	Ger- many[b]	United States	Italy	Sweden	Japan	USSR
			Index numbers of industrial output, 1953=100						
1860	4	15	15	6	2	..	..	..	..
1870	5	19	20	8	3	5	2	..	(1)
1880	8	23	24	10	5	7	3	..	(1)
1890	12	28	31	18	8	12	7	..	1
1900	16	33	40	29	12	17	16	10[c]	3
1910	24	36	56	42	20	30	23	12	4
1913	28	43	66	51	23	35	26	16	5
1920	26	43	45	30	30	32	25	28	1
1925–29	38	45	80	53	39	50	33	44	5
1932	30	45	67	35	24	41	34	49	12
1938	51	64	74	77	36	61	59	88	31
1950	..	94	87	72	84	79	97	55	69
1953	100	100	100	100	100	100	100	100	100
1958	133	114	150	151	102	142	118	168	172
1959	..	120	159	162	115	158	121	208	191
			Population in millions						
1850	1200	28	36	36	23	24	3.5	..	60
1900	1600	42	39	56	76	33	5.1	47	111
1950	2400	51	42	(50)	152	47	7.0	83	..
1958	2800	52	45	(54)	174	49	7.4	92	(206)

Sources: Industrial output: 1860 from Rolf Wagenführ, *Die Industriewirtschaft, Entwicklungstendenzen der deutschen und internationalen Industrieproduktion, 1860 bis 1932,* Institut für Konjunkturforschung (Berlin, 1932); 1870–1900 from League of Nations, *Industrialization and Foreign Trade* (Geneva, 1945), except for Sweden and Russia up to 1910, Japan up to 1932 and the world up to 1938; 1910 to recent years from O.E.E.C., *Industrial Statistics 1900–1957* (Paris, 1958), and United Nations, *Statistical Yearbook* and *Monthly Bulletin of Statistics;* also United States, *Historical Statistics: 1789–1945,* U.S.S.R., *Narodnoye Khozyaistvo* (Moscow, 1956); I. Svennilson, *Growth and Stagnation in the European Economy* (Geneva, 1954) and Y. Kotkovsky, *International Affairs,* No. 2 (1959). For population, W. S. Woytinsky and E. S. Woytinsky, *World Population and Production* (New York, 1953).

· · · · ·

[a] Including U.S.S.R., eastern Europe and China.
[b] Western Germany only for post-war years.
[c] 1905.

PATEL: *Rates of Industrial Growth in the Last Century* /71

of industrial output for the world as a whole and for the major industrial countries. As can be seen from Table 2, world industrial output has expanded by about 3.6 percent per year over these hundred years. Whatever the period chosen, the rate has varied little, except during the inter-war period (1918–1938) of stagnation and the great depression, when the rate fell to 2.4 percent per annum. But these years of inhibited growth seem to have piled up such a vast backlog of demand for capital and consumer goods that under its pressure the recent post-war decade was a period of very rapid industrial growth. Consequently, if the whole period from 1913 to 1958 is considered, the rate of 3.5 percent per year is not substantially different from the rate of 3.6 percent per year for the century as a whole.

The relative constancy of the rate of growth of industrial output for the world as a whole does not imply that all countries expanded their output at the same rate. The factors responsible for different rates of economic growth are complex and beyond the scope of this study. Broadly speaking, industrial output grew rather slowly in the countries where industrialization started earlier. Thus, for instance, the lowest growth rates are found in the United Kingdom and France. On the other hand, the rate of growth of industrial output attained by each new entrant in the field of industrialization has tended to be successively higher. As can be seen in Table 2, where the countries are arranged from left to right in the approximate chronological order in which they began industrializing, this trend is maintained in the period before as well as after the first world war.

For the period of 33 years (1880 to 1913) the rate of growth of industrial output rises from about 2 percent per year in the United Kingdom, to 3 percent for France, 5 percent for Germany, the United States and Italy, and to about 6 percent for Sweden and Russia. For the 45-year period from 1913 to 1958 the rates rise from about 2 percent for the United Kingdom and France to 2.4 percent for Germany, over 3 percent for the United States, Italy and Sweden, 5.4 percent for Japan and over 8 percent for the U.S.S.R.—and in these crowded 45 years there were two world wars and an international depression! The list of countries is not, of course, complete; but it does include nearly all the major countries, which accounted throughout the period for eighty to ninety percent of the world's industrial output.

One explanation for this rise in the rate of industrial growth for each successive new entrant into the industrial field might be the fact that the volume of its industrial output in the initial stage was so small that relatively limited additions to it would appear large in percentage terms. But this seems an inadequate explanation, for two reasons. First, the high rates would continue for the initial years only; they would not be almost consistently maintained, as they were, for a rather long period. Second, it would then be reasonable to expect that in some early phase of industrial development in the advanced industrial countries the rate of growth was also very high and that it declined subsequently as the volume of their industrial output rose. But the available evidence does not seem to support this. In the early stage of industrial expansion in Great Britain—the forty years (1820 to 1860) following the Napoleonic wars—the rate of growth of industrial output was a little over 3 percent per year, which was very close to the rate of 3 percent for the 31 years (1925–29 to 1958) following the first World War. Examination of the

TABLE 2

ANNUAL RATES OF GROWTH IN INDUSTRIAL OUTPUT IN SELECTED COUNTRIES, 1860–1958, PERCENT (COMPOUNDED)

Period	World[a]	United Kingdom	France	Ger- many[b]	United States	Italy	Sweden	Japan	USSR
1860– 1880	3.2	2.4	2.4	2.7	4.3	..	..	..	..
1880– 1900	4.0	1.7	2.4	5.3	4.5	4.5	8.1	..	6.4
1900– 1913	4.2	2.2	3.7	4.4	5.2	5.6	3.5	3.8[c]	4.8
1913– 1925/29	2.2	0.3	1.4	0.3	3.7	2.6	1.6	7.5	1.1
1925/29– 1938	2.8	3.1	–0.7	3.5	–0.9	1.7	5.4	6.5	17.2
1913– 1938	2.4	1.4	0.4	1.7	1.7	2.2	3.3	7.1	7.8
1938– 1958	4.9	2.9	3.6	3.5	5.3	4.3	3.5	3.4	8.9
1860– 1913	3.7	2.1	2.8	4.1	4.6	..	..	..	..
1880– 1913	4.1	1.9	3.1	4.9	4.8	4.9	6.3	..	5.7
1880– 1958	3.8	2.1	2.3	3.5	3.9	3.9	4.6	..	7.2
1900– 1958	3.7	2.2	2.3	2.9	3.7	3.7	3.5	5.0[c]	7.5
1913– 1958	3.5	2.2	1.9	2.4	3.3	3.1	3.4	5.4[d]	8.3
1925/29– 1958	4.1	3.0	2.1	3.5	3.1	3.4	4.2	4.4	11.8

Sources: Same as Table 1.

[a] Including U.S.S.R., eastern Europe and China.
[b] Western Germany only for post-World War II years.
[c] 1905–58.
[d] 1938 level reached only in 1952. If these 14 years are excluded, the rate would be 8.2 percent.

long-term development suggests that there was a fair amount of almost monotonous continuation of nearly the same per capita rate of growth in the United Kingdom, France, Germany and the United States; disregarding a few years of slow growth—due to either a war or a depression —even the older industrial countries do not seem to have suffered from what Keynes called "the rheumatics of old age." Although rates of growth after the first World War were in most countries somewhat lower than those before it, with the notable exception of Japan and the U.S.S.R., this is—as shown below—almost entirely explained by changes in the rate of population growth—not to speak of the influence of the years spent in war and the depression.

Perhaps a more valid explanation of the progressively higher rates of growth of industrial output for each new entrant to the process of industrialization lies in the opportunity of benefiting from accumulated technological advance—a factor which was so emphatically stressed by Veblen. It is reasonable to suppose that the rate of growth in the United Kingdom and France was determined in the main by the pace of technological advance. These countries could only apply new techniques as they evolved; whereas for each new entrant there was already an accumulated body of technological progress to assimilate. The newly industrializing countries did not have to follow religiously the slow and necessarily step-by-step developments in techniques common to the countries which set out early on the road to industrialization. Nor did they have to bear the costs and delays of evolving and industrially trying out the new techniques; the countries which were ahead continued doing most of this. The later a country entered the field of industrialization, the larger was the fund of technological advance upon which it could draw, and hence the faster its possible rate of growth. So long as the technological gap between the pioneering countries and the newcomers was not bridged, the high rate of growth in the latter could be maintained.

It would follow that, in technological terms, the rates of industrial growth could not have been much higher in the pioneering countries. For the same reason—and again technologically speaking—the rates of growth in the countries just starting industrialization in the second half of the twentieth century can be higher (depending upon the ability to assimilate and spread advanced technology) than the rates attained by the countries industrializing in the first half of the twentieth century, and substantially higher than the rate of growth attained by countries which began industrializing earlier.

As to growth in per capita output—during the last century, population increased by less than 1 percent per year in the older industrial countries (and much less in France) or at about the same rate as the population of the world as a whole. The increase was in general faster in the first half than in the second half of the century. Only in the United States, where Europeans migrated in large numbers in this period, was the rate of growth of population for the century as a whole as high as about 2 percent per year. As in the other countries, in the United States the rate of growth during the first half of this period—nearly 3 percent per year—was more than twice as high as that during the second period.

As shown in Table 2, the rate of growth of industrial output in the older industrial countries in the period 1913 to 1958 was somewhat lower than in the period 1860 to 1913. This decline has often been attributed to two causes: the expectation of a slowing down in the rate of growth as the industrial base became larger; and the disturbances caused by the two wars and the great depression. However, when the rate of growth of industrial output is deflated by changes in the rate of population growth, there is relatively little difference in the per capita annual rate of growth for both the periods, before and after the first World War. This is strikingly borne out by the experience in the United States, where the growth of industrial output was 4.6 percent in the period of 1860–1913 and 3.3 percent in the period 1913 to 1958; but the rate of growth of population was about 3 percent a year in the first period and 1.3 percent in the second period. Per capita industrial output thus grew at roughly the same rate—in fact slightly faster in the second period —despite the fact that the volume of output in the period after 1913 was substantially higher than in 1860 and that there was a decade of depression. Analysis of per capita rates of growth of industrial output in the United Kingdom, Germany and France shows that in each country the rate was not significantly different in either of the two periods.

Viewed over this long period, the differences in the rates of growth of population and industrial output bring out forcibly the immense power of compound growth at higher rates. The differences in rates of growth of 1 to 2 percent (population) and 3 to 7 or more percent (industrial output) are indeed large. But they may not appear spectacular. Only when these rates are compounded over a long period—say a century—can one see the full impact of the staggering force of compound growth at higher rates. Over a century, a given quantity (population or output) will increase 2.7 times at 1 percent, 7.2 times at 2 percent, 19 times at 3 percent, 50 times at 4 percent, and 130 times at 5 percent. The extent of the growth during a hundred years at still higher rates is almost incredible: 340 times at 6 percent, 870 times at 7 percent, and —just to underline the spectacular effect of high compound rates— nearly 14,000 times at 10 percent in a century. If the rate of growth of industrial output is some 2 to 4 percent higher than population growth, the rise in per capita output over a century would be much higher than might be suggested by the rather modest difference in the rates of growth.

II. THE PATTERN OF INDUSTRIAL GROWTH

In recent years a number of countries have initiated programmes and plans of economic development in which special attention is paid to industrial growth. For them, decisions concerning the patterns of industrial development have assumed great practical importance. In view of the wide difference in the endowment of natural resources in various countries, a study of the development of specific industries in the industrial countries is not likely to furnish a useful guide to determining investment priorities in the pre-industrial countries at the present time. But a study of the historic evolution of the over-all sectoral pattern—the relationship between producer goods and the consumer goods—in the major industrial countries may be more relevant. Consumer goods, as defined here, include all those finished goods and also semi-finished goods (e.g., yarn) which, although often used in industry, are largely bought by the public in a finished form—primarily for consumption in the home. Producer goods include raw materials, semi-manufactured articles and capital goods which are used by manufacturers.[3]

It is indeed striking that in all the major industrial countries for which data are known there was a continuous decline over time in the share of consumer goods in total industrial output. At the beginning of industrialization in these countries, consumer goods accounted for two-thirds or more of total industrial output, and producer goods for the remainder. In the course of industrial development, however, the relative position of these two sectors was almost completely reversed— the share of consumer goods falling to around one-third of total industrial output and that of producer goods rising correspondingly. The rate of growth of the producer goods sector was thus throughout this period higher than that of the consumer goods sector.

---

[3] The definition, and part of the data used in this section, are from Dr. W. Hoffmann's two studies, *British Industry, 1700–1950* (Oxford, 1955), and *Stadien und Typen der Industrialisierung* (Jena, 1931). The latter book has recently been published, in a somewhat revised and expanded version, in English translation under the title, *The Growth of Industrial Economies* (Manchester, 1958). The consumer and producer goods industries are defined to include four broad groups of industries under each—the consumer goods sector includes food, drink and tobacco, clothing (including footwear), leather goods and furniture (excluding other wood-working industries); the producer goods sector includes ferrous and non-ferrous metals, machinery, vehicle building and chemicals. These groups account for "two-thirds of the net output of all industry." For details, see *The Growth of Industrial Economies*, pp. 8–17.

In the early phase of industrialization—stretching from a few decades to half a century in the United Kingdom, France, Germany, the United States, Italy, Japan, and the U.S.S.R.—the producer goods sector grew one and a half to more than two times as fast as the consumer goods sector . . . Once industrialization had reached a fairly high level and the proportion of consumer goods in total industrial output had fallen to around one-third, the differences in the rates of growth of both these sectors narrowed down significantly, with the producer goods sector expanding only a little faster than the consumer goods sector. This general pattern of industrial growth—producer goods expanding nearly twice as fast as consumer goods in the early phase of industrialization and the gap between the rates of growth for the two sectors narrowing down later on—appears to have been a characteristic feature of economic development in all the major industrial countries. Among these countries, there were very real differences in their natural resources endowment, in the accumulation of technical skills, in the period when they began industrialization, in the speed of their growth, in their attitude and actual experience regarding international trade and capital movements, in the proportion of capital goods output devoted to exports, in the fiscal and other forms of economic policies pursued, and in how industrial growth was promoted—through private enterprise (and therefore without a strict pre-determination of sectoral priorities) or through state encouragement and central planning. Despite these differences there was nevertheless a striking uniformity in the evolution of the sectoral pattern of their industrial growth.

In a broad historical sense, there is nothing surprising in such a development. It is only a common sense proposition that since output of producers goods is the least developed segment in the early phase of industrialization, it should expand much faster than the consumer goods sector. Moreover, the share of investment (and hence producer goods) in national output and expenditure usually rises in the process of economic growth and calls for a more rapid expansion of the supplies of producer goods than of consumer goods. This process is generally reinforced by an increasing substitution of imported producer goods by domestic output. The relatively faster expansion of producer goods often continues even at a later stage of economic growth when the share of investment in national expenditure becomes more or less stable largely due to a rise in the actual machinery and equipment content per unit of fixed asset formation and in the share of producer goods in exports.[4] Many economic historians have regarded such a development as an essential feature of industrial growth, although other

---

[4] This may also be explained to some extent by the fact that a part of the final output of the metal, vehicle and chemical industries is destined for consumers.

economists, perhaps owing to their limited acquaintance with long-term experience and their preoccupation with contemporary concerns, have been less than clear on this point.

III. CHANGING SHARES IN THE WORLD'S INDUSTRIAL OUTPUT

Differences in the rates of growth of industrial output, described above, have led to important changes in the relative position of various countries and areas in total world industrial output. An analysis of these changes is of great interest in elucidating the conditions under which the gap between the most advanced industrial nations and the late-comers was closed. Its relevance to the contemporary problem of closing the gap between rich industrial countries and poor pre-industrial areas needs no emphasis.

Great Britain was the seed-bed for the early phase of the industrial revolution. Although it had only about 2 percent of the world's population, more than one-half of the world's industrial output was con-

TABLE 3

RELATIVE POSITION OF SELECTED COUNTRIES IN WORLD INDUSTRIAL
OUTPUT, PERCENTAGE SHARE IN WORLD INDUSTRIAL OUTPUT

	PRIVATE ENTERPRISE ECONOMIES							CENTRALLY PLANNED ECONOMIES			
Period	Total	US	United King-dom	Ger-many[a]	Total Western Europe	Japan	Others	Total	USSR	Eastern Europe	China
1870	97	23	32	13	62	..	12	3	..	..	—
1896–1900	96	30	20	17	53	..	13	4	..	..	—
1913	95	36	14	16	44	1	14	5	..	..	—
1926–1929	95	42	9	12	35	2	16	5	(2)	..	—
1953	77	41	6	6	25	2	9	23	14	(7)	(2)
1958	69	31	5	7	25	3	10	31	18	..	..

Sources: Same as Table 1. Data for 1870 to 1926–1929 from League of Nations, *Industrialization and Foreign Trade* (Geneva, 1945), p. 13, and for 1953, as indicated in the general note to Table 1; those for 1958 derived by deflating the relative weights by the movement of the index of industrial output; the weight assigned in the League of Nations' study to the industrial output in the U.S.S.R. in 1926–29 adjusted to agree with the movement of the index for the U.S.S.R. in Table 1.

Note: The relative shares of countries are based on very crude data and any inter-country comparisons should be limited to broad order of magnitude rather than precise statistical measurement.

[a] All of Germany up to 1926–29 and only western Germany thereafter.

centrated in these islands throughout the first half of the nineteenth century. In a world in which the growth of output in relation to population was almost stagnant, Great Britain attained a decisive superiority by realizing rates of growth of 2 to 3 percent per year. Although these rates appear very modest in comparison with those current in many parts of the world in the last few decades, they were a powerful engine of massive expansion—particularly when cumulated over a long period—in a more or less stagnant world. The benefits they yielded in the nineteenth century to Great Britain in terms of wealth and power are now a matter of common knowledge. This was the period of which it is rightly said that England was the workshop of the world.

The growth of industrial output in other countries in Europe and in the United States at rates twice as high as in Great Britain had started making inroads into British industrial supremacy during the second half of the nineteenth century. To the contemporary Europeans, the economic race between Great Britain and Germany was not just a subject of idle curiosity; it was intimately bound up with the realities of power and influence over the rest of mankind. While this contest constituted a center of attention for the historians of the late nineteenth century, the rapid emergence of the United States as a world industrial power was of far greater significance.[5] Already by the close of the nineteenth century the United States had surpassed Great Britain in total volume of industrial output (see Table 3), which by the end of the century was one and a half times higher than in Great Britain, and total German output was not far behind the British. Since the First World War the United States has remained the center of the industrial world, accounting for nearly 40 percent of its output.[6] Less than half a century was needed to accomplish this change.

During the first half of the twentieth century, other countries— Italy, Japan and the U.S.S.R.—began industrializing. Their pace of growth was still higher, but their share in world output in the initial period was so low that until the middle of this century their growth had little effect on the relative positions of other countries. This, how-

---

[5] To the historians who study the present economic competition between the United States and the U.S.S.R., it may be suggested that the economic developments in contemporary China may not have an altogether dissimilar significance for the twenty-first century.

[6] Whatever the shift in the relative position of Great Britain and the United States, the total industrial output in these two English-speaking countries has continued to account for one-half or more of the world's industrial output throughout the nineteenth century and the first half of the twentieth century. Economics—the whole body of theoretical premises, the neat schemes of internal balances and disturbing elements, the bundle of logical deductions and policy conclusions—is in no small measure associated with this; for economics is for the most part a product of the English-speaking countries with occasional contributions from the outside.

ever, was no longer the case by the end of the fifties. By then, the division of the world into two zones or regions was a fairly settled affair: the private enterprise economies, which basically maintained—although with considerable modifications in recent years—private ownership of means of production and depended on private enterprise for economic growth; the other, the centrally planned economies, where the resourcefulness and the financial ability of the individual daring entrepreneur of the Schumpeterian type was replaced by the leadership of the state in planning and promoting industrial growth. The precise measurement of the rates of growth which the latter group has attained remains a subject of considerable controversy among western scholars, but there is general agreement that these rates have been high—they are usually placed in the range of 8 to 10 percent per year, or more than twice as high as in the United States and nearly four times the rate common in the older industrial countries.

The relative position of the two groupings shown in Table 3 is very approximate, in fact only illustrative, and no attempt should be made to read into it any statistical precision. For the purpose of a broad survey of this type, it is not very important whether a few percentage points are added to or subtracted from either region. What is of decisive importance is the present relationship between their respective rates of growth. Given this relationship and given its continuation over the next decade or two, little arithmetical skill is needed to indicate that the industrial output of the centrally planned economies could approximate that of the rest of the world 15 to 25 years hence. Whether the level of industrial output in the centrally planned economies in recent years is taken as one-half, one-third or one-fourth (and these relative positions have been suggested by various scholars) of that in the private enterprise economies makes a difference of only a decade to the period— 15 years or 25 years—in which the industrial output in both groupings could become approximately equal.

Whether the present differential in the rates of growth in these two areas will continue or will narrow is not the main concern of this paper. The important point is this: once the continuation of the differential in the rates is assumed, the closing of the gap in a relatively short period is an arithmetically inevitable consequence. It would merely be a repetition of what Great Britain attained in the first half and the United States and Germany in the second half of the nineteenth century. In all these countries the underlying conditions were also the same, that is, the rate of growth of the newcomer was twice (or more) as high as that of the old-timer; and the period needed for closing the gap was less than half a century—the lifetime of a man in his twenties.

One further observation of some relevance may be made in this connection. Although a number of countries have become industrially strong over the last century, over 90 percent of the world's industrial output has continued to be concentrated in areas (including eastern Europe and the U.S.S.R.) inhabited by peoples of European origin— peoples now accounting for rather less than one-third of the population of the world. There have been varying degrees of industrialization in other countries (Japan, India, and China) but the share of these countries in world output was very small until recent years. An unfortunate consequence of observing such a concentration was the cultivation of a belief in some quarters that industrial growth was somehow an exclusively European plant which might be grown with great care in a few and specially selected gardens in the rest of the world but could hardly be expected to become a matter of mass cultivation.

It is true that all new technical developments require attaining adequate training and in many instances adaptation of habits of thought and behavior. But in a wide historical perspective, industrial growth, or more precisely the application of machinery to productive use, would seem to be no more the exclusive hall-mark of a particular geographic (and hence ethnic) region than were all the past landmarks in mankind's long development—early use of fire and later the taming of it, domestication of animals, agriculture and irrigation, smelting of ores and use of metals, invention of scripts, paper and the art of printing, ship's sternpost rudder and marine-compass, gunpowder, Indian numerals and the methods of calculation, and many others. Many areas of the world would recognize in such a list their own contribution—which was carried forward, enriched and brought to fruition in some other parts at another time. The experience of industrial growth in Japan, and in more recent years in India and China, should indicate that the idea of industrialization as an exclusive possession of the peoples of European origin is based on an arrogant ignorance of history rather than on facts.

3

The Take-Off
into Self-Sustained Growth

by

WALT W. ROSTOW

<hr />

[*Editorial note:* The following study is taken from Chapters III and IV of Professor Rostow's *The Stages of Economic Growth.* In order to emphasize those parts which seemed most relevant to the rest of this book, I reluctantly decided not to include direct mention of the full sweep of Professor Rostow's framework. Nevertheless, it should be remembered that this framework is much broader than the following excerpt suggests.

In summary, Professor Rostow identifies five stages of growth: (1) the traditional society, (2) the preconditions for take-off, (3) the take-off, (4) the drive to maturity, and (5) the age of high mass consumption. The traditional society is one in which techniques of production are of a low order of efficiency, in which scientific knowledge is limited and unsystematic, in which the bulk of society's resources

Reprinted from *The Stages of Economic Growth*, by Walt W. Rostow (pp. 17–58, with omissions), copyright © 1960 by Cambridge University Press, by permission of the publishers and author.

and efforts are devoted to agriculture, in which the social structure is hierarchical and rigid, and in which there is a low ceiling on productivity. The second and third stages are dealt with in detail in this selection. The fourth stage, the drive to maturity, is one in which sustained expansion over a long period extends modern technology over the entire range of a country's economic activity. Professor Rostow suggests that maturity is normally attained about sixty years after the take-off begins. The fifth stage, the age of high mass consumption, is one in which there is an increasing emphasis upon durable consumers' goods and services. It has also frequently been associated with the devotion of large amounts of resources to social welfare and security.

For a critique of Professor Rostow's analysis of the take-off, see Selection 22.]

I. THE PRECONDITIONS FOR TAKE-OFF

We consider in this [section] the preconditions for take-off: the transitional era when a society prepares itself—or is prepared by external forces—for sustained growth.

It is necessary to begin by distinguishing two kinds of cases history has to offer.

There is first what might be called the general case. This case fits not merely the evolution of most of Europe but also the greater part of Asia, the Middle East, and Africa. In this general case the creation of the preconditions for take-off required fundamental changes in a well-established traditional society: changes which touched and substantially altered the social structure and political system as well as techniques of production.

Then there is the second case. This case covers the small group of nations that were, in a sense, "born free":[1] the United States, Australia, New Zealand, Canada, and, perhaps, a few others. These nations were created mainly out of a Britain already far along in the transitional process. Moreover, they were founded by social groups—usually one type of non-conformist or another—who were at the margin of the dynamic transitional process slowly going forward within Britain. Finally their physical settings—of wild but abundant land and other natural resources—discouraged the maintenance of such elements in the traditional structure as were transplanted, and they accelerated the transitional process by offering extremely attractive incentives to get on with economic growth. Thus the nations within the second case never became

---

[1] A phrase used by Louis Hartz in *The Liberal Tradition in America* (New York, 1955).

so deeply caught up in the structures, politics and values of the traditional society; and, therefore, the process of their transition to modern growth was mainly economic and technical. The creation of the preconditions for take-off was largely a matter of building social overhead capital—railways, ports and roads—and of finding an economic setting in which a shift from agriculture and trade to manufacture was profitable; for, in the first instance, comparative advantage lay in agriculture and the production of food-stuffs and raw materials for export.

The distinction between the two cases is real enough; but looked at closely the lines of demarcation turn out to be not all that sharp. The United States, for example, created for itself a kind of traditional society in the South, as an appendage to Lancashire, and then New England's cotton mills; and the long, slow disengagement of the South from its peculiar version of a traditional society belongs clearly in the general rather than the special case. Canada, moreover, has had its regional problem of a sort of traditional society in Quebec. The take-off of the American South is a phenomenon of the last two decades; while the take-off in Quebec may only now be getting whole-heartedly under way.

There are other types of fuzziness as well. Are the Latin American states to be regarded as in the general case, or among the lucky offspring of already transitional Europe? On the whole, we would judge, they belong in the general case; that is, they began with a version of a traditional society—often a merging of traditional Latin Europe and native traditional cultures—which required fundamental change before the mixed blessings of compound interest could be attained; but the Latin American cases vary among themselves. Similarly, Scandinavia, somewhat like Britain itself, faced less searching problems than many other parts of Europe in shaking off the limiting parameters of the traditional society. Sweden is almost in the second rather than the first category. . . .

This [section] is concentrated on the general case; that is, on the process, within a traditional society, by which the preconditions for take-off are created.

The Nature of the Transition

The transition we are examining has, evidently, many dimensions. A society predominantly agricultural—with, in fact, usually 75% or more of its working force in agriculture—must shift to a predominance for industry, communications, trade and services.

A society whose economic, social and political arrangements are built around the life of relatively small—mainly self-sufficient—regions must orient its commerce and its thought to the nation and to a still larger international setting.

. . . . .

The income above minimum levels of consumption, largely concentrated in the hands of those who own land, must be shifted into the hands of those who will spend it on roads and railroads, schools and factories rather than on country houses and servants, personal ornaments and temples.

Men must come to be valued in the society not for their connexion with clan or class, or, even, their guild; but for their individual ability to perform specific, increasingly specialized functions.

And, above all, the concept must be spread that man need not regard his physical environment as virtually a factor given by nature and providence, but as an ordered world which, if rationally understood, can be manipulated in ways which yield productive change and, in one dimension at least, progress.

. . . . .

The Analysis of the Transition

The modern economist—or perhaps one should say, given the recent shift of interest to growth, the modern economist of a decade ago— might have been inclined to say to the historian something of this sort: "This complexity about whole societies is all very well; and it is no doubt of some interest to you and your kind; but don't make such heavy weather of it. What you are talking about is a rise in the rate of investment and in the *per capita* stock of capital. Get the investment-rate up to the point where the increase in output outstrips the rate of population increase—to, say, a rate of investment over 10% of national income—and the job is done. The difference between a traditional and a modern society is merely a question of whether its investment-rate is low relative to population increase—let us say under 5% of national income; or whether it has risen up to 10% or over. With a capital/output ratio of about 3, a 10% investment-rate will outstrip any likely population growth; and there you are, with a regular increase in output per head."

And what the old-fashioned modern economist might have said was, of course, quite true.

But to get the rate of investment up some men in the society must be able to manipulate and apply—and in a closed system they must be able to create—modern science and useful cost-reducing inventions.

Some other men in the society must be prepared to undergo the strain and risks of leadership in bringing the flow of available inventions productively into the capital stock.

Some other men in the society must be prepared to lend their money on long term, at high risk, to back the innovating entrepreneurs—not in money-lending, playing the exchanges, foreign trade or real estate—but in modern industry.

And the population at large must be prepared to accept training for —and then to operate—an economic system whose methods are subject to regular change, and one which also increasingly confines the individual in large, disciplined organizations allocating to him specialized narrow, recurrent tasks.

In short, the rise in the rate of investment—which the economist conjures up to summarize the transition—requires a radical shift in the society's effective attitude toward fundamental and applied science; toward the initiation of change in productive technique; toward the taking of risk; and toward the conditions and methods of work.

. . . . .

Having peered briefly inside the process of investment in a world of changing production functions, we can conclude by agreeing that, in the end, the essence of the transition can be described legitimately as a rise in the rate of investment to a level which regularly, substantially and perceptibly outstrips population growth; although, when this is said, it carries no implication that the rise in the investment-rate is an ultimate cause.

Two Sectoral Problems

The rise of the investment-rate, as well as reflecting these more profound societal changes, is also the consequence of developments in particular sectors of the economy, where the transformation of the economy actually takes place. The analysis of economic growth can, then, proceed only a short and highly abstracted way without disaggregation.

To illustrate the need to pierce the veil of aggregative analysis in the transitional period we shall look briefly now at two particular problems shared, in one way or another, by all societies which have learned how to grow: the problem of increased productivity in agriculture and the extractive industries; and the problem of social overhead capital.

Agriculture and the Extractive Industries

Although a good deal of the early growth process hinges on the food-supply, the first of these two sectoral problems is properly to be defined as that of agriculture and the extractive industries. The general requirement of the transition is to apply quick-yielding changes in productivity to the most accessible and naturally productive resources. Generally, this means higher productivity in food-production. But it may also mean wool, cotton, or silk—as in nineteenth-century New Zealand, the American South, and Japan. And in Sweden it meant timber; in Malaya, rubber; in the Middle East, oil; and in certain American regions, Australia, and Alaska, gold helped to do the trick.

The point is that it takes more than industry to industrialize. Industry itself takes time to develop momentum and competitive competence; in the meanwhile there is certain to be a big social overhead capital bill to meet; and there is almost certain to be a radically increased population to feed. In a generalized sense modernization takes a lot of working capital; and a good part of this working capital must come from rapid increases in output achieved by higher productivity in agriculture and the extractive industries.

More specifically the attempt simultaneously to expand fixed capital —of long gestation period—and to feed an expanding population requires both increased food output at home and/or increased imports from abroad. Capital imports can help, of course, but in the end loans must be serviced; and the servicing of loans requires enlarged exports.

It is, therefore, an essential condition for a successful transition that investment be increased and—even more important—that the hitherto unexploited back-log of innovations be brought to bear on a society's land and other natural resources, where quick increases in output are possible.

Having made the general case in terms of requirements for working capital, look for a moment more closely at the question of agriculture and the food-supply. There are, in fact, three distinct major roles agriculture must play in the transitional process between a traditional society and a successful take-off.

First, agriculture must supply more food. Food is needed to meet the likely rise in population, without yielding either starvation or a depletion of foreign exchange available for purposes essential to growth. But increased supplies and increased transfers of food out of rural areas are needed for another reason: to feed the urban populations which are certain to grow at a disproportionately high rate during the transition. And, in most cases, increased agricultural supplies are needed as well to help meet the foreign exchange bill for capital development: either positively by earning foreign exchange, as in the United States, Russia, Canada, and several other nations which generated and maintained agricultural surpluses while their populations were growing (and their urban populations growing faster than the population as a whole); or negatively, to minimize the foreign exchange bill for food—like a whole series of nations from Britain in the 1790's to Israel in the 1950's.

The central fact is that, in the transitional period, industry is not likely to have established a sufficiently large and productive base to earn enough foreign exchange to meet the increments in the nation's food bill via increased imports. Population increases, urbanization, and increased foreign exchange requirements for fixed and working capital are all thus likely to conspire to exert a peculiar pressure on the agricultural sector in the transitional process. Put another way, the rate of increase in output in agriculture may set the limit within which the transition to modernization proceeds.

But this is not all. Agriculture may enter the picture in a related but quite distinctive way, from the side of demand as well as supply. Let us assume that the governmental sector in this transitional economy is not so large that its expanded demand can support the rapid growth of industry. Let us assume that some of the potential leading sectors are in consumers' goods—as, indeed, has often been the case: not only cotton textiles—as in England and New England—but a wide range of import substitutes, as in a number of Latin American cases. In addition, the modern sector can—and often should—be built in part on items of capital for agriculture: farm machinery, chemical fertilizers, diesel pumps, etc. In short, an environment of rising real incomes in agriculture, rooted in increased productivity, may be an important stimulus to new modern industrial sectors essential to the take-off.

The income side of the productivity revolution in agriculture may be important even in those cases where the transition to industrialization is not based on consumers' goods industries; for it is from rising rural incomes that increased taxes of one sort or another can be drawn—necessary to finance the government's functions in the transition—without imposing either starvation on the peasants or inflation on the urban population.

And there is a third distinctive role for agriculture in the transitional period which goes beyond its functions in supplying resources, effective demand or tax revenues: agriculture must yield up a substantial part of its surplus income to the modern sector. At the core of the *Wealth of Nations*—lost among propositions about pins and free trade—is Adam

Smith's perception that surplus income derived from ownership of land must, somehow, be transferred out of the hands of those who would sterilize it in prodigal living into the hands of the productive men who will invest it in the modern sector and then regularly plough back their profits as output and productivity rise.

In their nineteenth-century land-reform schemes this is precisely what Japan, Russia, and many other nations have done during the transition in an effort to increase the supply of capital available for social overhead and other essential modernizing processes.

It is thus the multiple, distinctive, but converging consequences of the revolution in agriculture which give to it a peculiar importance in the period of preconditions. Agriculture must supply expanded food, expanded markets, and an expanded supply of loanable funds to the modern sector.

Social Overhead Capital

Where data exist on the level and pattern of capital formation in pre-take-off societies—and for the take-off as well—it is clear that a very high proportion of total investment must go into transport and other social overhead outlays.

Aside from their quantitative importance, social overhead outlays have three characteristics which distinguish them from investment in general, as usually presented in aggregative models. First, their periods of gestation and of pay-off are usually long. Unlike double-cropping or the application of chemical fertilizers, a railway system is unlikely to yield its results in a year or two from the time its construction is undertaken, although it will yield large benefits over a very long time. Second, social overhead capital is generally lumpy. You either build the line from, say, Chicago to San Francisco or you do not: an incomplete railway line is of limited use, although many other forms of investment —in industry and agriculture—can proceed usefully by small increments. Third, of its nature, the profits from social overhead capital often return to the community as a whole—through indirect chains of causation—rather than directly to the initiating enterpreneurs.

Taken together, these three characteristics of social overhead capital —the long periods of gestation and pay-off, the lumpiness, and the indirect routes of pay-off—decree that governments must generally play an extremely important role in the process of building social overhead capital; which means governments must generally play an extremely important role in the preconditions period. Put another way, social overhead capital cannot be formed—in some of its most essential forms —by an enlarging flow of ploughed-back profits from an initially small base. You cannot get well started unless you can mobilize quite large initial capital sums.

Thus, even in so highly capitalist a transitional society as the United States between 1815 and 1840, state and local governments played a major role in initiating the build-up of social overhead capital. The Erie Canal was built by the New York State legislature; and the great American continental railway networks were built with enormous federal subsidies in the form of land grants.

The argument about agriculture and social overhead capital in transitional societies underlies a point of method and a point of substance. The point of method is that orderly disaggregation is necessary for an analysis of economic growth that comes to grips with the key strategic factors. Aggregates which may be useful for purposes of short-run income analysis conceal more than they illuminate when carried over into the analysis of growth. The point of substance is that the preparation of a viable base for a modern industrial structure requires that quite revolutionary changes be brought about in two non-industrial sectors: agriculture and social overhead capital, most notably in transport.

Non-Economic Change

We turn, now, to the non-economic side of the preconditions for take-off.

The broad lines of societal change necessary to prepare a traditional society for regular growth are becoming familiar enough. It would be widely agreed that a new élite—a new leadership—must emerge and be given scope to begin the building of a modern industrial society; and, while the Protestant ethic by no means represents a set of values uniquely suitable for modernization, it is essential that the members of this new élite regard modernization as a possible task, serving some end they judge to be ethically good or otherwise advantageous.

Sociologically this new élite must—to a degree—supersede in social and political authority the old land-based élite, whose grasp on income above minimum levels of consumption must be broken where it proves impossible simply to divert that income smoothly into the modern sector.

And more generally—in rural as in urban areas—the horizon of expectations must lift; and men must become prepared for a life of change and specialized function.

Something like this group of sociological and psychological changes would now be agreed to be at the heart of the creation of the preconditions for take-off. But this is an insufficient view. While in no way denying the significance of some such changes in attitude, value, social structure and expectations, we would emphasize, in addition, the role of the political process and of political motive in the transition.

As a matter of historical fact a reactive nationalism—reacting against intrusion from more advanced nations—has been a most important and powerful motive force in the transition from traditional to modern societies, at least as important as the profit motive. Men holding effective authority or influence have been willing to uproot traditional societies not, primarily, to make more money but because the traditional society failed—or threatened to fail—to protect them from humiliation by foreigners. Leave Britain aside for a moment and consider the circumstances and motives that set traditional societies in other regions on the road to modernization.

In Germany it was certainly a nationalism based on past humiliation and future hope that did the job: the memory of Napoleon, and the Prussian perception of the potentialities for power of German unity and German nationalism. It was German nationalism which stole the revolution of 1848 at Frankfurt and made the framework within which the German take-off occurred—the Junkers and the men of the East, more than the men of trade and the liberals of the West. In Russia it was a series of military intrusions and defeats, stretching out over a century, which was the great engine of change: Napoleon's invasion, the Crimean War, the Russo-Japanese War, and then, finally, the First World War. In Japan it was the demonstration effect not of high profits or manufactured consumers' goods, but of the Opium War in China in the early 1840's and Commodore Perry's seven black ships a decade later that cast the die for modernization. And in China, the deeply entrenched traditional society yielded only slowly and painfully; but it did, in the end, yield to a century of humiliations from abroad that it could not prevent.

And so also, of course, with the colonial areas of the southern half of the world. But there, in the colonies, a dual demonstration effect operated.

Although imperial powers pursued policies which did not always optimize the development of the preconditions for take-off, they could not avoid bringing about transformation in thought, knowledge, institutions and the supply of social overhead capital which moved the colonial society along the transitional path; and they often included modernization of a sort as one explicit object of colonial policy.

In any case, the reality of the effective power that went with an ability to wield modern technology was demonstrated and the more thoughtful local people drew appropriate conclusions. Ports, docks, roads, and later, railways were built; a centralized tax system was imposed; some colonials were drawn into those minimum modern economic activities necessary to conduct trade to produce what the colonial power wished to export and what could profitably be produced locally for the expanding urban and commercialized agricultural markets; some modern goods and services were diffused sufficiently to alter the conception of an attainable level of consumption; the opportunity for a Western education was opened to a few, at least; and a concept of nationalism, transcending the old ties to clan or region, inevitably crystallized around an accumulating resentment of colonial rule.

In the end, out of these semi-modernized settings, local coalitions emerged which generated political and, in some cases, military pressure capable of forcing withdrawal; coalitions created by both the positive and negative types of demonstration.

Xenophobic nationalism or that peculiar form of it which developed in colonial areas has not, of course, been a unique motive in bringing about the modernization of traditional societies. The merchant has been always present, seeing in modernization not only the removal of obstacles to enlarged markets and profits but also the high status denied him—despite his wealth—in the traditional society. And there have almost always been intellectuals who saw in modernization ways of increasing the dignity or value of human life, for individuals and for the nation as a whole. And the soldier—an absolutely crucial figure of the transition—often brought much more to the job than resentment of foreign domination and dreams of future national glory on foreign fields of battle.

. . . . .

The Alternative Directions of Nationalism

Now we come to the crux of the matter. Nationalism can be turned in any one of several directions. It can be turned outward to right real or believed past humiliations suffered on the world scene or to exploit real or believed opportunities for national aggrandizement which appear for the first time as realistic possibilities, once the new modern state is established and the economy develops some momentum; nationalism can be held inward and focused on the political consolidation of the victory won by the national over the regionally based power; or nationalism can be turned to the tasks of economic, social, and political modernization which have been obstructed by the old regionally based, usually aristocratic societal structure, by the former colonial power, or by both in coalition.

. . . . it is clear that the length of time and the vicissitudes of transition from traditional to modern status depend substantially on the degree to which local talent, energy, and resources are channelled on to the domestic tasks of modernization as opposed to alternative possible objectives of nationalism; and this channelling must, in the general case, be in substantial part a function of political leadership.

This is so because the central government has essential, major technical tasks to perform in the period of preconditions. There is no need for the government to own the means of production; on the contrary. But the government must be capable of organizing the nation so that unified commercial markets develop; it must create and maintain a tax and fiscal system which diverts resources into modern uses, if necessary at the expense of the old rent-collectors; and it must lead the way through the whole spectrum of national policy—from tariffs to education and public health—toward the modernization of the economy and the society of which it is a part. For, as emphasized earlier, it is the inescapable responsibility of the state to make sure the stock of social overhead capital required for take-off is built; and it is likely as well that only vigorous leadership from the central government can bring about those radical changes in the productivity of agriculture and the use of other natural resources whose quick achievement may also constitute a precondition for take-off.

II. THE TAKE-OFF

We turn now to analyze narrowly that decisive interval in the history of a society when growth becomes its normal condition. We consider how it comes about that the slow-moving changes of the preconditions period, when forces of modernization contend against the habits and institutions, the values and vested interests of the traditional society, make a decisive break-through; and compound interest gets built into the society's structure.

As suggested in [the previous section], take-offs have occurred in two quite different types of societies; and, therefore, the process of establishing preconditions for take-off has varied. In the first and most general case the achievement of preconditions for take-off required major changes in political and social structure and even in effective social values. In the second case take-off was delayed not by political, social and cultural obstacles but by the high (and even expanding) levels of welfare that could be achieved by exploiting land and natural resources. In this second case take-off was initiated by a more narrowly economic process as, for example, in the northern United States, Australia and, perhaps, Sweden. And, you will recall, as one would expect in the essentially biological field of economic growth, history offers mixed as well as pure cases.

The beginning of take-off can usually be traced to a particular sharp stimulus. The stimulus may take the form of a political revolution which affects directly the balance of social power and effective values, the character of economic institutions, the distribution of income, the pattern of investment outlays and the proportion of potential innovations actually applied. Such was the case, for example, with the German revolution of 1848, the Meiji restoration in Japan of 1868, and the more recent achievement of Indian independence and the Communist victory in China. It may come about through a technological (including transport) innovation, which sets in motion a chain of secondary expansion in modern sectors and has powerful potential external economy effects which the society exploits. It may take the form of a newly favourable international environment, such as the opening of British and French markets to Swedish timber in the 1860's or a sharp relative rise in export prices and/or large new capital imports, as in the case of the United States from the late 1840's, Canada and Russia from the mid-1890's; but it may also come as a challenge posed by an unfavourable shift in the international environment, such as a sharp fall in the terms of trade (or a war-time blockage of foreign trade) requiring the rapid development of manufactured import substitutes, as with the Argentine and Australia from 1930 to 1945.

What is essential here is not the form of stimulus but the fact that the prior development of the society and its economy result in a positive, sustained, and self-reinforcing response to it: the result is not a once-over change in production functions or in the volume of investment, but a higher proportion of potential innovations accepted in a more or less regular flow, and a higher rate of investment.

The use of aggregative national-income terms evidently reveals little of the process which is occurring. It is nevertheless useful to regard as a necessary but not sufficient condition for the take-off the fact that the proportion of net investment to national income (or net national product) rises from, say, 5% to over 10%, definitely outstripping the likely population pressure (since under the assumed take-off circumstances the capital/output ratio is low),[2] and yielding a distinct rise in

---

[2] Capital/output ratio is the amount by which a given increase in investment increases the volume of output: a rough—very rough—measure of the productivity of capital investment; but since the arithmetic of economic growth requires some such concept, implicitly or explicitly, we had better refine the tool rather than abandon it. In the early stages of economic development two contrary forces operate on the capital/output ratio. On the one hand there is a vast requirement of basic overhead capital in transport, power, education etc. Here, due mainly to the long period over which investment yields its return, the apparent (short-run) capital/output ratio is high. On the other hand, there are generally large unexploited back-logs of

real output *per capita*. Whether real consumption *per capita* rises depends on the pattern of income distribution and population pressure, as well as on the magnitude, character and productivity of investment itself.

As indicated in the accompanying table, we believe it possible to identify at least tentatively such take-off periods for a number of countries which have passed into the stage of growth.

TABLE 1

SOME TENTATIVE, APPROXIMATE TAKE-OFF DATES

Country	Take-Off	Country	Take-Off
Great Britain	1783–1802	Russia	1890–1914
France	1830–60	Canada	1896–1914
Belgium	1833–60	Argentina	1935–
United States[a]	1843–60	Turkey	1937–
Germany	1850–73	India	1952–
Sweden	1868–90	China	1952–
Japan	1878–1900		

[a] The American take-off is here viewed as the upshot of two different periods of expansion: the first, that of the 1840's, marked by railway and manufacturing development, mainly confined to the East—this occurred while the West and South digested the extensive agricultural expansion of the previous decade; the second the great railway push into the Middle West during the 1850's marked by a heavy inflow of foreign capital. By the opening of the Civil War the American economy of North and West, with real momentum in its heavy-industry sector, is judged to have taken off.

The Take-Off Defined and Isolated

The take-off is such a decisive transition in a society's history that it is important to examine the nature of our definition and the inner mechanism of take-off somewhat more closely.

There are several problems of choice involved in defining the take-off with precision. We might begin with one arbitrary definition and consider briefly the two major alternatives.

For the present purposes the take-off is defined as requiring all three of the following related conditions:

(1) a rise in the rate of productive investment from, say 5% or less to over 10% of national income (or net national product (NNP));

known techniques and available natural resources to be put to work; and these back-logs make for a low capital/output ratio. We can assume formally a low capital/output ratio for the take-off period because we are assuming that the preconditions have been created, including a good deal of social overhead capital. In fact, the aggregate marginal capital/output ratio is likely to be kept up during the take-off by the requirement of continuing large outlays for overhead items which yield their returns only over long periods. Nevertheless, a ratio of 3:1 or 3.5:1 for the incremental capital/output ratio seems realistic as a rough bench-mark until we have learned more about capital/output ratios on a sectoral basis.

(2) the development of one or more substantial manufacturing[3] sectors, with a high rate of growth;

(3) the existence or quick emergence of a political, social and institutional framework which exploits the impulses to expansion in the modern sector and the potential external economy effects of the take-off and gives to growth an on-going character.

The third condition implies a considerable capability to mobilize capital from domestic sources. Some take-offs have occurred with virtually no capital imports, for example, Britain and Japan. Some take-offs have had a high component of foreign capital, for example, the United States, Russia and Canada. But some countries have imported large quantities of foreign capital for long periods, which undoubtedly contributed to creating the preconditions for take-off without actually initiating take-off, for example the Argentine before 1914, Venezuela down to recent years, the Belgian Congo currently.

In short, whatever the role of capital imports, the preconditions for take-off include an initial ability to mobilize domestic savings productively, as well as a structure which subsequently permits a high marginal rate of savings.

This definition is designed to isolate the early stage when industrialization takes hold rather than the later stage when industrialization becomes a more massive and statistically more impressive phenomenon. In Britain, for example, there is no doubt that it was between 1815 and 1850 that industrialization fully took hold. If the criterion chosen for take-off was the period of most rapid overall industrial growth, or the period when large-scale industry matured, all our take-off dates would have to be set later; Britain, for example, to 1819–48; the United States, to 1868–93; Sweden, to 1890–1920; Japan, to 1900–20; Russia, to 1928–40. The earlier dating is chosen here because it is believed that the decisive transformations (including a decisive shift in the investment-rate) occur in the first industrial phases; and later industrial maturity can be directly traced back to foundations laid in these first phases.

This definition is also designed to rule out from the take-off the quite substantial economic progress which can occur in an economy before a truly self-reinforcing growth process gets under way. Consider, for example, British economic expansion between, say, 1750 and 1783; Russian economic expansion between, say, 1861 and 1890, Canadian economic expansion between 1867 and the mid-1890's. Such periods

---

[3] In this context "manufacturing" is taken to include the processing of agricultural products or raw materials by modern methods: for example, timber in Sweden, meat in Australia, dairy products in Denmark. The dual requirement of a "manufacturing" sector is that its processes set in motion a chain of further modern sector requirements and that its expansion provides the potentiality of external economy effects, industrial in character.

—for which there is an equivalent in the economic history of almost every growing economy—were marked by extremely important, even decisive, developments. The transport network expanded, and with it both internal and external commerce; a revolution in agricultural productivity was, at least, begun; new institutions for mobilizing savings were developed; a class of commercial and even industrial entrepreneurs began to emerge; industrial enterprise on a limited scale (or in limited sectors) grew. And yet, however essential these pre-take-off periods were for later development, their scale and momentum were insufficient to transform the economy radically or, in some cases, to outstrip population growth and to yield an increase in *per capita* output.

With a sense of the considerable violence done to economic history, we are here seeking to isolate a period when the scale of productive economic activity reaches a critical level and produces changes which lead to a massive and progressive structural transformation in economies and the societies of which they are a part, better viewed as changes in kind than merely in degree.

Evidence on Investment-Rates in the Take-Off

The case for the concept of take-off hinges, in part, on quantitative evidence on the scale and productivity of investment in relation to population growth. Here we face a difficult problem; for investment data are not now generally available for early stages in economic history. Below is set out such a case as there is for regarding the shift from a productive investment-rate of about 5% of NNP to 10% or more as central to the process.

1. A *Prima Facie* Case   If we take the marginal capital/output ratio for an economy in its early stages of economic development at 3.5:1 and if we assume, as is not abnormal, a population rise of 1–15% per annum it is clear that something between 3.5 and 5.25% of NNP must be regularly invested if NNP *per capita* is to be sustained. An increase of 2% per annum in NNP *per capita* requires, under these assumptions, that something between 10.5 and 12.5% of NNP be regularly invested. By definition and assumption, then, a transition from relatively stagnant to substantial, regular rise in NNP *per capita*, under typical population conditions, requires that the proportion of national product productively invested should move from somewhere in the vicinity of 5% to something in the vicinity of 10%.

2. The Swedish Case   In the appendix to his paper on international differences in capital formation,[4] Kuznets gives gross and net capital

---

[4] [In Universities-National Bureau Committee for Economic Research, *Capital Formation and Economic Growth* (Princeton, N.J., 1955).—Ed.]

formation figures in relation to gross and net national product for a substantial group of countries where reasonably good statistical data exist.
Excepting Sweden, these data do not go back clearly to pre-take-off
stages. The Swedish data begin in the decade 1861–70; and the Swedish
take-off is to be dated from the latter years of the decade, as shown in
Table 2. (GCF: Gross Capital Formation; GNP: Gross National
Product; NCF: Net Capital Formation; DGCF: Domestic GCF.)

TABLE 2

KUZNETS' TABLE OF CALCULATIONS FOR SWEDEN

Decade	Domestic GCF/GNP (%)	Domestic NCF/NNP (%)	Depreciation to DGCF (%)
1. 1861–70	5.8	3.5–	(42)
2. 1871–80	8.8	5.3	(42)
3. 1881–90	10.8	6.6	(42)
4. 1891–1900	13.7	8.1	43.9
5. 1901–10	18.0	11.6	40.0
6. 1911–20	20.2	13.5	38.3
7. 1921–30	19.0	11.4	45.2

. . . . .

3. *The Canadian Case* The data developed by O. J. Firestone[5] for
Canada indicate a similar transition for net capital formation in its take-
off (say 1896–1914); but the gross investment proportion in the period
from Confederation to the mid-1890's was higher than appears to have
marked other periods when the preconditions were established, due to
investment in the railway network (abnormally large for a nation of
Canada's population), and to relatively heavy foreign investment, even
before the great capital import boom of the pre-1914 decade (see
Table 3).

4. *The Pattern of Contemporary Evidence in General*[6] In the years
after 1945 the number of countries for which reasonably respectable
national income (or product) data exist has grown; and with such data

[5] O. J. Firestone, *Canada's Economic Development, 1867–1952, with Special
Reference to Changes in the Country's National Product and National Wealth*,
paper prepared for the International Association for Research in Income and Wealth
(1953), to which Mr. Firestone has kindly furnished me certain revisions, shortly to
be published. By 1900 Canada already had about 18,000 miles of railway line; but
the territory served had been developed to a limited degree only. By 1900 Canada
already had a net balance of foreign indebtedness of over $1 billion. Although this
figure was almost quadrupled in the next two decades, capital imports represented
an important increment to domestic capital sources from the period of Confederation
down to the pre-1914 Canadian boom, which begins in the mid-1890's.
[6] I am indebted to Mr. Everett Hagen for mobilizing the statistical data in this
section, except where otherwise indicated.

TABLE 3

CANADA: GROSS AND NET INVESTMENT IN DURABLE PHYSICAL ASSETS AS PERCENTAGE OF GROSS AND NET NATIONAL EXPENDITURE (FOR SELECTED YEARS)

	GCF/GNP	NCF/NNP	Capital Consumption as Percentage of Gross Investment
1870	15.0	7.1	56.2
1900	13.1	4.0	72.5
1920	16.6	10.6	41.3
1929	23.0	12.1	53.3
1952	16.8	9.3	49.7

there have developed some tolerable savings and investment estimates for countries at different stages of the growth process. Within the category of nations usually grouped as "underdeveloped" one can distinguish four types.[7]

(*a*) Pre-take-off economies, where the apparent savings and investment-rates, including limited net capital imports, probably come to under 5% of net national product. In general, data for such countries are not satisfactory, and one's judgment that capital formation is low must rest on fragmentary data and partially subjective judgment. Examples are Ethiopia, Kenya, Thailand, Cambodia, Afghanistan and perhaps Indonesia.

(*b*) Economies attempting take-off, where the apparent savings and investment-rates, including limited net capital imports, have risen over 5% of net national product.[8] For example, Mexico (1950), Net Capital

---

[7] The percentages given are of net capital formation to net domestic product. The latter is the product net of depreciation of the geographic area. It includes the value of output produced in the area, regardless of whether the income flows abroad. Since indirect business taxes are not deducted, it tends to be larger than national income; hence the percentages are lower than if national income was used as the denominator in computing them.

[8] The Department of State estimates [Office of Intelligence Research, Report No. 6672, August 25, 1954.—*Ed.*] for economies which are either attempting take-off or which have, perhaps, passed into a stage of regular growth include:

	%		%
Argentina	13	Colombia	14
Brazil	14	Philippines	8
Chile	11	Venezuela	23

Venezuela has been for some time an "enclave economy," with a high investment-rate concentrated in a modern export sector whose growth did not generate general economic momentum in the Venezuelan economy; but in the past few years Venezuela may have moved over into the category of economies experiencing an authentic take-off.

Formation/Net Domestic Product 7.2%; Chile (1950), NCF/NDP 9.5%; Panama (1950), NCF/NDP 7.5%; Philippines (1952), NCF/NDP 6.4%; Puerto Rico (1952), NCF (private)/NDP 7.6%; India (1953), NCF/NDP perhaps about 7%. Whether the take-off period will, in fact, be successful remains in most of these cases still to be seen; although Mexico, at least, would appear to have passed beyond this historical watershed.

(*c*) Growing economies, where the apparent savings and investment-rates, including limited net capital imports, have reached 10% or over; for example, Colombia (1950), NCF/NDP 16.3%.

(*d*) Enclave economies: (i) cases where the apparent savings and investment-rates, including substantial net capital imports, have reached 10% or over, but the domestic preconditions for sustained growth have not been achieved. These economies, associated with major export industries, lack the third condition for take-off suggested above (pp. 89–90). They include the Belgian Congo (1951), NCF/NDP 21.7%; Southern Rhodesia (1950), GCF/GDP 45.5%, (1952) GCF/GDP 45.4%.

(ii) Cases where net capital exports are large. For example, Burma (1938), NCF/NDP, 7.1%; net capital exports/NDP 11.5%; Nigeria (1950–1), NCF/NDP 5.1%; net capital exports/NDP 5.6%.

5. *The Cases of India and Communist China* The two outstanding contemporary cases of economies attempting purposefully to take off are India and Communist China, both operating under national plans. . . . The Indian Planning Commission estimated investment as 5% of NNP in the initial year of the plan, 1950–1. Using a 3.1 marginal capital/output ratio, they envisaged a marginal savings rate of 20% for the First Five Year Plan, a 50% rate thereafter, down to 1968–9, when the average proportion of income invested would level off at 20% of NNP. As one would expect, the sectoral composition of this process is not fully worked out in the initial plan; but the Indian effort may well be remembered in economic history as the first take-off defined *ex ante* in national product terms.

So far as the aggregates are concerned, what we can say is that the Indian planned figures fall well within the range of prima facie hypothesis and historical experience, if India in fact fulfils the full requirements for take-off. The Chinese Communist figures are somewhat more ambitious in both agriculture and industry.

As of 1959, the momentum achieved over the past six years in China appears somewhat greater than that in India; but it will be some time before the accounts of progress in the two countries can be cast up with confidence—notably, with respect to agricultural development, which must play so large a role in each. What can be said is that the plans of both countries, in their overall investment goals and sectoral composition, are consistent with the take-off requirements; and, perhaps more important, the commitment of both societies to modernization appears too deep to permit more than temporary set-backs.

The Inner Structure of the Take-Off

Whatever the importance and virtue of viewing the take-off in aggregative terms—embracing national output, the proportion of output invested, and an aggregate marginal capital/output ratio—that approach tells us relatively little of what actually happens and of the causal processes at work in a take-off; nor is the investment-rate criterion conclusive.

Following the definition of take-off, we must consider not merely how a rise in the investment-rate is brought about, from both supply and demand perspectives, but how rapidly growing manufacturing sectors emerged and imparted their primary and secondary growth impulses to the economy.

Perhaps the most important thing to be said about the behavior of these variables in historical cases of take-off is that they have assumed many different forms. There is no single pattern. The rate and productivity of investment can rise, and the consequences of this rise can be diffused into a self-reinforcing general growth process by many different technical and economic routes, under the aegis of many different political, social and cultural settings, driven along by a wide variety of human motivations.

The purpose of the following paragraphs is to suggest briefly, and by way of illustration only, certain elements of both uniformity and variety in the variables whose movement has determined the inner structure of the take-off.

The Supply of Loanable Funds

By and large, the loanable funds required to finance the take-off have come from two types of source: from shifts in the control of income flows, including income-distribution changes and capital imports; and from the plough-back of profits in rapidly expanding particular sectors.

The notion of economic development occurring as a result of income shifts from those who will spend (hoard[9] or lend) less produc-

---

[9] Hoarding can, of course, be helpful in the growth process by depressing consumption and freeing resources for investment, if, in fact, non-hoarding persons or institutions acquire the resources and possess the will to expand productive investment. A direct transfer of income is evidently not required.

tively to those who will spend (or lend) more productively is one of the oldest and most fundamental notions in economics. It is basic, for example, to the *Wealth of Nations*.[10]

Historically, income shifts conducive to economic development have assumed many forms. In Meiji Japan and also in Czarist Russia the substitution of government bonds for the great landholders' claims on the flow of rent payments led to a highly Smithian redistribution of income into the hands of those in the modern sector. In both cases the real value of the government bonds exchanged for land depreciated; and, in general, the feudal landlords emerged with a less attractive arrangement than had first appeared to be offered. Aside from the confiscation effect, two positive impulses arose from land reform: the State itself used the flow of payments from peasants, now diverted from landlords' hands, for activity which encouraged economic development; and a certain number of the more enterprising former landlords directly invested in commerce and industry. In contemporary India and China we can observe quite different degrees of income transfer by this route. India is relying to only a very limited extent on the elimination of large incomes unproductively spent by large landlords; although this element figures in a small way in its programme. Communist China has systematically transferred all non-governmental pools of capital into the hands of the State, in a series of undisguised or barely disguised capital levies; and it is drawing heavily for capital resources on the mass of middle and poor peasants who remain.[11]

In addition to confiscatory and taxation devices, which can operate effectively when the State is spending more productively than the taxed individuals, inflation has been important to several take-offs. In Britain of the late 1790's, the United States of the 1850's, Japan of the 1870's there is no doubt that capital formation was aided by price inflation, which shifted resources away from consumption to profits.

The shift of income flows into more productive hands has, of course, been aided historically not only by government fiscal measures but also by banks and capital markets. Virtually without exception, the take-off periods have been marked by the extension of banking institutions which expanded the supply of working capital; and in most cases also by an expansion in the range of long-range financing done by a central, formally organized, capital market.

---

[10] See, especially, Smith's observations on the "perversion" of wealth by "prodigality"—that is, unproductive consumption expenditures—and on the virtues of "parsimony" which transfers income to those who will increase "the fund which is destined for the maintenance of productive hands." Routledge edition (London, 1890), pp. 259-60.

[11] W. W. Rostow *et al., Prospects for Communist China* (New York and London, 1954), Part 4.

Although these familiar capital-supply functions of the State and private institutions have been important to the take-off, it is likely to prove the case, on close examination, that a necessary condition for take-off was the existence of one or more rapidly growing sectors whose entrepreneurs (private or public) ploughed back into new capacity a very high proportion of profits. Put another way, the demand side of the investment process, rather than the supply of loanable funds, may be the decisive element in the take-off, as opposed to the period of creating the preconditions, or of sustaining growth once it is under way. The distinction is, historically, sometimes difficult to make, notably when the State simultaneously acts both to mobilize supplies of finance and to undertake major entrepreneurial acts. There are, nevertheless, periods in economic history when quite substantial improvements in the machinery of capital supply do not, in themselves, initiate a take-off, but fall within the period when the preconditions are created: for example, British banking developments in the century before 1783 and Russian banking developments before 1890.

One extremely important version of the plough-back process has taken place through foreign trade. Developing economies have created from their natural resources major export industries; and the rapid expansion in exports has been used to finance the import of capital equipment and to service the foreign debt during the take-off. United States, Russian and Canadian grain fulfilled this function, Swedish timber and pulp, Japanese silk, etc. Currently Chinese exports to the Communist bloc, wrung at great administrative and human cost from the agricultural sector, play this decisive role. It should be noted that the development of such export sectors has not in itself guaranteed accelerated capital formation. Enlarged foreign-exchange proceeds have been used in many familiar cases to finance hoards (as in the famous case of Indian bullion imports) or unproductive consumption outlays.

One possible mechanism for inducing a high rate of plough-back into productive investment is a rapid expansion in the effective demand for domestically manufactured consumers' goods, which would direct into the hands of vigorous entrepreneurs an increasing proportion of income flows under circumstances which would lead them to expand their own capacity and to increase their requirements for industrial raw materials, semi-manufactured products and manufactured components.

A final element in the supply of loanable funds is, of course, capital imports. Foreign capital has played a major role in the take-off stage of many economies: for example the United States, Russia, Sweden, Canada. The cases of Britain and Japan indicate, however, that it cannot be regarded as an essential condition. Foreign capital was notably useful when the construction of railways or other large overhead capital items with a long period of gestation played an important role in the take-off or the late preconditions period. Whatever its strategic role, the proportion of investment required for growth which goes into industry is relatively small compared to that required for utilities, transport and the housing of enlarged urban populations. And foreign capital can be mightily useful in helping carry the burden of these overhead items either directly or indirectly.

What can we say, in general, then, about the supply of finance during the take-off period? First, as a precondition, it appears necessary that the community's surplus above the mass-consumption level does not flow into the hands of those who will sterilize it by hoarding, luxury consumption or low-productivity investment outlays. Second, as a precondition, it appears necessary that institutions be developed which provide cheap and adequate working capital. Third, as a necessary condition, it appears that one or more sectors of the community must grow rapidly, inducing a more general industrialization process; and that the entrepreneurs in such sectors plough back a substantial proportion of their profits in further productive investment, one possible and recurrent version of the plough-back process being the investment of proceeds from a rapidly growing export sector.

. . . . .

The Sources of Entrepreneurship

It is evident that the take-off requires the existence and the successful activity of some group in the society which is prepared to accept innovations. As noted above, the problem of entrepreneurship in the take-off has not been profound in a limited group of wealthy agricultural nations whose populations derived by emigration mainly from north-western Europe. There the problem of take-off was primarily economic; and when economic incentives for industrialization emerged commercial and banking groups moved over easily into industrial entrepreneurship. In many other countries, however, the development of adequate entrepreneurship was a more searching social process.

Under some human motivation or other, a group must come to perceive it to be both possible and good to undertake acts of capital investment; and, for their efforts to be tolerably successful, they must act with approximate rationality in selecting the directions toward which their enterprise is directed. They must not only produce growth but tolerably balanced growth. We cannot quite say that it is necessary for them to act as if they were trying to maximize profit; for the criteria for private-profit maximization do not necessarily converge with the criteria for an optimum rate and pattern of growth in various sectors. But in a growing economy, over periods longer than the business cycle, economic history is reasonably tolerant of deviations from rationality, in the sense that excess capacity is finally put to productive use. Leaving aside here the question of ultimate human motivation, and assuming that the major overhead items are generated, if necessary, by some form of State initiative (including subsidy), we can say as a first approximation that some group must successfully emerge which behaves as if it were moved by the profit motive, in a dynamic economy with changing production functions.

In this connexion it is increasingly conventional for economists to pay their respects to the Protestant ethic.[12] The historian should not be ungrateful for this light on the grey horizon of formal growth models. But the known cases of economic growth which theory must seek to explain take us beyond the orbit of Protestantism. In a world where Samurai, Parsees, Jews, North Italians, Turkish, Russian, and Chinese civil servants (as well as Huguenots, Scotsmen and British north-countrymen) have played the role of a leading élite in economic growth, John Calvin should not be made to bear quite this weight. More fundamentally, allusion to a positive scale of religious or other values conducive to profit-maximizing activities is an insufficient sociological basis for this important phenomenon. What appears to be required for the emergence of such élites is not merely an appropriate value system but two further conditions: first, the new élite must feel itself denied the conventional routes to prestige and power by the traditional less acquisitive society of which it is a part; second, the traditional society must be sufficiently flexible (or weak) to permit its members to seek material advance (or political power) as a route upwards alternative to conformity.

Although an élite entrepreneurial class appears to be required for take-off, with significant power over aggregate income flows and industrial investment decisions, most take-offs have been preceded or accompanied by radical change in agricultural techniques and market organization. By and large the agricultural entrepreneur has been the individual land-owning farmer. A requirement for take-off is, therefore, a class of farmers willing and able to respond to the possibilities opened up for them by new techniques, landholding arrangements, transport facilities, and forms of market and credit organization. A small purposeful élite can go a long way in initiating economic growth; but, especially in agriculture (and to some extent in the industrial working force), a wider-based revolution in outlook must come about.

---

[12] See, for example, N. Kaldor, "Economic Growth and Cyclical Fluctuations," *Economic Journal* (March 1954), p. 67.

Whatever further empirical research may reveal about the motives which have led men to undertake the constructive entrepreneurial acts of the take-off period, this much appears sure: these motives have varied greatly, from one society to another; and they have rarely, if ever, been motives of an unmixed material character.

Leading Sectors in the Take-Off

... The overall rate of growth of an economy must be regarded in the first instance as the consequence of differing growth rates in particular sectors of the economy, such sectoral growth-rates being in part derived from certain overall demand factors (for example population, consumers' income, tastes etc.); in part, from the primary and secondary effects of changing supply factors, when these are effectively exploited.

On this view the sectors of an economy may be grouped in three categories:

(1) Primary growth sectors, where possibilities for innovation or for the exploitation of newly profitable or hitherto unexplored resources yield a high growth-rate and set in motion expansionary forces elsewhere in the economy.

(2) Supplementary growth sectors, where rapid advance occurs in direct response to—or as a requirement of—advance in the primary growth sectors; for example coal, iron and engineering in relation to railroads. These sectors may have to be tracked many stages back into the economy.

(3) Derived-growth sectors, where advance occurs in some fairly steady relation to the growth of total real income, population, industrial production or some other overall, modestly increasing variable. Food output in relation to population and housing in relation to family formation are classic derived relations of this order.

In the earlier stages of growth, primary and supplementary growth sectors derive their momentum essentially from the introduction and diffusion of changes in the cost-supply environment (in turn, of course, partially influenced by demand changes); while the derived-growth sectors are linked essentially to changes in demand (while subject also to continuing changes in production functions of a less dramatic character). In the age of high mass-consumption leading sectors become more dependent on demand factors than in the earlier stages . . .

At any period of time it appears to be true even in a mature and growing economy that forward momentum is maintained as the result of rapid expansion in a limited number of primary sectors, whose expansion has significant external economy and other secondary effects. From this perspective the behavior of sectors during the take-off is merely a special version of the growth process in general; or, put another way, growth proceeds by repeating endlessly, in different patterns, with different leading sectors, the experience of the take-off. Like the take-off, long-term growth requires that the society not only generate vast quantities of capital for depreciation and maintenance, for housing and for a balanced complement of utilities and other overheads, but also a sequence of highly productive primary sectors, growing rapidly, based on new production functions. Only thus has the aggregate marginal capital/output ratio been kept low.

Once again history is full of variety: a considerable array of sectors appears to have played this key role in the take-off process.

The development of a cotton-textile industry sufficient to meet domestic requirements has not generally imparted a sufficient impulse in itself to launch a self-sustaining growth process. The development of modern cotton-textile industries in substitution for imports has, more typically, marked the pre-take-off period, as for example in India, China and Mexico.

There is, however, the famous exception of Britain's industrial revolution. Baines's table[13] on raw-cotton imports and his comment on it are worth quoting, covering as they do the original leading sector in the first take-off (see Table 4).

TABLE 4

RATE OF INCREASE IN THE IMPORT OF COTTON-WOOL, IN PERIODS OF
TEN YEARS FROM 1741 TO 1831

	%		%
1741–51	81	1791–1801	67.5
1751–61	21.5	1801–11	39.5
1761–71	25.5	1811–21	93
1771–81	75.75	1821–31	85
1781–91	319.5		

From 1697 to 1741 the increase was trifling; between 1741 and 1751 the manufacture, though still insignificant in extent, made a considerable spring; during the next twenty years, the increase was moderate; from 1771 to 1781, owing to the invention of the jenny and the water-frame, a rapid increase took place: in the ten years from 1781 to 1791, being those which immediately followed the invention of the mule and the expiration of Arkwright's patent, the rate of advancement was prodigiously accelerated, being nearly 320%: and from that time to the present, and especially since the close of the war, the increase, though considerably moderated, has been rapid and steady far beyond all precedent in any other manufacture.

Why did the development of a modern factory system in cotton textiles lead on in Britain to a self-sustaining growth process, whereas it failed to do so in other cases? Part of the answer lies in the fact that by the late eighteenth century the preconditions for take-off in Britain were

---

[13] E. Baines, *History of the Cotton Manufacture* (London, 1835), p. 348.

very fully developed. Progress in textiles, coal, iron and even steam power had been considerable throughout the eighteenth century; and the social and institutional environment was propitious. But two further technical elements helped determine the upshot. First, the British cotton-textile industry was large in relation to the total size of the economy. From its modern beginnings, but notably from the 1780's forward, a very high proportion of total cotton-textile output was directed abroad, reaching 60% by the 1820's.[14] The evolution of this industry was a more massive fact, with wider secondary repercussions, than if it were simply supplying the domestic market. Industrial enterprise on this scale had secondary reactions on the development of urban areas, the demand for coal, iron and machinery, the demand for working capital and ultimately the demand for cheap transport, which powerfully stimulated industrial development in other directions.[15]

Second, a source of effective demand for rapid expansion in British cotton textiles was supplied, in the first instance, by the sharp reduction in real costs and prices which accompanied the technological developments in manufacture and the cheapening real cost of raw cotton induced by the cotton-gin. In this Britain had an advantage not enjoyed by those who came later; for they merely substituted domestic for foreign-manufactured cotton textiles. The substitution undoubtedly had important secondary effects by introducing a modern industrial sector and releasing, on balance, a pool of foreign exchange for other purposes; but there was no sharp fall in the real cost of acquiring cotton textiles and no equivalent rise in real income.

The introduction of the railroad has been historically the most powerful single initiator of take-offs.[16] It was decisive in the United States, France, Germany, Canada, and Russia; it has played an extremely important part in the Swedish, Japanese and other cases.

The railroad has had three major kinds of impact on economic growth during the take-off period. First, it has lowered internal transport costs, brought new areas and products into commercial markets and, in general,

---

[14] The volume (official value) of British cotton-goods exports rose from £355,060 in 1780 to £7,624,505 in 1802 (Baines, *op. cit.* p. 350). See also the calculation of R. C. O. Matthews, *A Study in Trade Cycle History* (Cambridge, 1954), pp. 127-9.

[15] If we are prepared to treat New England of the first half of the nineteenth century as a separable economy, its take-off into sustained growth can be allocated to the period, roughly, 1820–50; and, again, a disproportionately large cotton-textile industry based substantially on exports (that is, from New England to the rest of the United States) is the regional foundation for sustained growth.

[16] For a detailed analysis of the routes of impact of the railroad on economic development see Paul H. Cootner, *Transport Innovation and Economic Development: The Case of the U.S. Steam Railroads* (1953), unpublished doctoral thesis, M.I.T. (Cambridge, Mass.).

performed the Smithian function of widening the market. Second, it has been a prerequisite in many cases to the development of a major new and rapidly enlarging export sector which, in turn, has served to generate capital for internal development, as, for example, the American railroads before 1914. Third, and perhaps most important for the take-off itself, the development of railways has led on to the development of modern coal, iron and engineering industries. In many countries the growth of modern basic industrial sectors can be traced in the most direct way to the requirements for building and, especially, for maintaining substantial railway systems. When a society has developed deeper institutional, social and political prerequisites for take-off, the rapid growth of a railway system, with these powerful triple effects, has often served to lift it into self-sustained growth. Where the prerequisites have not existed, however, very substantial railway building has failed to initiate a take-off, as for example in India, China, pre-1895 Canada, pre-1914 Argentina, etc.

It is clear that an enlargement and modernization of armed forces could play the role of a leading sector in take-off. It was a factor in the Russian, Japanese and German take-offs; and it figures heavily in current Chinese Communist plans. But historically the role of modern armaments has been ancillary rather than central to the take-off.

Quite aside from their role in supplying foreign exchange for general capital-formation purposes, raw materials and food-stuffs can play the role of leading sectors in the take-off if they involve the application of modern processing techniques. The timber industry, built on the steam-saw, fulfilled this function in the first phase of Sweden's take-off, to be followed shortly by the pulp industry. Similarly, the shift of Denmark to meat and dairy products, after 1873, appears to have reinforced the development of a manufacturing sector in the economy, as well as providing a major source of foreign exchange. And as Lockwood notes, even the export of Japanese silk thread had important secondary effects which developed modern production techniques.[17]

> To satisfy the demands of American weaving and hosiery mills for uniform, high-grade yarn, however, it was necessary to improve the quality of the product, from the silkworm egg on through to the bale of silk. In sericulture this meant the introduction of scientific methods of breeding and disease control; in reeling it stimulated the shift to large filatures equipped with machinery; in marketing it led to large-scale organization in the collection and sale of cocoons and raw silk . . . it exerted steady pressure in favor

---

[17] W. W. Lockwood, *The Economic Development of Japan* (Princeton, 1954), pp. 338–9.

of the application of science, machinery, and modern business enterprise.

The role of leading sector has been assumed, finally, by the accelerated development of domestic manufacture of consumption goods over a wide range in substitution for imports, as, for example, in Australia, the Argentine and, perhaps, in contemporary Turkey.

What can we say, then, in general about these leading sectors? Historically, they have ranged from cotton textiles, through heavy-industry complexes based on railroads and military end-products, to timber, pulp, dairy products and finally a wide variety of consumers' goods. There is, clearly, no one sectoral sequence for take-off, no single sector which constitutes the magic key. There is no need for a growing society to recapitulate, for example, the structural sequence and pattern of Britain, the United States or Russia. Four basic factors must be present:

(1) There must be enlarged effective demand for the product or products of sectors which yield a foundation for a rapid rate of growth in output. Historically this has been brought about initially by the transfer of income from consumption or hoarding to productive investment; by capital imports; by a sharp increase in the productivity of current investment inputs, yielding an increase in consumers' real income expended on domestic manufactures; or by a combination of these routes.

(2) There must be an introduction into these sectors of new production functions as well as an expansion of capacity.

(3) The society must be capable of generating capital initially required to detonate the take-off in these key sectors; and especially there must be a high rate of plough-back by the (private or state) entrepreneurs controlling capacity and technique in these sectors and in the supplementary growth sectors they stimulated to expand.

(4) Finally, the leading sector or sectors must be such that their expansion and technical transformation induce a chain of requirements for increased capacity and the potentiality for new production functions in other sectors, to which the society, in fact, progressively responds.

The Take-Off in Perspective

This view of the take-off is, then, a return to a rather old-fashioned way of looking at economic development. The take-off is defined as an industrial revolution, tied directly to radical changes in methods of production, having their decisive consequence over a relatively short period of time.

This view would not deny the role of longer, slower changes in the whole process of economic growth. On the contrary, take-off requires the massive set of preconditions, going to the heart of a society's economic organization, its politics, and its effective scale of values, considered in [the previous section].

What this argument does assert is that the rapid growth of one or more new manufacturing sectors is a powerful and essential engine of economic transformation. Its power derives from the multiplicity of its forms of impact, when a society is prepared to respond positively to this impact. Growth in such sectors, with new production functions of high productivity, in itself tends to raise output per head; it places incomes in the hands of men who will not merely save a high proportion of an expanding income but who will plough it into highly productive investment; it sets up a chain of effective demand for other manufactured products; it sets up a requirement for enlarged urban areas, whose capital costs may be high, but whose population and market organization help to make industrialization an on-going process; and, finally, it opens up a range of external economy effects which, in the end, help to produce new leading sectors when the initial impulse of the take-off's leading sectors begins to wane.

In non-economic terms, the take-off usually witnesses a definitive social, political, and cultural victory of those who would modernize the economy over those who would either cling to the traditional society or seek other goals; but—because nationalism can be a social solvent as well as a diversionary force—the victory can assume forms of mutual accommodation, rather than the destruction of the traditional groups by the more modern; see, for example, the role of the Junkers in nascent industrial Germany, and the persistence of much in traditional Japan beyond 1880. By and large, the maintenance of momentum for a generation persuades the society to persist, and to concentrate its efforts on extending the tricks of modern technology beyond the sectors modernized during take-off.

4

The Historical Experience on the Basic Conditions of Economic Progress

by

H. J. HABAKKUK

⌄⌄

The historical experience I propose to consider is primarily that of Western Europe (including England), the U.S.A., Russia and Japan before 1914, i.e. the group of countries which there is some reason to believe experienced a marked acceleration in the trend of their output at some period in the preceding 100 or 150 years. I shall take it for granted—though it might well be debated—that the main stimulus to growth came from changes in industry, and that the advance in agriculture can most plausibly be regarded as a response to such changes. I know of no reason why industry should necessarily make the pace, and indeed Adam Smith thought that "the cultivation and improvement of the country . . . must necessarily be prior to the increase of the town"; but it seems in fact to have done so. This essay is therefore primarily an enquiry into the conditions which, in these areas, favored industrialization. It would be possible to shed light on this subject by

Reprinted from *Economic Progress: Papers and Proceedings of a Round Table Held by the International Economic Association*, ed. Leon H. Dupriez (1955) (pp. 149–169, with omissions), by permission of the author and of The International Economic Association.

considering the reasons for the absence of economic progress during most of human history over most of the world. But here I am concerned with the different question of why growth did occur in certain areas.

At the present stage of knowledge it is possible to explain, though only in a rough and ready fashion, the economic fortunes of any single economy, but the conditions favorable to growth are so varied, and combine in so many different ways, that it is not possible to give a list of essential requisites that is more than a string of platitudes. And since some of the conditions cannot be quantitatively conceived, and many which can be so conceived cannot, because of the deficiency of our sources, be measured, it may very well be that we shall never be able to make generalized statements about them.

It is probable that the most important of the conditions which made Europe the cradle of economic advance originated very far back in her history. Since early medieval times, parts of Europe exhibited economic progress of a kind which so far as we know did not take place in other continents—progress which was slow by the standards of the last 200 years, which affected only a small sector of the economy, which was for long periods retarded or reversed, but which is evidence of favorable conditions absent elsewhere. Thus, by the early eighteenth century many parts of Europe already had in some measure many of the facilities, the absence of which is often supposed to account for the failure of the backward areas of the present day to generate economic progress; credit, distribution and transport facilities, supplies of relatively skilled labor, acquisitive attitudes were already to be found in certain parts of Britain, Germany, the Low Countries and Italy. However deficient these facilities were, entrepreneurs did not have to provide them *ab initio* as they would in the undeveloped areas of today.

Adam Smith's explanation of the mechanism by which this type of economic advance was achieved is still the most reasonable. Given initial differences in aptitude or equipment, man's propensity to trade would extend the market and promote a greater division of labor; this increased the efficiency of labor directly, and also facilitated the invention and improvement of machines. To this must be added two other elements of explanation: (a) As society by this means became wealthier it was able to afford an increasing amount of those types of long-lived equipment whose capital content was heavy in relation to its annual yield; in the societies under discussion this meant primarily improved transport facilities. (b) The increase in total demand and/or the shifts in demand brought out and identified those branches of production in which improvement was possible, and sometimes created stringencies in the supply of particular commodities which stimulated the search for new methods. Most of the economically important inventions of the

Industrial Revolution–period can more plausibly be ascribed to the pressure of increasing demand rather than to the random operation of the human instinct of contrivance, changes in factor prices, or the Schumpeterian innovator (who became an important agent of advance only at a relatively late stage).

Though its working would be accelerated by changes in religious belief which enhanced the value of material success, or by accessions of scientific knowledge, the mechanism was autonomous, and, in the absence of destructive wars and natural disasters and so long as the supply of labor and capital was elastic, the advance tended to be sustained though of course not necessarily uniform. The progress depended on the extent of the market but itself promoted the extension of the market; each advance created the conditions for a further advance and indeed positively stimulated it; each successful solution of a production problem contributed to the general body of experience and knowledge which could be drawn on for the solution of further problems. In the process, skills and attitudes favorable to economic growth were developed.

This seems to me, at this very low level of generalization, the model which most corresponds with what happened in Europe up to the eighteenth century. In this sort of slow cumulative growth, many of the problems which face contemporary undeveloped countries in their attempt to industrialize did not arise. Advances took place gradually in many parts of the economy—it is striking in how many fields of activity in eighteenth century England new methods were being adopted —and so they tended to provide their own markets. The complementarity of different industries which new industrializing countries attempt to establish by policy was here product of spontaneous growth.

The generative power was provided by trade, and the ultimate explanation of the progressive economic history of Europe compared with other continents is that the simple facts of geography—river systems, proximity to the sea, great differences of natural advantage in a relatively small area—were exceptionally favorable to trade and a progressive extension of the market; and there is a good deal to be said for the old view that the acceleration of economic changes in the late eighteenth century was primarily the result of the great expansion of overseas trade in the two preceding centuries.

THE CONDITIONS OF ENGLAND'S INDUSTRIAL LEADERSHIP

I now turn to attempt a more detailed explanation of this acceleration of economic advance, which is associated with changes in the iron and cotton textiles industries and with the development of steam power. These changes were not made simultaneously in the parts of Europe in which they were ultimately adopted; they were made within small areas of a single country, England, and then diffused. Why?

English trade, both internal and external, was exceptionally favored by geography, and less impeded by destructive wars, disorder and political instability than that of continental countries: and this may well be the crucial reason why the mechanism worked more effectively in England than elsewhere, and why the momentum of her economy in the century before the great industrial changes was on balance greater than elsewhere.

Then again the barriers presented by state policy and by social institutions to the exploitations of any given range of economic opportunities were much smaller in England.

(a) In almost every continental country the state attempted in its own interests to maintain detailed regulation of economic life—regulation which, since it was designed mainly to preserve the existing structure, was unfavorable to spontaneous change. In this scheme of things, advance was to come from state-promoted and state-aided concerns exempted from the regulations. For a variety of reasons this did not prove a successful method of promoting industrial growth—political considerations determined the choice of the men to whom the concessions were granted, and they were protected by their privileged position from the stimulus of competition. A system in many ways similar existed in England in the sixteenth and early seventeenth centuries and was destroyed by the Civil War. Compared with the continent therefore, the English state did not exert its power to prevent the discarding of old types of activity in favor of those which yielded a higher return.

(b) Social mobility was very much greater in England. In many parts of the continent the peasants were still subject to various forms of serfdom, and the guilds were still key institutions. Large numbers of the population were tied to the soil, and entry into trades was not free. For both these reasons the scope for men of relatively obscure origin with bright ideas and enterprising temperament was very much greater in England.

The factors which were in some sense, external to the mechanism were exceptionally favorable to its operation in England. The size and nature of the market, on which more than on anything else the working of the mechanism depended, were also exceptionally favorable. The geographical size of the market available to English manufacturers was wide —transport costs were lower, marketing facilities better, internal tariffs, tolls, etc., such as existed in most continental countries, were absent.

The nature of the market, i.e., the purchasing power and tastes of the individuals who composed it, was more favorable; and this was of crucial importance when transport costs severely restricted the geographical market for many products. Japan, in the 1890's, could, by producing at low prices, rapidly acquire a very wide market; eighteenth century industrial areas could not.

(a) In the first place average per capita incomes were higher than on the continent. There were large numbers of people with a reasonable margin above subsistence for the consumption of manufactured goods. The inducement to expand an individual industry was not therefore impeded by the very inelastic demand which faces an industry in the poorer countries of the modern world.

(b) Moreover, the English consuming public were more likely to make use of any increase in their command over goods, rather than hoard, or take it out in increased leisure. A large eighteenth century literature was devoted to the factors which, by frustrating the flow of new demands for goods, would deprive the mechanism of its stimulus. The brake most commonly feared was laziness: instead of using their increased productive power to purchase more of the old goods and/or new goods, thus stimulating further advance, people would just take more time off, and the advance would consequently lose momentum. This undoubtedly happened in England, and it has happened in most countries in the early stages of industrialization. But the sector of English society characterized by a high preference for leisure was probably smaller than elsewhere. There was a large sector of English society which was willing to work harder to acquire the increasing range of goods available.

Both these features of the English market were primarily due to the importance of the middle group incomes. English society at the end of the seventeenth century was distinguished from the societies of the continent by the large part of the national income which accrued to people with moderate sized incomes—according to Gregory King, as much as half. The relatively great importance of this middle group is due, in turn, partly to social causes of long standing, and partly to differences of tax systems. The middle-income groups were relatively large in England for the same reasons as they were large in all the great trading centers of the pre-industrial age. Secondly, taxation on the continent was not only heavier, but was highly regressive and taxed the mass of the population for the benefit of a very small class.

(c) Moreover, this large middle market was a market for solid substantial goods as opposed to fine quality goods, i.e., for just the sort of goods suitable for machine production.

It is easy to see that the mechanism we have outlined might in favorable conditions produce a leap in economic activity, and this is what seems to have happened in the late eighteenth century. Both in the primary iron industry and in cotton there were exceptionally strong stimuli to the invention and adoption of new methods: in the former, the shortage of timber and the consequent dependence on foreign supplies for a large part of a munition of war, wrought iron; in the latter, the lack of balance between the spinning and weaving sections. The solutions to the problems so created made possible very much larger production at lower costs and the whole momentum of economic advance was thereby accelerated.

These seem to me the main reasons why the Industrial Revolution happened in England rather than in, for example, France. Except in so far as it may have had some part in directing investment into transport facilities, I do not think that the English priority can be attributed to greater availability of capital, and even transport facilities were primarily a response to prior industrial development, and—there is every reason to suppose—would have been built sooner or later, even if capital had been scarcer. Even more obviously, the economic advance of this period was not due to superior supplies of labor. The extent to which once economic advance had acquired momentum, it was not held up by inelasticities of labor and capital is a point I shall consider later.

THE CONDITIONS OF SUCCESSFUL "IMITATION"

There were broadly two reactions to the English Industrial Revolution.

1. In some countries there was direct imitation stimulated in varying degrees by the competition of English exports. The new technology was predominantly, though by no means exclusively, an English product and the first stages in the industrialization of other countries generally consisted in taking over this technology.

2. There were other countries whose economic growth was stimulated by increased British demand for imports. Since this was a demand for primary products the economic growth did not, for the most part, take the form of rapid industrialization. In some countries the increased demand may very well have retarded industrialization; in Sweden, possibly, where, until the last quarter of the century, growth primarily took the form of the expansion of her traditional timber and iron production. On the other hand, the increase in the home market which the growth made possible helped to create a basis for possible industrialization.

I propose to confine myself to the imitators. There are certain general observations to be made.

(a) Their problem differed from that of England in that there was a large stock of new techniques they could take over. But the difference in this respect is not one of principle. The commonest pattern of industrialization is for a country to take over the techniques already employed elsewhere, start to produce goods hitherto imported and win its home market. The English industrialization conforms in several respects to this pattern. It starts with the establishment in England of industries and techniques long established elsewhere.

(b) The period of absorption of foreign techniques was very long in England, but the adoption of English techniques by continental countries was nowhere rapid by modern standards. Compared with the sort of industrializations of underdeveloped areas which are contemplated at the present day, the industrialization of Germany, Japan and the United States was slow.

(c) The areas in which the new techniques were successfully adopted all possessed, at the start, supplies of skilled craftsman labor, and a nucleus of initiative and organizing ability; they were all rich in natural resources in relation to their populations; even Russia had a level of income per head very much above that of modern India. Most of them had textile and primary iron industries not widely dissimilar in organization and level of development to the corresponding English industries before their advance in the later eighteenth century. Except for Russia the level of skill was sufficiently high to present few technical difficulties in the way to imitation, and any gap in cultural standards was small. For this reason, nineteenth century experience is of doubtful relevance to the industrialization of undeveloped areas in the modern world.

I now propose to consider why some countries imitated with more success than others. The attempt confronts a major difficulty, for while it is possible to say that certain minima of economic achievement and technical skill were basic conditions of economic growth it is difficult to assess the importance, in determining the relative rates of growth, of differences above these minima.

THE FACTOR EQUIPMENT OF THE IMITATORS

One source of difference was the difference of return which the introduction of new techniques offered in the various countries. The most important of the new methods relied heavily on coal, and where coal was dear and charcoal cheap, as was the case in France, the scope for cost-reduction by the introduction of the new methods may very well have been small. The consequences of dear coal can be traced throughout the French economy. Because coke was slow to replace charcoal in the primary iron industry, this industry failed to achieve the opportunities for increased specialisation which geographical concentration might have afforded. Because of this lack of industrial concentration the incentive to build railways was less. The slow introduction of steam power was partly responsible for the deficiencies of the French metal working and machine industries. A more rapid introduction of the methods would clearly have been to the advantage of the French economy as a whole, but it is not clear that it would have yielded returns to the industry introducing them in the period ahead which it is reasonable for entrepreneurs to consider. There is no way of assessing precisely the responsibility of dear coal but it has still to be demonstrated that the French adoption of the new technique was slower than was warranted by her natural economic advantages. Similarly, over wide areas of the continent efficiency wages were so low that it is not at all clear that it would have paid entrepreneurs to introduce the new methods, a main advantage of which was that they economised labor. The common assumption, however, which I accept for the purposes of this argument is that the most important disparities cannot be explained in this way.

THE STRENGTH OF THE INITIATIVE

There were obvious social conditions, as essential to industrialization as the new techniques, which, except in U.S.A., did not exist, and which could only be established by state action. The state power in each of these countries was sufficiently strong to undertake the necessary drastic reconstructions of the social structure (*e.g.* abolition of serfdom in Prussia, of serfdom and the mir in Russia). This was in some sense a basic condition. Then there had to be a large number of potential native entrepreneurs. Though in Russia, Japan and Germany the state took the initiative in developing certain industries, and though the initial impetus so given was important, it is very doubtful whether the resources of any state in the 19th century would have been sufficient to carry through an industrial revolution. Moreover, though English enterprise played a significant part in the early phases of French, German and Russian industrialization, there is no case before 1914 of a major industrialization being carried far on the basis of foreign enterprise. The international mobility of enterprise seems to have been low. Some native source of initiative therefore was a basic condition, and it is often argued that some countries had more venturesome entrepreneurs for such reasons as national character, cultural background and institutions; political and social attitudes, *i.e.*, for non-economic reasons. Thus, the rapid industrialization of Japan compared with that of India and China is often attributed (where it is not attributed to the existence in Japan of a state prepared to initiate economic change) to the Samurai, "a ruling class which possessed prestige and self-confidence," but which "was not rigidly demarcated from the rest of the population nor . . . conservative in its outlook." The contrast of Japan with India is certainly one which requires explanation, since India had many of the basic conditions of industrialization—a merchant class, banking, and transport facilities, considerable production for the market—and perhaps in this case difference in character and quality of the native entrepreneurs was the decisive factor.

The slow growth of the French economy in the nineteenth century has been attributed to the social attitudes of the French entrepreneurs. The characteristic firm was the exclusive family firm; the motive of the family was not to maximize wealth, but to maintain a position, and even the most progressive firms exhibited this attitude. The argument is sometimes supported by the assertion that the army and the administration attracted a large amount of entrepreneurial ability, in contrast to Germany where, because of the exclusive tendency of the Prussian military and political system, the loss of potential entrepreneurs was smaller. It is also suggested that, for reasons which have nothing to do with the economic endowments of the two countries, the typical German entrepreneur was better educated, and therefore had wider horizons than his French counterpart.

It is extraordinarily difficult to know how much weight to attach to this factor since it is impossible to test entrepreneurial ability except by achievement and this begs the question. There is no *a priori* reason why it should not sometimes have been the major factor. But in the French case, the one that has been argued in most detail, it looks as if the character of enterprise was primarily a product of the economic environment rather than the reverse. For foreign concerns of France behaved in much the same way as the French, and the great corporations behaved in much the same way as the family. Moreover, the family firm was a common feature of nineteenth century capitalism, and elsewhere proved not only not incompatible with rapid progress but its main agent.

THE NATURE OF THE MARKET

There were important differences in the internal market conditions in respect of (a) the type of goods demanded, (b) the degree of homogeneity of the market, and (c) the character of its response to the availability of new goods. In the U.S.A. conditions under all three heads were exceptionally favorable.

   (a) Primarily because the new land was opened up in ways favorable to a wide distribution of landownership, there was a large market for substantial simple goods of a sort which lent themselves to standardized machine production. (In South America a large class of medium-sized property owners did not develop because, at an early stage, the land was occupied by great estates, and this is one reason why areas not deficient in natural resources failed to exhibit economic growth.)

(b) There was an absence of deeply grained traditional tastes, regional and social, which, in Europe, impeded the process whereby the competition of the more efficient firms forced the adoption of new methods and equipment throughout the economy.

(c) There was little desire to hoard, and a low value was placed on leisure.

All the European continental countries had suffered in the 18th century from social and fiscal arrangements which made their agricultural populations poor markets for substantial simple goods, and which deflected industry towards meeting the luxury demands of a small upper class market. Arrangements of this sort persisted in Russia far into the 19th century, and even in France, where they had been destroyed by the Revolution, they left their mark on industry—the differential advantages of French industry tended to be in the luxury lines. It seems however that, except perhaps in Russia, average per capita income was by the middle of the century sufficiently high in these countries to provide a market for substantial industries goods. Industrialists were not faced with the highly inelastic demand which results from extreme poverty.

They were however unhomogeneous markets with deeply rooted regional and social tastes. It was these forces of market imperfection, I am inclined to think, which were mainly responsible for the very slow diffusion in most countries on the continent of the new techniques, particularly in textiles, and for the failure of those firms which did adopt them to make more rapid progress; this rather than the ability of the workers in the old forms of industry to endure increasing misery. (Similarly, the stability and rigidity of tastes, the conservative attitude to new tastes, throughout the East and particularly in China—witness the difficulty of Western traders in finding exports, other than bullion and opium, acceptable to these markets—was a factor in limiting the growth of their industries.)

The characteristic of the market they served was primarily responsible for the sort of oligopolistic structure of French industry Mr. Landes has described. Why market imperfections were—as appears to have been the case—a less important impediment in Germany, also a predominantly peasant country, is a question to which I have no satisfactory answer. Possibly something is to be attributed to the fact that the French industrial structure had got set in an oligopolistic pattern *before* the building of the French railways, and was strong enough to resist the pressures set up by falling transport costs; whereas in Germany, where industrial development was later and the railways earlier, the pattern had less chance to establish itself. It is clear that hoarding was more prevalent in the peasant societies of the continent than in either England or the U.S.A., and it is possible that, in the early stages of industrialization, the elasticity of demand for goods in terms of effort was lower. And in so far as these two conditions prevailed, the market for manufactured goods in these countries failed to expand as rapidly as their natural resources and technical potentialities warranted. But I know of no evidence which would enable one to compare the various continental countries on this point.

A further market condition may be considered. Industrialization was accompanied by a rapid increase in population, and, in the early stages, the increase in national income was predominantly an increase in the number of individual incomes rather than in income per head; there was a widening rather than a deepening of consumption. This, though not a basic condition of growth, certainly made the task of entrepreneurs easier.

CAPITAL SUPPLIES

How far was the momentum of economic progress retarded by shortage of capital and finance? It is a striking fact that, though all these countries at the start of the process had very small savings, the process of capital accumulation does not appear to have involved a reduction in consumption. Though for the period under review there are no reliable figures, the extent to which this was due to borrowing from abroad was probably small. The borrowing of France, Germany and Japan in relation to their total capital formation was quite modest. The reasons for this—not of course equally important in all countries— were: (a) all these countries possessed before industrialization a substantial industry of the domestic type, (b) the initial stages of industrialization were gradual. These countries were able, therefore, to provide a very large part of their own capital equipment, and also meet out of their own resources the additional demand resulting from the income created by the investment. They did not, that is to say, need large foreign loans to cover deficits in their current account. (In the case of Japan, the need for foreign loans was further reduced by an increase, which in this context was fortuitous, of her exports of raw silk.) There is an obvious contrast with the development of the regions of recent settlement, most of which in the early stages were incapable of producing their own capital equipment, depended very heavily on imports for their consumer goods, and were developed very rapidly. Most of these latter drew heavily on foreign capital—Canada, for example, in the decade 1900–1910 drew almost half its aggregate net investment from abroad—but this is not true of the pre-1914 industrializations, except for Russia, where 80–90% of the capital in iron and steel and oil was foreign-owned.

Probably the main reason why capital formation did not involve a reduction in consumption levels is that there were, at the start of the process, reserves of unused capacity which could be brought into use with relatively little additional capital, land not exploited well below the level of existing techniques, disguised agricultural unemployment. Because of these reserves, the resources for capital investment were provided not only out of the products of that investment, but also out of the increase in output (primarily agricultural output) stimulated by the increase in demand. This argument does not of course hold to the extent to which the employment of these unused resources involved capital outlay; but it appears that considerable increase in yields per acre and in effective acreage could be achieved with very little additional capital.

The speed and size of the response depended, not only on the extent of the unused resources available, but on the agrarian structure, the existing transport and marketing facilities etc. The U.S.A. was exceptionally well placed, not only because of her large supplies of land, but because these had been developed in the first place to meet the needs of the market, and her agriculture, therefore, responded rapidly to any increase in demand. Among European countries, England was best placed, less because of her ratio of men to land than because of her system of land tenure; the landlord/tenant-farmer system is much better adapted than peasant agriculture to change the character and increase the output of its agriculture. Peasant systems are relatively unresponsive, and partly for this reason industrialization has often involved the attempted destruction of the peasantry. Where the response was slow, but the forces of expansion were strong, we should expect inflations to have occurred, and possibly for conditions to be less favorable to growth; and it is conceivable that further investigation will show that differences in response did influence the speed of growth in these countries. My impression, however is, that with the possible exception of Russia the response was sufficient for the rate of growth permitted by the other limiting factors.

Where the additional output was entirely absorbed by an increase in population, there would, of course, have been nothing available to contribute to capital investment, and it is clear that in some societies this is what happened. In the Balkans, indeed, it appears that increase in demand, though it stimulated an increase in agricultural output, stimulated a proportionately greater increase of population, and a consequent fall in income per head. But in none of the Western European industrializing countries did this happen, though in Germany something like it might have happened but for emigration.

Once the early stages had been passed, the rapid rise of real income itself provided the capital; mid-Victorian England, Germany after 1890, Japan in the inter-war period all proved capable of very high rates of saving.

My conclusion is that, for these reasons, the rate of capital investment actually achieved did not involve a fall in consumption. This, however, does not dispose of the question—was this rate retarded by shortage of finance? Were there a large number of projects which entrepreneurs actively wanted to undertake but which they were prevented from undertaking by the nature of the terms on which they could obtain funds? This is a question which it is not possible to answer with precision. Entrepreneurs completely frustrated by lack of funds leave no trace, and though many cases can be cited of well-known industrial figures who at one time or another faced finance difficulties, it is difficult to say how important these cases were. Moreover though the rates of interest on first-class securities can be compared country by country, it is extremely difficult to obtain information about the structure of rates in the different countries. The differences in the first-class security rate from area to area were not sufficiently great, one would have supposed, to have had much influence on the level of investment, but there may very well have been great and influential differences, as between the various areas, in lenders' assessment of the riskiness of industrial borrowers. My general impression, however, is that finance was not a major influence on the rate of growth. My reasons for believing this are

I) It was relatively easy for an entrepreneur in the early stages of industrialization to start a project with his private savings and those of his friends and relations, and to finance subsequent growth by ploughing back profits. Two conditions of his ability to do this were

a) The state of existing techniques of production. The means of production required for the smallest unit of investment which was technically and economically feasible, were small in relation to the savings of the potential entrepreneur. This was obviously more true of the initiating country than of the imitators, who had the opportunity of taking over in a single step projects which in the initiating country had taken several stages. But I should be inclined to argue that none of the European nineteenth century imitators lagged behind the initiator in technique sufficiently far to make a very significant difference. I except Russia and Japan from this generalization.

b) A high rate of profit. It has been argued that a condition of rapid accumulation from ploughed-back profits was the stickiness of wages when prices were rising. Possibly, too, it had something to do with the slow entry, for reasons not connected with availability of capital, of new firms, which allowed the leaders a period of exceptionally high profits. For these two reasons, the need of entrepreneurs to obtain funds from outside sources was limited. But

c) in all these areas, except Russia, there were loan markets, imperfect, of course, compared with those of the late nineteenth century, but highly developed compared with those of modern India and the Middle East. A borrower who could offer good security could borrow at a rate which was approximately uniform over a wide area; and for reasons given in (a) and (b) above, it was fairly easy for entrepreneurs to accumulate the assets which would enable them, when plowed-back profits were inadequate, to offer good security for a loan.

There was one project characteristic of the early stages of industrialization, where, in certain countries, these sources of finance were clearly inadequate—the railway—and here the state intervened and either built the railways, providing the finance partly out of taxation, or guaranteed the interest on loans issued by private entrepreneurs. Some states took the necessary action earlier than others, and the differences of timing obviously had a powerful effect on the rate of economic growth (viz. the importance of the fact that Germany had her railway system a decade before France); but if lack of finance influenced the government, it was usually to accelerate rather than retard state intervention.

II) In the later stages of industrialization, there was some tendency, the strength of which varied widely of course from industry to industry, for the smallest practicable unit to become large in relation to the funds available to a single industrialist from the sources we have discussed. And, in so far as this happened, the possibility increases that fruitful developments may have been retarded or frustrated by shortage of finance. The fact that the self-financing family firm continued to prevail over so much of European industry—including some of the most rapidly growing industries—can be used in evidence both for and against rating this possibility high, it may be taken as a sign either of the adequacy of the older sources of finance, or of the inadequacy of any alternative. A less ambiguous piece of evidence is the great resourcefulness and ingenuity shown where there was a marked shortage of funds in relation to available opportunities, in adapting or devising institutions to provide entrepreneurs with funds; witness the invention of the preference share, the developments in banking (particularly the German industrial banks), the adaptation of forms of joint-stock organization, and the role of the Zaibatzu in Japan. There may, of course, have been a considerable time-lag between these developments and the needs to which they were a response, the fact that these adaptations were made in the end is no proof that there was not a long period in which economic growth was retarded for the lack of them. But on the whole what impresses is the speed of the adaptation.

The suggestions which for purposes of discussion I wish to make are therefore, that so far as the nineteenth century industrializations are concerned 1) societies in which other conditions were favorable were usually capable of devising adequate financial institutions; 2) where the agricultural sector was responsive to an increase in demand, the real resources devoted to investment did not involve a contraction of consumption.

LABOR SUPPLIES

To what extent and in what ways was the momentum of economic progress affected by availability of labor? Can a certain sort of labor market be said to have been a "basic condition" of economic progress. In the classical version of things, the rising real wages of labor were the major internal force tending to halt accumulation, and the argument depended mainly on the unresponsiveness of food supply. There are really two quite distinct questions.

(1) How responsive was population to an increase in demand? This is partly a question of how favourable natural resources were to an expansion of food production—a question we have already discussed; it is partly a question of social structure, nature of crops, inheritance laws, etc.

(2) On what terms was the increase made available to industry? which is mainly a question of the legal and social impediments to movement.

In all these countries, except France, industrialization was accompanied by rapid natural increase. It is in dispute how far, in each case, this was due to (a) the effect of medical improvements on death rates, (b) the effect of higher living standards on birth-rates, (c) the effect of increased demand for labor (working mainly through marriage rates) on birth rates. But there might be general agreement that the increase was primarily a response to industrialization, rather than vice-versa, and that, in the period before labor became geographically mobile, some population-response was a basic condition of industrialization. (There is no contradiction between this and the belief that shortage of labor was a stimulus to labor-saving inventions in early 18th century England and to the installation of labor-saving machinery in 19th century U.S.A.)

The population-response varied widely, according not only to the elasticity of food supplies, but to general cultural patterns, age at marriage, inheritance customs, etc. The increase was exceptionally rapid in the U.S.A. It was weak only in France, where wide distribution of property coupled with equal division of inheritance provided strong inducement to postpone marriage. This seems, therefore, to have been a basic condition that was easily satisfied.

Much more important were the variations in the strength of the institutional impediments to the movement of population. The wide distribution of property rights in continental Europe made labor everywhere rather immobile. This was less of an impediment in Germany, where the emancipation of the serfs east of the Elbe was carried out in such a way as to create a substantial proletariat. The impediment to movement was greatest in Russia, where, even after the abolition of serfdom, the communal ownership of land and communal responsibility for taxation which survived almost until 1914, made permanent movements of labor exceptionally difficult. Probably the main influence of this immobility in the early stages of industrialization was on the gap between the terms on which labor was available to the factory and to domestic industry. In both Russia and France, but particularly in the former, the relatively high cost of attracting permanent labor into the industrial areas was one of the main factors depriving the factory of the power to compete the older forms of industry out of existence, but I know of no evidence sufficient to determine the importance of this factor as compared with the market imperfections already discussed.

To what extent was skilled labor a basic condition? The most intractable shortage was of the skill to construct and service the new machines, but there was also a shortage of the semi-skilled labor required to operate them. Though all these countries, except Russia had many skilled craftsmen of the locksmith type, a very high premium on skill persisted throughout the early stages of industrialization. The problem was met in part by direct attempts to train labor (in Germany the adaptation of gild apprenticeship rules, the various forms of technical education), and partly by adjusting the machinery to suit the capacity of the labor force (the early development of fool-proof mass-production machinery in the U.S.A., which was less well supplied with craft skills). There appear to be no significant differences on this point between initiator and imitators. The later mechanizations were more rapid and therefore the demand for skilled labor larger; but, for the same reason, the skilled craftsmen were more easily uprooted for work in the factory. Furthermore the imitators drew on the supplies of skilled English labor to alleviate exceptionally severe shortages. The nineteenth century industrializations experienced great difficulties not only in training skill, but in adapting labor to the exigencies of work in the factory. From its very nature, the acquisition of skills and of new attitudes to work was a slow process, and the deficiencies of labor were a more important retarding factor than shortage of finance.

. . . . .

5

International Investment To-day in the
Light of Nineteenth-Century Experience[1]

by

RAGNAR NURKSE

To many Americans to-day the problem of international investment is doubtless a source of perplexity and even of some irritation. Ever since the last world war great expectations have been placed on the export of private American capital as a means of bridging the dollar gap as well as financing world economic development. In reality, private foreign investment throughout the period since 1945 has fluctuated at a low level and without any sign at all of an upward trend.[2] This is most disappointing. We suspect that the export of capital from Great Britain was one reason why the international economy of the Victorian era did not know of a chronic sterling shortage. We recognize, above all, that foreign investment was associated during that era with a tremendous spurt in world production and trade. There is in America

Reprinted from *The Economic Journal*, LXIV, 256 (December, 1954) (pp. 744–758, with omissions) by permission of the Royal Economic Society and Professor Nurkse's executrix.

[1] A paper prepared for discussion at the Conference of the Association of University Teachers of Economics at Sheffield on January 2, 1954. My thanks are due to Mr. David Butt and Sir Donald MacDougall for a number of valuable and helpful comments.

[2] Cf. *Federal Reserve Bulletin*, October 1953, pp. 1039–42.

a feeling of nostalgia for the nineteenth-century environment that made this flow of capital possible. The question is: why can we not re-create that environment?

The answer, I submit, must start from the fact that the circumstances in which overseas investment, and more especially British investment, went on in the nineteenth century (which I take to have ended in 1914) were in some ways quite exceptional. To realize this is of more than historical interest. So long as the peculiar features of that experience are not fully appreciated, memories of wonders worked by foreign investment in the past can only lead to false hopes and frustration.

Recent researches have made it possible to estimate approximately the percentage share of her national income that Britain used to lend abroad. Occasionally one finds the same proportions being applied to the present American national income as an indication of what the United States could or should do. Over the fifty years that preceded the outbreak of the First World War, it seems that Great Britain invested overseas an amount equal to about 4% of her national income. In the later part of the period (1905–13) the ratio was as high as 7%. If the United States today were to devote similar percentage portions of her national income to the same purposes, she would be exporting funds to the tune of $12 billion or, if we apply the higher percentage, some $20 billion each year. These figures are almost absurdly large and tend to confirm the view that there was something unique about Britain's foreign investment.

It was unique in that the greater part of it—roughly two-thirds—went to the so-called "regions of recent settlement": the spacious, fertile and virtually empty plains of Canada, the United States, Argentina, Australia and other "new" countries in the world's temperate latitudes. It was unique in that it went to these places together with a great migration of about 60 million people,[3] including many trained and enterprising persons, from the British Isles as well as Continental Europe. The conditions that made this flow of private capital possible do not exist to any great extent today, and probably cannot be re-created.

It was in the newly settled regions, which received two-thirds of the capital exports and practically all the emigrants, that nineteenth-century international investment scored its greatest triumphs. The remaining third of British capital exported (or more accurately a quarter, since some went to Continental Europe) was employed in a different type of area, where its achievements were much more dubious: tropical or subtropical regions inhabited, often densely, by native populations endowed in some cases with ancient civilizations of their own. The areas that

---

[3] This is a gross figure; some of the migrants returned.

formed a minor field for overseas investment before 1914 are the major problem today: the truly backward economies, containing now about two-thirds of the world's population. The empty and newly settled regions, from which international investment derived its brilliant general record and reputation, are today, in *per capita* income, among the most prosperous countries in the world.

Labor and capital are complementary factors of production, and exert a profound attraction on each other. The movement of labor to the new regions attracted capital to the same places at the same time. And the other way round: the flow of capital stimulated the migration of people to these places. To some extent, it is true, the parallel movements of capital and labor might plausibly be interpreted as two separate effects of a common cause; namely, of the opening-up of the vast reserves of land and other natural resources. But the complementary nature of the labor and capital movements, based on the complementarity of the two factors, is equally plain. Any barrier to the transfer of one would have reduced the flow of the other. Labor and capital moved along side by side, supporting each other.

In the twentieth century the situation is totally different. The capital exports from the United States can be viewed rather as a *substitute* for the movement of people. Capital and labor are still complementary, and still basically attract one another. But as things now are, restricting the movement of labor in one direction increases the need, if not the incentive, for capital to move in the opposite direction. Cheap labor, instead of being allowed to come to the United States to work with American capital there, is to some extent supplied with American capital abroad (supplied by the American Government as in the years since 1945, if not by private profit-seeking investors, as in the 1920s). The underlying pressure—not necessarily the profit motive, but what we might call the global social pressure—is very strong for more capital to move out from the United States to work with the cheap labor in the world's backward economies. But notice that in this situation, in sharp contrast to the predominant nineteenth-century pattern, capital is being urged to go out to work with people that have not grown up in a capital-minded milieu, and may not be culturally prepared for the use of western equipment, methods and techniques.

With this situation in mind, we can perceive what I think is the basic rationale of the present American emphasis on direct business investment as a means of financing economic development. The advantages rightly attributed to it are, first, that it goes out with American enterprise, tied up with American "know-how," and, secondly, that it is likely to be productively used, not swallowed up—directly or indirectly —by immediate consumption in the receiving country. Since, however, in the low-income areas the domestic market is small, this type of investment tends inevitably in such areas to concentrate on extractive industries—mines, plantations, oil wells—producing raw materials for export mainly to the advanced countries. This is, in effect, the so-called "colonial" pattern of foreign investment, of which American oil operations abroad are now an outstanding example. It has its drawbacks as well as its virtues. But, in any event, the stress laid—even in the original Point Four programme—on direct investments in economically backward countries should not, in my opinion, be dismissed as merely a product of conservative business ideology; it reflects in part an essential difference in the present-day environment of international investment as compared with the nineteenth century.

In the aggregate flow of capital in the nineteenth century, the "colonial" type of venture played a minor role. Looking at Britain's foreign investment portfolio in 1913, we find that, of an estimated total of about £3,700 million outstanding at that time in nominal value, 30% was in loans to governments, as much as 40% in railway securities and some 5% in other public utilities, so that no less than three-quarters of the total was in public or public-utility investments. The rest includes banking, insurance and manufacturing companies, as well as investments directly in raw-material extraction. The total should be increased by making some allowance (say, £300 million) for private holdings and participations not represented by securities listed on the London Stock Exchange; but that would make little difference to the proportions indicated. It is therefore far from correct to assume, as is sometimes done, that the "colonial" form of enterprise in the extraction of mineral and plantation products for the creditor country was the typical pattern of foreign investment. To call it the "traditional" pattern might be justified in view of its history in earlier centuries. But in the nineteenth century its total amount was comparatively small; and what little there was of it appears to have been concentrated, as one would expect, in colonial and predominantly tropical areas.

To the new countries, by contrast, capital moved chiefly through the medium of securities carrying a fixed return (*i.e.*, bonds and preference shares) issued by public authorities and public-utility undertakings. To these countries, it appears, capital could safely be sent in the form of relatively untied funds, with a good chance that it would remain capital there, because the people in these places, having come from Europe themselves, knew what to do with capital and how to handle it. Cultural adaptation was no problem.

These countries—the "regions of recent settlement" that absorbed the bulk of British overseas investment—were offshoots of European civilization.[4] For Britain, or at any rate for Europe as a whole, investment

---

[4] The precise composition of this group may give rise to some debate, though essentially the line is clear. It takes in Canada, the United States, Australia, New

in these areas was essentially a process of capital widening rather than deepening. Indeed, when Britain sent capital out to work with Swedes, Poles, Germans and Italians emigrating overseas, she may have done so at the expense of the deepening which her own economy is said to have needed in the period just before the First World War. But international investment in the nineteenth century was, of course, unplanned, and was determined by private rather than national advantages. French and German activities in Eastern Europe and the Near East were an exception in this respect. As Professor Viner has remarked, "the French loans to Russia . . . bore a close resemblance to the programme of military aid to Western Europe which we are now embarking on."[5]

Great Britain's national advantage, apart from the return flow of interest and dividends, seemed to be handsomely served through cheaper food and raw materials, though this benefit was shared by other importing countries that had made no corresponding investments and, besides, as we now realize, was derived in part from *Raubwirtschaft*, through soil depletion and erosion in some of the rich new plains (for example, in the virgin grasslands of the Mississippi valley).

Production of primary commodities for export to the industrial creditor countries is characteristic of the "colonial" pattern of direct investment in economically backward areas. In the regions of recent settlement foreign investment can also be said to have been induced essentially by the raw-material needs of the industrial centers—especially by Great Britain's demand for the wheat, wool, meat and dairy products, which she decided not to try to produce for herself, and which these temperate regions were particularly well suited to produce. The capital that came into these regions did not, however, enter into primary production itself, but was employed above all in building up the costly framework of public services, including especially transport, which laid the basis for domestic industrial development, as well as for the production of raw commodities for export. These areas are now, and have been for some time, predominantly industrial,[6] a fact entirely compatible with the large or even preponderant share of primary products in their export trade.

Nineteenth-century foreign investment centered on the railway—

Zealand and South Africa. In South America it certainly includes Argentina and Uruguay, rich farm and grazing lands in temperate latitudes settled predominantly by recent immigration from Europe. I would perhaps include also the southern tip of Brazil, to which the same description largely applies, and in which most of Brazil's productive capacity, including immigration as well as foreign capital, has been concentrated since the middle of the nineteenth century.

[5] "America's Aims and the Progress of Underdeveloped Countries," in *The Progress of Underdeveloped Areas*, edited by B. F. Hoselitz (Chicago, 1952), p. 184.

[6] See F. Hilgerdt, *Industrialization and Foreign Trade* (League of Nations, 1945), pp. 26, 39 and *passim*.

that "great instrument of improvement," in Lord Dalhousie's phrase. If account is taken not only of railway securities but also of the use to which many government loans were put, it seems that well over half of Britain's external investment before 1914 went into railway construction. The great bulk of this was in the newly settled countries. The Indian railways, though an important individual item, accounted for less than one-tenth of the total of overseas railway securities held by British investors in 1914. The United States and the Argentine alone accounted for more than half of that total. In the new countries the railway was important as a means of migration. The great pioneer lines —first in the United States, later in the Argentine and elsewhere—were deliberately planned and built *in advance* of current traffic needs; they themselves created the settlement and economic growth that eventually led to a full demand for their services.

Although individual promoters sometimes played the most conspicuous part, the railways in the new countries were built, as a rule, if not directly by governments, at any rate with extensive government assistance in the form of land grants, subsidies and guaranteed returns to the investors. In view of this fact, one can safely say that the bulk of international investment in the nineteenth century depended on government action in the borrowing countries. In French and German capital exports, some of which also went to the new world, the proportion of government loans and other public investments was even higher than in the British case.

It is true that the transport revolution, to which the cheapening of British food imports (especially in the years 1880–1900) was largely due, was a matter of steamships as well as railways. While railway construction overseas was a major object of international financing, British shipbuilding counted almost entirely as part of British home investment. Since ship and railway building had much the same effects on international trade and the terms of trade, the distinction between home and foreign investment appears in this case somewhat arbitrary. In the internal economic expansion of the new countries, however, the railways had, of course, a very special part to play, rather different from that of the ships. And so we hear, for example, that "in the Argentine, the railway is like a magic talisman: for wherever it goes it entirely transforms the economic and productive conditions of the country."[7]

[7] A. B. Martinez and M. Lewandowski, *The Argentine in the Twentieth Century* (London, 1911), p. 108. A statement such as this applies to a type of region with the particular physical and human characteristics already noted. It would not apply in the same way to a country like India, where, for reasons that cannot be entered into, the railway "did not give rise to a flood of satellite innovations" and "destroyed more employment opportunities [*e.g.*, in traditional village industries] than it opened up" (L. H. Jenks, "British Experience with Foreign Investments," *Journal of Economic History*, 1944, Supplement, p. 75).

Overseas railway investment became predominant from about 1870 onwards. But this does not mean that the earlier part of the century can be ignored. While the total of foreign investment was much smaller then, so was everything else. We should note that by 1870 Britain's overseas assets had already grown to about the same order of magnitude as her annual national income. Capital imports were a prominent feature in the economic history of the United States for many years before the Civil War.

It is clear that the main flow of capital in the nineteenth century was not to the neediest countries with their "teeming millions," which were indeed neglected, but to sparsely peopled areas where conditions for rapid growth along familiar western lines were exceptionally favorable. If we were to look round for similar opportunities in the twentieth century, I do not know where we should find them if not in the further development of the same regions of recent settlement; or else perhaps in Siberia—a vast area reputedly rich in natural resources, which may be longing for an injection of skilled labor from Europe and capital from the United States.

Once the main facts about the nineteenth-century capital flow are set out in something like their true proportions, it is curious to see how little they fit in with some pre-conceived notions that have been widely current. Bernard Shaw, for example, in Act I of *The Apple Cart*, made one of his characters talk about England sending her "capital abroad to places where poverty and hardship still exist: in other words, where labor is cheap. We live in comfort on the imported profits of that capital." Consider, more seriously, the summary which Mrs. Joan Robinson gives (in *The Rate of Interest and Other Essays*, 1952, pp. 157-8) of the views of Rosa Luxemburg:

> The capitalist nations are surrounded by primitive economies, each insulated from the others like a nut within its shell, waiting to be cracked. The capitalists break open a primitive economy and enter into trade with it, whether by enticing its inhabitants with commodities they have never seen before, by political cunning or by brute force. Now exports to the primitives provide an outlet for the product of the last batch of capital goods created at home. After a little while another nut is broken, a use for more capital is thereby found, and so on, as long as the supply of untouched primitive economies lasts. . . . When the stock of unbroken nuts is exhausted, the capitalist system collapses for want of markets.

This is one variant of neo-Marxist doctrine and, like others, it neglects some crucial facts. No pre-existing markets were conquered in the new countries. Markets were *created* there by labor, enterprise and capital all drawn from Europe. In the industrially primitive countries markets were and have remained unattractive because of mass poverty. Why is it, for example, that in the 1920s Canada, Australia and New Zealand, with already quite highly developed industries of their own and with a combined population of only 17.4 millions, imported twice as much manufactured goods as India with her 340 million people?

The American public also, perhaps because it lives in one of the new countries itself, does not always appreciate the peculiar nature of the nineteenth-century investment experience. Some of us are too apt to forget—or to take for granted—all that went with it and to assume, from that experience, a "simple equivalence of the pace of capital transfer and the pace of development."[8] Keynes in 1922 made a remark that is worth recalling: "The practice of foreign investment, as we know it now, is a very modern contrivance, a very unstable one, and only suited to peculiar circumstances."[9] He cautioned against extending it by simple analogy to a different set of circumstances. Private foreign lending in the 1920s can be viewed in part as a backwash of the great momentum which it had gathered before 1914. Was it because in Central Europe foreign investment was applied to a situation to which it was unsuited that it came to grief there? It might perhaps have worked; Hitler did not give it a chance. Yet the fact is that it did not work.

Will it work, and if so, how will it work, in the "underdeveloped" areas of which we hear so much today? The preceding remarks have all been leading up to this question. My purpose here is to present the question, against the background of past experience, rather than try to answer it. In the time that remains I will only hazard a few brief comments on three general topics: direct business investment, public-utility investment and governmental grants.

. . . . .

For reasons mentioned earlier, direct investments by American business firms—usually financed from corporate reserves rather than security issues on the capital market—are thought to be particularly well suited to the economically backward countries. But they have their shortcomings also. In the life of an industrially primitive community they are apt to create not only a dual economy[10] but also a dual society, in which conditions for the diffusion of western technology may actually be the reverse of favorable. Foreign business investment is not always a

---

[8] Honor Croome, "The Dilemma of Development," in *New Commonwealth*, November 9, 1953, p. 487.

[9] *A Revision of the Treaty*, p. 161.

[10] Cf. H. W. Singer, "The Distribution of Gains between Investing and Borrowing Countries," *American Economic Review, Papers and Proceedings*, May 1950.

happy form of encounter between different civilizations. Besides, if techniques are to be of wide and permanent use, they must be adapted to local conditions. The methods of giant corporations, whose foreign operations are sometimes only a side-show, are often too standardized to favor such adaptation. And so the local economy may not get much help from the example they give; the example is often inapplicable. Let us remember that the Japanese acquired industrial techniques very effectively before they began to receive any substantial foreign business investments. Also the technical assistance programs now in operation remind us that there are other ways of spreading technical knowledge.

As a rule, when foreign business enterprise is attracted to economically backward areas, it is mainly for the production of raw materials for export markets, for the simple reason that the domestic market in such areas, even if protected by import restrictions, is generally too poor to afford any strong inducement to invest.[11] The natural result is a "colonial" investment pattern, open to the familiar criticisms that it tends to promote lopsided rather than "balanced" growth, and that it makes for instability due to high dependence on foreign demand for one or two staple products. If this type of direct investment is to take place in any considerable volume, it presupposes a long-run prospect of rapidly expanding demand in the industrial centers for the raw materials which it seeks to provide. Despite the forecasts of the Paley Report, there is no firm assurance of such an expansion except for certain minerals. Governmental purchase agreements alone cannot give this assurance in the absence of favorable basic demand conditions. A temporary stimulus might be got from the removal of United States tariff protection on primary products (such as sugar, copper, wool), but little can be hoped for in this direction.

In the last few years one of the chief economic obstacles to a greater flow of business funds to low-income countries has been the high level of business profits obtainable at home, from developing American natural resources and catering to the American mass market. Conditions

---

[11] From the latest comprehensive figures for American direct investments (*Survey of Current Business*, December 1952), it can be seen that of the total invested in Canada and Western Europe at the end of 1950, 23% was in extractive industries, as much as 60% in manufacturing and trade, 6% in public utilities and 11% in miscellaneous activities, including cinemas and other entertainments. Of the investments outstanding on the same date in all other countries, which with a few exceptions are economically backward, 60% was in extractive industries, mostly petroleum and mining, with 20%, 17%, and 3% respectively in the other groups. This pattern is by no means new. We know that in 1929 only one-fifth of total American direct investment was in manufacturing, and 84% of this was in Western Europe, Canada, Australia and New Zealand. "Only to a very small extent, therefore, did American direct investments enter into manufacturing for the domestic market in under-developed countries." (United Nations, *International Capital Movements in the Inter-War Period*, 1949, p. 32.)

may change. It is not inconceivable that business investment abroad might greatly increase in the future, and that it might bring substantial benefits to the poorer countries. Yet, on the whole, it seems unlikely that direct investment alone can become anything like an adequate source of international finance for economic development. It played, as we saw, a minor part in the nineteenth century. Can we rely on it to play a major part today? I doubt it.

What is most urgently needed today is a revival of the public or public-utility type of international investment that used to dominate the scene. The International Bank has hardly begun to fill the gap left by the disappearance of this type of private foreign lending. If the past cannot be reproduced, it is all the more imperative to devise a new pattern suited to present needs and conditions. Critics have wondered how much of nineteenth-century foreign investment would have survived the tests and rules laid down by the International Bank. The Bank, being dependent on the private capital market for most of its loanable funds, inevitably reflects to some extent the attitudes of the private investor. And the private American investor is still waiting for a change in the weather, and remains unimpressed by statistics showing that only 15% of the dollar bonds (not counting direct investments) floated in the 1920s by under-developed countries—that is, aside from Central Europe—have proved a permanent loss.

It is said that there are not enough productive projects in the low-income countries to absorb much more money than is now going out. It is pointed out that the Marshall Plan, which accustomed the world to the sight of a large dollar outflow, was not a plan of new development so much as one of reconstruction, in an area where a solid industrial foundation and the "know-how" of a skilled population already existed.[12]

No doubt this point has considerable force. But if there are not enough projects, can we not ask for international technical assistance to design them and to draw up the blueprints? Lack of basic services, such as transport, power and water supply, is a particularly serious bottleneck in the poor countries. Because of this the *physical* environment—quite apart from the obvious difficulties arising from the political or social climate—is unfavorable to private investment. A large foreign firm producing raw materials for export may find it profitable to set up incidental facilities such as roads or waterworks, of which the local economy, too, can make some use. But the general utility of such things often depends in haphazard fashion on the technical features of the

---

[12] It will be remembered, however, that some of the Marshall Aid was in effect passed on to "under-developed" countries (especially by way of the United Kingdom, whose overall balance was in equilibrium in 1948–49 and in surplus in 1950).

firm's main activity. It may be fairly high in the case of a railway built by a mining company from the interior of Peru to the sea-coast. It is virtually zero in the case of the pipe-line in which Arabian oil is pumped to the Mediterranean.

In the United States a hundred years ago public authorities, as well as private promoters, played a leading role in the drive for "internal improvements," financed in part by foreign capital. There is no question that ample scope exists for international financing of public improvements in the poor countries to-day. Until these countries have acquired a skeleton framework of such facilities, conditions will not be particularly attractive for the more varied and smaller-scale business investments there. Even with such basic improvements, of course, the individual business investments, domestic as well as foreign, may fail to materialize, because of other obstacles. It is conceivable, therefore, that some of these public works would turn out to be white elephants. But the risk has to be taken; any form of capital investment is, in the last analysis, an act of faith. However hard it may be for the pioneering spirit that opened up the new countries to apply itself to the low-income areas today, not much can be achieved without that spirit, and no international organization concerned with development can remain untouched by it.

Apart from the distribution of the promoter-function, there still remains the question of finance. If the profitability of American business at home has kept down direct investments abroad, a simple comparison of bond yields does not explain why "portfolio" lending cannot get started again. However, while the private investor has been standing on the side-lines, we may have witnessed the beginnings of a system of international grants-in-aid and low-interest loans from government funds. The reference to the principle of Equal Sacrifice with which Roosevelt defended the Lend-Lease program may some day appear significant in retrospect. I need not point to other signs and landmarks. Let me just quote a few recent expressions of opinion. The man who gave his name to the Marshall Plan, in accepting the Nobel peace prize [in December 1953] said that it was "of basic importance to any successful effort towards an enduring peace that the more favored nations should lend assistance in bettering the lot of the poorer."[13]

Dr. Herbert Feis, the historian of nineteenth-century foreign investment, has expressed himself as follows:

> A sense of obligation has won its way in the world to the effect that a wealthy country has a call of vague dimensions to provide means to assist poorer and suffering countries. To give free ad-

---

[13] *The Times,* December 12, 1953.

mission to [it] would bankrupt us and demoralize others; but to ignore the obligation wholly would be . . . out of accord with the effort in which we are engaged, to bring together the nations of the world in peaceful and co-operative understanding.[14]

Even if we hesitate to accept the assumption that world peace can be bought or that material progress makes for contentment the fact of growing pressures for international income transfers must nevertheless be recognized. It may be precisely because the problem of international investment is now, unlike what it was in the Victorian era, concerned in the main with the backward economies that the need for such transfers is felt to arise.

· · · · ·

---

[14] "International Economic Outlook," *Proceedings of the Academy of Political Science*, New York, May 1953, p. 59.

PART
· III ·

THE PIONEER OF
ECONOMIC GROWTH:
GREAT BRITAIN

INTRODUCTION

As was implied in Part I, any survey of economic growth in general must start with the British industrial revolution because the transformation of the British economy in the late eighteenth and early nineteenth centuries was the first of its kind in the history of the world. This does not mean that every (or, indeed, *any*) subsequent example of growth in other countries followed precisely the same course and pattern as the British. But the British case merits the closest attention because, being the pioneer, it provided a touchstone as well as a source of technology, capital, and ideas for economies which developed at later dates. The significance of the British industrial revolution has, of course, long been recognized, and there are many excellent studies of its particular aspects. Nevertheless, from the viewpoint of the modern interest in economic growth, by no means all of these are satisfactory. This is partly because they were written within a different framework (so that their emphases do not coincide with those which modern students of the subject prefer), and partly because British growth started too early for there to be a satisfactory basis for measuring its rate and structure. On the other hand, in the last decade or more the intensive academic interest in development has produced some searching new appraisals of some aspects of the classic industrial revolution (see the Selected Bibliography).

In an attempt to encompass as much material as possible, the first two Selections in this Part are taken from two general studies of British economic history. Selection 6 comes from Professor T. S. Ashton's brilliant study, *The Industrial Revolution*, which, although published in 1948, is still directly relevant to most of the problems of economic growth which have received so much emphasis in the years since then. Professor Ashton, formerly of the London School of Economics, now retired, is the leading authority on the economic history of the eighteenth century and the industrial revolution. His essay is offered here as a brief but penetrating survey of the salient characteristics, human as well as material, of the revolutionary process of industrialization. That process did not terminate in the first decades of the nineteenth century, but, rather, surged onward well beyond 1850. Indeed, the student should take care not to exaggerate the extent to which the British (or any) economy could be transformed in the initial generations of growth. For example, Professor J. D. Chambers, of Nottingham University, in his survey of the British economy from 1820 to 1880 (*The Workshop of the World*), from which Selection 7 is drawn, makes it clear that economic development was a continuing process in which there was still scope for vast and significant changes. In many respects the course of British industrialization after 1820 is just as interesting as its birth in the four or five decades before that date.

Whenever economic growth occurs, and no matter how long it continues, the role of the entrepreneur in generating and sustaining it is obviously an important one. It is for this reason that of all the specialist studies available, one referring to the nature of enterprise in the industrial revolution has been included here. Selection 8 is an article by Mr. C. H. Wilson, of Cambridge University, originally published in *Explorations in Entrepreneurial History*, a journal devoted to the study of enterprise. Mr. Wilson's essay abundantly demonstrates the wealth of information and analysis which is open to this particular approach. It serves to remind us that economic growth is preëminently the product of human action. But while human action can best be analyzed in terms of the individual, its outcome in economic processes assumes a regularity which typifies the economy as a whole. This is true of the aggregate phenomenon which we know as growth, and it is also true of one of the most typical features of nineteenth-century development: fluctuations. These fluctuations (in production, prices, trade, etc.), occurring with more or less regularity, are of various types. That is to say, they extend over differing periods of time. No attempt will be made here to deal with the short- or medium-run variations identified as business cycles. Instead, we reprint Professor Rostow's study of long-term trends in the British economy from 1790 to 1914 (Selection 9). Since that study was first published, in 1948, far more attention has been devoted to trends and "long swings" in economic life—particularly in research on the United States economy (see the Selected Bibliography and Selections 11 and 15)—and in measure as more information has become available, so analytical interpretations of the phenomenon have changed and become more complex. The essay is nevertheless reprinted here because it was an admirable attempt to identify and systematize a most important subject, and because in concentrating on the amount and nature of investment as a causal factor, it emphasized an element which clearly lies at the heart of the process of aggregate economic evolution.

The final Selection in this Part consists of excerpts from two articles and is representative of a large body of literature which has grown up concerning the nature and causes of the retardation in British economic growth in the late nineteenth century. Historians have long acknowledged that in the last part of the century the British economy seems to have lost a good deal of the momentum and dynamism which characterized it in the period up to the 1870's.[1] This retardation, moreover, seems to go beyond what one might normally expect from the late stages of growth. (It should also be distinguished from the almost inevitable process by which high growth rates in countries like the United States or Germany enabled them to overtake Britain's economic lead.) A wide variety of explanations have been suggested for this phenomenon—ranging from low level of technical education or conservative entrepreneurship to the rigidifying effects of trade unions or the overcommitment of the economy to "old-fashioned" staples such as cotton textiles and the iron and steel industry. In Selection 10 two opposing although related views of the "climacteric" of the British economy are presented. Professor E. H. Phelps Brown is at the London School of Economics, Mr. S. J. Handfield-Jones is at Glasgow University, and Mr. D. J. Coppock is at Manchester University.

---

[1] This is indicated in the data of industrial production reproduced in Selection 9, Table 1.

6

The Industrial Revolution
in Great Britain

by

T. S. ASHTON

⌄⌄⌄

In the short span of years between the accession of George III
[1760] and that of his son, William IV [1830], the face of England
changed. Areas that for centuries had been cultivated as open fields,
or had lain untended as common pasture, were hedged or fenced; ham-
lets grew into populous towns; and chimney stacks rose to dwarf the
ancient spires. Highroads were made—straighter, stronger, and wider
than those evil communications that had corrupted the good manners
of travellers in the days of Defoe. The North and Irish Seas, and the
navigable reaches of the Mersey, Ouse, Trent, Severn, Thames, Forth,
and Clyde were joined together by threads of still water. In the North
the first iron rails were laid down for the new locomotives, and steam
packets began to ply on the estuaries and the narrow seas.

Parallel changes took place in the structure of society. The number
of people increased vastly, and the proportion of children and young
people probably rose. The growth of new communities shifted the balance of population from the South and East to the North and Mid-

lands; enterprising Scots headed a procession the end of which is not yet in sight; and a flood of unskilled, but vigorous, Irish poured in, not without effect on the health and ways of life of Englishmen. Men and women born and bred on the countryside came to live crowded together, earning their bread, no longer as families or groups of neighbors, but as units in the labor force of factories; work grew to be more specialized; new forms of skill were developed, and some old forms lost. Labor became more mobile, and higher standards of comfort were offered to those able and willing to move to centers of opportunity.

At the same time fresh sources of raw material were exploited, new markets were opened, and new methods of trade devised. Capital increased in volume and fluidity; the currency was set on a gold base; a banking system came into being. Many old privileges and monopolies were swept away, and legislative impediments to enterprise removed. The State came to play a less active, the individual and the voluntary association a more active, part in affairs. Ideas of innovations and progress undermined traditional sanctions: men began to look forward, rather than backward, and their thoughts as to the nature and purpose of social life were transformed.

Whether or not such a series of changes should be spoken of as "The Industrial Revolution" might be debated at length. The changes were not merely "industrial," but also social and intellectual. The word "revolution" implies a suddenness of change that is not, in fact, characteristic of economic processes. The system of human relationships that is sometimes called capitalism had its origins long before 1760, and attained its full development long after 1830: there is a danger of overlooking the essential fact of continuity. But the phrase "Industrial Revolution" has been used by a long line of historians and has become so firmly embedded in common speech that it would be pedantic to offer a substitute.

The outstanding feature of the social history of the period—the thing that above all others distinguishes the age from its predecessors—is the rapid growth of population. Careful estimates, based on figures of burials and christenings, put the number of people in England and Wales at about five and a half millions in 1700, and six and a half millions in 1750: when the first census was taken in 1801 it was a round nine millions, and by 1831 had reached fourteen millions. In the second half of the eighteenth century population had thus increased by 40 per cent, and in the first three decades of the nineteenth century by more than 50 per cent. For Great Britain the figures are approximately eleven millions in 1801, and sixteen and a half millions in 1831.

The growth of population was not the result of any marked change in the birth rate. During the first four decades of the eighteenth century, it is true, the number of births per thousand people seems to have risen a little. Farm laborers tended to set up households of their own instead of boarding with their employers, and a decline of the system of apprenticeship in industry also led to earlier marriage and larger families. But from 1740 to 1830 the birth rate appears to have fluctuated only very slightly: for no decade does the estimate rise above 37.7, or fall below 36.6. Throughout the industrial revolution fertility was high but steady.

Nor can the increase of people be attributed to an influx from other countries. In every decade men and women took ship from Ireland to England and Scotland, and at times of dearth the trickle became a stream. But there was no such torrent of Irish immigration as was to come in the last five years of the eighteen-forties. On the other hand, during the eighteenth century perhaps a million people left Britain to seek a living overseas, mainly in the colonies. Among them were some 50,000 criminals transported to Maryland or Botany Bay, and a number of artisans who defied the law by carrying their technical knowledge and skill to Europe. . . . On balance, Britain was not a receiving center but a breeding-ground for new communities across the seas.

It was a fall of mortality that led to the increase of numbers. In the first four decades of the eighteenth century excessive indulgence in cheap gin and intermittent periods of famine took a heavy toll of lives; but between 1740 and 1820 the death rate fell almost continuously —from an estimated 35.8 for the ten years ending in 1740 to one of 21.1 for those ending in 1821. Many influences were operating to reduce the incidence of death. The introduction of root crops made it possible to feed more cattle in the winter months, and so to supply fresh meat throughout the year. The substitution of wheat for inferior cereals, and an increased consumption of vegetables, strengthened resistance to disease. Higher standards of personal cleanliness, associated with more soap and cheaper cotton underwear, lessened the dangers of infection. The use of brick in place of timber in the walls, and of slate or stone instead of thatch in the roofs, of cottages reduced the number of pests; and the removal of many noxious processes of manufacture from the homes of the workers brought greater domestic comfort. The larger towns were paved, drained, and supplied with running water; knowledge of medicine and surgery developed; hospitals and dispensaries increased; and more attention was paid to such things as the disposal of refuse and the proper burial of the dead.

. . . . .

The increase of the population of Britain occurred at a time when the output of commodities was also increasing at a rapid rate, and this coincidence has led to hasty generalizations. Some writers have drawn the inference that it was the growth of industry that led to the growth of numbers. If this were true the growth of industry must have exerted its influence, not through the birth rate (which, as we have seen, remained steady), but through the death rate. Some of the improvements in the arts of living mentioned above certainly depended on a development of industry, but it would be rash to assign to this a major part in the reduction of mortality. For population was growing rapidly, not only in Britain, but also in most other countries of western and northern Europe, where nothing in the nature of an industrial revolution occurred.

Other writers, reversing the causal sequence, have declared that the growth of population, through its effect on the demand for commodities, stimulated the expansion of industry. An increase of people, however, does not necessarily mean either a greater effective demand for manufactured goods or an increased production of these in the country concerned. (If it did we should expect to find a rapid economic development of Ireland in the eighteenth, and of Egypt, India, and China in the nineteenth century.) It may just as well lead to a lower standard of life for all. The spectre of the pressure of population on the means of subsistence which oppressed the mind of Malthus in 1798 was no chimera. It is true that the immediate pressure was less than Malthus supposed. But if, after the middle of the nineteenth century, there had been no railways in America, no opening up of the prairies, and no steamships, Britain might have learnt from bitter experience the fallacy of the view that, because with every pair of hands there is a mouth, therefore every expansion of numbers must lead to an increase of consumption and so of output. In Britain, in the eighteenth century and later, it so happened that, alongside the increase of population, there was taking place an increase of the other factors of production, and hence it was possible for the standard of life of the people—or of most of them—to rise.

There was an increase in the acreage of land under cultivation. Much attention was given to the draining of fens and marshes, to the breaking up and turning to arable of the old, rough, common pastures (which were usually spoken of as the waste), and to the hedging of land, so as to make it more productive of both crops and livestock. . . . Several new crops were introduced. The turnip made it possible to increase the size of the herds of cattle, and the potato, which was becoming a popular food in the North, brought substantial economies in the use of land. More will be said later about the agricultural and agrarian changes. It is sufficient here to make the point that land previously outside the system of economic activities was being drawn in, and put to better use. The lines of the moving frontier can be discerned on the hillsides today by those with eyes to see.

At the same time there was taking place a rapid increase of capital. The number of people with incomes more than sufficient to cover the primary needs of life was growing: the power to save was increasing. Stable political and social conditions, following the settlement of 1688, encouraged men to look to more distant horizons: what economists call time-preference was favorable to accumulation. The class structure also was favorable to it. It is generally recognized that more saving takes place in communities in which the distribution of wealth is uneven than in those in which it approaches more closely to modern conceptions of what is just. Estimates of statisticians, from Gregory King in 1688 to Colquhoun in 1812, exhibit wide variations in the incomes of different social classes; and the rise of new institutions, including that of the National Debt, intensified the disparities that had been handed down from earlier generations.

The public debt, as we know it today, arose out of the exigencies of the wars of William III [at the end of the seventeenth century]. It grew steadily—almost entirely as the result of successive wars—until, by 1815, it had reached a figure of £861 millions. Not all of it was held by the British people themselves: in 1776, it was estimated, about three-sevenths of it was in the hands of the Dutch. But, after 1781, when Holland became involved in war with Britain, the great bulk of the debt came to be held in [Britain]—by noblemen, squires, lawyers, retired merchants, and widows and spinsters of the well-to-do classes. In 1815 perhaps about one-eleventh, and in 1827 (according to the estimate of Sir Henry Parnell) one-twelfth, of the money income of the people of the United Kingdom consisted of sums raised from the taxpayers, including the poor, and transferred to the relatively rich holders of government bonds. In this way, increasingly, wealth came into the hands of those whose propensity was to save, rather than to spend.

Accumulation does not of itself, however, lead to the creation of capital goods: it was not only a willingness to save, but also a willingness to employ savings productively, that increased at this time. In the early eighteenth century, landlords had used saved resources to improve their own estates, merchants to extend their markets, and manufacturers to engage more labor; and some of the savings of the retired and leisured classes had been lent on mortgage to local landowners, farmers or tradesmen, or invested in the shares of a turnpike trust. Gradually the market for capital widened, aided by the rise of country bankers (who existed long before they took the name). The offer by the State of a mass of gilt-edged stock accustomed men to the idea of impersonal investment, and so they came to put their savings into enterprises distant in space and speculative in character. That the results might not always be advantageous was made manifest when the South Sea Bubble burst in 1720 and brought ruin to thousands. But, in general, the increased mobility of capital was socially beneficial, leading as it did to a substantial fall in the rate of interest.

For centuries the attitude of the State to the taking of interest had been one of hostility or, at least, of suspicion. The State was an habitual debtor—and laws had been passed prohibiting the making of loans at more than a prescribed rate. In 1625 the legal rate had been lowered from 10 to 8 per cent; in 1651 it was reduced to 6, and in 1714 to 5— in each case following upon a fall in the "natural" rate. In the early eighteenth century the abundance of loanable funds made it possible for finance ministers to reduce the interest paid to the creditors of the State. During the wars, the Government of William III had been obliged to offer 7 or 8 per cent (the Usury Laws did not apply to the State); but in 1717 the rate on the perpetual annuities was reduced to 5, and in 1727 to 4 per cent. Finally, in the 1750s, Pelham lowered it once more, and, by converting a number of issues into a single one, brought into being, in 1757, the 3 per cent Consolidated Stock which, for short, we call Consols. These conversions were not imposed on an unwilling public: they reflected, rather than initiated, a fall of the rate of interest in the community generally. There was, at this period, no single market rate to which reference can be made, but the process can be observed in the rising price of Bank of England stock; and the ledgers of merchants and manufacturers afford further evidence of what was taking place. Much economic activity at this time was controlled by small groups of partners, each of whom was entitled either to receive his share of the annual profits or to leave it, wholly or in part, to earn interest in the concern. During the early part of the eighteenth century the rate allowed on money reinvested in this way was falling steadily. A firm of ironmasters of Worcestershire, Edward Knight and Company, for example, credited each partner with 5 per cent on the undistributed profit during the 'twenties and early 'thirties, but in 1735 the rate was reduced to 4, and in 1756 to as little as 3 per cent. If a group of men were considering the investment of their savings in some new, large capital enterprise, such as a turnpike, they would first make an estimate of the number of years it would take for their capital to be restored to them in full. If the current rate of interest were 5 per cent it would be worth while embarking on an undertaking that would return the capital in twenty years; at 4 per cent investment might be extended to one that would take twenty-five years, and at 3 per cent to one that would take up to thirty-three and a third years, to reimburse the initial outlay. The lower the rate at which capital could be obtained—the smaller the advantage forgone in locking it up in a fixed form—the futher would capital works be extended.

As early as 1668 Sir Josiah Child remarked that "all countries are at this day richer or poorer in an exact proportion to what they pay, and have usually paid, for the Interest of Money." He went on to observe that "the bringing down of Interest from 6 to 4, or 3 per cent will necessarily . . . double the Capital Stock of the Nation" and added that "the Nobility and Gentry, whose estates lie mostly in Land, may presently upon all they have, instead of fifty write one hundred." In spite of this early exposition of the relation between interest, capital, and well-being, the importance of the lowering of the rate of interest in the half-century before the industrial revolution has never been properly stressed by historians. If we seek—it would be wrong to do so—for a single reason why the pace of economic development quickened about the middle of the eighteenth century, it is to this we must look. The deep mines, solidly built factories, well-constructed canals, and substantial houses of the industrial revolution were the products of relatively cheap capital.

One thing more was necessary: the increasing supplies of labor, land, and capital had to be co-ordinated. The eighteenth and early nineteenth centuries were rich in entrepreneurs, quick to devise new combinations of productive factors, eager to find new markets, receptive to new ideas. "The age is running mad after innovation," said Dr. Johnson; "all the business of the world is to be done in a new way; men are to be hanged in a new way; Tyburn [the site at which public executions were held] itself is not safe from the fury of innovation." The sentiments and attitudes of mind of the period were propitious. The religious and political differences that had torn society apart in the two preceding centuries had been composed; and if the eighteenth century was not markedly an age of faith, at least it practiced the Christian virtue of tolerance. The regulation of industry by gilds, municipalities, and the central government had broken down or had been allowed to sleep, and the field was open for the exercise of initiative and enterprise. It was perhaps no accident that it was in Lancashire and the West Riding, which had been exempted from some of the more restrictive provisions of the Elizabethan code of industrial legislation, that the development was most marked. It was certainly no accident that it was the villages and unincorporated towns—places like Manchester and Birmingham—that grew most rapidly, for industry and trade had long been moving away from the areas where some remnants of public control were still in operation.

During the seventeenth century the attitude of the Law had changed: from the time of Coke judgments in the courts of Common Law had become tender indeed to the rights of property, but hostile to privilege. In 1624 the Statute of Monopolies had swept away many vested interests, and a century and a half later Adam Smith was able to say of Englishmen that they were "to their great honor of all peoples, the least subject to the wretched spirit of monopoly." Whether or not the patent system, the lines of which had been laid down by that same Statute, was stimulating to innovation in industrial practice is not easy to determine. It gave security to the inventor, but it allowed some privileged positions to be maintained for an undue length of time, and it was sometimes used to block the way to new contrivance: for nearly a quarter of a century, for example, James Watt was able to prevent other engineers from constructing new types of steam engine, even under license from himself. Many manufacturers—not all from disinterested motives—opposed the application of the law and encouraged piracy. Associations were brought into being in Manchester and other centers of industry to contest the legality of rights claimed by patentees. The Society for the Encouragement of Arts, Manufactures and Commerce, founded in 1754, offered premiums to inventors who were willing to put their devices at the free disposal of all. And Parliament itself made awards (for example, £14,000 to Thomas Lombe when his patent for silk-throwing expired, £30,000 to Jenner for the discovery of vaccine inoculation, £10,000 to Edmund Cartwright for various contrivances, and £5,000 to Samuel Crompton for his invention of the "mule" [an improved spinning machine]) in addition to the substantial annual grants it voted for the use of the Board of Agriculture and the Veterinary College. Without any such monetary incentive, one of the outstanding industrialists, Josiah Wedgwood, resolved "to be released from these degrading slavish chains, these mean, selfish fears of other people copying my works"; and, at a later stage, the inventors of the safety lamps, Sir Humphry Davy, Dr. Clanny, and George Stephenson, all refused, in the interest of the miners, to take out patents for their devices. It is at least possible that without the apparatus of the patent system discovery might have developed quite as rapidly as it did.

Some accounts of the technological revolution begin with the story of a dreamy boy watching the steam raise the lid of the kettle on the domestic hearth, or with that of a poor weaver gazing with stupefaction at his wife's spinning wheel, overturned on the floor but still revolving. These, needless to say, are nothing but romantic fiction. Other accounts leave the impression that the inventions were the work of obscure millwrights, carpenters, or clockmakers, untutored in principles, who stumbled by chance on some device that was destined to bring others to fame and fortune and themselves to penury. It is true that there were inventors—men like Brindley and Murdoch—who were endowed with little learning, but with much native wit. It is true that there were others, such as Crompton and Cort, whose discoveries transformed whole industries, but left them to end their days in relative poverty. It is true that a few new products came into being as the result of accident. But such accounts have done harm by obscuring the fact that systematic thought lay behind most of the innovations in industrial practice, by making it appear that the distribution of rewards and penalties in the economic system was wholly irrational, and, above all, by overstressing the part played by chance in technical progress. "Chance," as Pasteur said, "favors only the mind which is prepared": most discoveries are achieved only after repeated trial and error. Many involve two or more previously independent ideas or processes, which, brought together in the mind of the inventor, issue in a more or less complex and efficient mechanism. In this way, for example, the principle of the jenny was united by Crompton with that of spinning by rollers to produce the mule; and the iron rail, which had long been in use in the coal mine, was joined to the locomotive to create the railway. In such cases of what has been called cross-mutation the part played by chance must have been very small indeed.

Yet other accounts of the industrial revolution are misleading because they present discovery as the achievement of individual genius, and not as a social process. "Invention," as a distinguished modern scientist, Michael Polanyi, has remarked, "is a drama enacted on a crowded stage." The applause tends to be given to those who happen to be on the boards in the final act, but the success of the performance depends on the close co-operation of many players, and of those behind the scenes. The men who, together, whether as rivals or as associates, created the technique of the industrial revolution were plain Englishmen or Scots,

Being neither demigods nor heroes,
But ingenious, hard-working descendants of homo sapiens,
Who had the luck to plant their seedlings in fine weather,
Not in the frost or storm, but when the slow ripening of time, the felicitous
    crossing of circumstance
Presented unimagined opportunities,
Which they seized. . . .

(The words are those of a master cotton-spinner, Godfrey Armitage, of our own day.)

Invention appears at every stage of human history, but it rarely thrives in a community of simple peasants or unskilled manual laborers: only when division of labor has developed, so that men devote themselves to a single product or process, does it come to harvest. Such division of labor already existed when the eighteenth century opened, and the industrial revolution was in part cause, and in part effect, of a heightening and extension of the principle of specialization.

Invention, again, is more likely to arise in a community that sets store by things of the mind than in one that seeks only material ends. The stream of English scientific thought, issuing from the teaching of Francis Bacon, and enlarged by the genius of Boyle and Newton, was one of the main tributaries of the industrial revolution. Newton, indeed, was too good a philosopher and scholar to care whether or not the ideas he gave to the world were immediately "useful"; but the belief in the possibility of achieving industrial progress by the method of observation and experiment came to the eighteenth century largely through him. Natural philosophy was shaking itself free from its association with metaphysics and—again the application of the principle of division of labor—splitting up into the separate systems of physiology, chemistry, physics, geology and so on. The sciences were not, however, as yet so specialized as to be out of contact with the language, thought, and practice of ordinary men. It was as a result of a visit to Norfolk, where he had gone to study the new methods of farming, that the Scottish landowner, James Hutton, became interested in the constitution of soils; and the discoveries that made him the most famous geologist of his day owed something to the navvies who were cutting the clays and blasting the rock to provide England with canals. Physicists and chemists, such as Franklin, Black, Priestley, Dalton, and Davy, were in intimate contact with the leading figures in British industry: there was much coming and going between the laboratory and the workshop, and men like James Watt, Josiah Wedgwood, William Reynolds, and James Keir were at home in the one as in the other. The names of engineers, ironmasters, industrial chemists, and instrument-makers on the list of Fellows of the Royal Society show how close were the relations between science and practice at this time.

Inventors, contrivers, industrialists, and entrepreneurs—it is not easy to distinguish one from another at a period of rapid change—came from every social class and from all parts of the country. Aristocrats, like Lord Lovell, in the early part of the century, and Coke of Holkham in the later, initiated improvements in agriculture; others, such as the Duke of Bridgewater and Earl Gower, created new forms of transport; and yet others were responsible for innovations in the chemical and mining industries. Clergymen and parsons, including Edmund Cartwright and Joseph Dawson, forsook the cure of souls to find out more efficient ways of weaving cloth and smelting iron. Doctors of medicine, among whom were John Roebuck and James Keir, took to chemical research and became captains of large-scale industry. Under the influence of a rationalist philosophy, scholars turned from the humanities to physical science, and some from physical science to technology. Lawyers, soldiers, public servants, and men of humbler station than these found in manufacture possibilities of advancement far greater than those offered in their original callings. A barber, Richard Arkwright, became the wealthiest and most influential of the cotton-spinners; an innkeeper, Peter Stubs, built up a highly esteemed concern in the file trade; a schoolmaster, Samuel Walker, became the leading figure in the north of England iron industry. "Every man," exclaimed the ebullient William Hutton in 1780, "has his fortune in his own hands." That, it is needless to say, has never been true, or even half true; but anyone who looks closely at English society in the mid- and late eighteenth century will understand how it was possible for it to be said, for at this time vertical mobility had reached a degree higher than that of any earlier, or perhaps any succeeding, age.

It has often been observed that the growth of industry was connected historically with the rise of groups which dissented from the Church by law established in England. In the seventeenth century the congregation of Puritans gathered about Richard Baxter at Kidderminster included the Foleys, the Crowleys, and the Hanburys, who were to set up great establishments in places as far afield as Staffordshire, Durham, and South Wales. In the following century members of the Society of Friends played a prominent part in the development of corn-milling, brewing, pharmacy, and banking; and the Quaker families of the Darbys, Reynolds, Lloyds, and Huntsmans came to direct the destinies of the iron and steel industries at a period of rapid change. There were Baptists, like Thomas Newcomen, and Presbyterians, like James Watt, in engineering; Independents, like John Roebuck and Joseph Dawson, alongside the Quakers, in iron-smelting; and Unitarians, including the M'Connels and the Gregs, in cotton-spinning. In cotton, moreover, the greatest inventor, Samuel Crompton, was a disciple of Emmanuel Swedenborg—who himself, it may be recalled, was an authority on metals and the technique of mines. Other industrialists, among whom were the Guests of South Wales, drew strength from the teaching of John Wesley. But Wesley's first appeal was to the poor and unprivileged, and the effects of Methodism are to be seen less in the quickening of enterprise than in the greater sobriety, diligence and self-discipline of the workers who came under its influence.

Many explanations have been offered of this close association between industry and Dissent. It has been suggested that those who sought out new forms of worship would also naturally strike out new pathes in secular fields. It has been argued that there is an intimate connection between the tenets peculiar to Nonconformity and the rules of conduct that lead to success in business. And it has been asserted that the exclusion of Dissenters from the universities, and from office in government and administration, forced many to seek an outlet for their abilities in industry and trade. There may be something in each of these contentions, but a simpler explanation lies in the fact that, broadly speaking, the Nonconformists constituted the better educated section of the middle classes. This view is supported by a consideration of the part played in the economic movement by the stream of energy that poured into England from Presbyterian Scotland after (though not immediately after) the Union of 1707. The greatest inventor of the age, James Watt, came from Scotland, as also did seven of his eight assistants in the business of erecting engines. Sir John Sinclair, Thomas Telford, John Macadam, David Mushet and James Beaumont Neilson brought their Scottish vigor of mind and character to English agriculture, transport, and iron-making. Highlanders and Lowlanders, alike, tramped to the Lancashire cotton area, many of them pausing at the little village of Chowbent, where a fellow-countryman named Cannan directed them to centres which offered scope for their several abilities. . . . These . . . immigrants were not illiterate peasants. Some were sons of the manse, and even those of humbler station had been given at least the rudiments of a sound education in the village or burgh school of their native place.

If the Scottish system of primary education was in advance of that of any other European country at this time, the same was true of the Scottish universities. It was not from Oxford or Cambridge, where the torch burnt dim, but from Glasgow and Edinburgh, that the impulse to scientific inquiry and its practical application came. Many young men, attracted by the learning and personality of Joseph Black, Professor of Chemistry at Glasgow and later at Edinburgh, were trained to methods of thought and experiment which were afterwards directed to industrial ends. . . .

In a humbler way the academies established by nonconformist zeal for education—at Bristol, Manchester, Northampton, Daventry, Warrington and elsewhere—did for England in the eighteenth century something of what the universities did for Scotland. Open to all, irrespective of creed, they provided a curriculum which, weighted, it is true, with Divinity, Rhetoric and Jewish Antiquities, included Mathematics, History, Geography, French, and Bookkeeping. Among their pupils were Daniel Defoe (and a contemporary named Cruso), John Cope, John Howard, Thomas Malthus, and William Hazlitt—to name only a few of those who were to rise to distinction in letters and public life. What is more to our immediate purpose, they were nurseries of scientific thought. Several of them were well equipped with "philosophical instruments" and offered facilities for experiment: their teachers included men of the quality of Joseph Priestley and John Dalton; and from them proceeded a stream of future industrialists, among whom were John Roebuck (who was trained at Northampton before proceeding to Edinburgh and Leyden), Matthew Boulton, John Wilkinson, Benjamin Gott, and—of a later generation—Joseph Whitworth.

Apart from the dissenting academies, there were in many towns institutions which, like the national Society of Arts, were devoted to the improvement of methods of production. Informal groups of scientists and manufacturers came into being in Lancashire and the Midlands, as well as at Edinburgh and Glasgow. Who can say how much the master cotton-spinners gained from their contact with Thomas Percival and John Dalton in the Literary and Philosophical Society of Manchester; or how much Birmingham and its province owes to the Lunar Society, in which Erasmus Darwin, R. L. Edgeworth, Joseph Priestley, James Watt, Matthew Boulton, and Josiah Wedgwood brought their powerful minds to bear on the problems of life and, no less, on those of getting a living?

The conjuncture of growing supplies of land, labor, and capital made possible the expansion of industry; coal and steam provided the fuel and power for large-scale manufacture; low rates of interest, rising prices, and high expectations of profit offered the incentive. But behind and beyond these material and economic factors lay something more. Trade with foreign parts had widened men's views of the world, and science their conception of the universe: the industrial revolution was also a revolution of ideas. If it registered an advance in understanding of, and control over, Nature, it also saw the beginning of a new attitude to the problems of human society. And here, again, it was from Scotland, and the University of Glasgow in particular, that the clearest beam of light was thrown. It is, no doubt, an academic error to overstress the part played by speculative thought in shaping the lives of ordinary men and women: it is arguable that John Wesley, Tom Paine, William Cobbett, and Orator Hunt were of as much immediate consequence as David Hume, or even Jeremy Bentham. But, at least, there is one product of Scottish moral philosophy that cannot pass without mention in any account of the forces that produced the industrial revolution. The *Enquiry into the Nature and Causes of the Wealth of Nations*, which appeared in 1776, was to serve as a court of appeal on matters of economics and politics for generations to come. Its judgments were the material from which men not given to the study of treatises framed their maxims of conduct for business and government alike. It was under its influence that the idea of a more or less fixed volume of trade and employment, directed and regulated by the State, gave way—gradually and with many setbacks—to thoughts of unlimited progress in a free and expanding economy.

7

Great Britain Becomes the Workshop
of the World, 1820–1880

by

J. D. CHAMBERS

~~~~~~

I. FACTORS IN THE TRANSITION TO MACHINE INDUSTRY

The period during which Britain can be described as the workshop of the world is open to a variety of definitions. In this book it is taken to lie roughly between the financial crisis of 1825 and the onset of what is known as the Great Depression in 1873, or in round figures, between 1820 and 1880. That is not to imply that by the last quarter of the century British economic supremacy was at an end; on the contrary, in some important respects it grew to a new peak of grandeur. It rested on the world-wide services Britain provided through her shipping and credit agencies and the mutually advantageous relations she had established with her dependent empire. By these means she was able to meet the gap between her exports and the imports which poured into her free market and thus to provide funds for the lubrication of the wheels

Reprinted from *The Workshop of the World: British Economic History from 1820 to 1880*, by J. D. Chambers (pp. 1–24, with omissions), copyright © 1961 by Oxford University Press, by permission of the publishers and author.

of the world's commerce; but she no longer held a virtual monopoly of the supply of manufactured goods, and two vital components of her export trade consisted of raw materials: the products of her coal mines and the re-exported products of Australian ranches. Britain as the pioneer of the world industrial revolution had given place to Britain the world's banker, trader and collier, and a competitor with other industrial giants whom she herself had materially assisted to adult stature.

At the beginning of the period so defined, Britain was in the throes of the transition . . . from a primarily agricultural and commercial economy to a modern industrial state. For the first time in history, the life of a great nation had become geared to machine production for the international market; economic output over the long period was rising substantially faster than population growth and the foundation was being laid for a spectacular rise in the standard of living. It was the first transition of its kind, and since it was the product of natural growth and only marginally dependent on outside sources of capital and skill, it was also the last. Historians have sometimes complained that the change was managed badly; in view of the anxious efforts of undeveloped economies today to achieve the same end, the question to which historians are now more inclined to turn their attention is how it was managed at all.

In 1820, when this book takes up the story, the political face of the country remained unchanged though it reflected an entirely new mood; its geographical face, especially in the Midlands and North, appeared, to contemporaries, to be in process of transformation. In 1822, one of the earliest of the geological surveys reported that a traveller from London to the west or north-west would cross bands of clay and chalk and oolite and a broad zone of red marly sand, and beyond this he would find himself in the midst of coal mines and iron furnaces "—in South Wales, the Forest of Dean, the Black Country, in North Warwickshire and West Leicestershire and so through Nottinghamshire and Derbyshire to the coal and iron of Yorkshire and the North." The Trent and Soar marked the eastern boundary, the Warwickshire Avon and the Severn the southern boundary, of the land of coal mines and iron furnaces. To the south of it most of the old industries were dying and, except in London, new ones were little more than desperate stopgaps to take the place of the spinning and weaving and the metallurgical industries which in former times had been the staple of the industrial economy of the nation but which could no longer provide a return on capital or yield a livelihood to labor. To the north and west of it, a succession of startling successes had been won in the production of high quality goods at prices which brought them within the reach of constantly widening sectors of the market. Innovation had led to innovation, making possible an incalculable saving of time and labor and releasing circulating capital for investment in more machines or the production of more goods, "a process," says Professor Ashton, "which is at the centre of what is called the industrial revolution."[1] Moreover, a major contribution to this vital process of transforming circulating into fixed capital had been made by the completion of a road system and a network of waterways which permitted the carriage of goods to all parts of the country with speed and safety and an absence of internal tolls that was known in no other country in Europe.

To a German visitor in 1828, Britain appeared to be an extraordinary land in which "the new creations springing into life every year bordered on the fabulous"; a Frenchman walking through the Black Country on a dark night had found the horizon "bounded by a circle of fire. From all parts, columns of smoke and flame rose on the air and the whole country around seemed as if lighted by an intense conflagration." An American, after a tour of the northern textile towns and villages, spoke of the new workmen's stone cottages fresh from the mason's yards which met his eyes on every side.

These travellers could have found equally significant evidence of Britain's economic power nearer home. In 1789, an ambitious young man, Samuel Slater, quietly left his home in Belper and was next heard of in Pawtucket, Rhode Island, where he built a replica of the Arkwright machine from memory (since to take out plans was illegal) and so became the founder of the American power textile industry. The Cockerill Brothers, who had been transforming the Belgian textile industry since the last years of the eighteenth century, turned, after the war, to the production of the latest steam engines, pumps, hydraulic presses at their engineering works at Seraing—perhaps the greatest works of their kind in Europe—and boasted that they had all the latest inventions within ten days of their appearance in England. A young Westphalian locksmith was sent in 1819 by the Prussian government to learn the latest English methods of machine production; and as far away as Vienna the directors and foremen of cotton mills were chiefly British emigrants. Britain was already qualifying for the title of workshop of the world.

As an episode in economic history, the transition to industrialism in Britain has a special significance. It represents the classic example of self-generated take-off from a traditional, basically agricultural and commercial economy to sustained economic growth through specialization of processes, technological innovations—sometimes in alliance with scientific discoveries—and the exchange of a surplus of manufactured

---

[1] See T. S. Ashton, *An Economic History of England in the 18th Century*, p. 112, for the classic statement of the economics of the innovating process.

goods for food and raw materials in other parts of the world. It implied, also, a new phase of capital investment which called for the plowing back of at least 10 per cent of the national income in investment instead of the customary 4 per cent or 5 per cent per annum in order to maintain a rate of production sufficient to keep ahead of the increase of population. It involved the community in a simultaneous creation of new forms of industry and transport and in an immense effort in agriculture and building to feed and house a new industrial population; and it placed new strains on a social and political system which had to reconcile the demand for increased output with the dawning awareness on the part of labor that industrialization held the key to economic advance for all and not only for the privileged few. The change was accomplished peacefully; and thanks to the labors of scholars at home and abroad it is possible to present the results of the national effort in broad outline in statistical form: Dr. W. Hoffman calculates that the output of British industries, taken together, grew at the rate of from 0.5 per cent to 1 per cent per annum between 1700 and 1780, but from 1780 to 1870 the rate of growth was more than 3 per cent. Miss Phyllis Deane of the Oxford Bureau of Statistics thinks that from 1740, when the rise of the national income from the late seventeenth-century levels became noticeable, the average real income per head probably rose by half; between 1800 and 1850–60 it may have doubled, and by 1900 it had probably doubled again.

To contemporaries who watched, not without apprehension, the process of economic transformation taking place, the main agent of growth was the accumulation of capital, and the factors which favored it were accorded a place of special importance. To Adam Smith (who took his stand in the pre-transition period) "every prodigal appears to be a public enemy and every frugal man a public benefactor"; and to Ricardo, impressed—perhaps obsessed—with the rise in population, the continuous growth of capital and its embodiment in new forms of machinery were necessary for the maintenance of profits, rents and wages alike. As we know now, Ricardo and his followers took an unnecessarily gloomy view of the prospects of industrial society, and many of their contemporaries refused to share it, but all agreed on the paramount need of capital accumulation and technical improvements and the necessity of removing obstacles that might interpose themselves between the productive process and the market or impede the efficient use of capital resources.

A particularly important role, therefore, fell to the man of business, the merchant or manufacturer or improving farmer and landlord—the entrepreneur as the classical economists called him—who undertook the work of directing capital resources to their alternative uses. It was mainly his own capital that he was directing, and he was usually responsible, along with his partners if he had any, to his last shilling for the debts of the firm in the event of failure. In return for the profits of enterprise, he set his own and sometimes other people's capital in motion by employing labor at subsistence wages and providing tools and materials with which they were enabled to supply the needs of the market. In the eyes of contemporary theorists, he was relatively a passive agent of market forces of which the consumer was king.

In the light of recent studies based on the records left by some of the pioneer firms, modern historians would accord the entrepreneur a wider and more human role, especially in the case of the large new firms which took the lead in the advance to machine production. Such firms broke new ground not merely in the application of technical innovations to existing processes, but through improvements in organization and management of labor and in the study of market forces. . . .

Improvement in organization involved the early factory master in problems of recruitment and management for which the traditional system of putting-out through irresponsible middlemen was by no means the best preparation. Arkwright and Strutt, who initiated the revolution in cotton spinning, owed their success not only to their business acumen but to the imagination which they brought to the human problems of machine industry. They were community builders as well as organizers of production, and they and their successors, the Gregs of Styal, Benjamin Gott of Leeds, John Fielden of Todmorden, John Heathcoat of Tiverton, the Ashtons, Ashworths, Whiteheads of Cheshire and Lancashire, combined outstanding efficiency in the management of their concerns with a rudimentary system of welfare which has a place of importance in the history of labor relations. Robert Owen, the chief of the community builders, was the first to realize that output did not necessarily vary directly with the length of the working day, and that the appallingly long hours that were possible under the more flexible domestic system were not only inhuman but might be relatively unprofitable under conditions of factory production. Sir Robert Peel, the leading factory master of the day, who had already been instrumental in passing the Act of 1802 to regulate the hours of parish apprentices, joined forces with Owen to initiate the proceedings that culminated in the Acts of 1819–20; and under the leadership of these two highly successful manufacturers, the long-sustained effort of the State to curb the rapacity of the average factory master was launched.

. . . . .

The leading figures in the transition to machine industry (whatever may be said of the rank and file) cannot easily be fitted into the classical and Marxist mold of the capitalist inexorably confined by the cash nexus and mechanically adjusting himself to the movement of the market under the stimulus of marginal costs. Many industrial leaders could more easily be classified as products of religious dissent and perhaps more particularly, of the superior education which dissenting schools provided.[2] . . . The supreme self-confidence of the leaders of enterprise who were not only managers but the chief risk-takers of their concerns may have had its roots in the same source. They were acting in accordance with the character of a society in which the qualities of personal decision and responsibility were rooted in a long tradition of individualism in its most private and sacred aspects.

Not only the masters, but the men, especially in the new industrial communities of the North, the Midlands and South Wales, were also coming under these influences. The sanctifying virtues of hard work, thrift and self-denial were now being carried into the lives of the working classes themselves through a multitude of chapels and Sunday schools under the influence of the evangelical revival. It contributed also to the rise of effective working-class organization through the qualities of integrity and moral leadership which it evoked and on which durable trade unionism rested; and even the voices raised in indignant protest against the injustices and cruelties which industrialism brought in its train, struck the authentic note of the age of self-discipline for moral as well as material ends. "An idle man," said the redoubtable Parson Bull to the miners of Yorkshire, his neighbors and friends, *"is the devil's man.* Apply yourselves diligently to your calling—be not like some who *work hard* a few days, *drink hard* the rest—Three things then let me recommend—Religion as *the root,* and Industry and Patriotism as the *branches.*" Men and masters shared a common tradition and understood, if they did not always speak, a common language. The process of industrialization on which they were both engaged was a social as well as an economic process, and it reflected the energies of a whole people pursuing their material ends in a framework of values which accorded special importance to the qualities which could be turned to account in an age of unprecedented economic and social opportunities.

In agriculture the main emphasis of change was on the more efficient use of the land itself. To regard this change in land use as a mere undifferentiated drive towards enclosure for higher rents is to obscure its essential character. The introduction of the turnip and artificial grasses made possible the spread of arable cultivation of light soils that had hitherto lain idle; and while heavy soils were being put down to grass or

---

[2] [See Selection 6, pp. 156–158—*Ed.*]

cultivated in long leys for animal husbandry to satisfy the growing market for meat and particularly for tallow, lighter soils were being given over to mixed farming.

The special character of the British agrarian revolution—a revolution in land use involving appropriate advances in animal breeding and crop rotation—has important implications both on the side of capital formation and on that of labor supply. The English tenurial system, in accordance with which the landlord provided and usually maintained the fixed capital, implied a quasi-co-operative relationship between landlord and tenant which enabled the latter to retain a proportion of the profits of the joint investment and frequently encouraged the tenant to plow back his profits in improvements even though he might have no certain security of tenure or legal redress for loss of unexhausted improvements. The factor of confidence between landlord and tenant must be numbered among the imponderables that contributed to the process of capital formation in the period of transition.

Within the peculiar—and probably unique—context of the English agrarian system, the opportunities for saving were very wide. They were open not only to the owners of the soil but to a growing body of substantial tenant farmers; and the increasing volume of agricultural production fertilized intermediate areas of trading activities carried on by those involved in processing the raw materials of agriculture for milling, brewing, distilling, starch making, tallow candling and the like. A more direct impact of agricultural savings was made through rural and urban building and through the part which great landowners played, along with the great industrialists, in the development of transport, especially inland navigation.

Landowners were not slow to respond to the opportunities offered them in the nineteenth century when their resources were greater than ever before, being swollen by urban rentals, although at the same time being burdened in some cases by unprecedented debts incurred in the course of patrician living. Few of the gentry of the north of England and the Midlands and South Wales failed to enlarge their incomes by means of leases of mineral rights, and some mined their own coal directly and even leased coal from others. Earl Fitzwilliam in Yorkshire, and the Earl of Crawford in Lancashire, managed their own enterprises; the Lowthers of Cumberland sank £500,000 in mines, harbor and general development of Whitehaven. They easily—indeed inevitably—passed from coal to railways, and helped to promote companies that were likely to serve the needs of their own enterprises or enhance the value of their properties. (They could also obstruct development, and in other parts of the country railway companies often went out of their way to placate aristocratic opposition or to attract aristocratic investment by reserving a proportion of the shares to landowners on the route of the railway: the reservation of one-third of the shares of the Liverpool and Manchester and one-fifth of the Great Western are two outstanding examples.) Lord Durham passed from railways to sea transport and marketed the products of his mineral empire in his own ships from the port of Sunderland; the Marquis of Londonderry converted Seaham into a port and a steel town, and the seventh Duke of Devonshire took the lead, not only as chief risk-taker but as paramount managerial influence in the development of Barrow-in-Furness which grew from an isolated village of 150 inhabitants in 1846 to an industrial center of 40,000 people in 1873, equipped with the largest and most efficient Bessemer steel plant in the world, a shipyard planned to employ 6,000 men, and a prosperous railway system which linked this previously unknown corner of England with the national railway network.

$$\cdot \ \cdot \ \cdot \ \cdot \ \cdot$$

Powerful as the internal market was, it had also the reinforcement of a growing export trade to support the structure of machine industry. A population of less than twelve million people, according to the British census of 1801, was an insecure base for the doubling of the rate of investment; no more than 40 per cent of the output of the cotton industry, for instance, was absorbed by the home market in the first half of the nineteenth century; and it was fortunate—though not fortuitous —that the field of manufacture in which innovation had made its most spectacular advance coincided with the area of most elastic demand. Under the stimulus of rising war-time incomes and falling textile prices, the appetite for machine-made textiles grew with what it fed on, and, as a result of the invention of the cotton gin by Eli Whitney in 1793, the problem of supply was solved at a moment when shortage of raw material might have had disastrous results. From an average of 16 m. lb. in the period 1783–7, the import of raw cotton rose to 28.9 m. lb. in 1787–92 and 56 m. lb. in 1800, and while the total of domestic exports nearly doubled (from £10.7 m. in 1783–7 to £19.7 m. in 1796–1800 according to Professor Ashton's figures)[3] the exports of cotton manufactures in the same period more than quadrupled, representing a ratio of 13 per cent of the total; by 1806 the proportion was 40 per cent. At the same time, and in spite of wartime wages and prices, the price of cotton yarn showed a spectacular fall—from 38s. in 1786 for No. 100 yarn to 6s. 9d. in 1807. The British take-off, it has been well said, was launched on a wave of war inflation and cotton exports.

---

[3] T. S. Ashton, *Economic Fluctuations in England 1700–1800* (1959), p. 184.

II. INDUSTRIAL SOCIETY AND THE COMING OF MACHINE INDUSTRY

This widening of commercial horizons both at home and abroad called for a reorganization of the structure of industry and an adaptation of the labor force on a radical scale; but both the variety of forms of organization and the length of time during which the adaptation took place were greater than is sometimes realized. Birmingham, which claimed, through the famous firm of Boulton and Watt, to provide the world with steam engines, required very few for its own manufacturing processes. Here the "garret master," with a £100 capital and his traditional skill was still the typical figure; the great factory at Soho remained a "magnificent exception," and it was not until the last quarter of the nineteenth century that machinery was devised (or imported from America) which could enable standardized factory production to compete with the products of the myriad small masters who supplied the highly specialized products of the finished metal trades: light arms, jewelry, sporting guns, japanned products, etc. In Sheffield it was much the same with the making of scythes, sickles, table knives, where craftsmen, as in Birmingham, worked for middlemen except in times of bad trade when they launched out on a desperate gamble of their own. The cheapness of the metal on which they worked was such that unemployed journeymen would sometimes establish themselves on credit as small masters and contrive to dispose of their product—often of the lowest quality—as best they could "through new and strange channels on the meanest terms, for money, for stuff, for anything, for nothing." The first cutlery factory which embodied all processes from steel making to the hafting of the knife appeared in 1832, but owing to the variety of style and quality of the finished product, there was still room for the little man, and the factory product remained the exception for many years.

The extraction of the coal on which the national economy rested was not only non-mechanized but, except in the northern coalfield, continued to depend on small sub-contractors (butties in the Midlands and West Country) who engaged to get coal at an agreed price and employed their own labor; the production of iron was often undertaken in the west Midlands by "overhands" with their own gangs of day laborers; even in the highly organized cotton spinning the operative spinner belonged to a higher order of workers than his "piecer" whom he employed at wages half his own; the building of a locomotive might be subcontracted to a piece master who would employ his own craftsmen and these in turn would employ and pay their own workmen. In the textile industries, there was an army of hand workers who were as much part of the "great industry" as the factory workers themselves, though more susceptible to the ebb and flow of its commercial mechanism. There were probably half a million weavers[4] in 1830 working for cotton, silk, woolen and linen firms, and not less than 50,000 framework knitters usually working for middlemen and many of them for large firms operating through a system of departmental managers. Such forms of employment were not widely different from those of the factory except that the operatives had to provide or pay for their own fixed capital equipment, so absolving the employer from the burden of initial investment and subsequent overheads. In cotton, the firm of Horrocks had 700 spinners working in factories at Preston in 1830 but an army of out-workers numbering over 6,000; silk throwsters at Congleton might have half their men in factories and half out; in hosiery I. and R. Morley had 2,700 framework knitters and a host of seamers and finishers of all kinds and no factory at all until after 1860.

To define the conditions which produced factory production is not easy, but it may be said that concentration was most advanced where power machinery could be applied and where numerous delicate processes called for co-ordination under skilled supervision in order to capture or to extend a known area of the market. This was especially the case when finishing processes involving new techniques of dyeing and printing were brought together by the merchant with his eye on the market, or in the manufacture of glass, soap, pottery, paper, which depended on the direct application of chemical knowledge, and in the machine tool shops and the metal industries calling for large investment of fixed capital as well as specialized skill.

Important and indeed revolutionary as these processes were, the advance was not such as to affect directly more than a small proportion of the population. In 1834, the historian of the cotton industry, Edward Baines, estimated the workers in cotton mills at about 210–230,000; that is, one in every eighty of the population, less than one-third of the female domestic servants, and perhaps one-eighth of those engaged in agriculture. Apart from the handloom weavers and framework knitters who were on the fringes of the "great industry," there were tens of thousands of tailors, shoemakers, metal workers, country blacksmiths, cobblers, carpenters, sewing women, and between three and four hundred thousand workers in the building trades, almost untouched by the new machinery. Many other local industries had been touched and turned to decay. . . .

The representative Englishman, it has been said, was still a countryman in 1831, and the representative workman was still a handicraftsman

---

[4] See J. H. Clapham, *An Economic History of Britain*, I, p. 179.

in a traditional workshop, working with traditional tools. In 1851, the distribution of the population had changed in favor of the townsman, but the representative Englishman was still far from being a worker directly employed in machine industry. The victory of the factory over the older forms of industrial organization was slow and it was not until the last decades of the century that it became the dominant form of organization in a majority of industries. In 1851, those employed in the principal non-mechanized categories comprised about five and a half million workers and outnumbered those in the mechanized industries (including coal) by three to one; and of the one and three quarter million in the mechanized groups, half a million were cotton workers. The most numerous group after agriculture were the domestic servants. In 1851, their number had risen to over a million and was still twice as large as the cotton workers. At 1,039,000 they were drawing nearer to the agricultural group which now numbered 1,790,000 and together these two groups numbered more than double those engaged in manufacturing and mining. When Britain was the undisputed workshop of the world, the "great industry" on which it was based actually employed 1.7 m. out of a total British population of 21 million.

The relative numerical weakness of the "great industry" emphasizes its revolutionary character. In 1851, it absorbed less than one-quarter of the principal occupation groups, but it made an essential contribution to an economy which now had to provide for a population that had nearly trebled in the course of a hundred years. In 1751, the British population is thought to have been 7½ million; in 1831, it was 16½ million; by 1851, it had grown to 21 million. It was, also, by this time, a predominantly urban population; in 1831, the proportion of British people in towns of over 20,000 was one-quarter; within a generation the proportion had risen to a half and was rapidly growing. By 1851, the representative Englishman was becoming a townsman.

The British "take-off" had involved, in its early stages, not only the mobilization of resources for industrial growth—machinery, transport, agricultural improvements, public utilities—but for fighting a twenty years' war with France. Investment on this gigantic scale could not be undertaken without a sacrifice of current consumption; it was impossible to have both guns and butter and at the same time to build the factories and farms that produced them. The transition from war to peace in 1815 which cut off government expenditure coincided with the end of a phase in long-term investment in agriculture and transport and imposed therefore a double strain. Moreover, between 1814 and 1817, 400,-000 ex-service men sought re-entry to civil life and population was rising by more than 200,000 a year; there was a temporary collapse of the iron industry following the cessation of government orders; the export industries were facing the resistance of tariffs after a post-war spree of dumping of accumulated stocks. Surplus labor organized hunger marches and clamored for the vote; political economists talked of the need to check population growth; a handful of merchants petitioned for free trade; George and Robert Stephenson wrestled with the problem of the locomotive, but they were balked of success until 1829. If the engineers had reached their goal a generation earlier, the quota of misery might have been less. The logic of economic growth, with its disparity between the relentless growth of numbers and the sporadic advance of innovation, took its course. The astonishing resilience of cotton and iron and the flow of funds into harbor installations, gas, water and other utilities, saved the situation, and the period 1815–30 ranks as one of the most troubled yet one of the most productive of the century. Still wider fluctuations were to follow; the first railway mania raised the boom of 1834–6 to record heights, but the accumulated miseries of the down swing made the period 1837–42 the most critical of the century, and there is some reason for thinking that the real national income per head in 1840 was lower than in 1830. Between 1840 and 1850 the "industry state," to use Sir John Clapham's expression, began to experience the invigorating effects of a rapidly expanding railway network and of a fleet of iron ships of which a growing proportion consisted of iron screw steamers, the fruits of long-term investment and innovation of a previous generation; the reform of the tariff and the reintroduction of the income tax in place of the heavy excise duties helped to stimulate the home and foreign markets; and the time was approaching when the British standard of living would be carried forward on a tide of exports which exchanged at a premium in terms of food, especially meat and dairy produce. The harvest of a mature economy was at last beginning to be gathered.

8

The Entrepreneur in the Industrial
Revolution in Britain

by

CHARLES WILSON

The causes that produce genius in individual men, and outbursts of activity in nations, are mysteries which only become more impenetrable as one theory after another is flung out to account for that which is beyond knowledge. But though he may make no pretense of having penetrated the laws of the spiritual world, the historian is bound to describe the manner of life and the intellectual atmosphere which shaped and colored, whether or not they occasioned greatness of deed and mind.

—G. M. TREVELYAN (1904)

〰〰〰〰〰〰〰〰〰〰〰〰〰〰〰〰〰〰〰〰〰〰〰〰〰〰〰〰〰〰〰〰〰

I

The study of modern industrial change in Britain has passed through a number of phases. A hundred years ago it was still in the full flowering of what may be termed the "Heroic" phase: the organizers of change were still regarded by observers like Samuel Smiles with the respect and even awe properly attributable to those who had been instrumental in delivering society from the fate predicted for it by Malthus. Less favorable comment was not wanting but in so far as criticism was not purely conservative it remained tolerably open-minded. And apart from the pure Marxians, the growing body of socialist humanitarian critics con-

Reprinted from *Explorations in Entrepreneurial History*, VII, 3 (February, 1955) (pp. 129–45, with omissions), by permission of Professor Arthur H. Cole and the author.

centrated their energies against industrial capitalism for its defects as a system of distribution of wealth rather than as a mode of production.

Side by side with such criticisms, which tended to encourage tacit assumptions that the growth of wealth was a virtually automatic process, there took place a narrowing of the focus of professional historians not unconnected (I think) with the former process. If the business organizer's function was otiose, who deserved to be studied? The answer came easily enough: it was the inventor. And from Toynbee down to Usher inventions took pride of place in the study of industrial history. Only with the comparatively recent impact (in England) of sociology and economic theory on historical method has the inventor's place in the process been re-assessed. . . .

The notion that the total process was a complex interweaving of scores of influences, trends and pressures—a study in economic counterpoint—has been most fully realized in Professor Ashton's short but brilliant study published in 1948.[1] Here the contemporary cluster of activities—affecting finance, transport, social relations and markets as well as technology—is brilliantly described and analyzed. From the point of view of this paper, not the least important of Professor Ashton's contributions is his clear perception of the economic and social role of the entrepreneur. Refuting the errors of those who have written of the "disasters of the industrial revolution" Professor Ashton has pointed out that "the central problem of the age was how to feed and clothe and employ generations of children outnumbering by far those of any other time." If England had remained a nation of cultivators and craftsmen she must have shared the fate of Ireland and submitted to the remedies of emigration or starvation. "She was delivered," he writes, "not by her rulers, but by those who, seeking no doubt their own narrow ends, had the wit and resource to devise new instruments of production and new methods of administering industry."

Here is a starting point for further inquiry. Professor Ashton has himself suggested some of the diverse considerations which led employers to reorganize industry on new lines. In the iron and cotton industries technology suggested large scale production and the application of power in the factory. Elsewhere, economic rather than technological considerations prevailed. In the chemical and engineering industries, supervision was necessary to insure quality of workmanship. In textiles, too, oversight was necessary and Benjamin Gott, the great woolen manufacturer at Leeds, saw the factory system as a preventive against the waste and embezzlement of materials. Wedgwood's *Etruria* was devised partially to exploit the economies to be derived from the division and subdivision of labor. And so on.

---

[1] [See Selection 6—*Ed.*]

Such are a few of the suggestions which the student of the entrepreneur must take up. The inquiry remains, nevertheless, in an early stage. What were the "ends" which the entrepreneur of that age had before his eye? How "narrow" were they? Why was he moved to devise new instruments of production and new types of industrial organization? And what was the social background against which this great increment of wealth was created? The ensuing paper does not attempt to do more than suggest possible lines of study in the light of evidence which though obvious enough has had less careful study than it seems to warrant.

II

First let us remind ourselves of a few elementary generalizations. In the first place, the writer agrees with Professor Ashton as to the usefulness of the phrase "Industrial Revolution." It would, as he says, be pedantic to question it, but it is important to realize that abrupt change is not in fact characteristic of the economic process, certainly not in the 18th and 19th century. Late 18th century Britain was an old commercial society, highly skilled and sophisticated in certain economic techniques. The new industrial changes were linked organically and personally with an older economic world at every stage. Landowners provided land and money for canals, and for factories, from fortunes expanded by incremental site values. Much—perhaps too much—has been made of the fact that many of the new industrialists were recruited from the ranks of the yeoman farmers. But the weavers who equally turned into industrialists were also an integral part of the older order. Capital came to industrialists in need from merchants of an older generation, especially in Lancashire. The Baltic tallow merchant became in his own person the largest manufacturer of those candles—nightlights—which illuminated millions of early Victorian homes. The "navvies" skilled in canal building were switched to railway construction just as clockmakers were brought in to solve problems of building industrial machinery. Brewers and drapers of Dr. Johnson's London became suppliers of capital for industrial development. Everywhere there is unbroken continuity.

Yet continuity does not mean uniformity. Each industry had its own rate of progress. The cotton industry was early subjected to rapid change and by 1811 four-fifths of the cotton goods produced in Lancashire were made of mule yarn spun largely in urban mills. Yet even in this industry, other sections of production were slower to respond and Edmund Cartwright's power loom, invented in 1784, was still too primitive to be used in the best manufactures thirty years later. The woolen industry was even slower to respond. As Sir John Clapham has remarked, many accounts of the industrial revolution would hardly suggest that in 1830 only one person in 80 worked in a cotton mill. In the England of George IV, out-work was still the predominant form of capitalist industry. Indeed, it is only in very recent times that some important industries have entered the stage that cotton entered 150 years ago. The problems of industrial discipline that attended the coming of the factory in the Northampton boot and shoe industry are still within living memory and one does not need to be middle-aged to remember the eclipse of the bespoke tailoring trade by factory-made suits bought off the peg.

The economic historian who deals with the industrial revolution without reservation in terms of period will therefore do so at his peril. He will do well to remember too that he is dealing with a society which, though growing, was still relatively small and compact, and in which a more abstract and generalized system of economic relationships was only just beginning to encroach on one based largely on local and often family relations. The intimate connections between the growth of industry and the several kinds of religious Dissent—especially the older sects—have been fairly fully investigated and proven. It was not only the better (and more practical) education that Dissenters provided for themselves but the necessary solidarity they felt between themselves that helps to explain the phenomenon. The Meeting House or the Chapel extended the ties of the family, and you lent and borrowed within your known community with a confidence hardly yet to be extended beyond such limits. The parochial character of industry seems to me to go on much longer than is usually supposed: perhaps it still goes on. A knowledgeable businessman could write in 1903 as if the spread in industry of limited liability was a recent thing, and about the same time a soap maker could write to a Bristol rival: "personal knowledge of each other is a great factor in the cohesion of the soap trade. . . ." He was only repeating what earlier makers had said: that "good fellowship" in the trade was worth ten shillings a ton.[2]

The entrepreneur was not, that is to say, operating in an anonymous world. Nor, on the whole, for all its difficulties, was it an unfriendly world. An observer trying to explain the rapid growth of the British economy in 1800 ascribed it to the improvements in public utilities and cost-reducing inventions applied in industry. To greater output and better quality was due "the universally increasing demand" for British goods. But, he added significantly, "All these advantages she owes to her social system, which gives equal respectability to trade and equal security to the capital invested in it."[3] The tradition had deep roots: Thomas Deloney, the Elizabethan writer, remarked "the younger sons

---

[2] Charles Wilson, *History of Unilevers* (London, 1954), I, 70.
[3] Henry Beeke, *Observations on the Produce of the Income Tax* (London, 1799).

of knights and gentlemen, to whom their fathers would leave no lands, were most commonly preferred to learn this trade [cloth making] to the end that thereby they might live in good estate and drive forth their days in prosperity." But in the early 18th century Defoe noted that the social stream ran in both directions and "many of the great families who now pass for gentry in the Western counties have been originally raised from and built up by this truly noble manufacture."

III

Such was the background to what Dr. Johnson called "an age of innovation," and such are a few of the limits and circumstances, local and special, which must be borne in mind as the particular context within which the entrepreneur of the industrial revolution worked. The nature of the entrepreneur's function has been defined shortly by Professor [Arthur H.] Cole[4] as "the utilization by one productive factor of the other productive factors for the creation of economic goods": the motive or result being an increase of profit or efficiency, or an accession or shift of personal power, or the growth or survival of the business as a unit. Enough evidence is readily available to suggest that this definition may well suggest new modes of inquiry into the industrial revolution. As Mantoux pointed out in his classic study [*The Industrial Revolution in the Eighteenth Century*], the great figures of the movement made their reputations as *organizers*. Their distinctive characteristic was that they fulfilled in one person the functions of capitalist, financier, works manager, merchant and salesman. Here was "a new pattern of the complete business man." So much is common knowledge: we usually assume that such men, though far from common, were responsible for changing the climate of opinion amongst the manufacturing class as a whole. Yet, oddly enough, there has been relatively little attempt to bond their total function into the economic context. A dozen biographers from Samuel Smiles onward have rendered tribute to Wedgwood, Boulton, and many others. Yet Wedgwood's fame rests largely on his application of the principle of division of labor. Boulton is famous for his association with and promotion of Watt and his invention. So with the others. Yet further survey of the field of their labors prompts the question whether here, as so often in history, we are not allowing our eye to be attracted by the spectacular difference, while ignoring the common quality shared by all these great entrepreneurs and not for that reason of less significance but perhaps more. If too rigid a pattern is not to be imposed on the bewildering variety of circumstances, our sense of this common characteristic must be kept as general

---

[4] F. C. Lane and Jelle C. Riemersma (ed.), *Enterprise and Secular Change* (Chicago, 1953), pp. 183–4.

as possible. I should define it thus: *a sense of market opportunity combined with the capacity needed to exploit it.* The conventional accounts of change have in reality concentrated so much on the exploitation of opportunity as to obscure the nature of the opportunity itself. The fact that Wilkinson was the best and most reliable borer of cylinders in England is no doubt a technical fact of some importance, as is the fact that Hargreaves' jenny could spin 80 threads at once. Yet economically such facts are quite useless unless it is explained why the accurate boring of cylinders or the greater output of yarn was not only necessary but seen by some men "of wit and resource" to be necessary and potentially profitable.

. . . . .

IV

"To study the entrepreneur," Professor Cole has written, "is to study the central figure in modern economic history and to my way of thinking, the central figure in economics."[5] Certainly a legitimate approach to modern economic history might be to trace the development from . . . the slow gathering of control over the different processes within a single industry to that outward seeking after control not merely of one industry but of the ancillary industries and processes on which the so-called "central" manufacture depends—in short to the vertical combine in which modern industrial development has reached (some might say, passed) its peak of self-fulfillment.

If we narrow our focus, for the moment, to the textile industries of Britain in the period of revolution, certain general features of change will be seen to emerge. First, for nearly a century before industry itself was revolutionized by the new technology, there had proceeded an expansion of markets which, though small in relation to what was to follow, was very large indeed by comparison with what had gone before. The "official" value of British exports in 1760 was twice that of 1700 and nearly eight times that of 1660, and though the proportionate importance of cloth declined steadily, its actual value rose rapidly and remained (till 1802) the most valuable single export. This moreover in a period when the price revolution is no longer available as a convenient *deus ex machina* in the historian's apparatus of analysis and explanation. The falling rate of interest was certainly an important factor in expansion: but it seems to me to have been rather in the nature of an enabling condition for those prepared to take advantage of it. It did not prevent the decline and virtual extinction of well-established industries in some areas. It is, however, not merely an expansion of production, linked no

---

[5] *Ibid.,* p. 187.

doubt to an increase of population, fundamental developments in public finance, and better facilities for transport, that is significant. There is besides a marked shift of emphasis in the nature of the articles produced, and a new phase of interregional competition for market supremacy. In this battle—and especially in the battle for exports—the East Anglian industry slowly overcame the weakening resistance of the West, only to be overwhelmed in turn by the ingenuity and assiduity of the Yorkshire industry.

The movement away from the older heavier woolens to lighter and brighter worsteds (extended later in the growth of demand for printed calicoes and cottons) clearly represents a phase of social and economic change: in this the development of an urban middle class demand and the growth of tropical and semi-tropical exports were to combine. Sir John Elwill, a great Exeter cloth merchant, wrote in 1714 to a Dutch client that the manufacture of "mixt Serges" was declining and would "never flourish as heretofore." The reason was that they were "not worn by Many Sort of People as formerly": but "Some new sorts of Drapery were invented . . . which are used by many that formerly used Serge." Yet the West was to fail utterly in the struggle for the market in the new cloths and it is not altogether fanciful to seek part of the explanation of her failure in the relative weakness of the link between manufacturer and merchant. In Devonshire, the two functions were often separate: in Norwich and Yorkshire they were often combined. After a brief glory, Norwich gave way to Yorkshire, where the link was most strong. There, by the end of the 18th century, as Professor Heaton has shown,[6] "many merchants had gained absolute control over production by becoming manufacturers themselves." Merchant and manufacturer were united in one person and a term was put to the friction between the former, who alone knew what the customer would buy, and the latter, who was often more interested in persuading the merchant to take what he had always made. Equally there is evidence here of the commercial sense of the industrialists less evident elsewhere. Professor Heaton has shown us the indefatigable Sam Hill, toiling and sweating to imitate the latest worsteds from Norwich and ending triumphantly on a note of pushful confidence that defied contemporary depression and becomes enterprise personified. "I think it now evident these manufactories . . . will come in spite of fate into these northern Countries."

It is difficult not to see a relationship between the growth of the worsted market (which by the 1770's was on the point of overtaking the older production of woolens) and the change in industrial organization which brought carding, slubbing, spinning, and in some cases finish-

---

[6] H. Heaton, *Yorkshire Woollen and Worsted Industry* (Oxford, England, 1920), p. 388.

ing and dyeing—but not yet weaving—into the factory between 1790 and 1825. These developments in technology and industrial organization fill in the framework sketched by Mantoux: it was the continental demand for English worsted which enabled the enterprising clothier to profit from circumstances. A petition from the weavers presented to the House of Commons in 1794 spoke of the large numbers of merchants who were turning clothiers, especially in and near Leeds and Halifax, setting up large factories for making woolen cloth.

It must be evident that the most progressive of these men who were to set the pattern for future development owed as much to their grasp of commercial opportunity as they did to their capacity to apply and develop the new inventions. Benjamin Gott, the first of the great Leeds spinners, was a merchant whose mind turned first to the nature of demand and secondly to the means of satisfying it. His most important innovations were the application of new chemical techniques to the vital finishing and dyeing sections of the cloth-making process. Here thousands of pounds and infinite patience were expended in developing an industrial process scientifically controlled throughout. In the early 19th century the process of concentration can be taken a step further in the worsted business of William Foster at Queensbury, then a small village half-way between Bradford and Halifax. In his own lifetime the founder saw his industry change from a domestic affair into one where all the numerous processes were comprised and controlled within Foster's own factories. The special feature of Foster's, however, was their development of high grade fabrics for dresses from mohair and alpaca. These, his Victorian biographer tells us, "were dispersed over all the countries of the world, lending new charms to female loveliness wherever they are seen, whether it be to form a chastely flowing garment for an Eastern beauty, or to adorn the figure of the most fashionably attired Parisian belle." And at this point we may watch the vital transition from market sense to advertisement proper. For faced by the wiles of the Paris fashion dictators Foster decided to invoke the aid of an aristocratic beauty, the Countess of Bective, in support of a patriotic movement in female fashions. What became known as the Bective movement was in fact the first essay in what was later to become a regular feature of advertising: the ingenious exploitation of snob appeal. The Countess of Bective must go into the history of industrial change as clearly as the spinning jenny. For the charms of aristocratic beauty were to be no less an instrument to the hand of the entrepreneur than the steam loom itself.

That invention and organization were intimately related to possibilities and changes in demand is no less clear from the history of cotton than from that of wool. The 18th century yielded nothing to the 20th in the extravagance and caprice of its tastes and fashions in clothing. Within a matter of months a fad would take hold which called for immediate response and the most flexible commercial and industrial organization. It was presumably through such a series of changes that the great markets for Lancashire goods were built up. The general trend in Europe at any rate was an extension of the demand for lighter, finer fabrics and in particular for fabrics which imitated the qualities of those previously imported from the East. The ingenuity of the entrepreneurs who seized this opportunity to develop a local imitative industry has been traced by Wadsworth and Mann,[7] and their application of chemical knowledge to their production problems by Mr. and Mrs. Clow.[8] Thus behind the staggering increase in Lancashire exports to Europe— from practically nothing in 1750 to £218,000 by 1770—lies the story of the experiments in dyeing by John Wilson of Ainsworth (near Manchester) and others. Most of the increase was accounted for by cotton velvets and checks. The correspondence of Samuel Oldknow with his London agents about this time brings out clearly the relationship between markets and manufacturer. The manufacturers were advised which types of fabric were a poor sale and should be dropped, which sold well and should be developed. "We want as many spotted muslins and fancy muslins as you can make, the finer the better. . . . You must give a look to Invention, industry you have in abundance. We expect to hear from you as often as possible and as the sun shines let us make the Hay." And later: "We rather wish you to drop the Sattinets, they are not new here and only fit for 2 months sale. The Buff stripes are liked best but still do not pursue it, turn the loom to something else. They are not fine enough for People of Fashion, for which they are only calculated for . . . try your skill at Table Linen . . . Arkwright must lower his Twist and he must spin finer, tell him the reputation of our Country against Scotland is at stake." These pressures of the market and competition were bearing in on the industrialist from every direction. What came to be a widespread muslin industry in Lancashire and Scotland depended on the ability of the mule to produce a thread even finer than the best hand spun yarn from India. Only with the water frame could English calico weavers compete with Indian calicoes. Only the water frames of Arkwright's mill at Derby could produce the strong thread for Strutt's specialty—the ribbed stocking and so on.

It is evident that if manufacturers were to be able to rise to these exacting occasions their control of the productive process must be firm and flexible. Herein lies, it seems to me, one of the most important

---

[7] A. P. Wadsworth and Jean de L. Mann, *The Cotton Trade and Industrial Lancashire* (Manchester, England, 1931).
[8] A. and N. Clow, *The Chemical Revolution* (London, 1952).

facts behind the movement to include all the several processes of manufacture—spinning, weaving, dyeing, finishing—under the control of
single entrepreneurs . . . It was illustrated most strikingly in the development of Horrockses of Preston where the whole process from sorting out
American and Egyptian cotton bales down to dispatching their special
finished cotton products—sheetings, shirtings and long cloths—to merchants at home and abroad was gathered into one organization by the
1830's.

It was as true of other industries producing consumer goods as of wool
and cotton that the entrepreneur's first effort had to be concentrated on
innovation and organization designed not merely for quantity production but for quality appropriate to the existing or potential demand.
What an observer said of Crossleys, the great carpet makers of Halifax,
might have been said of many others. "No amount of cheapening of
production would have availed them anything if they had not also been
able to take the lead in the beauty and originality of their designs." The
best known achievement of Josiah Wedgwood, one of the classical
entrepreneurs of English industrial history, was to found his factory
Etruria on the principle of division of labor. But mass production *in
vacuo* might well have been a failure, even given the growing demand
for crockery from which to drink coffee and tea, had it not been combined with a shrewd perception of the contemporary appeal of pseudo-
classical designs. Having provided all Europe with table china his commercial imagination was by no means exhausted and in the late 1770's
he wrote of his intention to develop a new line of manufacture—
"earthen water pipes, for London first, and then for all the world."

Perception of a small but important need in an expanding commercial
society—the steel pen—led Josiah Mason to establish a factory at
Birmingham which became the largest of its kind in the world. Mason
was not himself an inventor but he had (as his biographer observed) a
"quickness in seizing a new idea, sagacity in realizing its possibilities
of development and courage in bringing it within range of practical
application." It was these qualities which later attracted his attention
to the invention of electro-plating and its usefulness in the manufacture
of cheap table ornaments and spoons and forks, ". . . knowing, as he
shrewdly said, that the reputation as well as the solid profit of the
enterprise must rest upon articles capable of being made by the hundred
thousand and requisite for common household use." Much later, in the
1880's, a similar perception that a new type of customer, the working
class housewife, "clean, saving and thrifty," was available, led William
Lever to launch a patent "washer" soap with qualities which had
a special appeal to this type of user. Backed by every kind of advertising
—mostly borrowed from North America—he built up in less than 20

years a business which surpassed in scope and size all other British competitors.[9]

The qualities and capacities which have been stressed in the entrepreneur are most clearly discernible in those industries and trades producing goods for a wide range of consumers. Yet it would be rash to assume that they were less important in industries like the iron industry, an important part of which—and that most swiftly revolutionized— manufactured capital goods or munitions. In the course of the 18th century an industry which was splintered into a vast number of small separate enterprises—furnaces, forges and slitting mills—became increasingly concentrated in large "integrated" establishments in which all those processes from the mining of the ore down to the delivery of cannon mortars, bombs, cannonades, boilers, mill-gear and the like were carried out. The great iron masters like Richard Crawshay, Anthony Bacon and John Roebuck, though their market may have been less capricious in some ways than those for which the textile makers catered, had their own problems of quality which could only be mastered by trial and error, in a concern where (as a French visitor to the Carron works noted) "everything is arranged and carried on with exact precision and nothing is left to mere routine or chance." The quality of iron used in making an iron railing would be different from that suitable for making a horse-shoe or a cart wheel. Not the least of the problems of an industry in which vast amounts of capital had to be sunk was the uncertain character of its wartime market. It needed the passionate, single-minded, almost ludicrous faith of a John Wilkinson in his product to transfer the new material to peacetime use, not only in bridges, ships, and cast iron pipes for public water supply but in numerous more or less suitable architectural uses. The inside story of the partnership between the iron masters and those architects of the Gothic Revival who sent clustering columns and high traceried windows soaring up in cast iron in hundreds of fashionable buildings has yet to be told. But it could hardly fail to record remarkable deeds of entrepreneurship.

Similarly, if a point had to be chosen from which Bessemer's later invention sprang it might well be the day in France when he, knowing little at the time of iron metallurgy, saw that the type of iron used in gun-making left much to be desired. Likewise John Brown of Sheffield, to whose faith in steel Bessemer owed an incalculable debt, owed his own fame to his vision of the railway system. "He saw boundless demand in this new adjunct of civilization." And on the railway companies he thrust his invention of the conical spring buffer (1848), bullied the doubting Admiralty into adopting iron plates and cajoled the railways into adopting steel rails by distributing free samples.

[9] Wilson, *op. cit.*, Vol. I, chap. iii.

The drift of these detailed inquiries seems to me to be clear: it is the tendency, powerful yet in the period of industrial revolution far from ubiquitous, for the entrepreneur's intervention in certain important fields of industry to widen into an all-embracing function. This was necessary, it seems to me, if stability of costs, assured production in point of quantity or quality, and the requisite flexibility with regard to markets were to be achieved. A detailed examination of those markets suggests that it is misleading to consider the industrial revolution (as many text books do) merely in terms of undifferentiated commodities called cotton or woolens or iron. Such a treatment obscures the fundamental fact that the need to be met was for highly specific versions of such general categories of commodities and the relation between this fact and the consequential changes in industrial organization. It might be argued that in the last analysis it was a commercial flair that was basic. "The tradesman," as an 18th century writer put it, "stands at the head of the manufacurer." Or as a later German historian wrote: "Every commercial capitalist, whether he understands the technical side of his business or not, is always a trader. It is trade which decides what commodities shall be produced, where they shall be produced and how they shall be produced." And perhaps the classic instance of the captain of industry who owed his success to his commercial gifts as much as anything was Boulton who dared to risk financing Watt because, as Mantoux has said: "He was a bold and clever trader versed in the needs and possibilities of the market." The fact that the lineage of many of the new entrepreneurs may be traced through generations of yeomen or artisans does not necessarily damage the claims such a theory may have to our consideration.

V

Much ink has been spilt in attempts to identify the sources from whence came the entrepreneurs and the capital they disposed. Yet the evidence remains too flimsy and incomplete to conclude with confidence more than this: that they came from every social source and every area. A great landowner like the Duke of Bridgewater created new forms of transport; merchants came to make the things they had previously only sold, scientists turned into industrialists, parsons into inventors, small farmers and weavers became captains of industry. Arkwright was a barber, Samuel Walker of Rotherham turned from schoolmastering to become a great iron master. The capital required likewise came from a variety of sources. In many enterprises from those of the early entrepreneurs—Wedgwood, Gott and Crawshay—down to that of the last of the line—William Lever—personal saving played a great part. The great iron business of Walkers at Rotherham rose in the 1740's largely on capital amassed from plowed back profits. And in the 1880's Lever was making £50,000 a year, living modestly on £400 a year and with the remainder creating and purchasing his own Ordinary Shares. In yet other instances, capital was raised by means of partnership deeds and mortgages while short-term funds came from the banks. Only great public enterprises—turnpikes, canals, docks and the like—were public companies drawing on a national capital market. For the rest, investment was (and often long remained) local and even sectarian.

The brakes which early centuries had placed on the economic freedom of the entrepreneur—the restrictive and paternal legislation of guilds, muncipalities and states—had largely disappeared from the world of Boulton and Watt. Here natural philosophy was itself being dissolved into its component applied sciences which in turn became technology; but even in the 1730's the poet's theme was already a philosophy which seemed eminently suitable to the entrepreneur:

> That REASON, PASSION, answer one great aim;
> That true SELF-LOVE and SOCIAL are the same. . . .[10]

Thus long before economic freedom became rationalized and systematized into a doctrine, the climate of opinion was becoming favorable to its practical development. An attempt in 1690 to set up an *omnibus* "Guild or Fraternity" under the control of the Leeds Corporation for controlling cloth-working was recognized by 1720 to be a dead letter "by long disuse and failure." Companies of this type—and they were tried in many places—could not exercise effective supervision over materials, workmanship, hours, wages and quality which in the Middle Ages had been partially controlled by specialized guilds, partially by the entrepreneurs. Apprenticeship and supervision of wage rates by the Justices of the Peace were likewise falling into desuetude in the century before the industrial revolution proper began. The idea of regulation persisted very much longer in regard to external trade. The cotton industry grew up behind the shelter of the Calico Act (1721), designed to protect the woolen industries from India silks, and it was not until a century or more after the nominal date usually assigned to the beginning of industrial revolution (1760) that all the remains of the old mercantilist system were finally swept away. Even at Manchester, where ideas of economic freedom were most strongly developed, sectional opposition, obstinate and prolonged, was still evoked by proposals to export textile machinery. Even here, however, there are signs in the 18th century that the demand of entrepreneurs for adequate supplies of cheap materials was raising up a strong body of opposition to the monopolies of the

---

[10] Alexander Pope, *Essay on Man.*

great importing companies which had long formed an integral part of the old system.

On the whole, the entrepreneur was empirical in his economic views. The nearest thing to a general economic philosophy evolved in the transitional stage from the mercantile system to the full doctrine of laissez-faire was probably enshrined in the sub-title to Mandeville's *Fable of the Bees* (1714). It ran: "Private Vices, Public Benefits." This economic application of Pope's equation of self-love and social welfare was frequently elaborated by popular philosophers like Dr. Johnson and others. The "evil of luxury," said Johnson, was one of those false things "transmitted from book to book." The truth was that luxury produced much good: the expense went to the industrious poor and the demand gave rise to "so much general productive exertion" that it could not fail to be beneficial. In short, here is the beginning of a philosophical divorce between ethics and economic doctrine. It remained, nevertheless, far from complete so far as the entrepreneur was concerned. It may be, as some have attempted to show, that the new capitalism was relatively free from social controls and rested on a theoretical basis of the operation of natural law rather than on a system voluntarily developed by men. Yet those who saw (and no doubt with good reason) much virtue in the operations of the Hidden Hand often acted in practice in ways which denied its claim to be the sole regulator of human affairs. As E. H. Carr has observed: ". . . the ingrained and irrational habits of personal abstinence and public service . . . played a more important part in building up the *laissez-faire* and liberal society of the nineteenth century than the rational morality of the harmony of interests."[11] Even Adam Smith's economic man was to act within the limits of justice and self-command, restrained by the quality of "sympathy" which was an integral part of man's nature. "When Mrs. Crossley entered her works at 4 A.M. she made a daily vow: 'If the Lord does bless us at this place, the poor shall taste of it.' And she left this advice with her sons on the conduct of business in bad times: 'If you can go on giving employment in the winter, do so, for it is a bad thing for a working man to go home and hear his children cry for bread when he has none to give them.' "

Humanitarian and Fabian preconceptions in our writing of economic and social history have tended to obscure the older tradition of philanthropy and welfare that runs like a continuous thread through the operations of the greatest of the entrepreneurs. Plans for the welfare of adult workers and the care and education of child labor were not a monopoly of Robert Owen. Boulton and Wedgwood were not only

---

[11] *The Conditions of Peace* (London, 1942), chap. v. Also see Charles Wilson, "Canon Demant's Economic History," *Cambridge Journal* (February, 1953).

cultivated men but just employers who regarded a humane code of labor relations as an efficient system of production and gave a lead to others in such matters as the provision of schemes of social welfare and education. They were imitated by scores of others even unto the second and third generations; so that even in the 1850's when elementary education was a recognized public charge, Price's Patent Candleworks were still running an elaborate and expensive set of schools for their boy and girl employees at Battersea. Early Victorian England was for many a hard and cheerless world: but there seems at the moment to be less danger of exaggerating the sense of responsibility that the best entrepreneurs possessed than of assuming that their outlook was typified by the worst. The age of domestic industry was not the Golden Age it once seemed nor was the factory town exclusively a society of juvenile chimney sweeps and cadaverous spinning elves.

The leading entrepreneurs may well turn out to have a just claim to rank high amongst those who not only swept and garnished their own houses but initiated a national process of social amelioration in an age facing insuperable problems of social adjustment. Some of the most vigorous social reformers, like Robert Peel, Samuel Whitbread, and Harriet Martineau, came from this class and the tradition lasted down to the enlightened capitalists of the late 19th and early 20th century like the Levers and the Cadburys with their new housing schemes. It was not merely their own success but their palpable contribution to material national well-being and their consciousness of social responsibility which drew to them popular esteem and social prestige. They were associated by partnerships and friendships with nobility. Wedgwood and Boulton both joined in business enterprises with Lord Stamford, Lord Grey, Lord Gower, the Duke of Bridgewater, Lord Anson, Lord Cathcart and Lord Talbot. In Scotland Lord Dundas and Lord Dundonald were far from negligible figures in the movement to apply chemical knowledge to industry. In South Wales Lady Charlotte Guest, the daughter of the 8th Earl of Lindsey, played no small part in managing the great Dowlais iron works of her husband. Royalty itself made a point of conferring its patronage and interests. George III and his Queen several times received Boulton and encouraged Catherine II to visit this national prodigy at his Soho works. In 1787 the Royal visitors were received at Whitbread's great brewery at Chiswell Street where half an hour out of a two-hour visit was spent examining the steam engine recently supplied by Boulton: ". . . in which it was apparent this was not the first half hour thus usefully employed on economic arts, for His Majesty, with becoming science, explained to the Queen and the Princesses the leading movements in the machinery."

The entrepreneurs and their new industries had become a matter for high favor and national pride.

The generally favorable conditions thus described did not however prevent the innovators from running into serious problems and rigidities in the contemporary economy. Of serious shortage of capital we hear strangely little: presumably the traditions of thrift and mutual confidence deep rooted in a commercial and often dissenting society worked to the advantage of the entrepreneur, leaving him only the lesser though not unimportant problems of temporary shortages of working capital and a defective coinage. This latter led many employers to issue token coins or "shop-notes" convertible (theoretically) into cash by shop-keepers, or to resort to truck payments. To obtain a factory labor supply was more difficult. Dr. Ure noted that it was "nearly impossible to convert persons past the age of puberty, whether drawn from rural or handicraft occupations, into useful factory hands." The need was supplied by the new millions of children who quickly acquired the new manual skills. It was longer before the problems of skilled supervision were solved but slowly a code of discipline and organization was shaped to match the productive process itself. Managers and foremen emerged, schemes for piece rates and bonuses were devised, with fines for drunkenness, carelessness and idling.

Such problems have received less attention than those posed by the attacks made on the new industrial system. Those who employed physical violence in machine-breaking and the like—the Luddites who smashed stocking frames and power looms and the unemployed hand-loom weavers who met at Peterloo—have had their story told many times. Their ranks were filled from the workers whom the new technology left on the scrap-heap. But scarcely less important, and continuous rather than spasmodic, was the growing power of organized labor. Trade Clubs and Unions in the guise of friendly societies are found everywhere in the 18th century. By 1800 when an Act made it generally illegal for any person to join with another to obtain increased wages or reduced hours of work, there were already many Acts on the Statute Book forbidding such practices in individual industries. But the new Act, like its predecesors, seems to have had little effect. Employees, then as now, had to reckon with much organized interest and natural conservatism; so that when William Fairbairn, the founder of the great Fairbairn Engineering business of Manchester and Leeds, first came to London in 1811 as an almost penniless lad seeking work with Rennie, then building Waterloo Bridge, he found the trade unions were masters of the situation. "I had no difficulty in finding employment; but before I could begin work I had to run the gauntlet of the trade societies; and after dancing attendance for nearly six weeks, with very little money in my pocket . . . I was ultimately declared illegitimate and sent adrift to seek my fortune elsewhere."

Scarcely less obstructive were the activities of those who saw their own interests being affected by the innovators. The small manufacturers threatened by Arkwright's improved production invoked doubtful legislation against him, but when he had won this battle there ensued a series of others, against rival inventors and producers who challenged the validity of his patents. All in all Arkwright, a litigious customer admittedly, spent a not inconsiderable part of his time, energies and capital in Parliamentary and Court actions on such accounts. Boulton likewise had to petition Parliament to extend the rights for his engine in face of Burke, who protested in the name of liberty against this new monopoly. And like Arkwright, he and Watt were engaged in interminable law suits against users of the engine (like the Cornish copper mine owners) and rival Soho manufacturers to protect their rights.

The way of the innovator though theoretically cleared for him at many points was thus far from smooth; yet so strongly was the tide running with him and so remarkable was the combination of qualities which, at his best, he evinced, that opposition of the kind adumbrated—partial, sectional, but on the whole ill-organized—did little to check the swift growth of his enterprise. He did not yet control, nor was he ever to control, the whole of the economic process. Yet where he did, his grasp was hard to shake. Men of this kind came to speak with a new tone of authority—new because they were exercising a new and comprehensive kind of economic control, capable of indefinite extension. Lifted on to the plane of philosophy, his voice became what Victorian England recognized, rightly or wrongly, as the voice of progress. ". . . he knew," the historian of early Victorian England has written, "that in the essential business of humanity, the mastery of brute nature by intelligence, he had outstripped the world, and the Machine was the emblem and instrument of his triumph. The patriotism of early Victorian England . . . was at heart a pride in human capacity, which time had led to fruition in England. . . ."[12] It is difficult—impossible I would say—to understand the momentum behind the process unless it is realized that Arkwright, Boulton, Wedgwood and the rest shared with the ferocity of enthusiasm in a faith which they managed to raise to the status of a sort of *Zeitgeist*; a faith which was finally enshrined in the historical philosophy of the most honored child of the age, Macaulay. The opportunity to direct such a large part of the economic and social process brought forth both good and evil. On the whole the best among them rose to their responsibilities. Their motives swiftly came to outrun the mere desire for profit. At worst their passion might degenerate into

---

[12] G. M. Young, *Portrait of an Age* (London, 1936), p. 8.

a desire for personal power: but it often remained a genuine delight in quality for those who bought from them—perhaps even for its own sake—and a better life for their work-people. "I don't work at business," a later one cast in the same mold wrote, "only for the sake of money. I am not a lover of money as money and never have been. I work at business because business is life. It enables me to do things."[13] It was the enlarged scope which the new type of business organization offered for "doing things" which perhaps helps to explain the character of those who did them.

The system of capitalist industry established by the entrepreneurs of the first century of change retained the confidence of the society geared to it so long as it was unquestionably efficient and so long as it was successful in providing not only profits but increasing employment. Doubts on the second point had arisen at earlier dates but from the 1890's they were joined to anxieties on the first. The difficulties of analyzing the problem are magnified by the simultaneous appearance of two major problems: foreign competition and managerial competence. The first has been exhaustively examined; the second hardly at all. We do not know, from the inside, what problems of internal conflict of policy may have been generated by the disappearance of the first and second generations of entrepreneur (who often insisted on complete personal ownership of risk capital and thus of policy) and their replacement by managers, family or professional, endowed only with limited powers of decision by a growing body of shareholders. Neither with shareholders nor with employees was their prestige as high as that of their predecessors. From outside began the attacks by publicists and the industrial system had to sustain not only volleys from the artillery of the Marxists but also the sniping of the Fabians and Liberals. Increasingly the popular assumption tended to be that the function of the entrepreneur had merely been to mind (and occasionally sabotage) an automatic machine. It was the division of wealth, not its production, that called for urgent thought and action. The assumption has died hard.

---

[13] Wilson, *op cit.*, I, 187.

9

Trends in the British Economy, 1790–1914

by

WALT W. ROSTOW

▼▼▼

I

British industrial production, and the national income, did not expand continuously from 1790 to 1914, nor was the trend rate of increase constant. In some phases, further, the trends in commodity prices and interest rates were upward, in others they declined. The rate and the direction of the movement of real wages and the terms of trade varied as well. It is the view here that the diverse movements among the principal variables within the economy can be related to each other in a co-ordinate way, and to the whole character of economic development in Britain, and in the world economy.

In order to examine trend movements the era 1790–1914 is divided into five phases. The first runs from about 1790 to 1815; the second to the end of the forties; the third to 1873; the fourth to 1900; the fifth

Reprinted from *British Economy of the Nineteenth Century*, by W. W. Rostow (pp. 7–28, with omissions), copyright © 1948 by The Clarendon Press, Oxford, by permission of the publishers and author.

to 1914. No very special connotations attach to the particular years chosen as points of demarcation. They do roughly mark, however, moments when the direction or rate of movement of certain principal variables within the economy altered; and the periods they contain form useful analytic units for the examination of trends.

The accompanying Table 1 sets out annual average percentage rates of change for a number of series which reflect, with greater or lesser

TABLE 1

TRENDS IN THE BRITISH ECONOMY: 1793–1912

The following table gives measurements for annual average percentage rate of change in the case of certain key economic variables within the British economy, on which reasonably accurate quantitative data exist for continuous periods. Except where indicated below the rates are averaged as between five-year intervals centred on the indicated year; e.g. figures for the period ending "1815" represent the rate of change between 1791–5 and 1813–17.

ANNUAL AVERAGE PERCENTAGE RATE OF CHANGE
(Plus, Unless Otherwise Indicated)

For Period Ending	Population U.K.	Total Industrial Production	Consumers-Goods Production	Producers-Goods Production	Volume Imports
	%	%	%	%	%
"1815"	1.4	2.1	1.9	2.3	2.6
"1847"	1.1	3.5	3.2	4.4	3.7
"1873"	0.7	3.2	2.6	4.1	4.4
"1900"	0.9	1.7	1.3	2.2	2.8
"1912"	0.9	1.5	1.0	1.9	1.2
"1793–1912"	1.0	2.6	2.2	3.2	3.1

For Period Ending	Volume Exports	Gross Barter Terms of Trade	Yield on Consols	Bank Rate	General Prices	Real Wages Tucker	Wood	Output per capita Employed
	%	%	%	%	%	%	%	%
"1815"	4.1	1.6	0.8	..	1.8	−0.5	..	..
"1847"	2.8	−0.8	−1.1	−1.2	−1.4	0.7	..	(0.6)
"1873"	4.9	0.6	−0.05	0.3	0.6	0.6	1.1	1.1
"1900"	1.7	−1.0	−0.7	−0.1	−1.5	1.2	1.3	1.6
"1912"	2.7	1.5	1.5	0.7	1.5	−0.5	−0.5	0.6
"1793–1912"	3.3	..	..	..	..	..	..	..

Note: 1. The gross barter terms of trade represent the volume of exports over the volume of imports. A "favorable" movement—that is, an increase in imports with respect to exports—is represented by a decline.

2. Output *per capita* figures are those of Colin Clark (*National Income and Outlay*, pp. 232, 247); the rate for the period up to 1847 is limited in the time covered, and is particularly suspect, given the nature of available data. From "1815" to "1847" consists of the rate from 1830–9 to 1840–9; "1873" consists of 1870–6; "1900," of 1894–1903; "1912," of 1911–13.

accuracy, the movements of certain variables believed relevant to trend analysis. These variables are calculated between five-year averages, rather than between individual years, in order to avoid arbitrary bias due to short-run fluctuations; and the center year is, in each instance, at or close to the peak year in the proximate major cycle.

It will be noted that the turning-points employed here conform, generally, to those in price trends, which have for long been familiar. The rise in prices during the period of the French wars; the falling trend to the late forties; the rise to 1873; the fall to the late nineties; and the rise to the outbreak of the First World War have, for some time, been the subject of remark and speculation. Although the trend periods chosen here conform to the long movements of prices, the analysis employed is not concerned exclusively, or even primarily, with the level of general prices.

Nor is any considerable attention given to the long-run forces determining the level of the real national income. Its rate of increase, like that of population, to which it closely relates, appears to be subject to laws of growth outside the scope of the present analysis. The focus is, rather, the complex of forces affecting the course of real wages; and in exposing those forces emphasis is placed on the scale and character of investment, the course of interest rates and commodity prices, and the terms of trade.

Such an investigation would, of course, be much strengthened if adequate data on the national income were available: its real size, composition, and distribution; but the national-income statistics, in their present form, are inadequate. . . .

II

At its core the theoretical framework employed in this analysis of trends is exceedingly simple, however complex the body of fact it is designed to inform. It might be described as a dynamic version of the elementary theory of diminishing returns.

In a closed community, with constant population, working force, and money incomes, with full employment maintained by private or communal action, with all expenditures except those on consumption going into productive investment, and with no changes in knowledge, we would expect prices to fall, over a period of time, and real wages to rise. We would also expect the yield on new investment to fall, as the expected return on new investment fell towards the point where known possibilities of new productive investment were exhausted or the return so small that leisure was preferred to further investment outlays.

If such a community were to divert the whole of its income, over and above consumption, to the prosecution of a civil war, or to the building of pyramids or churches, we would expect prices to cease their decline. And if such enterprise were expanded to a scale larger than the previous allocation to new productive investment, we would expect prices to rise and real wages to fall.

Assume that the closed community is an island, devoted exclusively to the production and consumption of wheat, which has been devoting a fixed amount of its labor and other resources to the clearing and planting of additional inferior wheat land, on the island. The land brought into cultivation is progressively less productive; but, nevertheless, the productivity of labor, and the total wheat supply is increasing each year. The wheat price is falling, if at a diminishing rate, so long as the fixed labor supply is not spread so thin that additional increments of land fail to yield some positive increase in production.

Assume, further, that another island is discovered nearby, with virgin soil, of distinctly higher potential productivity. It is found that two years' work by the whole normal investment forces is required to clear the first plot on the island, and another year will pass before the first harvest is in. Over the period when the new island is being prepared and planted, the fall in the wheat price and rise in total consumption would cease; and it would be resumed, at an accelerated rate, when the crop from the new island was, at last, harvested. If, excited by the vista, the islanders were to devote an increased proportion of their total effort to clearing the new island, the wheat price would rise over the shortened period of development.

The data are not sufficient, of course, progressively and systematically to relax the assumptions governing this primitive parable to a point closely approximating the turbulent developments of the British economy in the nineteenth century. It is evident that the British economy was not closed; that the population and working force and money incomes were not constant; that full employment was not continuously maintained; that the proportion of the national incomes spent for purposes other than consumption varied; and that the state of knowledge was almost constantly enlarged. The parable has been cited, however, because it is central to the subsequent analysis that outlays for purposes other than consumption be distinguished with respect to their being productive or non-productive; and that attention be focused on the relative productivity of the productive outlays, and the quantity of resources and time periods required before they yielded their productive results. It is the view here that the main trends in the British economy, over the period 1700–1914, are best understood in terms of the shifting balance between productive and unproductive outlays; and among types of productive outlays with differing yields and differing periods of gestation.

This approach to the British economy, or to virtually any other economy in modern times, has what is perhaps an important implication for the study of economic history. Much of Britain's investment was foreign investment, related to developments on distant continents, in which Britain participated, but which British initiative did not wholly determine. And the course of events at home, in other respects as well, derived in part from forces generated abroad. The fluctuations and trends in Britain were shared, with variations, by most other areas in the world. It is likely that the optimum unit for the study of economic history is not the nation, but the whole inter-related trading area; certainly that is the frame within which many of the most important national, regional, or even industrial problems must be placed, if they are fully to be understood.

III

The trend movements that must be explained, over the period from about 1790 to 1815, are the following: a rapid rise in production, within both industry and agriculture; a substantially greater increase in exports than in imports; a rise in interest rates and prices; a falling tendency in real wages.

The central economic characteristic of these years is that it was a period of war. From that fact the following four consequences may be traced:

1. The establishment of British men regularly in service was raised well over 500,000, perhaps 400,000 more than the peace-time establishment. Depending on the population base taken, the mobilized force constituted between 3 per cent and 5 per cent of the total population and, of course, a much larger proportion of the total working force.

2. The real cost of certain basic commodities rose: imports, because of the circuitous and often dangerous routes followed, the necessity for convoys, and the consequently very large increases in freight rates; foodstuffs, because of the obstruction of imports from the Baltic, and the necessity for diverting resources into expansion of British agriculture caused by this factor in conjunction with a rapidly rising population. The rise in the prices of foodstuffs was accentuated by chronically bad harvests over the war years.

3. Large resources were diverted into ship-building, to replace war losses and to support an artificially expanded foreign trade; into the expansion of dock facilities; into armament manufacture, and to other manufactures consumed by British and Allied armies.

    4. Substantial general resources were diverted abroad, by means of loans and subsidies to allies on the Continent.

The British foreign balance was kept in equilibrium, without large bullion movements, by an extraordinary increase in British exports and especially in re-exports.[1] Britain enjoyed a virtual monopoly in West Indian products which, for the most part, were sold through the various entrepot ports: at first Hamburg, and then the arc of peripheral ports, from Scandinavia to the Ionian islands. The profits in this trade, coupled with those in the export of British manufactures, largely financed the war-time outlays abroad. There was, indeed, a great boom in trade; but the resources needed to sustain it, in ships, manpower, and newly constructed docks served simply to meet the deficit in the foreign balance caused by the extent and character of the war effort. They did not generate an equivalent rise in imports for the British economy. Thus exports increase more than imports; that is, the gross barter terms of trade turn unfavorable.

    And, on the whole, the behavior of the variables in the economy follows closely that which one would expect from a shift in investment to what are called, above, unproductive outlays, or to outlays which did not yield fully their productive results within the trend period. The course of the British economy during the French wars conforms well to what textbooks in international trade would call "a case in capital exports"; or to the pattern of lend-lease.

    There was, of course, a very substantial increase in total production, related to and required by the great population increase of this period. These were the years when the effects of abundant American cotton, released by the invention of the cotton gin, in combination with the new textile machinery and the steam engine, began to transform the cotton industry. The volume of exports of British cotton goods rose at an annual rate of 10.6 per cent, from 1793 to 1815. Iron output, freed of its dependence on Swedish ore, also increased rapidly. But on balance the wastes of the war years, and the diversion of resources to uses less productive than those of peace, were so great that the level of real wages could not be fully maintained; and there are evidences, as well, that various types of investment at home languished, under competition from more profitable adventures in agriculture, foreign trade, and the limited portion of industry directly affected by war contracts. . . .

    It is easy, in the examination of trends, to lapse into a vocabulary

---

[1] The extent and significance of the rise in re-exports may be seen from the fact that, whereas the volume of British goods exported, from 1793 to 1815, rose at an annual percentage rate of 3.8 per cent per annum, total exports, including re-exports, rose at an annual rate of 4.1 per cent. . . .

which appears to imply that the movements within the economy were smooth, and at constant rates. This is an incorrect conception for all the trend periods. In the French wars the decade from 1793 to 1803 is dominated by large outlays abroad, and a concomitant boom in foreign trade, based largely on Hamburg. Then there is an interval, to about 1808, when outlays abroad are on a modest scale, trade is inhibited, and a revealing passage occurs, in 1807, when frustrated investors turned briefly to the flotation of joint stock companies at home. Two cycles follow, with peaks in 1810 and 1815, against a background of steadily increasing outlays abroad: the first looking to Latin America, as a means of evading Napoleon's briefly effective warfare against the British balance of payments; the second, to American and continental markets, in successive years (1814, 1815) on the coming of peace. The bulk of the price rise occurred swiftly, in the period up to 1803; and the trend over the next decade was relatively steady. And within the general price-index the cost-reducing processes of the Industrial Revolution were already beginning to bring down the prices of cotton textiles and iron from about the turn of the century.

IV

Perhaps the most suggestive commentary on the trends of the economy during the French wars is their course in the three decades that followed. Without exception higher rates of increase in industrial production prevail than during the war years; and real wages, which actually fell to 1815, rise substantially. Brick production, stagnant in the previous quarter century, leaps forward, at an annual rate of 2.8 per cent, and with it a wide range of domestic investment. As can be seen in Table 1, this was the period when the rates of increase in industrial production were at a maximum for the whole era to 1914. These were truly years of Industrial Revolution.

The period between 1815 and 1847 was one of uninterrupted peace for Britain; and there were only minor wars elsewhere. Investment outlays were thus almost wholly productive. Investment was, for Britain, heavily concentrated, too, in enterprises which yielded their cost-reducing results within a fairly short period. The installation of machinery in cotton textiles; the enlargement and improvement of metallurgical plant; the introduction of Nielson's hot blast; the building of bridges, roads, and even of the British railways—all these brought lower real costs; and the period of gestation for such investment was relatively short. It was natural that the price trend should be downward. As a writer in the *Edinburgh Review* asked [in July, 1832], in reply to contemporary arguments for national policies of inflation and protection, "What but the facilitating of production, or, in other words, the reduc-

tion of price, is the object of inventions and discoveries of the arts?"
And the natural downward trend was strengthened by the tariff reformers, from the twenties onward.

The course of prices was not, of course, downward continuously, or
at a constant rate. There was a period of rapid decline, beginning
in the latter years of war and extending into the twenties; a slower
trend decline in the thirties and forties. Each of the major trade cycle
expansions yielded, for a part of their duration, upward breaks in the
powerful downward trend: in 1818, during the brief post-war boom;
in 1825, at the peak of the long expansion of the early twenties; then
most notably in the thirties. The great British railway boom of the
forties caused only a very slight rise in prices, until bad harvests and
the continued American boom, which affected the quantity and prices
of British exports, brought prices up in 1847, well after the British
cyclical turning point in 1845.

It is significant that the thirties saw the most substantial and sustained rise in prices of this whole trend period. For in that decade a
larger proportion of British investment was directed abroad than in any
other between the war years and the fifties. This was not, to be sure,
the first British adventure in foreign securities in the nineteenth century.
Immediately after 1815, with the Government removed as a borrower
from the capital markets, greatly developed by the experience of meeting the large requirements for war finance, London had granted loans
to various continental countries; and there had been the considerable
Latin American flotations of 1824–5. In the thirties, however, a great
and protracted wave of "internal improvements," sponsored by the
not wholly reliable American state governments, caught the eye of
British promoters and of the broadened investment public. The balance
of investment outlays shifted somewhat from home to abroad; and
from projects which would yield their cost-reducing results in a relatively
short period, to the relatively longer period involved in the opening up
of new territories, the building of its canals and roads, and the clearing
of its rivers. Thus, for a time, prices rose.

But over the period as a whole, not only prices in their downward
trend, but the course of interest rates, real wages, and the terms of
trade conform roughly to the stylized conception of these three post-
1815 decades as a period of intensive domestic development. Interest
rates fall; real wages rise; and the terms of trade shift favorably to
Britain.

These years, however, have a bad name in economic history. In part
that repute stems from factors which do not belong within the scope
of this analysis; namely, the conditions of housing and of health in
portions of the new industrial cities. In part it stems from intervals of

severe unemployment, bad harvests, and high food prices. In part it stems from the unhappy position of portions of the agricultural community, readjusting to the unfavorable position in postwar grain markets. In part, it stems from the pressure on industrial prices and profit margins, imposed by rapidly expanding industrial capacity, exploiting successively more efficient methods, in a régime of relatively free competition. Here, however, the focus of analysis is the rate of change in industrial production, the volume of imports and exports, and the level of real wages. And in terms of these related criteria the period emerges as one of extraordinary development, perhaps the most rapid rate of development of domestic resources throughout the whole of Britain's economic history.

· · · · ·

V

The third trend period embraces what is usually referred to, with some considerable ambiguity, as the great mid-Victorian boom, running from about 1850 to the crisis of 1873. As Table 1 indicates, the rates of growth in production were only slightly less than for the previous trend period. In the other variables we find a worsening in the gross barter terms of trade and a rise in general prices. The interest rates of which continuous record exists exhibit no clear-cut trend movement: the Bank rate, and the open market rate on good three months' bills, in net, rise very slightly; the yield on Consols falls very slightly. All that can be said firmly, from these rough measures, is that the previous downward trend in interest rates was arrested. And, from the sixties, at least, real wages rose.

As a first approximation, the period may certainly be characterized as one in which an increased proportion of the investment outlays, of the world community, went into unproductive ventures, or to ventures which yielded their results only over a long period of time. For Britain this was a notable period of capital exports, concentrated particularly in the fifties and the early seventies.

Taking the world economy as a whole three factors can usefully be distinguished. First, there were wars: principally, the Crimean War; the American Civil War; and the sequence of Prussian campaigns that ended with the French defeat in 1870. By present severe standards these wars—excepting the American Civil War—were minor affairs. They undoubtedly wasted, however, a significant portion of the resources normally available for productive investment, in the years over which they took place, and within the countries directly affected; and these effects were transmitted, through the international markets, to the rest of the world.

Second, there was gold-mining. The economic effects of gold-mining over this era have by no means been fully or satisfactorily explored. In general, however, its consequences are clear. Gold, for those who mined it, was a useful product, capable of exchange for goods and services, including imports. The United States financed a part of its trade deficit and capital imports by mining and exporting gold, as did Australia. India, which absorbed large quantities of the new-mined gold, surrendered for it exports of goods. The real effort required by Australia and the United States in mining gold was quite probably less than that necessary to purchase an equivalent volume of imports by growing and exporting, say, additional wheat or wool or cotton; although there were significant wastes of manpower and resources among the prospectors who did not strike it rich. On the whole, however, it is likely to prove the case, on close investigation, that in terms of the mining area the production of gold was a thoroughly reasonable enterprise, in the nineteenth century.

For the world as a whole, however, gold-mining constituted, in part, a tax on resources, capricious in its incidence, for the maintenance of the gold standard. Leaving aside, for the moment, the requirements of the banking systems for new gold, and its effects on the supply and terms of credit, it is evident that, except in its limited ornamental or industrial uses, gold supplied no service to the world: neither food, shelter, nor clothing. In this limited perspective the pursuit of gold absorbed resources without producing an enlargement or cheapening in supply of commodities or of services. To the extent, of course, that India wanted gold, and was satisfied to surrender other resources for it, and to the extent that gold elsewhere was used for ornamental or industrial purposes this stricture does not apply.

The issue, then, narrows to the question of whether the banking systems of the nineteenth century required gold on the scale in which it was mined, in order to avoid the imposition, for technical reasons, of deflationary policies. This, too, is a question which deserves further exploration; but the evidence strongly suggests that men in the past have, on the whole, and over a period of time, been sensible enough to adjust their monetary institutions to their requirements. Over the era under consideration here, it seems very doubtful if mankind was crucified on a cross of gold, except, perhaps, that too large a proportion of resources was expended in pursuing and mining it.

Even if one assumes that the new gold was, in fact, required for the successful working of the banking systems of the world, mining would still constitute a tax; a drain on resources from alternative uses. And in this aspect, like a war, or the building of a pyramid, gold was a price-raising factor, quite apart from any possible effects it might have had on central bank reserves, the rates of interest, and the willingness of banking systems to lend.

Nor is there satisfactory evidence that the effect of the new gold on bank lending was of any considerable significance. In this trend period, for example, one cannot trace an effect from the gold influx on short-term interest rates, through bank reserves, prolonging or accelerating cyclical expansions, beyond the point to which they would otherwise have proceeded, or shortening the periods of cyclical depression. Gold-mining in California and Australia, and the concurrent development of those territories in other directions, certainly constituted, at the time, a significant and attractive form of investment; and it was a form of investment tending to raise world prices, both because gold-mining was involved, and because of the considerable period of gestation involved in the opening up of new territories. On the other hand, the strictly monetary effects of the new gold, operating through central bank reserves and interest rates, do not appear to have been important.

The third great new factor in this trend period was, of course, railway building. Some 21,000 miles of railway-line were laid in the United States in the fifties, firmly binding the north-west to the north-east, on the eve of Civil War: a fact of political and military, as well as economic significance. At the time of the crisis in 1857 it was estimated that fully £80 million in American railway securities were held in Britain. This was also the period when Thomas Brassey crossed the Channel, and with British funds and even some British labor, began laying track on the Continent. In 1852 Brassey held contracts for 264 miles of French line; and later in the decade there was at least one British director on the board of nineteen Continental railway companies.

It is suggested, then, that the upward trend in prices, as well as the trend of the other variables, in the quarter century before 1873 was due mainly to a shift, essentially on a world-wide scale, towards unproductive outlays in war, and in a limited sense, in gold-mining; and to extensive investment, serving to lay railways and to open new territories, which yielded their consequences for the position of supply curves, in individual markets, more fully in the period after 1873 than in the quarter century which preceded it.

As in the other trend periods, the variables did not move continuously. Prices, for example, rise very rapidly from 1852 to 1854; but the trend, from that time until the final stages of the boom of the early seventies, some two decades later, is steady. The pattern of the sixties, like the first decade of the century and the thirties, constitutes in many ways an exception to the main trends of the period within which it lies.

The glamorous external developments of the fifties and the early seventies were lacking, inhibited in part by war in the United States, and the various enterprises of Prussia on the Continent. Britain turned, for the time, to homely domestic tasks. There was an expansion in ship-building which doubled the tonnage of steam vessels in British registry between 1860 and 1868. Another 5,000 miles of British railways were laid. And a wide variety of domestic developments were centered in a company flotation boom, which crashed in 1866. Whereas the crisis of 1866 was largely a British phenomenon, those of 1857 and 1873 were world-wide; and, in this, each conforms to the character of the expansion which preceded it. It was in this decade, significantly, that real wages resumed their rise. Over the fifties they had, in net, been stagnant.

The great cyclical expansion, from 1868 to 1873, in many ways repeated the phenomena of the fifties, with developments external to Britain commanding the stage, especially in the latter stages of the boom (1871-3). There is, however, an important exception to this parallelism. The powerful forces set in motion earlier, to open new grain lands, were already operative; and in the United States they were released from the obstructive influence of war. Food prices rose less than money wages, in the course of the expansion, and real wages continued the upward course of the early sixties. But prices in general rose, and exports increased more rapidly than imports.

VI[2]

The fourth of the trend periods runs from 1873 to the eve of the Boer War, in 1898. It is more usual practice to date the ending of this phase with the middle nineties. On close examination, however, the character of the expansion running from 1894 through 1898 belongs, in the character of its investment and the behavior of the principal variables, rather with the Great Depression period, than with the phase of war and capital exports, which give a distinctive character to the fifteen years preceding the outbreak of the First World War.

The phenomena to be explained here are essentially the same as those which dominated the period from 1815 to the end of the forties: a favorable shift in the terms of trade; a fall in interest rates and commodity prices; a maintained rise in real wages. In terms of the primitive model set forth earlier there is no doubt that Britain, over these years, turned on the whole to internal developments, yielding their results over a relatively short period. These were the years of steel, the iron and steel freighter, and the machine tool; of the telephone and the electricity company; and, in the nineties, of the bicycle. Gradually, in the eighties, South Africa and other parts of the Empire began to

---

[2] [Also see Selection 10—Ed.]

claim an increasing proportion of British enterprise; and in the late eighties, briefly, the trend movements were broken by the Argentine boom, which left the house of Baring tottering in its wake. But the evidence for a net shift toward intensive investment at home is undeniable; and, moreover, these were not only years of peace, but the world was spared until the nineties, any substantial new diversion of enterprise to the pursuit of gold. Falling prices and rising real wages are to be expected.

Nor was this simply a characteristic of British enterprise. The United States, recovered from Civil War, devoted itself to the exploitation of the great Western Empire. Grain prices fell almost steadily, which aided the working classes throughout the world, but turned the American farmer, for three decades, into something of a political radical. In the East great new industries, their foundations laid or strengthened during the Civil War, grew rapidly. And in Germany a similar process of domestic development and exploitation took place.

The rate of rise of total industrial production in Britain fell off sharply in this period; but it rose in output *per capita* and in real wages. The rate of increase of both imports and exports declined; but the gross barter terms of trade moved favorably to Britain. For these years there is available, as well, the net barter terms of trade; that is, the relation between import and export prices. These show, as would be expected, a greater fall in import than in export prices. The whole behavior of Britain's foreign balance conforms to what one would, theoretically, expect of a shift in the character of its investment flows from foreign to domestic enterprise, and to what one would expect in a world consolidating and exploiting, on the whole, its previously opened resources, rather than breaking new ground.

VII

The fifth trend period covers the interval from the outbreak of the Boer War to the First World War. Here there is a clean reversal in the trends of interest rates, prices, the terms of trade, and even in real wages.

The character of new enterprise reveals the same three elements that characterized the mid-Victorian quarter century. Again there are wars: the Boer War, the Spanish American War, the Russo-Japanese War, and the Balkan wars. In addition, military budgets claimed an increasing amount of the national expenditure throughout the world. Second, there was gold, not only from South Africa, but also an increased flow from the other producing areas, as more efficient techniques of mining were introduced. Third, there was another world-wide wave of extensive investment, involving Africa, South America, Canada, Australia, and India.

The capital market had no sooner freed itself of the brief but real burden of financing the Boer War when, roughly in 1905, foreign governments, railways, and mining enterprises came to London on a large scale, with attractive prospects. Interest rates rose, and British investors were, in part, driven from the capital market. Industrial flotations at home continued through the boom to 1907, on a small scale; but flotations by home railways, gas works, and water companies fell off very sharply, to reappear in the slump of 1908, when their modest but solid appeal again seemed attractive to the briefly disillusioned investor. Although the expansion which ran from 1908 to 1913 saw some increase in domestic investment, there is no doubt that the diversion of funds abroad was at some real short-run cost to the development of the British economy. G. T. Jones, tracing the course of the Lancashire cotton industry and the building industry in London, found a cessation in the decline of real costs at about the turn of the century.[3] And unemployment in the building trades, which had been down to less than 1 per cent in 1898, perhaps the last authentic year of the Great Depression, was never less than 3 per cent from 1901 to 1914; and it averaged almost 7.5 per cent throughout the general business expansion, from 1904 to 1907.

On the other hand, the export branches of British trade enjoyed very great prosperity, and the rate of increase in the volume of exports was considerably greater than in the previous trend period. The increase in imports, however, was at a lesser rate. Both the gross barter and the net terms of trade turned unfavorably to Britain; and real wages, in net, declined. This decline, although mitigated by a shortening of work hours, increased social services, and a more equitable tax structure, was real; and it can be seen in the figures for *per capita* consumption of sugar, meat, and beer, as well as in calculated indexes of real wages.

Whether Britain, in some sense, exported too much capital in the decade preceding 1914 is a matter for judgment. In any such calculus, however, the long-run effects of those investments, in strengthening the economies within the Empire, in opening new sources of supply for British imports, and in increasing the national holdings of negotiable international wealth would have to be taken fully into account. It is clear, however, that in the context of the development of the world economy as a whole, the rate of growth of capital within Britain, and the real wages of the British working classes, were adversely affected in this period.

---

[3] *Increasing Return*, pts. ii and iii.

10

The "Climacteric" in the British Economy of the Late Nineteenth Century: Two Interpretations

by

E. H. PHELPS BROWN,
S. J. HANDFIELD-JONES,

and

D. J. COPPOCK

[*Editorial note:* This Selection includes parts of two articles on the retardation of growth in productivity in the late nineteenth-century British economy. As will be noted, the second was written in response to and in criticism of the first. A good deal of the discussion in these two essays turns on the presentation and interpretation of statistics; however, it would have been inappropriate to reproduce here the complex quantitative data upon which the discussion is based—the general analyses of the retardation are far more relevant to our present purposes. On the other hand, in order to bring the text into better focus, and as an indication of the statistical considerations involved, we should note some of the prefatory material.[1]

1. Professor Phelps Brown and Mr. Handfield-Jones start by drawing attention to the familiar fact that the late nineteenth century witnessed a check to the rise of real wages, or of productivity, in a number of

---

[1] The reader should bear in mind that, owing to the imperfect nature of the surviving statistics (as the authors acknowledge), none of the quantitative evidence can be accepted entirely without qualm. Both articles discuss the validity of the statistics at some length, and the interested reader should consult the originals for the details which have been omitted here.

countries. Considering the case of the United Kingdom, they decide that this was not primarily due either to a decline in incomes from property held abroad or to the tendency of the terms of trade to move adversely after 1900. Having thus focused attention on domestic productivity, they obtain measures of output per worker in manufacturing and mining and find that after the 1880's the rate of increase slowed down very sharply. They acknowledge that this check was at somewhat different times evident in some industries (e.g., transportation by rail, coal mining, cotton textiles, beer, iron ore mining, and iron and steel smelting), and not in others (e.g., shipping, iron and steel manufactures, and woolen textiles). And they point out that although there were new and fast-growing industries (e.g., motor vehicles, chemicals, and electricity), they were still too small to affect aggregate figures in any substantial way. Finally, they note a comparable decline in agricultural productivity. On the basis of these data Professor Phelps Brown and Mr. Handfield-Jones put forward an analysis and explanation of the "climacteric" of the 1890's which is reproduced below.

2. Their interpretation of late nineteenth-century productivity trends was subsequently challenged by Mr. Coppock. His article, too, commenced with detailed statistical discussion. For example, he recomputed the statistics of industrial productivity in an attempt to eliminate the effects of the short business cycle, and from the consequent average growth rates of productivity found that there was a sharp downward break in the trend after 1866–74. (This was a retardation of the productivity figures; the check to the growth rate of per capita *income* did not come until after 1890–99.) Hence Mr. Coppock concludes that although there *was* a "climacteric" it came in the 1870's, not in the 1890's. He further explains the apparent paradox of a sustained rise in real income until the end of the century by noting the use of a price index which is heavily weighted with primary products and exports—both of which declined sharply in price from the 1870's to the 1890's. In the second part of this Selection appears the concluding section of Mr. Coppock's article, in which the author discusses the possible causes of the "climacteric" which he identifies as occurring in the 1870's.]

(a)

The Climacteric of the 1890's

by

E. H. PHELPS BROWN

and

S. J. HANDFIELD-JONES

Our estimates are subject to a wide margin of error at some points, but contain enough agreement of independent evidence to make it clear that some checks to the rise of productivity in industry and agriculture underlay the set-backs to real income a head and real wages in the United Kingdom about the turn of the century. Why did these things come about? We can narrow our search for causes, because we have good reason to believe that the check was not peculiar to the United Kingdom, but was also experienced in some measure by Belgium, France, Germany, and the United States. The most likely causes will be those which could have operated in all these countries. When, therefore, we consider the reasons given for the United Kingdom's falling behind other countries at this time, we must ask whether they mark factors common to the other countries but operative with greater intensity in the United Kingdom, or factors peculiar to the United Kingdom but

Reprinted from *Oxford Economic Papers*, New Series, IV, 3 (October, 1952) (pp. 279–89, with omissions), by permission of the editors, The Clarendon Press, and the authors.

working there to the same effect as different factors in the other countries.

To contemporaries these reasons seemed important: it was alleged that both management and labor were less efficient in Britain than they had been.

Criticism was directed against British management by comparison with other countries. Awareness of high productivity in American industry, and dispatch of teams to find out how it is achieved, go back at least to the 1850's in Britain,[2] but perhaps the first team to contain trade unionists was that of Mr. Alfred Mosely, who in 1902 took twenty-three trade union officers to visit their own industries in the United States.[3] Their observations have a familiar ring to readers of recent reports, whose findings they anticipate in some detail. The special correspondent of *The Times* who accompanied them endorsed the main points of contrast which they drew between British and American management.[4] American managers were chosen for their competence, not their family connections. "The American manufacturer realizes the supreme importance of order and system in the factory, and accordingly sees not only that every operation is simplified and sub-divided to the form in which it can be most efficiently performed, but also that each worker is always fully supplied with the kind of work which he or she can do best." Probably the American "has few, if any, machines that are utterly unknown in England, but he is more determined and wholesale in his use of mechanical appliances generally, and runs them for the utmost he can get out of them." "In America, employer and workmen seem to be closer together than they are in England, and in consequence the former is more able to benefit from the latter's knowledge and experience."

In the following year, 1903, [Alfred] Marshall noted the loss by Britain of the industrial leadership she had sixty years before. "It was not inevitable," he wrote,[5] "that she should lose as much of it as she has done. The greatness and rapidity of her loss is partly due to that very prosperity which followed the adoption of Free Trade." The combination of advantages which she enjoyed in those years encouraged "the belief that an Englishman could expect to obtain a much larger real income and to live much more luxuriously than anybody else, at all events in an old country; and that if he chose to shorten his hours of

---

[2] See D. L. Burn, "The Genesis of American Engineering Competition, 1850–70," *Economic History*, ii. 6, Jan. 1931.

[3] *Mosely Industrial Commission to the United States of America, Oct.-Dec. 1902. Reports of the Delegates* (Manchester, 1903).

[4] *The Times*, 16, 23, 25, and 26 Dec. 1902.

[5] Sec. L of *Memorandum on Fiscal Policy of International Trade*, completed Aug. 1903, published as H. of C. No. 321, Nov. 1908.

work and take things easily, he could afford to do it." Other causes of complacency lay in the distraction of competitors by civil war in America, and the wars which Germany fought in Europe; and in the bounty conferred upon the entrepreneur by rising prices consequent upon the influx of gold. "This combination of causes made many of the sons of manufacturers content to follow mechanically the lead given by their fathers. They worked shorter hours, and they exerted themselves less to obtain new practical ideas than their fathers had done; and thus a part of England's leadership was destroyed rapidly. In the 'nineties it became clear that in future Englishmen must take business as seriously as their grandfathers had done, and as their American and German rivals were doing."

The relative decline of British industry was also attributed to an increased enforcement of restrictive practices by trade unionists. This was the contention of eleven articles by E. A. Pratt which *The Times* printed in the winter of 1901–2 under the title of "The Crisis in British Industry." "The 'new' unionism, with its resort to violence and intimidation, has in turn been succeeded by a 'newer' unionism, which, although working along much quieter lines, is doing even more serious injury"— by enforcing restrictive practices. The articles contained instances of these practices, but little definite evidence that they had increased of late. [Sidney and Beatrice] Webb rejoined[6] that

> the complaints as to diminished quantity or energy of work, and of the tacit conspiracy to discourage individual exertion, occur with curiously exact iteration in every decade of the last hundred years at least. . . . To give one instance only, we have found exactly the same accusation of the bricklayers' limiting the number of bricks, and precisely the same belief that they were only doing "half as much" as they did twenty years before, in the great strikes of 1833, in those of 1853, again in 1859–60, and again in 1871.

It is probable none the less that the rise in the strength of trade unions between 1889 and 1901 did increase the practical effect of restrictive tendencies which had long been present. There is a distinct, and real, possibility, that wage-earners' standards of achievement were kept down, or even lowered, through emigration taking off many of the most energetic.

Yet with trade unionists as with management, what is well-founded in the charges does not seem enough to account for the severe check to productivity which came about in the 1890's. The fact that great advances in British productivity have been achieved in later years, when

---

[6] *The Times*, 6 Dec. 1901.

similar contrasts have been drawn between British and American management, and British trade unions have been stronger than ever, reminds us that these factors, though important, are not the only ones on which productivity depends. In accounting for the climacteric, moreover, we have to look not for persistent conditions which kept productivity down at all times, but for recent changes which could have halted its previously rising trend, and what change there was at this time in the qualities of management and labor does not seem commensurate with that effect. It was rather that through these factors Britain was denied some energies of industrial advance, which were active in America, and might have sustained the rise of productivity here when a pause came in other kinds of development. British labor generally was not prepared to risk job security and abandon bargaining weapons for the chance of higher earnings. British industrial society had not developed the morale and institutions which would accumulate the practical achievements of management as a doctrine, and impart them as a discipline, so as to maintain a general level of managerial performance not far below that of the best firms in each generation.

These seem to have been continuing deficiencies in the endowment of British industry, rather than the active causes of the check to British productivity in the 1890's, which are more likely to be found in factors affecting Britain in common with the other countries which experienced something of the same check.

Such common factors may reasonably be sought in the declining rate of extension at this time of the techniques of power, transport, and machinery comprised beneath the names of Steam and Steel. There is a varying but usually considerable lag between the inventions which first open the way and the massive applications which alone take effect on the productivity of whole peoples. So though the heroic age of the steam-engine lay far back, in the eighteenth century, and Bessemer's invention is usually assigned to 1856, it was not till after the civil war in America, and the Franco-Prussian war in Europe, that the general benefit began to be won of steam-engines driving steel machinery, and of transport by steam engines on steel rails and in steel ships. Our hypothesis is that the rapid and general extension of these techniques was coming to an end in the 1890's. The supersession of sail by steam at sea is a striking example. In 1860, nearly half a century after the first steamships had been tried, the tonnage of British shipping under sail was still growing, and was nearly ten times as great as the tonnage in steam; in 1880 the ratio was still about 3 to 2. But steam tonnage was now growing very rapidly, and in 1883 it overtook the declining tonnage under sail; by 1895 it was more than twice as great; and in carrying capacity of course the disparity was far wider than this. The replacement of each sailing-ship by a steamship makes a big advance in the productivity of transport, but once the sailing-ships have been replaced, such rapid improvements are no longer possible: only those annual advances remain which can be brought about by gradual improvements in the performance of the steamship itself.

The example brings out another point: the inventions which affect productivity most are those which improve processes common to many industries. All industries depend on power, transport, and the basic techniques of machine-making, and an invention which improves one of these is likely to raise productivity everywhere; unlike the inventions which are specific to particular industries. Even when technical improvements are coming forward fairly steadily, the inventions of widespread application may be made and brought into general use only discontinuously. The times of greatest rise in national productivity are those in which important inventions of widespread application have reached the stage of widespread installation.

Our knowledge of industrial history agrees with this. It shows, first,[7] that in manufacturing generally, about 1850 there was still much handwork, and outwork, the sailing ships, so to speak, of industry, giving the opportunity for a rapid rise in productivity when they were superseded by factory power and machinery. Second, it shows that the advance of power and mechanization in the 40 years after 1850 brought about changes in industrial methods which were widespread, far-reaching, and sometimes revolutionary. Third, it shows some continuing technical progress, and the opening of new possibilities, in the 20 years before the First World War, but no longer the massive application of new equipment to raise productivity throughout industries that were already large. In the previous period, steel had ousted puddled iron; working to gauge on steel had made machine parts interchangeable, and this "reacted continuously on the older mechanized industries";[8] spinning and weaving had been mechanized in the woolen industry; steel rollers had superseded millstones in the steam mills—the list might be longer. But the 20 years before the First World War do not see such widespread changes. The emphasis lies on "widespread." Much development was beginning now, which was to bring about the rise of nearly two-thirds in output per man-hour in British industry, which Rostas[9] has found between 1907 and 1937; but it took most of its effect only in its massive application after the war.

---

[7] [See above, Selection 6.—*Ed.*]

[8] J. H. Clapham, *Economic History of Modern Britain*, II, (Cambridge, England, 1932), 80.

[9] L. Rostas, *Comparative Productivity in British and American Industry* (National Institute of Economic and Social Research, Occasional Papers, xiii, 1948), p. 49. The coverage is manufacturing, mining, building, and public utilities. In this area output per wage-earner rose by 47 per cent between 1907 and 1937, by 37 per cent between 1924 and 1937 (ibid., pp. 42–43).

In sum, then, our main explanation of the check to the rise of real income in the United Kingdom about the end of the nineteenth century is that the previous rise had been carried forward by the massive application of Steam and Steel, which now had not much scope for extension; while the new techniques, especially of electricity, the internal combustion engine, and the new chemical processes, did not attain massive application until during and after the First World War.

. . . . .

The reduced rate of extension of new types of equipment in the United Kingdom suggests a lower rate of capital accumulation, and the great increase in capital export after 1904 also makes this seem likely. But [our] estimates of real capital per head . . . show a rise sustained to 1914 along a linear trend. We have used two methods, which have a common base in Stamp's estimate of the capital stock about 1912, but are quite independent in their estimates of the changes through earlier years. The first method is to estimate annual net investment, and after reducing this to £s of constant purchasing power, use it to decumulate the stock of 1912 and arrive by difference at the stocks of earlier years. The second method is to capitalize property incomes either (as Stamp did) by applying the appropriate number of years' purchase to each category of property income in the Inland Revenue returns, or by applying an average of years' purchase to profits as a whole. This

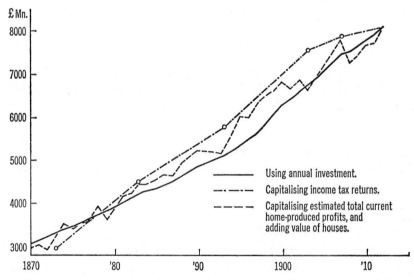

FIG. 1.   Total Revenue-Earning Capital (Excluding Farm Capital) Within U.K., in December, 1812 (£s).

second method has two drawbacks—the uncertainty of the right number of years' purchase for some property incomes, and the quasi-rent
nature of much of the income capitalized, which causes the capital
values obtained to swing above or below the current replacement cost
of the buildings, equipment, and stocks. The first method avoids
these snags of valuation, but has drawbacks of its own: it rests on a
relatively small number of series, and involves some rough estimating;
any bias in it, or defect of coverage, will take cumulative effect on the
estimates of capital stocks. But we can use the two methods as checks
on one another, and Fig. 1 shows that there is more agreement between
the results than we might expect, at least over the whole span; since
two independent methods have been used, and different price indexes,
the agreement confirms the magnitude of the movement. This magnitude is illustrated in Fig. 2, which shows that real capital a head rose
by 60 per cent during this period. This rise, moreover, appears to have

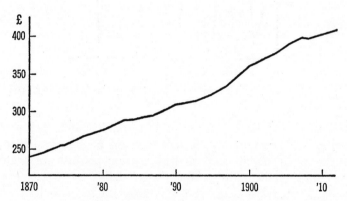

FIG. 2.   U.K.: Home Revenue-Earning Capital (Excluding Farm Capital)
per Occupied Person, in December, 1912 (£s).

been sustained through the 20 years before the First World War, so that
the average man at work in the United Kingdom in 1914 was working
with more equipment, even though he was not much more productive,
than his counterpart in 1895.

  This impression is borne out by Fig. 3, which shows total net home
investment each year, in £s whose purchasing power over investment
goods is about that of December 1912. So far from the nineties bringing
a slackening in home investment, they saw a rapid rise to an average
half as great again as that of the seventies and eighties, and except in
1908 a substantial increase was maintained down to the war. It has been
generally known that a housing boom began in the nineties, but our

estimates suggest that investment in industrial equipment rose then even
more rapidly than housing.

The continued and indeed accelerated growth of capital a head throws
doubt on an explanation of the check to productivity which otherwise
would seem likely to have something in it, namely, that the decline in

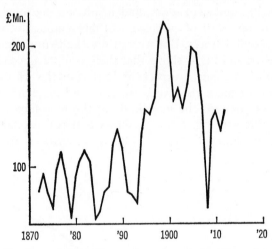

FIG. 3.   U.K.: Annual Net Home Investment, in December, 1912 (£s).

product wage-rates, i.e. the rise in prices of products relatively to money
wage-rates in Britain after 1899, relieved firms of the pressure to introduce labor-saving equipment, to which rising product wage-rates had
been submitting them throughout the preceding 40 years. Very likely
there was some relaxing effect, but it does not seem to have checked
the growth of equipment per occupied person.

Our findings do not conflict with the explanation of the check to
productivity put forward [above]—the tonnage of steamships, so to
speak, might continue to increase even faster than the occupied population, but adding one steamship to others would not make so much
difference as substituting a steamship for a sailing-ship had done. There
was no longer the innovation effect.

This working out of the innovation effect of Steam and Steel was
the more serious for the British people, because they had been gaining
so much from it as importers of food and raw materials.

It has been said, and it may with truth [wrote the signatories of
Part II of the report of the Royal Commission on Gold and
Silver],[10] that the development of machinery was as great in the

---

[10] C. 5512 of 1888; Part II, para. 26.

fifteen or twenty years which preceded 1874, as in the subsequent years, and that steam transport had been also largely developed in the earlier period. But not only has the actual extension of railways and the cheapening of land and sea freight been greater in the subsequent years, but the effect of railways which had been previously made has been more felt. . . . Large new districts of great natural fertility, and rich in minerals, have been opened up, and consequently civilized countries have been furnished with an unprecedented quantity of raw vegetable and mineral products.

Thus the ever-growing British population drew supplies whose rate of increase was even greater than its own, so long as Steam and Steel were opening new sources up; but when that opening up was done, though supplies continued to rise in total, their rate of increase fell, while that of population went on. The factory-worker's terms of trade with farmers and miners ceased to move in his favor.

This sort of check would have been bound to hold back the standard of living of the British people, even if it had not coincided with a reduced rate of progress in their own industrial productivity. British imports were largely of materials which we may call basic, because some quantity of them is indispensable to subsistence. Inventions and discoveries may be roughly divided into those on the one hand which open up new sources of basic materials, or increase the return to a unit of human work on the existing sources, or make transport from them easier; and those on the other hand which provide more of other materials, or increase our ability to work material up into useful and pleasing manufactures. A first rise in the standard of living above the level of subsistence requires an almost proportional rise in the intake of basic materials: it depends, that is to say, on inventions of the first class. No doubt, if the rise is maintained, and population is constant, the relative importance of the second class rises, and after some point has been passed there is no presumption that the one class is more beneficial than the other. But the population of Britain at this time was relentlessly increasing, and if only the existing standard of living were to be maintained, supplies of basic materials had to be increased as rapidly as the number of consumers. Sooner or later the ability of an expanding economy to do this is likely to be impaired by decreasing returns at its existing sources of supply, and this obstacle cannot be avoided by however vigorous a development of inventions of the second class. The consequent set-back to real income will generally be felt most by the wage-earners, because their consumption contains a higher proportion of basic materials than does that of the better off.

The relative unimportance in such circumstances of skill in working basic materials up, compared with the availability of those materials themselves, was put with unusual emphasis by Marshall in 1903.[11]

> The progress of the arts and resources of manufacture has bene-fited England more than almost any other country in one important but indirect way. It has so reduced the cost of carriage by land and sea that raw materials and food can come to her, even from the centers of great continents, at a less cost than they could come from the near neighborhood of the sea-shores and great rivers of the Continent sixty years ago; and the 300,000 miles of railways which have been built during the last sixty years in America, Asia, Africa, and Australia are rendering greater service to English-men than to any other people, except those in whose lands the several railways are placed.

So far "the progress of manufactures" as it provides inventions of our first class; now for the second.

> In almost every other respect the progress of the arts and resources of manufacture has benefited England less than any other country. For, even sixty years ago, the excess of the cost of the manufactures needed for her own consumption over that of the raw material by which they were made was small. If it could have been reduced to nothing, she would have gained by the change very much less than she has gained by the lowering of the cost of imported food and raw material for her own use.

The changed balance between the growth of population and the supply of basic materials seemed ominous to contemporaries. On the eve of the war D. R. Robertston[12] concluded "that the normal tendency for the ratio of exchange to alter against the manufacturing and in favor of the agricultural communities was in force in the 'seventies, was suspended in the 'eighties and 'nineties, and is now once more on the whole triumphing. This is perhaps the most significant economic fact in the world today." We know now that those conditions were fostering their own correction, and the balance swung back after the war, so that the years 1896–1914 have fallen into their place in an historical alternation. As W. W. Rostow[13] has said, "The three famous periods of extensive expansion, with rising price and interest trends

---

[11] Sec. L of his *Memorandum on Fiscal Policy of International Trade* (1903), H. of C. No. 321, Nov. 1908.

[12] At p. 169, n. 1, of his *Study of Industrial Fluctuation* (1915). (No. 8 in the London School of Economics series of Reprints of Scarce Works on Political Economy.)

[13] "The Historical Analysis of the Terms of Trade," *Economic History Review*, iv. 1, 1951, p. 64.

(roughly 1793–1815; 1848–73; 1896–1914) were part of the rough and ready process by which an appropriate balance of world production and a more or less appropriate distribution of population on the earth's land were maintained." Even the immediate effect, moreover, though it fell specially hard upon the wage-earners, was not so very great in proportion to national income. But since the Second World War we have learned again how an economy may be rapidly increasing the range and efficiency of its manufactures yet be held back by short supplies of foodstuffs, raw materials, and power.

In the greater scarcity of basic materials we may find a link between contemporary changes in the trends of productivity and of prices. The upturn of prices was facilitated by the increased supply of gold, but this other factor seems to have been at work to start the rise in prices and carry it on, and may well have made itself felt even without any increase in the output of gold. An initial rise in raw material prices tends to raise requirements of working capital, which in certain monetary conditions will be provided in such increased quantities as to support a general sympathetic rise of product prices and other factor prices. Consumers whose real income is reduced by scarcity of basic materials try to maintain it by getting higher money incomes; again in certain monetary conditions they will succeed, and another round of price rises follows. We have seen in recent years how in the absence of monetary constraint a price rise in one sector can spread outwards, and one set-back to real income can start a spiral of prices and money incomes. These processes, beginning with the greater scarcity of basic materials in the 1890's, may have been at work to draw out the monetary expansion and rise in prices which the increased gold supply made possible.

Some inferences may be drawn for the present prospects of Great Britain.

It seems that the substantial and general raising of productivity is brought about by the massive application of technical advances. The phase of massive application may follow that of pathbreaking invention only at a long remove. When it comes, it brings a high rate of advance, which falls off as the field of innovation is worked over. The progress of productivity, and the standard of living, thus appears to be very unstable. We cannot count upon the advance of productivity along a constant growth curve. Should at any time our standard of living not be much raised for 20 years, that would be only what has already happened in the lifetime of many people now living.

The raising of the standard of living generally requires increased supplies of basic materials. Improvements in our efficiency in working materials up into products of existing types, and fertility in designing new products, can compensate only partially for inability to increase these supplies. Such an increase can be achieved by capital investment which develops new sources of supply overseas, by success in exporting, or by inventions which liberate new sources of energy and basic materials within the country. If advances of these kinds can be made, a limiting factor can be lifted which otherwise will restrict the use of all other technical advances.

. . . . .

(b)

The Climacteric of the 1870's

by

D. J. COPPOCK

The causes of the climacteric of the 1870's will be discussed briefly since any explanation of this phenomenon must, for lack of adequate data, necessarily be of a tentative nature. Professor Phelps Brown and Mr. Handfield-Jones dating the climacteric in the 1890's find its causes to lie in

> . . . the declining rate of extension at this time of the techniques of power, transport, and machinery comprised beneath the names of Steam and Steel . . .
>
> . . . our main explanation of the check to the rise of real income in the United Kingdom about the end of the nineteenth century is that the previous rise had been carried forward by the massive application of Steam and Steel, which now had not much scope for extension . . .

Explanations in terms of declining efficiency of management and labor are rejected. The well-known complaints of reduced efficiency of

Reprinted from *The Manchester School of Economic and Social Studies*, XXIV, 1, (January, 1956) (pp. 21–31, with omissions), by permission of The Manchester School and the author.

management and labor during the last quarter of the 19th century are conceded but are not regarded as the "active cause" of the check to productivity. Capital accumulation is examined but is found to continue its trend without check and even with acceleration after 1900 and therefore the check cannot be explained in terms of a reduced rate of application of labor-saving equipment.

The explanation given above is inappropriate for two reasons. First, if the climacteric is dated in the 1870's, the event can hardly depend on the ending of the massive application of steel since this presumably requires the massive availability of steel, a condition hardly fulfilled in the 1870's. During this decade the average annual steel production was not much above ½ million tons. It is true that steel production grew considerably in the following twenty years but this period coincides with a decline in the rate of growth of productivity to levels well below those of the twenty years before 1870. If it is true that the massive application of steel was ending in the 1890's this does not seem to have produced any significant decline in the growth of productivity. Secondly, the explanation given seems to be contradicted by the behavior of their index of capital a head which shows continued growth throughout the period. It is difficult to see why the pace of capital accumulation should continue unchecked when a period of massive innovation had ceased. We should expect at least some rough association between innovation and accumulation. The perverse behavior of the capital series is explained away by Professor Phelps Brown and his colleague by postulating the end of the "innovation effect." But this would surely have implied a severe fall in the marginal productivity of investment after 1900 and it is difficult to see why capital accumulation should continue along its trend in the face of such a change. By dating the climacteric in the 1870's this difficulty is removed. Bearing in mind the differences in coverage and the fact that the capital index is not adjusted to allow for changes in its utilization there is no serious disagreement between the trend in capital a head and industrial productivity between 1870 and 1913.

It is easy to amend the hypothesis developed by Professor Phelps Brown to take account of the revised dating of the climacteric. Since the 1870's mark the transition from the Iron Age to the Steel Age let us suggest that the climacteric marks the end of the general application of steam power and iron machinery to the staple industries of Britain. This change was probably accompanied by a decline in the rate of capital growth per head in industry, since the ending of these profitable innovations would reduce the incentive to accumulate capital. The hypothesis does not require that the transition from iron to steel produced no increase in industrial productivity, only that the effects of steel were less powerful than those of iron. The substitution of steel machinery for iron would doubtless improve its precision and enable an increase in its speed of working; but the yield would probably be less significant than that from the original substitution of iron machinery for handwork. The hypothesis need not exclude an occasional case where the iron stage was omitted, as *e.g.*, in corn-milling. Nor need it exclude the use of steel (not necessarily mass-produced) in small quantities in key parts of iron machinery. In the case of at least one industry, that of coal-mining the climacteric may be explained by the ending of the application of steam and iron and the failure to apply steel effectively. The coal-mining industry exhibits the climacteric in a dramatic way. After rising from 1847/53 to 1866/74 at an average annual rate of about 2% the growth of productivity ceases to rise between 1866/74 and 1875/83 and thereafter declines at a rate approaching 1% per annum. The period of rapid growth can be explained by the application of steam power and iron to the tasks of winding, ventilation and underground haulage. Apart from improvements in these fields the obvious application of steel was to the problem of mechanical cutting; but though mechanical cutters were developed as early as the 1860's, by 1901 only 1½% of total output was cut by machinery. The Royal Commission of 1925 noted that in America at the beginning of the 20th Century some 25% of coal was mechanically cut. Of course, coal-mining is an industry subject to diminishing returns but need these have been encountered so dramatically? Whether or not mechanical cutting was economic in the 1880's and 1890's it seems possible to explain the decline in productivity objectively in terms of the ending of application of iron and the failure to apply steel.

This hypothesis of the ending of the massive application of steam and iron is plausible enough but there are two reasons for not being content with it. Firstly, it is rather a vague hypothesis and, as formulated, might prove difficult to verify. Secondly, the theory does not seem adequately to explain the relative stagnation of Britain as compared with the U.S.A. and Germany after 1870. In the U.S.A. the trend rate of growth of productivity in manufacturing industry was 1.6% per annum between 1873/83 and 1908/13.[1] For Germany the data is less reliable, but the trend of productivity may have been as high as 2.6% per annum.[2] If such rates of growth were possible in the Steel Age why was the

---

[1] Based on series 6 in B. Weber and S. J. Handfield-Jones, "The Rate of Economic Growth in the U.S.A., 1869–1939," *Oxford Economic Papers*, June, 1954, p. 127. [Parts of this article (although not the series mentioned) are reprinted as Selection 15 below—Ed.]

[2] Professor Lewis gives the trend of production as 4.7% (*Manchester School*, May, 1955, p. 149). The trend in employment is based on Census data given by G. Stolper, *The German Economy, 1870–1940* (Allen and Unwin, 1940), p. 41.

British rate of growth so low? The contrast may be explained by the later start of a period of rapid industrialization in the U.S.A. and Germany and their adaptation of steel machinery at the outset but this can hardly explain everything. Though the rate of growth of manufacturing production in the U.S.A. and Germany, between 1870 and 1913 was more than double that of the U.K.,[3] they were not negligible producers at the beginning of the period. In 1870 Britain accounted for 32% of world manufacturing production. The shares of the U.S.A. and Germany were 23% and 13% respectively.[4] The rapid growth of productivity in these countries could, therefore, equally plausibly be explained in terms of a more active replacement of obsolete machinery and a more rapid accumulation of newer types. Perhaps the potential innovations of the Steel Age were not as fully exploited by the U.K. as by Germany and the U.S.A.

Without rejecting the modified theory of Professor Phelps Brown, but rather to formulate it in more concrete terms, it is suggested that the decline in productivity in the U.K. after the 1870's, and its low level as compared with the U.S.A. and Germany is to be explained by a relatively low rate of growth of capital per head in industry after the 1870's. The fragmentary evidence available at present lends some support to this hypothesis. Using Professor Douglas's estimates, by decades, for the growth of capital in the U.K., and[5] excluding farmers' capital and railway capital before deflating, the average annual rate of growth of industrial capital between 1875 and 1914 is about 2.3%, or less than 1% per head of the occupied population in [about 70% of British] industries. The revised estimates by Professor Phelps Brown and Mr. Handfield-Jones give the same rate of growth when deflated by the Douglas price index number. If their price index number for capital goods is used the growth rate is raised by 0.4%; but this index, like their price index of final products is too much dependent on raw material and export prices. If the elasticity of output with respect to capital is of the order 0.25 to 0.5 it is not surprising that the rate of growth of industrial productivity between 1875 and 1913 should be of the order 0.5% per annum or less.[6] An interesting feature of the

---

[3] See W. A. Lewis, *Economic Survey*, p. 74.

[4] League of Nations, *Industrialisation and Foreign Trade*, p. 13.

[5] P. H. Douglas, "An Estimate of the Growth of Capital in the U. K., 1865–1909," *Journal of Economic and Business History*, 1930.

[6] It will be noticed that this implies a rising capital-output ratio which seems to conflict with popular beliefs that such ratios are constant. But these ratios are usually given for aggregate capital and income. It does not follow that all components of capital must grow at the same rate; for some periods of industrial evolution capital in houses and, *e.g.* railroads may grow at a lower rate than industrial capital. In money terms the capital-output ratio for the U.K. rose from 3.2 in 1875 to 3.9 in 1914 (using the values given by Phelps Brown, *Oxford Economic Papers*, p. 306,

Douglas capital estimates is that, for the decade 1865/75, they show an increase which is twice as great as that for any subsequent decade. It is curious that the trend of this admittedly approximate index of capital growth should display the same suggestion of a decline in growth after the 1870's as is found in the independent measures of production and productivity. Additional support for the argument of low capital growth may be found in data in power available per operative in manufacturing industry towards the end of the period. In 1907, horse-power available per operative in manufacturing industry in the U.K. averaged about 1.4. In the U.S.A. the roughly comparable figure for 1909 was 2.9. The objections to the use of measures of horse-power per head as indicators of capital equipment are well known[7] but the figures may give a rough indication of the relative amounts of capital available per worker. If American equipment was superior in quality the contrast is heightened. The figures quoted here do seem to lend support to the idea that, despite a later start, the rate of accumulation of capital per operative was faster than that of the U.K. and this may explain part of the difference in the rates of growth of productivity.

A rigorous test of the hypothesis proposed must await the accumulation of more accurate data on capital accumulation before and after the 1870's. The immediate problem is now to explain the postulated relatively low rate of capital growth per head in the U.K.

It seems clear that the low rate of accumulation cannot be explained by any deficiency of savings in view of the enormous export of capital during the period, which was of the order of £3,000 million between 1875 and 1914 or some 40% of total savings. Were these savings forced to migrate in search of higher yields than were available at home? It does not seem likely, since much of the capital export went into fixed interest securities, and the average yield may have been as low as 5%, compared with an average yield on real capital at home of some 11%. Of course, one could postulate various types of market imperfection which could reconcile this sort of yield discrepancy with superior expectations for given classes of investment, but the existence of savings on such a scale suggests that if the demand for savings at home had been greater the supply would have been forthcoming. The low rate of capital accumulation must therefore be explained by factors on the demand side.

and Prest's figure for national income, less dividends and interest from abroad). Comparisons in real terms are not possible until adequate estimates of real output are available. The figures quoted by Phelps Brown and Weber, *Economic Journal*, 1953, p. 266, seem to depend on their estimates of real income, which I have argued above are misleading.

[7] See Rostas, (*Comparative Productivity in British and American Industry*), pp. 54–5.

Was the low demand for savings accounted for by the alleged decline in the efficiency of British entrepreneurs? It would be possible to argue that the transition from the relatively crude technology of the Iron Age to the more advanced technology of the Steel Age could expose weaknesses in an entrepreneurial system, which did not place enough emphasis on technical and scientific education; but the evidence for this is hardly conclusive.

It seems clear enough that in the iron and steel industry there was a decline in entrepreneurial talent after the 1870's. In 1880 production of steel in Britain, the U.S.A. and Germany was around the level of 1 million tons. By 1913 British output stood at about 8 million tons whilst Germany and America were producing 17 and 31 million tons respectively.[8] It has been argued that the failure to develop mass-produced steel as effectively as our competitors was accounted for by a relative inferiority in British entrepreneurship in connection with the problems of mass-production of iron and steel.[9] This was a weakness in a fundamental industry. Equally fundamental was coal-mining in which the failure to apply steel may have been due to entrepreneurial weakness. Other examples would be the loss of initiative to Germany and the U.S.A. in the development of chemicals and electrical engineering and its applications.[10] It is not necessary, however, to lean heavily on this theory of entrepreneurial decline, since the low rate of capital accumulation in Britain can be explained by a more powerful factor arising from British dependence on international trade.

The decline in the growth of productivity after the 1870's is associated with a parallel decline in growth of production and exports. It seems evident that any discussion of the causes of the climacteric in productivity must have relevance to the causes of this generalized climacteric. The suggestion about to be made is that the decline in growth of British exports after the 1870's explains the low rate of industrial capital accumulation during this period and, as a result, explains the low rate of growth of productivity. The theory is based on the analysis of Pro-

---

[8] The necessary allowances must be made for distribution of resources. As Sir John Clapham puts it, in relation to the U.S.A., "Half a continent is likely in the course of time to mine more coal and make more steel than a small island." [*Economic History of Modern Britain*] Vol. II, p. 122). Something of the same applies to the German development, behind tariff barriers of basic steel, which Englishmen had made possible. But the fact remains that iron and steel produced per capita grew more slowly in Britain than in the U.S.A. and Germany, and even than in Belgium and France. See Burnham and Hoskins, *Iron and Steel in Britain, 1870–1930*, pp. 52–3.

[9] See D. L. Burn, *The Economic History of Steelmaking*, especially Chap. 10 and pp. 67–9 and 296–305. Also Burnham and Hoskins, *op. cit.*, especially Chap. 9.

[10] Cf. Clapham, *op. cit.*, Vol. II, pp. 106, 108–9, Vol. III, pp. 124, 130–1, 136–7, 313.

fessor Lewis who, in his *Economic Survey, 1919–1939,* suggested that the decline in production after 1870 and Britain's relative stagnation can be explained in terms of the declining trend in British exports.[11]

Taking the average annual growth rates of Schlote's measure of total home produced exports, the value from 1819/25 to 1866/74 is 4.7% and for 1866/74 to 1908/13 2.3%. The corresponding growth rates for industrial production are 3.3% and 1.7% respectively. The rates for some of the principal industries are as in Table 1.

TABLE 1

PERCENTAGE AVERAGE ANNUAL GROWTH RATES[a]

	1827/36 TO 1866/74		1866/74 TO 1908/13	
	Production	Exports	Production	Exports
Coal	4.0	8.3	2.1	4.4
Iron and steel	5.4	4.8	2.4	2.3
Machinery	5.1	8.1	2.8	5.1
Cotton	3.9	4.3	1.5	1.7
Wool	2.1	4.4	1.6	−0.2

[a] Series based on [W. Hoffman, *British Industry, 1700–1950* and W. Schlote, *British Overseas Trade from 1700 to the 1930's.—Ed.*]. Note that the production series for "machinery" is Hoffman's "Iron and Steel goods, machinery, tools, etc." which is really the Iron and Steel series plus net imports reweighted. The Cotton and Wool production series are combined yarn and cloth, which again are merely differently weighted measures of cotton and wool consumption subject to deductions for spinning losses and net exports of yarn. Schlote's volume estimates for individual exports do not extend beyond 1827.

If the growth rate of exports is regarded as an exogenous variable, the general decline in the growth of exports after the 1870's undoubtedly explains a decline in the rate of growth of production and in the required rate of investment. Given a reduction in the rate of investment a decline in the rate of growth of productivity will follow.

Two possible objections to the hypothesis must be dealt with. First it seems to require the assumption that the rate of growth of exports was exogenous, which needs to be justified. Secondly, it would be possible to argue that a decline in the growth of exports can only explain a decline in production and does not necessarily require a decline in productivity. In other words, whilst a reduced rate of growth of exports can explain a check to capital widening, it need go no further than that.

The assumption that the growth of exports was exogenous can be defended to some extent. Even if Britain's share of world trade in manufactures had remained unchanged the volume of exports was bound to reflect the declining growth in volume of world trade in manufactures during the 1880's and 1890's which was caused by the

---

[11] *Op. cit.,* p. 74.

adverse terms of trade for primary producers.[12] Superimposed on this basic trend was the effect of Britain's declining share of world trade in manufactures which was also partly exogenous, since it reflected the rapid industrial development of Western Europe and the U.S.A., the erection of tariff barriers and competition in international trade often accompanied by price discrimination. A rough idea of the effects of these factors on Britain's trade in manufactures can be gained by using Schlote's analysis of exports by volume to industrial and agrarian countries. The percentage increases in the volume of exported finished manufactures between selected dates are as in Table 2.[13]

TABLE 2

	1854/7 TO 1877/9	1877/9 TO 1908/13
Industrial Europe	122	47
U.S.A.	− 13	24
All agrarian countries	107	125

The figures illustrate the effects of the reversal of the free trade movement of the 1860's and 1870's on trade with Industrial Europe. In the case of the U.S.A. the big increase in tariffs dates from the 1860's. The combined total of exports to Industrial Europe and the U.S.A. was not insignificant, being about 50% of the trade with agrarian countries in 1877/79.

It seems reasonable, therefore, to regard some part, and perhaps a substantial part, of the climacteric in production as being caused exogenously by the effects of world factors on British export growth. But this cannot be the complete explanation since the share of British exports in world trade will depend on the type of goods which Britain produces and their relative prices as compared with foreign exports. These things in turn depend on the reaction to technological progress and the trend in productivity. Here we encounter the second objection. Can the decline in growth of exports explain the decline in growth of productivity or does the chain of causation work the other way? Do we need an independent explanation of the decline in productivity?

The answer is that, whilst an independent explanation need not be ruled out of an eclectic theory, a decline in productivity growth is bound

---

[12] See Lewis, *Economic Survey*, p. 74 and "World Production, Prices and Trade, 1870–1960," *Manchester School*, 1952.

[13] Based on Schlote *op. cit.*, Tables 32 and 34. The estimates are got by the crude method of applying the percentage of trade in manufactures from Table 34 to the volume of exports of home produced goods in Table 32. The dates fall in different stages of the trade cycle, but a comparison of the trend in the aggregates with the intercyclical growth rates suggests that the figures are reasonably good indicators of the trends.

to result from the check to investment caused by the check to exports. The reason is connected with the continuity of technological progress. A secular rise in demand for a product will require a secular growth in the capital equipment of producers. But, given the decision to add to capital, the efficient producer will take advantage of advances in technique with the result that reductions in real cost or improvements in quality will follow automatically. It follows that a decline in the rate of growth of exports can explain a decline in the rate of capital improvement and deepening and consequently a decline in the growth of productivity.[14]

If it is true that the period of the 1870's marks an end of the large scale and profitable application of the techniques of steam-power and iron machinery the explanation given above is reinforced. Exports react on productivity and productivity reacts on exports to explain a generalized climacteric of the 1870's.

The implications, for this theory, of the export of capital should be noted. To the extent that this raised the demand for British exports it raised the demand for capital at home; thus the relatively high capital export of the 1880's may have moderated the climacteric in exports and production. Also the rising rate of growth of British exports in the later part of the period, under the influence of improving terms of trade for primary producers and the surge of capital exports does not seem to have produced any effect on the growth of production. To some extent this is explained by the opposite trend in the building cycle; the theory presented above depends on the low average level of the growth of exports after the 1870's as compared with the period before. But the relative inefficiency of British entrepreneurship may have been more important in the later years of the period after 1870.

The larger question, whether it would have paid Britain to concentrate more on investment at home in the period after 1870, *e.g.*, by resorting to protection, has not been discussed since it involves the analysis of a hypothetical world. But from the unemployment data of the period it seems reasonable to argue that Britain could have had more investment of both kinds had the incentive or enterprise been present. In this case the rate of growth of production and productivity would have been higher and this in turn would have made more investment possible.

---

[14] It has, of course, been argued that a decline in demand ought to increase the incentive to instal cost-reducing equipment. Whilst cases of this may happen it cannot be general or the phenomenon of the business cycle would not exist.

PART
·IV·

THE TRANSFORMATION
OF A CONTINENT:
THE UNITED STATES

INTRODUCTION

Quite apart from anything else, the fact that the economic expansion of the United States in the nineteenth century was an example of *continental* growth distinguishes it sharply from the British case. It means, in addition, that it is difficult to find any brief studies which cover so broad a canvas—simply because historians and economists have generally found it much more fruitful to select a particular topic or period from the panoramic variety of nineteenth-century development. Nevertheless, the surface characteristics of that development are worthy of note.

Between 1800 and 1900 the population of the United States rose from some 5 million to 76 million. At the same time, owing to purchase, conquest, and treaty, its area more than tripled,[1] and population

---

[1] Between 1880 and 1860 the area of the continental United States rose from 888,811 to 3,022,387 square miles, the principal acquisitions being the Louisiana Purchase, 1803 (827,192 square miles); the annexation of Texas, 1845 (390,144 square miles); the Oregon Compromise, 1846 (285,580 square miles); and the Mexican Cession, 1848 (529,017 square miles).

streamed into the newly acquired lands to the west in one of the most spectacular migrations of modern history. The abundance of land and accessible natural resources helped give American economic growth a dual character, for it implied an enormous increase in primary production as well as an accompanying process of industrialization. This element was so important that it was not until the early 1880's that the net value of the output of manufacturing industry overtook that of agriculture—although it is worth noting that the absolute magnitudes involved were at the same time sufficient to make the United States the leading industrial nation with 29 per cent of the world's total manufacturing output.

On the side of the expansion of primary production a number of factors stand out. One has already been mentioned: the westward flow of population, that is, of labor. But capital and enterprise also moved from the Atlantic toward the Pacific, and, as regards the growth of both cotton production in the South and (perhaps even more) grain and livestock production in the North and West, they were of crucial significance. Capital moved not only into direct production, but also into the buildings, the trading facilities, and the transportation so essential to economic expansion. In this process the railroad has been traditionally considered as a dominant force, and some idea of the pace of construction can be gathered from the following figures of railroad mileage operated at various dates:[2]

1830	23	1870	53,000
1840	2,800	1880	93,000
1850	9,000	1890	167,000
1860	30,600	1900	207,000

The importance of a transportation system (both because it lowered costs, thus opening up new markets and sources of supply, and because its construction was a direct stimulant to a higher level of economic activity) in the United States also helps account for the far from negligible role of federal, state, and local governments in the development of the country. Thus it has been estimated by Professor Carter Goodrich[3] that before 1860 public authorities accounted for about 70 per cent of the investment in canals and perhaps as much as 30

[2] Bureau of the Census, *Historical Statistics of the United States* (Washington, D.C., 1960), pp. 427, 429. Figures for 1840–60 are rounded to the nearest 100; those for 1870–1900 to the nearest 1,000. Figures for 1890 and 1900 exclude yard tracks and sidings. Another measure of the growth of railroads is provided by investment figures: railroads in the 1870's and 1880's accounted for 20.4 per cent and 15.6 per cent of national gross capital formation, respectively (Melville J. Ulmer, *Trends and Cycles in Capital Formation by United States Railroads*, 1870–1950 [New York, 1954], p. 11).

[3] *Government Promotion of American Canals and Railroads*, 1800–1890 (New York, 1960), pp. 270–71.

per cent of the investment in railroads—achievements made possible by subsidies, public investment, the lending of public credit, and land grants.

Although the precise importance of each element has not yet been determined, it is clear that the growth of primary production had a variety of impacts upon overall growth and industrialization. It supplied a growing market for industrial products; through an increase in productivity it liberated a growing proportion of the labor force for secondary and tertiary industry; and, by the same means, it supplied a cheaper and greater flow of food and raw materials to towns and factories. In addition, since the United States was, for most of the period, an exporter of primary produce, it earned a great deal of foreign exchange and thereby helped finance necessary imports. Indeed, the role of the international economy in American economic growth was of very great significance (although it declined over time). This was true not only because of the importance of commodity exports and imports, but also by reason of the inflow of capital from Europe, the mass migration of people from the same source,[4] and (perhaps equally significant) the energizing consequences of continuous and intimate contact with European technology, techniques, and ideas.

This last factor was more important for industrial than agricultural development. Yet at almost every stage American mechanics and entrepreneurs demonstrated a dynamic ability to adapt as well as imitate, and, in the last resort, to develop entirely new techniques more suitable to their own environment. All this was especially true of the two broad developments which visitors judged to be most characteristic of the American economic genius: the use of machinery which was labor-saving, automatic, and standardizing, and the development of large-scale and ultimately integrated enterprises which pressed relentlessly for rationalization and low costs. These trends could be seen in embryo in the New England textile mills and in the machine-tool, armament, and timepiece industries of the first few decades of the century. But they came to spectacular fruition in the forty or fifty years before 1914 in the new (or newly important) areas of manufacturing in steel, petroleum, rubber, bicycles, electrical equipment, chemicals, tobacco, meat packing, and the like. And they came together conclusively in the modern system of mass production which was decisively inaugurated by the Ford Motor Company in the second decade of this century.

Apart from the foregoing, the other factors which facilitated economic

---

[4] Between 1830 and 1900 there was some $2,750,000,000 of foreign investment in the United States. In the same period about 16,000,000 immigrants entered the country. See Seymour E. Harris (ed.), *American Economic History* (New York, 1961), pp. 68, 89.

growth in nineteenth-century America are sufficiently well known not to need lengthy repetition here. The very "openness" of the country encouraged that flexibility of economic outlook and operation which is the best basis for development. In addition, American society, measured against that of Europe, welcomed both material strivings and the risks and changes which are its inevitable concomitants. Correspondingly, business enterprise and business achievement were acknowledged to have a central significance in American life—an acknowledgment which was matched by the appearance of generations of entrepreneurs who were more ambitious, more venturesome, more successful, and sometimes more ruthless than their European counterparts. On the other hand, it is plain that entrepreneurship was helped in its tasks by government action directed toward economic growth. This was most obvious in public policy toward the distribution of western lands, the construction of a transportation network, and tariff protection to industry. But this, too, reflected the fact that society as a whole not only welcomed the advent of rapid economic growth, but was, in general, more than willing to pay the relevant price in terms of change, dislocation, friction, and high profits.

That this price was perhaps not excessive is indicated by the fact that the nineteenth-century development of the United States was unprecedented both as to pace and scope. Unfortunately, reasonably accurate measures only became available after the 1830's. On this basis it appears that between 1839 and 1859 commodity production grew at an average rate of 57 per cent per decade (16 per cent per capita per decade). Between 1869 and 1899 the comparable decennial rates were 54 per cent and 24 per cent.[5] Taking a somewhat broader measure, the production of both goods and services grew at an average rate of 56 per cent (27.5 per cent per capita) per decade between 1870 and 1915.[6] These figures give an impression of relative constancy; but in fact, as with the British economy, both business cycles and trend movements or long swings were prominent features of long-run expansion. And, as is illustrated in Selections 11, 13, and 15, such fluctuations can be studied from two related viewpoints (even apart from short-run business cycles): as rhythmical or wavelike movements of important economic variables, or, in the case of upswings, as discontinuous forward surges in economic activity.

The five studies which have been selected for inclusion in this Part each represent a different approach to American economic growth.

---

[5] William N. Parker (ed. for the National Bureau of Economic Research), *Trends in the American Economy in the Nineteenth Century* (Princeton, N. J., 1960), p. 16.
[6] *Economic Development and Cultural Change*, V, 1 (1954), 13.

Selection 11 is taken from a most stimulating and broad study of economic growth in the United States between 1790 and 1860 by Professor Douglass C. North of the University of Washington. It exemplifies the integration of economic theory and detailed historical knowledge—with particular reference to the relationship between exports (either national or regional) and economic change. Selection 13, by Professor Alfred H. Conrad of Harvard University, is comparable in that it also brings together rigorous analytical tools and a wealth of historical data, but is contrasting in that the theoretical approach is quite different and the chronological scope is somewhat more extensive. Whereas Professor North concentrates primarily on the role of the market and the mechanisms by which it may (or may not) induce economic change, Professor Conrad is principally concerned with the consequences of structural change within a more complex economic model. Examples of a more "traditional" approach are provided by Selections 12 and 14. The former, by Professor George R. Taylor of Amherst College, is drawn from his well-known study of the American economy between 1815 and 1860 (*The Transportation Revolution*). It provides a succinct picture of the United States on the eve of the Civil War and of the significant changes which had taken place in the two previous generations. Selection 14, which examines the important institutional changes in the American economy after 1850, is an excerpt from a general survey of American history by a British scholar, Frank Thistlethwaite, Vice Chancellor of the University of East Anglia. Selection 15 represents the growing number of studies of long-run fluctuations in the American economy. Bernard Weber and S. J. Handfield-Jones are both at the University of Glasgow. It should be noted that although the statistical data is much more abundant for the period after the Civil War, long swings have also been conclusively identified in the decades before 1860.[7]

---

[7] See Selection 11, and the footnotes in it referring to the work of Moses Abramovitz; also see the Selected Bibliography.

11

Aspects of Economic Growth

in the United States, 1815-1860

by

DOUGLASS C. NORTH

I. THE ANALYTICAL FRAMEWORK

The analytical framework of this study is a composite of several propositions, the most important of which was a cornerstone of *The Wealth of Nations*. Taken together they reflect certain underlying features of economic behavior which have characterized the development of market economies over the past several centuries. These propositions emerged in the course of the give and take between some initial hypotheses about economic development,[1] the subsequent organization of statistical data and qualitative information to test these hypotheses, and their modification[2] in the light of this evidence. The gist of the

Reprinted from Douglass C. North, *The Economic Growth of the United States, 1790–1860* (pp. 1–14, 66–74, with omissions). © 1961. Prentice-Hall, Inc., Englewood Cliffs, N. J. Reprinted by permission of the publishers and author.

[1] Cf. Douglass C. North, "Location Theory and Regional Economic Growth," *Journal of Political Economy* LXII, No. 3 (June 1955), 243–58, and subsequent exchange with Charles Tiebout in the same journal, LXIV, No. 2 (April 1956), 160–69.

[2] Douglass C. North, "Agriculture and Regional Economic Growth," paper delivered before the American Farm Economics Association, Cornell, August 1959, and subsequently published in American Farm Economics Association, *Proceedings* XLI, No. 5 (December 1959), 943–51. This argument would require some modi-

argument is that the timing and pace of an economy's development has been determined by: (1) the success of its export sector, and (2) the characteristics of the export industry and the disposition of the income received from the export sector.

1

The expanding international economy of the past two centuries has provided the avenue by which one economy after another has accelerated its rate of growth. There are few exceptions to the essential initiating role of a successful export sector in the early stages of accelerated growth of market economies. The reason is that the domestic market has been small and scattered. These economies have been predominantly rural, with a high degree of individual self-sufficiency. Reflecting this aspect of the market, specialization and division of labor have been limited and rudimentary. An expanding external market has provided the means for an increase in the size of the domestic market, growth in money income, and the spread of specialization and division of labor. Under the favorable conditions outlined below (with respect to the disposition of income from the export sector), it has set in motion a chain of consequences leading to sustained growth. Before examining these factors it is important to explore in more detail the conditions underlying successful production of goods and services for export.

Credits earned from the exportation of goods and services can be seen from the country's balance of payments, but an explanation lies in the character of the demand for the export and in the nature of the supply function. The analysis must explore the determinants of the demand and shifts in demand as well as the shape of the supply function and shifts in supply. The supply response to a change in price plays an important role in the analysis. It is a central part of the argument with respect to long swings in prices and other economic activity that supply shifts in response to price changes proceeded irregularly, and, in conjunction with the speculative behavior which accompanied the latter phases of periods of accelerated growth, were important in the explanation of long swings in economic activity which characterized the United States development after 1815.

. . . . .

2

The first step in the analysis is an exploration of the determinants of the export sector of the economy. The next is an examination of the

---

fication for countries with population "pressure." Cf. Harvey Leibenstein's *Economic Backwardness and Economic Growth* (New York: Wiley and Sons, 1957), Chapter 10.

characteristics of the export sector and the disposition of the income received from outside the economy or region. Certainly one of the perplexing problems in the study of economic growth has been the varying progress of different economies as a result of an increment to income from the export sector. Why does one area remain tied to a single export staple while another diversifies its production and becomes an urbanized, industrialized economy? Regions or nations which remain tied to a single export commodity almost inevitably fail to achieve sustained expansion. Not only will there be a slowing down in the rate of growth of the export good or service which adversely affects development, but the fact that the economy remains tied to a single industry will mean that specialization and division of labor outside that industry are limited. Historically, it has meant that a large share of the populace has remained outside the market economy, the development of more effective factor markets has been limited, and inflow of additional productive factors has usually been confined to capital flowing into the export industry. The factors which appear to be most important in the sustained development of economies subsequent to expansion of the export sector can be subsumed under three headings:

1. The natural endowments of the region (at any given level of technology),
2. The character of the export industry, and
3. Changes in technology and transfer costs.

It is worthwhile to examine each of these in turn.

The natural endowments of a region dictate its initial export commodities. If these endowments result in a tremendous comparative advantage in one commodity over any other, the immediate consequence will be for resources to concentrate on its production. But if the region has broad production possibilities such that the rate of return on the production of a number of goods and services is not too much less than on the initial export commodity, with the growth of the region and accompanying changes in factor proportions such production is likely to be a simple process.

The character of the export commodity's influence on regional growth is more complicated. A number of important consequences stem from the technological nature of the production function. If the export commodity is a *plantation* type which is relatively labor intensive, with significant increasing returns to scale, then its development will be in marked contrast to one where the export commodity may be most efficiently produced on a family-size farm with relatively smaller absolute amounts of labor required.[3] In the first case, extremely unequal distribution of income will tend to result, with the bulk of the population devoting most of its income to foodstuffs and simple necessities (much of which may be self-sufficient production). At the other end of the income scale the plantation owners will tend to spend most of their income on imported luxury goods. There will be slight encouragement of residentiary types of economic activity. With more equitable distribution of incomes, there is a demand for a broad range of goods and services, part of which will be residentiary, thus inducing investment in other types of economic activities. Trading centers will tend to develop to provide these goods and services, in contrast to the plantation economy, which will merely develop a few urban areas devoted to export of the staple commodity and distribution of imports.

A natural consequence of these divergent patterns will be the attitude towards investment in knowledge.[4] Under the plantation system, with its marked inequality of incomes, the planter will be reluctant to devote his tax monies to expenditures for education or research other than that related to the staple commodity. In contrast, the region with more equitable income distribution will be aware of the stake in improving its comparative position through education and research, and be willing to devote public expenditures in these directions. This will improve its relative position in a variety of types of economic activity and broaden the resultant economic base. This does not imply that equal income distribution will produce optimum investment of this kind, but only that the distribution of income should not be extremely skewed, as in the plantation type economy.

Equally important is the investment induced by the export commodity or service. If the export requires substantial investment in transport, warehousing, port facilities and other types of social overhead investment, external economies are created which facilitate the development of other exports. If the export industry encourages the growth of complementary and subsidiary industries, and if technology, transport costs and resource endowments permit these to be locally produced, further development will be induced. In both social overhead investment and investment in complementary and subsidiary industry, urbanization and increased specialization are promoted, and additional residentiary activity geared to the increasing local demand for consumption goods and services develops. At the other extreme is the export

---

[3] Cf. R. E. Baldwin, "Patterns of Development in Newly Settled Regions," *The Manchester School of Economic and Social Studies* XXIV, No. 2 (May 1956), 161–79.

[4] I am in Professor Theodore Schultz's debt for focussing my attention on this problem.

industry, which requires only the immediate development of a few centers for collection and export and develops little subsidiary industry, or develops such subsidiary industry and marketing facilities, even though they are of a nature to be most efficiently imported.

Changes in technology and transport may completely alter the region's comparative advantage. Technological change may increase the potential rate of return from the production of other goods and services, and lead to exploitation of new resources and a shift away from the old export industry. The initial development of transportation facilities to implement the export industry tends to reinforce dependence upon it and inhibit more diversified economic activity. The early development of transport typically (under competitive conditions) leads to a rapid fall in the transport rate, increasing the comparative advantage of the export commodity. Moreover, with newly settled regions the outward shipment of a bulky product has no counterpart in the inward voyage, which must be made mostly empty or in ballast. Inward freights are consequently low and can compete with locally produced goods. Local industries which had been protected by high transport costs, or which might develop if high transport costs continued, face effective competition from imports.

The disposition of income earned from the export industry plays a decisive role in the growth of the region. Related to this argument is the region's propensity to import. To the extent that a region's income directly flows out in the purchase of goods and services rather than having a regional multiplier-accelerator effect,[5] it is inducing growth elsewhere but reaping few of the benefits of increased income from the export sector itself. The *successful* economy grows because the initial developments from the export industry lead to a widening of the export base and growth in the size of the domestic market. Growing demand in the domestic sector leads to an ever widening variety of residentiary industries. These industries (and services) producing for the local market vary in character. They range from those which must by necessity be residentiary (retail trade, some services, etc.) to those which—as the size of the market permits firms to achieve efficient scale of operations —become substitutes for some imports. In response to profitable opportunities in the economy, there is an inflow of labor and capital to augment the domestic increase. Changing factor proportions, along with the cost reducing consequences of social overhead investments and the improved skills, training, and knowledge that come from diversion of capital into investment in education, lead to a broadening of the export base. This usually occurs first in the processing of a wider variety

[5] Cf. J. S. Dusenberry, "Some Aspects of the Theory of Economic Development," *Explorations in Entrepreneurial History* III, No. 2 (December 1950), 63–102.

of raw materials and then in the fabrication of goods, typically entailing a greater use of capital and skills. Some of this manufacturing may develop initially for the export market, while other forms of manufacturing may be initially oriented to the expanding domestic market.

In the *unsuccessful* economy, the increment to income from expansion of the export industry leads to an increase in the supply of that export commodity, but not to broadening of the export base nor growth in the size of the domestic market. Income flows out of the area with little more than expansion of the export industry as a result.

3

The argument has thus far been aimed at what may be called the *extensive* growth of an economy. Growth in income from the export sector and its favorable disposition along the lines of the above arguments leads to an increase in the supply of productive factors from both domestic sources and immigration, the inflow of capital and entrepreneurial talent, and frequently from the acquisition of land. It leads to an increase in aggregate income, but the analysis has not been focussed directly on the increased efficiency of productive factors which is necessary to rising per capita real income.

To what extent were the productivity increases resulting from technological innovations, investment in research, training and education, and improved organization of economic activity simply a consequence of the activities of an acquisitive society in the context of the favorable conditions for extensive growth described above?

In the case of technological change we were followers in the process of industrialization and in the more fundamental beginnings of scientific development which underlay the rapid advances of the nineteenth century. Accompanying the economic expansion of the Western World was the development of science. This development provided a reservoir of knowledge that could be tapped to produce new techniques required by more pressing economic needs. This is not the place for the theory of societal change which would be necessary to support such an argument, but several specific points should be made:

1. There was available to us a reservoir of technological information as a result of the prior development in England, and to a lesser degree other western European countries, of these scientific innovations. Under the competitive market conditions which characterized our economy, the rewards awaiting the entrepreneur who successfully adapted these innovations to the American scene were sufficient incentive. Throughout this era, beginning with

Samuel Slater, such adaptations were made as it became profitable to do so.

2. In the case of indigenous innovations, the most striking aspect of many of them was that they emerged in the context of a mounting problem, reflecting the search for alternative uses of existing sunk capital or the rising price of a resource or productive factor, especially labor. Whether it was Eli Whitney's cotton gin—certainly the major domestic innovation for the economy's growth during the period—or the labor saving devices which impressed British investigators of American manufacturing in the 1850's, they clearly owed their origins to the deliberate search for solutions to economic problems, particularly in the export sector.

If the argument of the preceding paragraphs is accepted, it follows that productivity changes stemming from technological innovations are, in part at least, a nearly automatic response to successful expansion of industries in an acquisitive society under competitive market conditions. Not only was there available a reservoir of technological improvements, but the structure of a competitive market provided important rewards for successful innovation in a society whose value system prized such activity. This is not a complete explanation of technological change in America during this period. The role of the entrepreneur and innovator is an important one, but I would downgrade its significance for the study of growth in economies which: (1) followed in the process of industrial development, and (2) were acquisitively oriented under competitive market conditions.

Investment in knowledge represents a deliberate decision by a society to divert resources from more immediately productive pursuits. Implicitly or explicitly, a society makes assumptions about the returns on such investment which affect the level of expenditure of tax monies. The amount of capital diverted into investment in knowledge will depend upon the structure of political power and the attitudes of that group in a society which is in a position to enact legislation regarding taxes and public expenditure. Where extremely unequal income distribution is paralleled by unequal distribution of political power, the development of broadly based public education is less likely, since there are no obvious gains to those who must provide the bulk of the tax monies for such an investment. Such investment is likely to be a larger proportion of income under conditions of more equal income distribution, since the broader distribution of costs will be matched by an equally expanded distribution of benefits. Very unequal income distribution, *per se,* will only be a reinforcing factor in the unwillingness to invest in human capital where it is not obvious to the dominant political-economic group that such an investment will yield a high return to them. However, a substantial degree of income inequality is compatible with a relatively large investment in knowledge when the range of production possibilities may be enhanced and profitable opportunities increased by a better educated populace. It was not only the western farmer and mechanic in an atmosphere of egalitarianism who espoused educational investment, but also the eastern entrepreneur and employer who equally recognized the importance of such investment.[6] The striking difference between educational investment in the South and in the other two regions during the period 1815–1860 is explainable in terms of this argument. There is abundant contemporary evidence that Westerners and residents of the Northeast set a high value on such investment compared to the southern planter, who saw little return to himself from a better educated populace. Investment in knowledge partially reflected the economic structure of the region.

The most important *proximate* cause of increasing productivity of the economy during this period came from improved organization of economic activity. By this I mean the consequences of increasing specialization and division of labor which were responsible not only for growing efficiency in agriculture and transport, but which determined the pace, timing, and character of manufacturing development as well. The cause of increasing specialization was, of course, the size of the market, which permitted individual specialization of function in the productive process and specialization of the firm in the form of vertical dis-integration, and also encouraged the adoption of technological processes. It should not be necessary here to argue the cause of Adam Smith's theorem, but it is necessary to elaborate on a modern day re-statement of the theorem, which has widespread implications for economic growth. I am referring to the article by George J. Stigler which uses Smith's proposition as its title.[7] Stigler elaborates a case of external economies which provides the essential connecting link between extensive expansion and consequent growth in the size of the market, and increasing efficiency. He argues that a firm performs a number of functions, some subject to diminishing returns, others subject to increasing returns. With a limited market the firm necessarily performs all of these functions, from recruiting its labor force and constructing

---

[6] While incomes were certainly unequal in the North, political representation was of course far broader in the North than in the South, and the added pressure from lower income groups (and particularly immigrants) was a further impetus to educational investment in the North.

[7] "The Division of Labor is Limited by the Extent of the Market," *Journal of Political Economy* LIX, No. 3 (June 1951), 185–93.

its machinery to marketing its product. With expansion in the size of the market some of these functions with increasing returns split off from the firm and realize decreasing costs with expansion in their output. A cotton textile firm, which initially had to perform all the functions from machinery construction to retailing, gradually divests itself from all functions but spinning and weaving. Specialized textile machinery and retailing establishments develop as the market attains sufficient size. These new specialized firms, subject to increasing returns, effectively realize and pass on, under competitive conditions, the lower costs of machinery or retailing. This process of specialization of function with growth of the market size was one of the most striking features of industrialization in this country. The size of the market, of course, was basically a function of the success of the export sector and the disposition of income from this sector.

The answer to the question about the relationship between factors making for improved efficiency and those promoting extensive growth of the economy is that they stemmed in large part from the same causes.

4

. . . The business cycle is a poor framework for the analysis of economic growth. The shortness of the period, monetary disturbances, and speculative excesses combine to conceal rather than expose the underlying factors in the long-run growth of the economy. While business cycles must be integrated into the analysis, their proper position is as an inherent feature of a market economy in which underlying factors shape the proximate events and timing of cyclical activity.

A more promising temporal framework is the long cycle in economic activity which characterized the economy after 1815. Its pervasiveness in most of the time series for the period,[8] and the coincidence of most of the major turning points of these series with other evidence of important changes in the economy, makes it a useful chronological framework. No attempt is made here to offer a complete theory of long swings,[9] although the evidence suggests that this cycle is intimately connected with capital investments of a relatively long gestation period, such as transportation and construction. We do know that the growth of the economy has proceeded in a series of surges followed by periods

---

[8] See Moses Abramovitz, "Long Swings in United States Economic Growth," 38th *Annual Report* of the National Bureau of Economic Research (New York: National Bureau of Economic Research, 1958), pp. 47–56, which presents 24 series showing long cycles for the pre-1860 period.

[9] Abramovitz prefers the name "long swings" to describe these movements, although they are also sometimes referred to as secondary secular movements and trend cycles.

of slower growth, and that the length of these swings has usually been between eighteen and twenty years.[10] . . .

The chronology of long swings during this period is as follows. The trough of each cycle coincided with the trough of a serious depression. From this trough, the initial expansion was gradual. The substantial growth of capacity during the previous boom resulted in several years of depressed prices, modest profit expectations and only gradual reabsorption of unemployed or underemployed resources into production. As demand for the commodities in the export sector increased, existing capacity was finally utilized. It was not until prices began to rise that there began a significant redirection of productive factors into the export sector to increase supply. Initial redirection of productive factors was primarily within the region. At first it was a reabsorption of unemployed or underemployed (as in the case of self-sufficient farmers) factors. With increasing profit expectations, there was both an interregional and an international flow of labor and capital. The pace of expansion accelerated, and the boom was under way. It is during such periods that the real growth rate of the economy was greatest, because of both the addition of real resources to economic activity and increases of productivity. The latter resulted from the more efficient uses of productive factors in the export sector, or social overhead investment related to the export sector, as compared to their use in locally oriented or self-sufficient economic activity.

Each surge of expansion during this period consisted of extensive movement into new territory, with all the concomitant internal migration and investment in transportation and construction which accompanied the opening up, settlement, and integration of the area into the economy. In the new area itself there was induced growth in all the necessary residentiary industry and services, while in older areas there was increasing demand for consumer and capital goods for the new area.

An important part of the argument is that there is a lag in production as a result of the lengthy gestation period required to produce substantial increases in supply. Transportation developments in the West to open up new land and increased cotton production in the South were time consuming processes. In the interim, with full employment achieved, prices rose, reflecting both the diversion of productive factors from consumer goods and increased demand with rising income. The capital imports which directed resources into the export sector or into

---

[10] An excellent summary of the evidence on long swings is contained in Moses Abramovitz's testimony before the Joint Economic Committee, 86th Congress, 1st Session, *Hearings*, Part 2, "Historical and Comparative Rates of Production," pp. 411–33.

social overhead investment financed a high level of consumption goods imports, which mitigated the inflationary pressures.

The actual growth rate of the economy in the latter part of the periods of expansion was slower. With fully employed resources, growth in real output was limited to productivity increases. Productivity changes themselves occurred at a slower rate than during the earlier period, when productive factors were shifting into industries of higher productivity than those from which they had moved.

Two factors combined to bring a boom to a close, and since they did not necessarily coincide in their timing it was possible to have a sharp recession and brief revival, as in 1837–1839, before both coincided to end the period of expansion. Although both resulted in a decline in investment, one was primarily monetary and acted through the money supply, and the other was real and related to the realization of increases in capacity which had been under way.

There is no intention in this differentiation between monetary and real factors to imply that the two are not intimately related. The former, whether from political policies within the economy or from without, is more susceptible to exogenous influences, reacting upon the domestic money supply through exchange rates and specie flows.

The gold standard, which served as the most immediate sensitive tie in our international economic relations, resulted in changes in the domestic money supply. In each boom, a growing disparity between domestic and foreign price levels inevitably set in motion a domestic readjustment process to bring prices in line. United States prices rose relative to foreign prices as a result of the expansion and price effects described above. While specific domestic and foreign economic policies were proximately related to the contractions in the money supply, the more general reason lay in the price *distortions* from the boom itself.

While monetary effects were proximate forces in the downturn, factors resulting from the expansion in capacity during the boom are most important in the lengthy period of decline and readjustment which ensued. Construction, transportation and the integration of new areas into the economy all involved lengthy commitments of resources before substantial increases in supply resulted. The increase, when it did come about, typically resulted in such a substantial increment to capacity that supply increased disproportionately relative to the growth in demand. The result was not only a fall in the price of the commodity but a long period of depressed prices until demand had shifted to the right sufficiently to *catch up* with this capacity.

The drastic drop in the prices of leading export commodities was paralleled by declining prices in general. Downward price flexibility was a characteristic of the economy during this period. The fall in prices was rapid, and was followed by several years of depressed activity with only slight further declines in prices. The painful readjustment and re-valuation of assets that followed was extended by the very large increase in capacity of the previous boom until the trough was reached at the very bottom of the business cycle.

· · · · ·

II. THE ECONOMY 1815–1860—AN OVERVIEW

Between the end of the second war with England and the firing on Fort Sumter were nearly fifty years of peace, interrupted only briefly by the Mexican War on this continent and the Crimean War abroad. Neither was a major disturbing force, although the latter had repercussions upon economic stability in the 1850's. It was an era of tremendous expansion for the Atlantic economy as a whole and for the United States in particular.

The contrast between the sources of expansion in periods just before and after the War of 1812 is striking. In the former period the Western World was at war, and the rapid development of the American economy for fourteen years reflected our ability to take advantage of this war. The exigencies of war relaxed the mercantilist restrictions of European powers, and war created the demand for shipping and re-exports and the very favorable terms of trade that produced unequalled American prosperity up to 1808.

The period following 1815 was not only one of peace, but one in which artificial national barriers to the free movement of goods, services, productive factors, and ideas were being relaxed. An international economy was emerging in which the parts were interrelated by the forces of comparative prices of goods, services, and productive factors. An analysis of the United States economic development must necessarily be put into the context of the expansion of the Atlantic economy. Institutions and national policies which both impeded and fostered the international exchange of goods, services, productive factors and ideas must be continually brought into view. It was the "anonymous," impersonal forces of the evolving international economy which were the basic influence on the developing Atlantic economy and its constituent parts. National policies and institutional influences modified rather than generated the economic growth that ensued. The very forces of the Atlantic economy which were inducing expansion in the United States were thereby making this country increasingly independent of the international economic context, so that during these years there was a fundamental shift away from dependence upon the Atlantic economy toward dependence on our own internal economy as the mainspring of expansion.

In 1815 the international context was still critical. The expanding industrialization of England and Europe in the years after the Napoleonic wars was accompanied not only by the gradual relaxation of restrictions on trade and factor mobility, but the resultant structural changes accelerated the movement of productive factors in response to differential rates of return. While the immigration of people and particularly capital into the United States played an important part in our growth in the thirty years after 1815, it was the growth of the cotton textile industry and the demand for cotton which was decisive. In 1815 the previous sources of expansion, the re-export and carrying trade and manufactures, were declining as a result of peacetime competition. The West was still largely unintegrated into the national economy. The United States was left with only cotton as the major expansive force. The vicissitudes of the cotton trade—the speculative expansion of 1818, the radical decline in prices in the 1820's and the boom in the 1830's—were the most important influence upon the varying rates of growth of the economy during the period. Cotton was strategic because it was the major independent variable in the interdependent structure of internal and international trade. The demands for western foodstuffs and northeastern services and manufactures were basically dependent upon the income received from the cotton trade. This dependence resulted not only from the developing regional specialization, but from the characteristics of the South itself.

A marked characteristic of the South was that income received from the export of cotton (and sugar, rice and tobacco) flowed directly out of the regional economy again in the purchase of goods and services. The South provided neither the services to market its own exports nor the consumer goods and services to supply its own needs, and had a very high propensity to import. It was the West which provided food for the South and, since the South was the West's major market until the problems of cross-mountain transport had been solved, the growth of the market for western foodstuffs was geared to the expansion of the southern cotton economy.

The Northeast provided not only the services to finance, transport, insure, and market the South's cotton, but also supplied the South with manufactured goods, either from its own industry or imported and reshipped to the South. Major markets for the Northeast were the South and the West. Both depended, directly in the first case and indirectly in the second, on the income from the cotton trade.

It was cotton which was the most important influence in the growth in the market size and the consequent expansion of the economy: the slow development of the 1820's, the accelerated growth in the 1830's. In this period of rapid growth, it was cotton that initiated the concomitant expansion in income, in the size of domestic markets, and creation of the social overhead investment (in the course of its role in the marketing of cotton) in the Northeast which were to facilitate the subsequent rapid growth of manufactures. Cotton also accounted for the accelerated pace of westward migration as well as for the movement of people out of self-sufficiency into the market economy.

Cotton was not the only expansive influence in the economy during this period. Clearly there were others, and they will be considered. Had there been no cotton gin, it is certain that the resources directly and indirectly devoted to the cotton trade would have been at least partially absorbed in other types of economic activity. Given the social structure, attitudes and motivation of American society, and the rich quantity and quality of resources which made even the self-sufficient farmer well off as compared with his European counterpart, the United States economy would not have stagnated. But cotton was the commodity for which foreign demand was significantly increasing, it accounted for over half the value of exports, and the income directly or indirectly from cotton was the major independent influence on the evolving pattern of interregional trade. Without cotton the development in the size of the market would have been a much more lengthy process, since there was no alternative way to expand the domestic market rapidly without recourse to external demand. In short, cotton was the most important proximate cause of expansion, and by tracing out the resulting interrelationships light may be shed on the pace and character of the economy's development, particularly in the years up to 1843.

The argument advanced in [section I] with respect to the strategic role of certain industries is pertinent here. A great deal of economic activity is a passive rather than an active source of economic expansion. It grows up either dependent upon an "active" industry or in response to the growth of income initially generated by the carriers[11] of economic change. In the examination of economic change it is important to distinguish between an independent variable initiating the change and the expansion of dependent economic activity which is induced by the "carrier" industry. This distinction is undoubtedly more difficult to make today than it was before 1860, when transport barriers and distinct patterns of regional specialization and internal trade all pointed to the strategic role of cotton. Direct income from the cotton trade was probably no more than 6 per cent of any plausible estimate of national

---

[11] The term is Rutledge Vining's. See his article, "Location of Industry and Regional Patterns of Business Cycle Behavior," *Econometrica* XIV (January 1946), 37–68.

income which we might employ,[12] but when income from cotton exports, including shipments to textile mills in our own Northeast, grew from $25 million in 1831 to $70 million in 1836, it set in motion the whole process of accelerated expansion which culminated in 1839.[13] Certainly the views of contemporaries, northern observers as well as southerners, support the position that in this period cotton was indeed king.

The cotton trade remained an important influence upon the economy until 1860, but its role declined in relative importance after the boom and depression that followed 1839. It is not that income from cotton did not grow. On the contrary, the 1850's represented another prosperous era, though not as wildly speculative as former ones, in which the value of the cotton trade exceeded any former period. However, a major consequence of the expansive period of the 1830's was the creation of conditions that made possible industrialization in the Northeast. Transport facilities developed to connect the East and West more efficiently; a new market for western staples developed in the rapidly urbanizing East and, sporadically, in Europe. The dependence of both the Northeast and the West on the South waned.[14] The discovery of gold in California in 1848 created a third source of expansion outside the South. The Far West was not only a major market for the goods and services of the Northeast, but its one export, gold, played a vital role in the whole expansion of the 1850's.

It should not be forgotten that the United States expansion was taking place within the larger context of the Atlantic economy. While the demand for cotton in England and to a lesser extent in France played perhaps the most prominent part, the terms of trade, relative price levels here and abroad, the movement of productive factors, and the flow of ideas, particularly technological information, were all a part of the interrelated pattern of development.

Throughout the whole period the secular movement of the terms of trade became increasingly favorable. In the expansive surges of 1815–1818 and 1832–1839 they became very favorable, reflecting a rapid rise in the price of American exports. In these two periods, it was cotton that accounted for the rise and appeared to initiate the sub-

---

[12] However, if we took into account the income generated in the course of transport, financing, and marketing cotton (that is, the directly dependent industries) it would be significantly greater.

[13] And the era of depressed prices in the 1820's had an equally depressing effect on economic activity in that decade.

[14] The most striking evidence of the changing role of cotton is provided by its role in cyclical turning points. While cotton set the pace in the booms and depressions of 1815–1823 and 1823–1843, it lagged a full two years behind the recovery that began in 1843 and was clearly not a major influence in the cyclical downturn of 1857. In fact, the South was relatively unaffected by that depression.

sequent flow of capital in response to the increased profitability of opening up and developing new sources of supply of the export staple and western foodstuffs.[15] The consequent divergence of domestic and foreign price levels, and the increase in imports and specie movements, determined the timing of cyclical movements. Attractive employment opportunities during these surges of expansion were the pull which brought immigrants to American shores in increasing numbers.

Expansion in the 1850's, unlike that of the two previous booms, was not preceded by favorable movements of the terms of trade—instead it was the domestic price level which began to rise before the export price index. Cotton played a part in the boom, but it was industrialization in the Northeast and the opening up of the West and Far West which were primarily responsible for the growth of the 1840's and 1850's. The influence of the international economy was felt less in the flow of capital than in the flow of people with the first big wave of immigration coming in this period.

The foregoing summary has emphasized surges in growth followed by periods of depression, then gradual expansion preceding still another boom. The explanation of these long swings is that these movements are initiated by the movement of prices in the key "carrier" industries. Shifts in supply and demand result in a shift of resources into these areas in periods of rising prices. There is concomitant expansion in the wide variety of subsidiary, complementary, and residentiary activities whose fortunes are tied to the growth of the "carrier" industries and to the rise in income that is initiated by these surges of expansion. The process is a lengthy and cumulative one, ultimately overlayed with speculative excesses; the tremendous expansion in supply results in a painful period of declining prices and readjustment. In the first two expansive periods analyzed here, 1815 to 1818 and 1832 to 1839, cotton was the key industry in both the boom and the subsequent collapse and readjustment. In the last period the sources of expansion are more diffuse, but grain in the West played the most important role.

Underlying the uneven pattern of development were the shape of the supply curve of cotton (or grain) and the way in which the supply curve shifted. During each period of expansion, millions of acres of new land were purchased from the government for cotton production. Once this land had been cleared and a crop or two of corn planted to prepare the soil, the amount of cotton available could be substantially increased, and the supply curve of cotton shifted very sharply to the right. With the depressed cotton prices that followed such expansion,

[15] This argument is elaborated in my article, "International Capital Flows and the Development of the American West," *Journal of Economic History* XVI, No. 4 (December 1956), 493–505.

a good deal of this land was devoted to alternative uses. For the most part, it was put to crop and livestock use to feed slaves and reduce the costs of purchasing foodstuffs. In effect, it represented unused capacity with respect to cotton, and any slight increase in cotton prices could and did lead to shifting some of this land into cotton. In the old South, where slaves as such were an important intermediate good, this was clearly a rational redirection of resources during periods of depressed prices. . . . The supply curve of cotton . . . was highly elastic over a range of output which included all the available land that had been cleared and readied for crop production and was suitable for cotton. Even with the rapid growth in demand that characterized the cotton textile industry in the first half of the nineteenth century, it took a decade for demand to shift to the right sufficiently to absorb this potential supply. During this decade very little new land was sold in the cotton states, and the expansion of potential capacity was at a much slower rate than during the previous boom. When the growth of demand for cotton finally brought all this potential capacity into production, a further increase in demand resulted in substantial price increases as the supply curve became increasingly inelastic. With the readily available cotton land already in production, higher prices brought forth little additional production in the short run.

While there had been little incentive to buy and clear new land for cotton during the period of low prices, rising prices triggered a land boom in the new South. Millions of acres of virgin land were sold; planters and their slaves migrated in large numbers to open up and exploit the rich land in the Southwest—Alabama, Louisiana, Mississippi, and Arkansas were the major states. A lengthy period intervened between the initial impetus from rising prices and substantial output increases for putting this land into production. While imperfections in the capital market and land speculation partially explain this delay, the more important reasons were the time it took to obtain slaves from the old South, clear the land, and plant a crop or two of corn to prepare the soil. . . . In the five [newly important] cotton states [Alabama, Arkansas, Mississippi, Florida, and Louisiana] there was a lag of approximately four years between the peak in land sales and a large increase in cotton production. The consequence was a vast shift to the right in the supply curve of cotton and the beginning of a new period of depressed prices. Cotton output actually fell as some of this land was diverted into corn with the low cotton prices that prevailed after 1839.

In the West, the same general pattern prevailed with respect to wheat and corn. Land sales in the western states paralleled the prices of those staples, with one important difference. Little transportation or other social overhead investment was necessary to increase the supply of cotton in the South. In the West, transportation was the major limiting factor in increasing supply. The accessible lands close to water transportation were taken up first. Initially, the rise in prices brought into cultivation land further and further from cheap transportation. As a result, the supply curve of wheat and corn land was probably less inelastic than cotton as it began to slope upward. However, it also encouraged a boom in land sales and at the same time a growing agitation for large-scale investment in new transportation facilities. Canal and railroad building was a lengthy process, but a completed canal or railroad opened up large amounts of new land. The canal construction era of the 1830's and the railroad construction period of the 1850's each served to make possible, along with the land sales and influx of settlers that accompanied them, a large shift to the right in wheat and corn supplies, with much the same results as cotton.

. . . . .

12

The National Economy in 1860

by

GEORGE R. TAYLOR

RESOURCES AND EXTRACTIVE INDUSTRIES

Between 1815 and 1860 Florida, Texas, and the Far West were added to the territorial possessions of the United States, with a resulting increase in area of 1,307,000 square miles or about 76 per cent. Though significant for the future, the addition of this vast area had a relatively small influence on American industrial development before 1860. Some trade and agricultural activity appeared, and the discovery of gold in California in 1848 led to the rapid settlement of that region. But for the most part this newer territory remained but sparsely populated and largely unexploited until later in the century.

According to the census of 1860, the total population of the United States had reached 31,443,321, with 19,690,000 accredited to the North;

Reprinted from *The Transportation Revolution, 1815–1860*, by George Rogers Taylor (pp. 384–98, with omissions), copyright © 1951 by George Rogers Taylor. Reprinted by permission of the author and publishers, Holt, Rinehart and Winston, Inc.

11,133,361 to the South; and only 619,000 to the West.[1] Of every seven persons, one was a Negro and one was of foreign birth. Immigration, which had been small in the generation ending with the War of 1812, grew rapidly thereafter. More than 5,000,000 entered between 1819 and 1860, and of these more than half arrived during the fifties. Over one half of the immigrants came from Great Britain and Ireland, and about one third from Germany.

Resources in one extractive industry, fur trading and trapping, had been so fully exploited that the product had actually begun to decline. . . . Expanding settlement and destructive methods tended to reduce the supply, and, at the same time, there appeared seriously unfavorable demand developments. During the thirties the market fell off sharply as silk came to be preferred for hats. Also nutria, chiefly South American, became more fashionable than muskrat fur.

On the Great Plains the vast herds of bison afforded an increasing source of hides. Only small amounts of meat were salvaged. By the 1840's hundreds of thousands were being slain annually; 800,000 was the contemporary estimate for the 1859–1860 season. They were so numerous—the total number was estimated at 15,000,000—that this tremendous slaughter continued for two decades after 1860 before the herds were largely killed off.

Fishing, an activity even older than the fur trade, experienced a vigorous growth in the decades following the War of 1812. Expanding domestic markets took an increasing portion of the enlarged catch, and foreign markets, especially those of the West Indies, absorbed surpluses at advantageous prices. As in earlier years, the codfisheries remained most important. But productive new fisheries—mackerel, herring, halibut, and lobster—were added. The catch was taken chiefly off the coast of New England and the Maritime Provinces by Americans from fishing towns and villages scattered along the coast from Long Island Sound to Maine. . . .

Whaling grew phenomenally after 1812, and in some years its value product may have been about equal to that for the rest of the fishing industry. The demand for the products of this sea mammal, especially for illuminating oil, seemed insatiable. Whalers from the ports of New York and New England pursued their quarry to the remotest seas, with the result that the United States became the main producer of whale bone and oil. Whaling gave employment to more than 12,000 men in 1860. Over one half of these workers had their homes in New Bedford, the chief center of the industry.

---

[1] As in 1940 Census: North includes New England, Middle Atlantic, East and West North Central; South includes South Atlantic, East and West South Central; West, Mountain and Pacific states.

The total value of the product of American fisheries cannot be determined with any close degree of accuracy. . . . At any rate, the contribution of this industry to the national product appears to have been small, amounting to appreciably less than half that from either mining or lumbering.

Mineral production, which, just before the Civil War, stood on the threshold of its period of phenomenal growth, had made only a very small beginning in 1815. From early colonial times iron had been produced in small quantities in many places along the eastern seaboard. By 1860 this was still true, but more than half of the output now came from Pennsylvania, and production in the Ohio and Cumberland valleys was becoming especially important. Development of the rich ores of the Lake Superior region benefited from the opening of the St. Marys Canal in 1855. By 1860 ore from the lake region accounted for almost one tenth of total pig iron production in the United States.

Like iron, copper production had remained relatively small-scale and came from widely scattered deposits. But during the fifties output was considerably increased, both from the Ducktown district on the border where Tennessee joins Georgia and also from the fabulously rich mines of the Upper Peninsula of Michigan. Exploitation of this latter field began in the early 1840's but did not at first become profitable despite the uncovering of rich deposits. During the next decade, however, with the aid of Boston and Pittsburgh investors, Michigan mines showed handsome profits and by 1860 accounted for three fourths of the total national product.

Small quantities of lead had long been produced in the Missouri and the Wisconsin tristate areas. Following 1815 the output from the latter, often referred to as the Galena district, expanded considerably, reaching its maximum in the period 1845–1850. Thereafter output declined as the deposit of easily available ore became exhausted. The output from these two areas was valued at around $1,500,000 annually for the years 1845–1847. Small quantities of gold had been mined in the southern Appalachians before the discovery of the metal in California in 1848. Following that year, the California output grew so rapidly that during the fifties gold became the most valuable mineral product of the United States. In 1857 the output of the California mines was valued at nearly $50,000,000.

The existence of vast coal beds in the United States was known in the early national period and even before, but their exploitation awaited the development of cheap transportation and improvements in the technique of their use. Both of these difficulties were sufficiently overcome by the second quarter of the century as to permit a rapid extension of coal mining. For bituminous the chief development came in the mines of the Pittsburgh area, which greatly increased their output to meet the growing needs of the Ohio River Valley. As soon as canals and railroads brought the anthracite of northeastern Pennsylvania to tidewater, this fuel came rapidly into extensive use in the chief coastal cities, both for heating homes and for industrial use. By 1860 the coal production of the United States was valued at $20,000,000, and the great era of coal production had begun. In only twenty years after that date it had increased by about 400 per cent.

. . . . .

Lumber production was more than fourteen times greater in 1859 than it had been in 1819. Despite generations of exploitation, during which millions of acres of forest had been burned merely to clear the land for farming, much lumber was still being produced in 1860 in such older states as Connecticut, New York, and Pennsylvania. The census for that year shows the two last states as responsible for about one fourth of the total lumber output. Though regarded as an old lumbering area, the vast forests of Maine were far from exhaustion in 1860, and the industry was just entering upon its great period of rapid growth in Michigan, Wisconsin, and Minnesota. . . . By 1860 the output of Wisconsin forests had become so great that Chicago had become the greatest lumber center in the world. From as far north as the St. Croix River tremendous rafts of lumber and logs were being floated down the Mississippi to St. Louis. From southern forests hard pine and cypress shingles moved in growing quantities to northern markets, but the great period of southern exploitation was still to come. By the census referred to above, the gross value of lumber produced in the United States exceeded $100,000,000. In terms of hands employed, as well as value of product, it was, although much less important than agriculture, next to it the leading extractive industry of the United States.

URBANIZATION

It has often been noted that the rapidity of western settlement and the development of western agriculture reflected the revolutionary improvements in transportation . . . But with attention firmly focused on the western movement, students have tended to overlook the fact that this was the period in American history of the most rapid urbanization. Basic to this city growth was the increasing production of the expanding West and the growing specialization and exchange made possible by improved methods of transportation and communication.

. . . The proportion of the population living in cities (that is, places of 2,500 or more) was only 6.1 per cent in 1820, and there had been little change since the census of 1810. But from this time on until the Civil War, the cities grew at a more rapid rate than ever before or since in United States history. By 1860 close to 20 per cent of the population were city dwellers. In the forty years between 1820 and 1860 the total population of the United States rose by 226 per cent, but the proportion living in cities increased by 797 per cent. The most rapid urbanization took place in the two decades preceding the Civil War. Total population increased 35.9 per cent during the forties and 35.6 per cent in the fifties; during the same decades urban population grew 92.1 per cent and 75.4 per cent, respectively. In 1820, only 12 cities had a population exceeding 10,000 and only 2 were greater than 100,000. Forty years later, in 1860, 101 cities exceeded 10,000, 8 exceeded 100,000, and New York had passed 1,000,000.

The fifteen cities exceeding 50,000 in population, according to the census of 1860, are shown in [Table 1]. These cities, like those in 1820, owed their pre-eminence chiefly to the demands of commerce. The five largest cities in order of size were, as in 1820, the great seaports of New York, Philadelphia, Baltimore, Boston, and New Orleans. Each had benefited not only from the increase of foreign trade, but especially from the greatly increased domestic flow of goods which now moved coastwise and by river, canal, and railroad. Of the next seven cities in order of rank, only Newark was chiefly important as a seaport; all the others owed their growth in large part to the development of com-

TABLE 1

THE LEADING CITIES IN 1860

Rank in Order of Population	Name of City	Population	Percentage Engaged in Manufacture
1	New York	1,080,330	9.5
2	Philadelphia	565,529	17.5
3	Baltimore	212,418	8.0
4	Boston	177,840	10.8
5	New Orleans	168,675	3.0
6	Cincinnati	161,044	18.3
7	St. Louis	160,773	5.8
8	Chicago	109,260	4.9
9	Buffalo	81,129	6.9
10	Newark	71,941	26.2
11	Louisville	68,033	9.8
12	Albany	62,367	9.3
13	Washington	61,122	3.9
14	San Francisco	56,802	2.6
15	Providence	50,666	22.0

Source: *Eighth Census of the United States: Mortality and Miscellaneous Statistics,* p. xviii.

merce by river, canal, or lake, although for each the railroad rapidly began to play a major role.

By 1860 the great era of the industrial city had not yet arrived. However, manufacturing had already become a factor in urban growth and cannot be entirely ignored. New Orleans stands out as the one very large city which was almost completely commercial. Only 3 per cent of its total population was engaged in manufactures in 1860. In New York and Boston 10 and 11 per cent, respectively, of the population were so engaged. Two of the greatest commercial cities—Philadelphia with 17 per cent employed in manufactures, and Cincinnati with 18 per cent—owed their importance almost as much to industry as to commerce. Finally, predominantly manufacturing cities were already appearing with the comparable percentages running 26 for Newark, 36 for Lowell, and 45 for Lynn. Lynn was the smallest of these, with a population of 19,083. These were the forerunners of the industrial cities of a later period.

. . . . .

THE GROWTH OF WEALTH AND INCOME

Every record of the years from 1815 to 1860 testifies to the tremendous increase in national wealth, not only in terms of the annual volume of consumption goods and services produced, but also in the unprecedented additions to capital equipment—in roads, canals, ships and steamboats, railroads, factories, and machines. Unfortunately, accurate measurement of this growth in wealth and income is rendered impossible by the lack of adequate statistical records. Yet on the basis of the data available, estimates have been made which, although subject to substantial error, are worthy of brief notice.

A study which includes only the taxable value of property—and hence probably involves considerable understatement—indicates that national wealth, as so measured, rose from $3,273,000 in 1825 to $16,-160,000 in 1860, or nearly 400 per cent. Estimates for total realized national income show about the same percentage advance. Adjusted for changes in the general price level, they indicate that the average per capita income rose from $168 in 1819 to $300 in 1860. As 1819 was a year of deep depression, it may perhaps be roughly estimated that per capita real income in dollars of constant purchasing power rose by about 50 per cent from 1815 to 1860. About all that can be said as to the reliability of this figure is that, on the basis of what is generally known about the period, the estimate appears fairly plausible.

It would be interesting to know how the increased average per capita income was divided among different occupations and economic groups. According to [one] study, real wages increased nearly 40 per cent from 1820 to 1860. If this is compared with the 50 per cent rise in average per capita income, the implication is that wage earners shared somewhat less than proportionally in the increased income. But the statistical series is not sufficiently reliable to warrant confidence on this point, nor is general descriptive material available such as to justify confident generalization in this respect.

Certainly within the wage earning class marked variations appeared in the extent of the benefit received by different groups. The very poor, the paupers, and the handicapped appear to have been as badly off at the end of the period as they were at the beginning, and there were more of them—possibly even proportionally more—in part, at least, because of the heavy influx of immigrants during the fifties. At least the conditions of urban poverty . . . indicate that many on the lowest rungs of the economic ladder did not benefit from the increased productivity of the peroid. Some skilled craftsmen, like the hand-loom weavers, actually experienced a degradation of their living conditions as they found themselves forced to compete with the machine or to accept factory employment. On the other hand, workers who possessed mechanical skills—skilled metalworkers, tool makers, and those in the building trades—the demand for whose services expanded rapidly, appear to have gained more than other workmen.

Without attempting to deal with the extremely difficult problem of the extent to which agriculture shared in the gains of the transportation revolution, the question remains as to how the businessmen, the urban owners and managers of enterprises, fared. Two mutually reinforcing circumstances led to the rapid development of the role of the entrepreneur. In the first place, the transportation revolution and the beginnings of the industrial revolution in the relatively undeveloped economy opened up unique opportunities for risk taking and profit. And in the second place, Americans of that age, especially those in the northern states, met the rapidly developing opportunities for material gain with unusual energy and enthusiasm. The spirit of adventure, aggressiveness, and willingness to make sacrifices in the hope of economic advantage, which characterized American merchants in the foreign trade and drove settlers to develop the West so rapidly despite all obstacles and uncertainties, also dominated the businessmen who played so active a part in planning, organizing, financing, and managing new ventures in transporting and manufacturing goods.

The indications seem clear that this entrepreneurial group at least retained its proportionate share, and probably more, of the increase in wealth and income. It must not be forgotten, however, that risks were great and that there were many failures, especially during the recurrent financial crises. How far such business losses offset the gains is impossible to say, but certain it is, at least, that the number of wealthy men increased greatly between 1815 and 1860. By the close of the War of 1812 two men, Stephen Girard and John Jacob Astor, had already accumulated great wealth. Possibly there were three or four others like William Gray of Boston who could be regarded as millionaires in that they owned property valued at $1,000,000 or more. Girard's estate was valued in 1831 at about $8,000,000, Astor's in 1848 at more than $20,000,000.

According to a contemporary estimate, New York had 14 millionaires in 1846, 19 persons with property worth $500,000, and 137 whose wealth was estimated to reach at least $250,000. By 1855 the number of millionaires in New York had risen to 20. Three years later, 25 were claimed for Philadelphia. For Boston, 18 had been reported in 1850. Foreign trade and land speculation appear to have supplied the foundation for most of this wealth, but banking and manufacturing were increasingly important.

The well-to-do businessmen of the northern cities, like the great planters in the slave states, constituted the most powerful class in the community. And business success, never lightly regarded in the commercial centers of the North, became more than ever the prize sought by the able and ambitious. The leading merchants of the colonial period had often been men of broad culture and superior education. Many took an interest in politics and held important governmental positions. This became less true in the early national period after about 1810, as position and success came to be measured more and more by a purely monetary standard. Fewer of the business elite than ever before had more than an elementary education, and among some, at least, the feeling developed that it was hardly necessary for success. And the direct participation of businessmen in politics declined sharply.

Between 1815 and 1860 it was apparently somewhat easier than in earlier decades for farmers and laborers to rise in business to positions of wealth. Apprentices, those with little or no schooling, and those with only an elementary education, stood a better chance of business success than at any time before or since in American history. Yet, although this was true in a relative sense, the majority of successful businessmen continued to come from families ranking in the upper- and upper middle-income groups and from the sons of fathers who were business or professional men or government servants. It was still true, as C. Wright Mills has observed, that "the best statistical chance of becoming a member of the business elite . . . [was] to be born into it."[2]

---

[2] C. Wright Mills, "The American Business Elite: A Collective Portrait," *Tasks of Economic History* (December, 1945), p. 29.

A NATIONAL ECONOMY

By 1860 the colonial orientation of the American economy . . . had disappeared, and a national economy had taken its place. No longer were more than nine tenths of American agriculture and industry concentrated within a narrow strip extending no farther inland than a hundred miles from the Atlantic coast, nor was dependence upon foreign trade and European markets the almost universal characteristic of the economy. The changes described in the previous chapters, especially those of the transportation revolution, had resulted in the creation of a new and really national economic orientation.

It is true that London was still the financial capital of the world and that America still looked to Great Britain for large extensions of credit. Nevertheless, domestic sources of capital had expanded rapidly, and eastern merchants, although often still dependent on foreign capital, were increasingly able to assume the burden of granting the long credits still customary in domestic commerce. Even in foreign trade, American importers and exporters were beginning to compete on more nearly equal terms with British merchants.

Although foreign commerce had grown tremendously . . . it had become largely overshadowed by the domestic trade. The great export staples, cotton and tobacco, were still sent abroad in tremendous quantities, and wheat exports, which had declined after the years immediately following the War of 1812, were again rising to renewed importance in the fifties. But the extreme dependence on foreign markets for disposing of American wheat and tobacco had been greatly reduced. This followed not only from the increasing diversification of American agriculture and industry but also from the tremendously expanded home market for domestic products. Early in the period, home consumption had absorbed a very large part of the wheat production and, despite the greatly expanded tobacco output during the fifties, more than half of that crop was consumed in the United States.

Even for cotton, the exports of which grew so tremendously that this one product may be said to have dominated foreign trade, two developments must be noted. First, though just before the Civil War Great Britain was still absorbing more than half of the United States cotton crop and only about one fourth of the total production was being taken by American factories, American consumption, which had been annually under 100,000 bales until 1823, had risen to about 1,000,000 bales by the end of the fifties. Second, the financing and marketing of this staple had been taken over more and more by New York businessmen. So, although the South with its continued dependence upon cotton monoculture retained an economy of the colonial type, it did so increasingly as a part of the larger national economy of the United States.

The growth of domestic commerce had contributed to the decline of merchant capitalism, possibly already past its zenith in 1815, and by 1860 the organization of both foreign and domestic trade had reached a degree of specialization and a country-wide integration typical of modern national economies. Banking and finance had become a separate calling which was further differentiated with the rise of commercial banks, savings banks, insurance companies, note brokers, clearinghouses, and stock exchanges. With the rise of factories, manufacturing had become separated from marketing, and with the transportation revolution the actual moving of goods in foreign and domestic trade had become largely the responsibility of common carriers. Those who actually traded in goods, whether foreign or domestic, had also become highly specialized operators. Among those were the wholesale merchants who bought and sold goods in large quantities for their own account, and whose business had benefited from the decline of the auctions after the 1820's; commission merchants or factors often specializing in a particular product and buying and selling goods for others; brokers who did not actually receive the goods at all but brought buyer and seller together; and retailers, both those who had specialty shops in the large cities and those much more typical the country over who sold to consumers almost every conceivable product and service.

New York had firmly established itself as the great distributing center of the nation for both domestic and foreign goods. Here, centered in Pearl Street, were the jobbers and wholesalers to whose establishments came by coastwise vessel and railroad train country retailers from the South and West. Traveling salesmen, though increasing rapidly, were as yet relatively few in number. Retailers and wholesalers flocking to the metropolis on the Hudson divided their time between visiting the countinghouses to buy supplies for the coming season and enjoying a holiday in the big city. But not all storekeepers could afford an annual trip to New York. So regional jobbing centers grew rapidly, especially in the decade preceding 1860, with places like Augusta, Memphis, and Louisville in the South, and Cincinnati, St. Louis, and Chicago in the West, becoming of increasing importance. Certain cities became trading centers for particular commodities and developed highly specialized marketing procedures. Thus, by 1860 cotton was sold by sample in New York and New Orleans, and tremendous quantities of grain changed hands in Chicago and Buffalo merely on the basis of recognized grades. Boston had become the leading wool market of the country, St. Louis led in the marketing of furs, while Chicago and Albany were the leading marts for lumber.

This emerging national economy of 1860 had a new orientation. The great cities of the East no longer faced the sea and gave their chief attention to shipping and foreign trade. Their commerce centered increasingly now at the railroad stations rather than at the docks, and the commercial news from Mobile, Memphis, Louisville, Cleveland, and Chicago was awaited with greater interest than that from Liverpool, Marseilles, or Antwerp. But though the American economy now faced the rapidly developing West, the leadership and the organizing genius remained concentrated in the great eastern cities. There, on Wall Street, State Street, and Broad Street, the leaders of the emerging era of finance capitalism were beginning to appear. By means of well-placed investments, by speculation and manipulation on the stock and produce exchanges, and by membership on the boards of directors of banks, insurance companies, cotton mills, and railroads, these rising entrepreneurs, the successors of the older sedentary merchants, were soon to play the directing role in the emerging national economy of stocks and bonds and debentures.

13

Income Growth and Structural Change

by

ALFRED H. CONRAD

... *The great mass of nations is neither rich nor gay: they whose aggregate constitutes the people, are found in the streets, and the villages, in the shops and farms; and from them collectively considered, must the measure of general prosperity be taken. As they approach to delicacy a nation is refined, as their conveniences are multiplied, a nation, at least a commercial nation, must be denominated wealthy.*

—SAMUEL JOHNSON

. . . . .

I

The transformation of the American economy that took place during the nineteenth century was great enough to loom large in even the most impressionistic account of the period. But impressionism in economic history is not explanation. We know why salt meat, which would have seemed a daily luxury to the British laborer, seems coarse today. Economic history ought to tell us more than that, however; we should be able to say how we have approached this level of consumption. With the mass of data that has been turned out as a by-product of the industrial system and the flood of theories by which we try to explain ourselves, we ought to be able to describe more convincingly, if less colorfully than earlier historians, the process by which the conveniences of the American people were multiplied in the last century and a half. This chapter will attempt, therefore, to go beyond—or behind—the net prod-

Reprinted by permission from *American Economic History*, edited by Seymour E. Harris (pp. 26–60, with omissions). Copyright, 1961. McGraw-Hill Book Company, Inc.

uct indices. An index of income growth, even one much better than what we have for most of the period, is not a history of income. We want to show the factors—economic and noneconomic, if the reader has a taste for parochial taxonomy—that determined the rate of growth of income. For an explanation, we shall borrow heavily from theories of economic development that explain sudden jumps in the rate of growth as the results of sharp changes in the structure of the economy. The classic among these theories is Professor Schumpeter's hypothesis that innovation is the driving force of economic development. Innovations are not simply inventions or new products, for the innovation is a structural change that destroys old profitabilities (for firms, industries, and perhaps even regions), introduces new industrial interrelationships, and lifts the economy as a whole to new levels of output and of productive efficiency. The structural change may be institutional or organizational; it may be a series of corporate mergers or a major shift in the pattern of population movements to the frontier.

. . . . .

II

If we take the multiplication of conveniences as our criterion, then the growth of net national product provides a quantitative summary of the transformation of the economy. For roughly half the period of United States national history, that is, from 1869 to the present, the data on net product are continuous and, within the limits of the concept, comprehensive. For the first half, from 1780 to the Civil War decade, the data are patchy and incomplete and, where available, suspect, at best. What does this evidence show?

For the early period, before 1869, the only continuous national income estimates in constant prices are in the series compiled by Robert F. Martin. (The estimates, unfortunately, are probably not much better than crude impressions dignified by a show of numerical exactness.) . . . Martin's figures show an eightfold growth of real net income (in prices of 1926), from $1.1 billion in 1799 to $9 billion in 1869. But real income per capita increased from $216 in 1799 to only $237 in 1869, a percentage change of barely 10 per cent over a period of seventy years. For the first three decades, from 1799 to 1829, he shows a decline of 24 per cent in the income-per-head series, and it was not until 1849 that the rise was sufficient to carry past the initial-year level.

It will be argued in this chapter that the decade of the forties was the first upsurge in the process of industrialization in the American system. In a recent statement by Raymond Goldsmith before the Joint Economic Committee, 1839 or some date "not very long before 1839" was offered as the break in the trend of growth of real net product per capita. Since that year, he estimates, real income per head has grown at an annual rate of 1⅝ per cent. It would require evidence of implausibly low living standards in the eighteenth century to support the argument that incomes were rising at a rate of even 1 per cent for sustained periods before 1839. Goldsmith's guess for the average rate of growth from the mid-eighteenth century to 1839 is not above ½ per cent per year. It is hardly credible that there was a real worsening of living standards over the first third of the century, as Martin has stated. The impressionistic contemporary accounts of Harriet Martineau and Alexis de Tocqueville give no evidence that the country was going through a decline in living standards, much less do they speak of any changes in distribution unfavorable to the mass of the nation. On the other side, however, Professor Schumpeter characterized this period, to 1840, as the downswing of a long Kondratieff cycle, a period of absorption and derivative development rather than of strong, sustained growth. There were two severe commercial crises, both of which may have been primarily speculative and financial in origin but which had strong disruptive effects, especially upon the young industrial sectors. . . . There is some indication, then, that the first third of the century was a sluggish period in which the level of aggregate income may not have grown much faster than the population that produced it. The growth of population, 223 per cent from the turn of the century to 1839, is of course evidence of growth, but it hardly compares with the signs of development in the next forty years.

. . . . .

In spite of the extreme paucity of good data for the period, it may be useful to consider a suggestive theoretical view of the beginning of the century. In Schumpeterian terms, especially as extended by the work of the Swedish historian Erik Dahmén, the otherwise surprisingly low rate of per capita income growth would be typical of a period of industrial preparation. From that point of view, the first three decades of this history appear to have been a period in which structural tensions and disparities among the rates of development in different industries made a kind of breathing spell. This pause—an "incomplete development block"—was broken, initially and tentatively, by the canals and then, in the forties, by the great surge of industrial change set off by railroad expansion. Eastern industrial progress had been carried forward almost to the limit that water power, however efficient, could permit; its further progress, to be based largely upon steam power, waited for the supply of cheap coal. The availability of coal, in turn, waited upon the great transportation innovations of the fourth and fifth decades of the century. Similarly, the now-classic Schumpeterian description of conflict between the "new" and the "old" seems to fit the two major crises of the period. In each decline, but especially in the first, the panic came on the heels of an aggressive period of dumping by English merchants; after each, but especially after the second, the panic was followed by a period of rapid technological change and capital development. Finally, the conflict between Chestnut Street in Philadelphia and Wall Street in New York characterized the financial confusions and tensions from the last years of the Second Bank of the United States to the downturn of 1837. These lags and structural imbalances add some preliminary support to the impression given by admittedly imperfect statistical evidence. Later, in [section 4], we shall examine the structural changes in detail.

For the period since 1869, we are the beneficiaries of Professor Kuznets' massive researches on the net national product. From the decade 1869–1878 to the recent five years 1950–1954, his data indicate a rise in net national product, at 1929 prices, from $9.5 billion to $142.7 billion (annual averages), that is, an average rate of change of more than 4 per cent yer pear. During the same period, population rose from 44.6 million persons to 157.5 million, an increase of about 350 per cent. Real per capita product, therefore, increased more than four times, from $213 to $906 (in 1929 prices), an annual rate of change of 2 per cent. But the range about these averages is extremely wide, and the short-run details are therefore more interesting for the history of United States economic growth than is the single long-run index of change.

There were two periods of accelerated growth during the last part of the nineteenth century. The first and more dramatic surge took place in the two decades after the Civil War. Recall that this was a period generally characterized by the severe panic of 1873 and the long depression to 1879 and by the outcries of Greenback and silver agitation. From the minor contraction in 1869–1870 to the uncertain peak in 1881–1883, the average annual rate of growth was approximately 9 per cent. (The span, starting and ending at opposite phases of the business cycle, imparts some upward bias to the rate.) The remarkable aspect of the seventies is the continued growth in output, while the fall of prices and the level of unemployment dominated the commercial sense of the period. Average real net product in the decade 1874–1883 increased by almost 46 per cent over the average for 1869–1878. The national product in 1929 prices rose from $7 billion in 1869 to $14 billion in 1879; by 1884, it had passed $18 billion.

The second burst of development came as the economy recovered from the financial crisis of 1893. By the turn of the century, another upsurge was under way, less rapid than the first, but clearly different from any of the cyclical recoveries in the intervening period and more rapid than anything we have experienced since that time. The rate of growth between the decade averages for 1889–1898 and 1899–1908 was almost 6 per cent per year. From 1894 to 1903, national product grew from $22 billion to $37.7 billion, in 1929 prices. The per capita increase was 5 per cent per year in the first spurt and 3 per cent per year in the second; in between, it fell as low as 0.9 per cent in the late eighties and early nineties. These, then, were the second and third break-throughs in the process of industrialization, periods of advanced and structural change in which net product moved ahead much more rapidly than did population.

The rate of growth fell off sharply at the end of the first decade of this century and began to recover, though somewhat uncertainly, in the years of the World War. The spectacular rise in the twenties and the after-math, in which income fell sufficiently to give a negative rate of change for the interval 1924–1933 to 1929–1938, are sufficiently close to us in time to make detailed consideration here unnecessary. Quite apart from the experience of the Great Depression, there is some indication that the rate of growth has been declining since the post-Civil War decades of the nineteenth century. Professor Kuznets' data show a decline in the percentage change per decade in both national product and national product per capita since 1869. In the interval from the end of the Civil War to the eve of the World War, the average decadal rate of growth in the two indices was 56 per cent and 27.5 per cent, respectively. Be-tween the periods 1894–1903 and 1950–1954, the decade averages were 33.8 per cent and 16.4 per cent. But these long averages tell us very little, after all. It is extremely difficult to say now whether or not the de-pression years will continue to dominate the recent statistical picture for very long. The long postwar boom has not been sufficient to overcome the impression of secular decline in the growth rate.

In this chapter we shall concentrate upon an attempt to explain his-torically the three great surges of industrial growth during the nineteenth century.

III

What we have found, then, is a long period of sustained growth, punc-tuated by three sharp drives upward. During the process of industrializa-tion, the output series showed sudden discontinuities in the early forties, the seventies, and the late nineties. It is not entirely clear that the break identified here in the seventies is really distinct from the sustained push that began in the forties. However, since the Civil War decade did constitute a complete disruption and reorganization in the economy, it will be worthwhile, at least initially, to study the two periods separately.

.   .   .   .   .

This [Selection] was conceived as an attempt to explain historically the evolution of American living standards. The research was guided by the expectation that major variations in the rate of growth of national income could be explained by changes in the structure of the economy. *Structure* in this context refers to the technological and organizational relationships that determine how the system will respond to variations from outside itself, to population change, perhaps, or to the assumption of new responsibilities by the government. In more rigorous terms, the structure discussed in this chapter is the given part of a theory of income generation—that is, the fixed terms that define the relationship between income and the outside, or exogenous variables. If we think in terms of formal relationships, the structure may be defined by the numerical values of the constants in the familiar multiplier-accelerator equations (i.e., the parameters).

In multiplier-accelerator models of income growth there is a two-way relationship between investment and income. Increases in the production of goods and services can be achieved only with appropriate increases in the stock of capital equipment, given "the" capital-output ratio. Therefore, income changes will determine (in part) the required level of investment. On the other hand, investment in excess of intended saving will, via the multiplier process, cause further, magnified increases in the level of income. Within this capital-adjustment process, autonomous investment—that is, investment which is not simply called for by the growth of income—and other long-term exogenous developments, such as population growth and technological change, can set off and, if they are at all continuous, possibly maintain the growth of income. Now, in this context, structural changes will be looked upon as once-over developments that affect the way in which the economy's capital-adjustment process responds to the autonomous shocks or long-run developments. Following Professor Dusenberry, we shall list the most important changes, indicating in what way each will affect the income growth rate.

1. Increases in the propensity to consume (once the industrial growth process has begun and the system has advanced beyond near-zero saving ratios) or decreases in the lag between income and consumption will cause the rate of growth to rise. In the United States the initial relatively high degree of equality of income shares and later improvements in the payments mechanism were among the possibilities that operated in this direction.

2. A rise in the dividend pay-out ratio and, *a fortiori*, any development

that causes a reduction in the use of retained earnings (that is, an increase in borrowed funds) for investment will *cet. par.* cause the growth rate to increase.

3. A change in the rate of return will have a favorable effect on the marginal efficiency of capital; if it does not arise from a decrease in competition and limits on the entry of new firms, the change is almost certain to be fully favorable to more rapid growth of investment.

4. Improvements in techniques in the investment-funds markets, which were crucial through much of the nineteenth-century history, will cause both capital and income to respond more rapidly to outside changes.

5. Technological changes that increase the capital intensity of the economy will obviously heighten the response of the accelerator mechanism; to the extent that the innovations are financed by borrowing—and this is the Schumpeterian argument—the effect will be in the direction of even greater buoyancy. The nineteenth century of this economy is punctuated by a series of developments, within industries and among industries, that increased the capital intensity of the productive process.

6. It is simple enough to state that government expenditure will have a buoyant effect, just as an increase in private expenditure would, and that an increase in effective tax rates will act as a drag on the economy. But there is more to the impact of government activity, of course, and it will be necessary to watch for changes in debt position and in the management of the debt if we are to understand how the government impinged upon the growth process in the difficult surplus periods of the last quarter of the century.

Technological change has appeared in this list several times. Had we decided to discuss nineteenth-century income growth in terms of the technical relationships between physical inputs and outputs—the production function—the direct effect of technological improvement upon the efficiency of resource use would have been the central part of the story. Instead, by concentrating upon the level of income-generating activity, we are able to bring in productivity change largely in terms of the rate of return and the incentive to greater investment. . . .

These are the major structural changes that affect the way in which the dynamic multiplier-accelerator interaction responds to outside shocks. Some of these changes, in addition to altering the parameters or givens in the model, are themselves put into effect as outside shocks; technological change, since it cannot usually be realized without a burst of investment, is precisely of this nature. The income history of the United States in the nineteenth century will be explained in this chapter in terms of the structural changes just outlined. We shall be able to refer directly to the values of the constants only rarely, e.g., the capital-output ratio or the debt-income ratio. For the most part, we shall simply try to identify such changes as shifts in industrial composition, the appearance and development of new industries, and organizational and technological innovations, on the one hand, with the major increases in the growth rate during the period of industrialization, on the other.

. . . . .

This complicated description of the income growth process is not introduced on the chance that we might find the numerical values for the parameters in the income relationships and in that way describe the conditions necessary to generate a steady-growth path (although it would be an exciting and tempting possibility). Rather it is of interest in the setting of this study because of the suggestions that it makes toward combining structural change and dynamic processes. A dynamic process, like the simple multiplier-accelerator relationship just described, contains a law of change: Given appropriate initial conditions and parameters in the behavior relationships, it will, once started, generate by itself a path of growth (or decline, or fluctuation). . . . A fruitful procedure for historical explanation would seem to be to use a simple dynamic theory in which we can examine the changing numerical values of the income relationships much as if we had a whole set of comparative static equilibrium situations under scrutiny. The law of change in a dynamic process may itself change, of course; some of this will be expressed in changing parameters. When such changes do take place, or when the system is subject to sharp external shocks, there will be once-for-all variations in the rate of growth. The identification of such structural changes is the goal of this history.

. . . . .

The multiplier-accelerator process described above is not the only model "true" for the period we are examining, nor is it asserted that this model is equally true at all times. Rather, we have looked for a description of growth sufficiently general so that structural changes could be traced to their income-growth outcomes without having to scrap and replace the theory at every step of industrial development. If we find that the changes we observe would be expected to have brought about the variations in growth that did indeed take place, then we shall have an explanation for the historical growth path of income in the period since 1800.

IV

With this approach in mind, what is to be explained? We have said repeatedly "the rate of growth of income." But we have seen, too, that, while the rate of growth was sustained for quite long periods, there have been relatively short spurts of rapid increase surrounded, if not by stagnation, at least by stretches of more sluggish movement. We shall ask, then, what caused the first period of accelerated development after the depression of 1837 and the two great advances, in the seventies and at the turn of the century.

It would not do, here, to follow the recent analyses of economic development in their emphasis upon backwardness and the initial push or "take-off." The United States at the opening of the nineteenth century may have been growing slowly, in preindustrial fashion, but it would be difficult to find good evidence of stagnation, much more so for backwardness. Instead, we shall concentrate first upon the conditions behind the surge in the rate of growth that followed the rise out of the crisis of 1837, observing that the United States, as a late-comer *vis-à-vis* British industrialization, gained much from British technology.

. . . . .

We have attempted in section II to demonstrate that there was a significant upturn out of the crisis of 1837–1843. We can now look for the change in composition or concentration that the Gerschenkron or Rostow analyses would lead us to expect and then go on to consider the structural changes in more detail. In every real measure of industrial composition, there was a sharp change between the decades before and after the depression. The percentage of gainfully employed in agriculture, which had been going down by not more than two points in any previous decade, dropped by five points in the forties and again in the fifties. In the decade ending in 1849, manufacturing output (value added) grew at a rate of 152 per cent and in the overlapping decade (to 1854) 133 per cent; in the same periods agriculture grew at rates of 26 per cent and 39 per cent, respectively. The shares in value of total commodity output moved in comparable fashion: agriculture, from 72 per cent in 1839 to 55.5 per cent in 1859; manufactures, from 17.4 per cent in 1839 to 32 per cent twenty years later.

The expansion of primary metal manufactures and heavy industry is an important part of industrialization. But the production of iron and steel in the forties was dominated by tariff changes; between 1840 and 1847 annual output increased by more than 200 per cent. Then, under the influence of the tariff of 1846, importation increased and production declined by about 100,000 tons annually. Ezra Seaman estimated, however, that the annual consumption of iron and hardware increased from less than 400,000 tons to about 1 million tons, between 1840 and 1850. Finally, between 1850 and 1860, domestic manufactures of iron and steel increased by 40 per cent, and the fabrication of steam engines and agricultural implements by 66 per cent and 159 per cent, respectively.

In these statistics, fragmentary and of widely varying credibility, there seems to be an unmistakable and consistent picture of an economy changing its direction. The pace of industrialization did not leap up from zero; what did happen was a marked acceleration in the trend toward manufacturing and construction. Within the manufacturing sector, the trend turned toward the heavy industries. The increase in the rate of investment, measured in terms of fixed capital per worker ratios, was greater between 1849 and 1859 than in any comparable period in the century: from $50.60 to $69.60. This is the evidence. What can we say about the causes?

The most important institutional changes in the upsurge and during the preceding period of preparation were directed toward making credit more cheaply and efficiently available for the growing manufacturing and railway industries. However unfortunate the destruction of the Second Bank of the United States may have been from the point of view of the long-run development of central banking in this country, it did have a beneficial impact in shifting the locus of the money market from the mercantile business community of Philadelphia to the more aggressive manufacturing centers in New York and Boston. Loanable funds continued to be scarce and low interest rates almost unavailable. Long-term credit, especially, was in extremely short supply. But by 1850 the growth in intermediary banking institutions—savings banks and insurance companies, primarily in the East, and the wildcats and new state banks in the South and West—had been sufficient to make the accumulation of capital, even by small investors, much more feasible than it had been.

The investment history of the Massachusetts Hospital Life Insurance Company is very interesting in this respect. Before 1830 the company's investments were concentrated in western Massachusetts farm mortgages, rarely for a term longer than one year. About 1830 and especially after 1837, securities and business loans became more important in the portfolio, and the locus shifted to the neighborhood of Boston and to the textile industry. In the forties, when textile selling agents would not generally lend for more than six months, and commercial banks for only three or four, the savings banks and the Massachusetts Hospital Life were practically the only sources of funds at terms of a year or more. This evidence may be taken as having more than anecdotal significance, considering the expansion of savings bank capital in the late forties and the fifties and the singular importance of the Massachusetts Hospital Life in the textile capital market.

The first savings banks appeared in New York in 1817. By 1846, the New York institutions held deposits of $112 million; a decade later, in the single year 1857, there was a growth of $25 million more. The Massachusetts savings banks grew in number from thirty-one in 1839 to eighty-six in 1859; deposits increased from $5.6 million to $39.4 million. There was a similar growth in insurance companies; in New York, insurance capital increased from $16 million in 1827 to $75 million in 1860. Another important change took place in the emerging role of the note broker over this period. Having been a suspect "money-shaver" in 1819, by 1837 he was dealing among the banks and in 1857 began to deal in paper on his own account very much in the manner of the commercial paper house. In the same year, the newly formed New York Clearing House made a tentative effort toward dealing with the crisis by extending clearing-house certificates for the first time.

Throughout the prewar period, of course, the dependence upon foreign funds continued, especially in the financing of railway construction. But the changes in domestic banking that were taking place made a real difference in the form and availability of finance in the drive of the forties and fifties. A strong indication of this change is given in Lance Davis' study of the pattern of textile finance before 1860. Equity capital was the most important form over the whole period, although it declined from 1827 to 1860 while loans increased in significance. Although retained earnings obviously can only become important with advancing age of the corporations, they declined in weight over historical time (for given ages). Another measure of the change is the cost of capital: Average interest rates on prime commercial paper declined from 10.14 for the decade ending in 1840 to 8.14 in the following decade, in New York. The decline in Boston was from 8.68 to 7.68. But the availability of credit and especially of long-term loans was even more important for capital accumulation than interest costs in this period. And, in this respect, two special participants in the capital markets are significant: the Western wildcat banks and the state governments. The wildcats, by providing currency and credit for agriculture and local industry in the West, and the governments, by financing internal improvements, provided for long-term credit needs that could not have been met from the East without a serious strain on the supply of funds and a subsequent rise in the interest rates to industrial borrowers.

Two more influences in the capital market remain to be discussed: the government budget position and the most important source of funds for investment, the inflow of capital from London. In the thirties, largely under pressure of the fiscal surplus, the Federal government took an increasing share of the responsibility for road construction and internal improvements. Jackson's opposition and the fears for state sovereignty that prompted it are written into the Maysville veto. The fact remains, however, that from 1831 to 1835 Federal expenditures for roads and canals almost doubled the amount spent in the preceding five years. The Jackson administration spent over $25 million on public works, more than double the total for internal improvements by all previous administrations. But it was the state governments that played an active promotional if not entrepreneurial role during this period. To a large extent, the venture capital for transportation improvements came from the public treasury or at least was made more available on the basis of public credit. States, without using their tax power to service the loans, picked up the weak notes and securities of private companies and issued in turn the apparently stronger debt instruments of the government. One of the most important indirect effects of this state backing was to increase the willingness of foreign capitalists—British, primarily, but also in the French and Low Country markets—to invest in American transportation and land development.

In the forties, seven Federal budgets contained a deficit. Under free banking and the Independent Treasury, persistent surpluses caused a deflationary flow of currency into government vaults; the deficits, however poorly managed, at least had the advantage that they did not reduce circulation and cause a tightening of credit as the undistributed surplus did. It is especially significant, therefore, that in 1850 the Federal budget moved up to a surplus position and continued so for eight years and that in 1850, 1853, and 1854 the net United States commodity trade and specie balance was negative and relatively high. The previous heavy inflow of capital occurred in the thirties, of course, and reached peaks of $61 million in 1836 and $41 million in 1839. This observation is not intended as an assertion of causal connection between the Federal surplus and the negative balances in the early fifties. Rather it is intended to show that from the middle thirties until the middle fifties growth was accompanied by either a government deficit or net capital imports. British capital was far more important in providing the initial funds for the spurt of investment and maintaining the pace until the panic of 1857, but an undistributed surplus—rather than the actual deficit—might have caused a real drag on accumulation in the 1840s. Before leaving this discussion of the capital-market developments, it may be useful to warn the reader against the dangers of looking at these events from a rigid Keynesian position. Keep in mind that the fiscal consequences of a surplus obtained by high tariffs on imports are different from a surplus achieved by taxation; there is much less deflationary pressure. Indeed, to the extent that income was redistributed to the disadvantage of the working class, and by virtue of the protection afforded the textile industry, the tariff may have had a stimulating effect on capital accumulation in some sectors of the economy.

All these developments must have had the effect of increasing the availability of credit in the period under review and, therefore, of increasing the ratio of borrowing to income. Such changes increase the rate of investment, reduce the level of business saving relative to the demand for funds, and shorten the lags between changes in income and changes in investment demand. Indeed, after 1850 there appears to have been a sharp increase in the ratio of primary securities to income and a corresponding reduction in the ratio of money supply to primary securities. It was not until the second half of the century that the banking system began to approach maturity, and even then the period of adolescence was singularly chaotic. But through the episode from 1830 to 1860, the capital-market changes were sufficiently bunched and sufficiently in the right direction to have made possible the financing of a large investment block. In this respect, it is interesting to note during how much of this development the central government, far from taking over the functions of the banking system, struggled fitfully and unsuccessfully to stay out of the money market, in sharp contrast to the Italian and Russian experiences described by Professor Gerschenkron.

The second set of structural changes to be considered are much more familiar. They are technological rather than institutional innovations and operate directly upon the degree of capital intensity and the productive relationships. It has been pointed out by Victor Clark that the depression of 1837 was accompanied by changes in business conditions so great that we would be justified in making that year the dividing line between two industrial eras. There are really two kinds of change involved here: (1) changes in the nature and intensity of capital use in the manufacturing sectors, especially in textiles and primary metals, and (2) epochal expansions in transportation and, derived from this, in agricultural development.

In the manufacture of textiles, all the major technical difficulties holding back the introduction of steam power and the use of large-scale productive units had been cleared away by the thirties. By the 1840s, Clark reported, New England industries began to outgrow the available water power. The first technological change to make larger units possible came in hydraulic-turbine and water-wheel design. Then, in the period between 1840 and 1850, the Massachusetts mills became the scene of a conflict between steam and water power. Widespread utilization of the new steam-based methods waited another decade, however, until coal became cheaply available to New England. Between 1850 and 1860, the mechanical improvements were so extensive that the Lowell mills were said to have been stripped down to shells and practically reconstructed in the course of the decade. In primary metal production, between 1830 and 1850, a number of major innovations were introduced, either taken over from British technology or developed here as a result of the increased supply of mineral fuels. The basic change, perhaps, was the introduction of coke between 1837 and 1840, which, together with the use of anthracite, made a new era in iron technology. These changes made possible the use of hot blasts, with a saving of 40 per cent in fuel costs. Finally, in consequence of the adoption of the new fuels and the hot blast, there came increased furnace capacity, a much wider use of puddling and refining, and great economies in labor requirements.

These innovations appear to have increased the capital-labor ratio in New England cotton manufacture by roughly one-half between 1840 and 1850 and to have increased the capital-output ratio by one-third. For all mining and manufacturing, the rate of growth of value added was greater in the decade ending in 1849 than was the rate of growth of manufactured producers' durables over the same period, but the growth rate of total commodity output was much lower. In the following decade, producers' fixed capital increased much more rapidly than either total or manufactured output. Within a multiplier-accelerator model, technological changes that increase capital intensity will increase the rate of growth both of investment and of income. The first increase occurs since greater capital intensity requires more investment; the second is the result of the multiplier effect upon income. The technical changes in textiles and in iron and steel production, both of which had high capital coefficients relative to all other mining and manufacturing, meant an increase in the rate of growth in these sectors beyond the average for the economy and, therefore, an increase in the volume of investment and in the degree of capital intensity. (Almost two-thirds of the very high capital coefficient for agriculture consisted of the value of land in 1850. While agricultural expansion may have a strong effect in absorbing savings, it does not have a comparable impact upon the investment goods industries.) Finally, to the extent that iron and steel required large, relatively indivisible units, expansion in that sector took place to a large extent ahead of demand, thereby boosting further the impact of the multiplier.

It may be even more illuminating to consider the effect of these changes in the disaggregate setting of input-output analysis. Industries are not linked in simple sequences—from primary to intermediate to final. There is rather a complex set of interrelationships such that virtually all the sectors might be called "intermediate." The significance of this interdependence lies in the process by which structural changes reverberate through the economy; for example, changes in the cost of fuel made possible by the railroads affect the cost of primary metals which, in turn, affect capital costs throughout the economy (including the price of railway equipment and, therefore, the cost of delivered fuel). The changes in textile methods increased the demand for steam engines and other producers' hardware, thereby increasing pressures upon the iron and steel and metal-fabricating sectors and making more likely the achievement of further economies of scale in those primary sectors. The technical advances in iron and steel production, in turn, had even more important reverberative effects. The primary metals flow directly or indirectly into literally all other commodity-producing sectors in the economy. Therefore, a productivity increase in iron or steel becomes a productivity increase, in the sense of reducing (marginal) capital costs at given capital-output ratios, everywhere in the system. In addition, of course, the lower costs of the primary metals may provoke the use of more capital-intensive methods elsewhere.

There are, within these relationships, certain flows that are especially strategic. Savings in those industries whose output flows primarily to other producing sectors rather than directly to the ultimate consumers will exert a heavier, wider impact on the technical structure than would comparable direct savings in the "consumer goods" industries. The manufacturers of fabricated structural metal and textile-mill products, which we have been discussing, are among the first four industries in a complete list of forty-five ranked according to the proportion of the industry's total gross output in 1947 that went forth as interindustry inputs (including capital formation). The primary manufacturing sectors were (and are) in an extremely strategic position in the chain of innovation; the technical break-through and the cost savings introduced in those industries were especially important in closing the developmental block of the thirties, and, therefore, in releasing a Schumpeterian wave of innovation. The changes in textile production had another expansive effect in that they made American cheap cotton goods competitive in world markets from the 1830s on. To sum up: By virtue of their very high capital intensity, relative to mining and manufacturing as a whole, and their position in the input-output relationships of the economy, the technical changes in textiles and in primary metals had strong reverberative impact throughout the economy. In addition, of course, the rapid growth in these sectors, following upon the reduction in their costs, increased the average capital intensity of the whole system and, thereby, the rate of growth of aggregate capital and of income.

The classical explanations of growth in this period are correct, of course, in their emphasis upon the railroads. First, as a capital-intensive, heavy-borrowing sector, railroad construction (1) increased the rate of growth of capital directly and (2) provided a strong offset to business savings elsewhere in the economy. Secondly, in so far as they were built to the West ahead of demand, the railroads exerted an even stronger upward pressure upon the aggregate investment schedule. These are double-barreled effects similar to the impact of technical change in the textile and primary metals industries. In addition to the effects on capital intensity, however, the railroads, by lowering transport costs and pushing ahead of population into the West, changed the geographical focus and the nature of operations of the agricultural sector. First, the railroads held off the Ricardian effect mentioned earlier; by reducing shipping costs for the staple crops, the railroads made it still more advantageous for farming to move out of the low-yield Eastern sectors into the rich Northwest (now Middle West) region. In addition, by increasing agricultural productivity and reducing labor requirements on the farm, the population shift was, in effect, releasing farm labor for industrial employment in the manufacturing centers. Agricultural employment increased, of course, and immigrant Irish and German workers reduced the pressures in the industrial labor markets. But the point is that the flow of domestic and immigrant labor directly into nonagricultural occupations would not have been possible without major improvements in agricultural productivity.

It is impossible to separate the effects of the London cereal market from the effects of domestic supply and demand upon American agricultural prices. However, it is a sign of improved yields that agricultural prices should have declined more rapidly than construction prices in the face of the new demand pressures arising from immigration into the Eastern industrial centers during the late forties. This price decline was achieved in spite of the rising export of foodstuffs to England in the late years of the decade. The sharp rise that did occur in the middle fifties can be attributed as much to the Crimean War and the poor French and British harvests as to any Ricardian pressures on food prices in a rapid industrialization. There has been much attention lavished upon the effect of railroads in creating national markets for Eastern manufacturers by reducing transport costs. It seems clear, however, that what the rail-roads carried back from the West—for the manufacturing centers as well as for export—was more essential to industrialization than the manufactured goods that they carried out.

The squeeze upon manufacturers' profits that was predicted by Ricardo was made inoperable in the United States of the forties and fifties by the opening of new, fertile agricultural areas. But this is an exceedingly negative point of departure. First, agricultural produce—cotton, primarily, and cereals—formed the basis of the high trade balances in 1840, 1843, and, especially, 1846 and 1847. Second, the opening of new food-producing regions imposed a strong autonomous investment push within the multiplier-accelerator process. Considerable investment was required for urban service centers, ahead of demand, not balanced by previous savings, and with strong local multiplier effects. This increase in Western incomes, spent on goods that could be exported inter-regionally (in contrast to the services and marketing facilities that could not), increased the induced investment pressures in the East, which in turn made new jobs, absorbed more immigration, and made necessary the further development of food production in the new Northwest.

Granting the implications of this analysis, what was the timing of the impetus to capital formation? In the twenties and early thirties, the canals initiated the period of transport innovation. Then in 1841 there was a first peak in railroad mileage added, which was followed by a sharp decline to 1843 and 1844. From that time until the war and especially between 1849 and the peak in 1856, the increase in railway mileage was continuously and increasingly above the trend of growth for the period 1831–1910. The population shift to the marginal (in the geographical, not the productivity, sense) areas occurred a decade earlier, in the forties; for the territory added to the census enumeration after 1830, the population increase in the forties was 677,000 and in the fifties, 2.4 million. It seems clear, in the light of this analysis and this timing, that the railroads, however powerful they were in absorbing capital and promoting further mechanical innovation elsewhere in the system, may have had their most powerful effect in accelerating the tremendous innovation embodied in the shift of population and the industrialization of agriculture. As a measure of the change in the structure of farming, note that the share of agricultural equipment in the total of manufactured producers' durables doubled between 1839 and 1859 and that farm improvements grew at a rate of 45.4 per cent between 1849 and 1859. These agricultural innovations and the shift in population that supported them were an indispensable part of the industrialization of the American economy.

Beginning in the decade of the thirties and accelerating in the two decades following, a series of structural changes in the sources of capital, the new textile manufacturing sector, and the basic metal industries combined to raise the growth of capital at given capital-output ratios and to increase the capital intensity of the economy, directly and indirectly. The development of railroads absorbed capital, increased the borrowing-income ratio for the system, and was essential for the opening of the fuel and food-producing regions. The timing and concentration of these changes and the probable direction of their impact upon the parameters and exogenous variables in the multiplier-accelerator process provide both support and explanation for a surge of income growth in the American economy in the period of recovery after the depression of 1837.

V

When we pass the Civil War and enter the decade of the seventies, the way in which the war interrupted the press of development that had been under way since the early forties becomes clear. In the South activity was disrupted entirely, but in the North development and growth were in many ways spurred in the war years. Whether the data simply average these effects, masking the Northern industrialization, or whether the war did indeed set back the pace of development is a moot question. There was a remarkably slight depression beginning late in 1865. Then, after the low point in 1867, a railroad boom began which carried business through a brief contraction in 1870 to the precipitous break of 1873. But in spite of the panic and the severe decline in prices, per capita real income grew over the decade. Again, a railroad boom carried the drive, beginning in 1877, well before the turn in over-all activity in 1879. By the time it turned down in the early eighties, the spurt had raised the net output level at an annual rate higher than any experienced before or since. It is debatable whether this period is really distinguishable, in the sense of structural change, from the surge that characterized the two decades before the war. For example, Schumpeter considered the war to have been only an interruption in the upswing of the second, the "bourgeois," Kondratieff long wave. In his chronology, the peak was reached in the seventies, and from then until the turn of the century the system absorbed and adjusted to the great changes of the railroad era. We shall follow the calendar suggested earlier in examining the pace of change over the forty-year period after the war.

Schumpeter argued that the disruptions of the war were swamped by the rising tide of railroad expansion that began or continued immediately after the end of fighting. What were they? Destruction was limited entirely to the South, and it was also in the defeated region that the great social upheaval and inflation occurred. In fact, it is not difficult to make a strong argument for the hypothesis that the North conducted its war finance on a good Keynesian basis and that it was mismanagement *after* the war that created the intolerable strains in the money market. But in the South the breaking of normal capital flows and commercial relations intensified the tremendous organizational uncertainties and the difficulties of getting the large-scale, speculative cotton agriculture under way again. The result, a generation later, was that the South had settled into the role of a colonial economy, backward in every economic sense of the word. But there were other strains and imbalances outside the South. The pressure of rapid debt reduction and the general maladministration of the revenue surplus added to the confusion over monetary panaceas; these problems were not solved until the late nineties. However, the combination of war and tariff had fostered the manufacturing sector and brought about a greater independence of England than had been achieved in the whole first half-century. Industry emerged from the war in a highly liquid state, and we shall find that the impact of deflation in the time of prosperity fell largely upon the unfortunate farmers. The basic financial confusion helped nobody, but the regressive fiscal policy worked to the advantage of the saving classes in a period of strong demand for investment funds. With this background, we can summarize some of the important magnitudes of the postwar development and study the structural changes that might have caused it.

As was mentioned earlier, there were two periods of rapid growth, separated by almost two decades of relatively sluggish, absorptive activity. The first strong push began about 1867, stopped short in 1873, and then continued from 1877 to 1881 or 1882. The difference in rate of growth of income between the postwar boom and the low point in the early nineties was on the order of 3:1 for net national product (measured in decade averages) and about 7:1 for net product per capita. The drive starting in the late nineties was little more than half as rapid as the earlier one in the aggregates and much less than half as rapid in per capita terms.

Let us try now to relate these developments in the rate of growth to changes in the underlying structure of the economy. The change in industrial shares simply continued the trend that had started in the prewar burst of industrialization. Agriculture's value added, although it grew very rapidly in the late seventies, slowed down drastically in the late eighties. In terms of employment, the farm share of gainfully occupied barely declined in the seventies and then fell sharply in the next decade. The rate of growth of value added in mining and manufacturing rose through the seventies and eighties, while farm value added grew at a rate of 15.3 per cent in the war decade, 51.1 per cent in the next, and then slowed down to a rate of 24.6 per cent in the eighties. There was no great change in the ratio of farm value added per worker to the average for the whole commodity-producing sector in 1869 to 1879, and it is probably safe to conclude that agricultural productivity increased about as rapidly as productivity in the rest of the producing industries. In the eighties, however, the rate of growth of value added became negligible in agriculture, while in mining and manufactures the rate of increase was 2½ times what it had been earlier.

It is difficult to see any concentration upon capital formation as opposed to consumers' goods in the first postwar boom. Rather, the figures on aggregate capital intensity increase fairly steadily to the end of the century. The share of gross capital formation in gross national product (GNP) was 22.5 per cent from 1869 to 1878, less than one percentage point greater than it was in the succeeding decade. The share of capital formation in the seventies was almost two points less than the proportion in the nineties. There was, then, a fairly steady increase in the proportion of income that flowed into savings over the period. In marginal terms, that is, in the relative *changes* in investment and net product, there is an upward trend that reached its peak in the increase between the decades 1879–1888 and 1884–1893. Finally, capital intensity, measured by the ratio of reproducible capital to annual net product, increased from 2.83 in 1879 to 3.36 in 1899. We have remarked earlier that increasing capital intensity causes the growth rate to increase in multiplier-accelerator-income models. It is difficult to say what was the increase in capital ratios between the war and postwar decades, but the increase to the end of the century must have given added impetus to the second surge in the growth rate. Within Kuznets' capital-formation totals, the share of construction grew markedly between 1869–1878 and 1884–1893, while the share of producers' durables declined at first and then increased sharply in the first decade of the present century. This change supports Schumpeter's suggestion that the first part of this surge of industrialization was propelled by the railway expansion and the second part by technical change in the manufacturing sectors. We can now use these observations as a vantage point from which to consider the specific effects of growing industries on the rate of increase of income.

The postwar railroad boom started in 1867 and reached its peak in 1872. By then, the total value of road and equipment was over $8 billion, and the gross capital expenditure for the year $604 million. Expenditures turned down for the rest of the decade but were still sufficient to account for over 20 per cent of the total gross capital formation. The proportion fell to 15.6 per cent in the next decade and then fell to half of that until the twenties, when of course it declined even more. Between 1868 and 1871, the rate of growth of railway mileage averaged 12 per cent annually, not comparable to the 22 per cent around 1850 but not to be approached again except for the two years 1880–1881. The impact of this capital growth on the national average is obvious, and the reverberative effects have been discussed with respect to the earlier boom.

Two other aspects of railway development should be added to the discussion at this point: (1) the lead of railway building over population inflows in the postwar boom and (2) the manner in which the roads were financed. Whereas before the Civil War railroad construction lagged behind immigration and behind the movement of population into the West, after the war the railroads led both of these series. Part of the explanation for the change lies in the labor requirements and the dependence upon immigrant manpower for construction in the fifties. Part of it lies in the speculative, promotional, colonizing aspect of much of the Western railway development in the later period.

Even more important than the effect that railroad building ahead of demand had upon the investment-output ratio were the effects arising out of the financing practices of the railway companies. More than any other form of investment in the nineteenth century, although it was to be matched later by the utilities, railway expansion required tremendous creation of credit, at first by state governments, then by English banks and individuals, and, finally, as the major stock traded in the financial exchanges. The danger of this speculation is evident in the crisis of 1857 and more drastically, after the Northern Pacific failure, in the crisis of 1873. In the light of the capital intensity of railroad expansion, the high propensity to borrow, and the tendency to build ahead of demand, the impact of railroad investment upon the parameters of the multiplier-accelerator relationships in the postwar decade cannot be reasonably questioned.

The capital-intensive public utilities and street railways gave the second great impetus to capital formation, well after the first upsurge. In 1877, the telephone was introduced; in 1882, electric light and power; in 1887, the electric street railway. In each case, the expansion was rapid and together they were no doubt sufficient to make the recovery after the depression of 1893 carry on to become the upswing of the third Kondratieff. Whatever the development of electric power in manufacturing, which had become significant in cotton mills after 1882, Schumpeter dismissed this use of electricity as signifying little compared with the development of the electric tram. The role of capital intensity in these sectors in raising the level of capital formation in the nineties hardly bears repeating. What is less well recognized, however, is the strength of an organizational innovation that accompanied the street railway and raised all the parameters dependent upon the availability of credit: the holding company. In subsequent periods, the holding company (and other forms of combination and monopoly introduced about this time) might, by increasing profits and retained earnings and by increasing barriers to entry, reduce the rate of growth of investment and, therefore, of income. But at this point in the development of the industry, given the nature of the utility and the state of the capital markets, it is unlikely that the monopoly elements of the holding company counted for more in a depressing sense than did its usefulness in facilitating borrowing and the absorption of investable funds.

Within manufacturing, the scarcity of labor, which persisted despite the waves of immigration, was met by a series of innovations which, without exception, involved increased capital intensity. The capital-output ratio increased by 10 per cent in each of the two decades following 1874–1883, and the capital-labor ratio (limited to reproducible capital) rose from $2,320 per member of the labor force in 1879 to $2,770 in 1889, $3,560 at the end of the century, and $4,170 in 1909 (all in 1929 prices and without adjustment for the reduction in hours.) The result was an increase in value added per worker in mining and manufacturing of 18.4 per cent in the decade 1869–1879, 46 per cent in the following decade, and 9.3 per cent in the last decade of the century (all in prices of 1879). The value of output of fixed capital grew increasingly from the end of the Civil War to the decade of the nineties, when it declined. Where and when did these changes arise? Schumpeter lists the sources for us: efficient coking in the prosperity before 1873; use of petroleum for lighting at the end of the war and the development of petroleum for other purposes later in the period; manufactured gas and natural gas, especially in the late seventies and eighties; farm implements, the output of which rose four times between 1860 and 1890; the Singer sewing machine and the McKay shoe-sewing machine, especially after 1860; textile improvements which had started early and continued through the period. Iron mining did not change technically, but between 1870 and 1890, there was a shift from the Eastern states to the ore fields of the Central West and South which was sufficient (with some foreign imports) to bring the price down to one-third over the two decades. The Bessemer process and other technological changes in milling were increasingly adopted up to the late eighties. Finally, the iron and steel industry may stand as an example of the development of another of the great innovations of the end of the century: the vertical combination.

Manufacturing and mining have the lowest capital-output ratio among the major groups in the economy, so that the producers' goods innovations, simply as a source of investment activity and increased capital intensity for the system, might not have been sufficient to carry the two periods of increasing growth rates without the expansion of railroads and utilities and the shift in population. What is unquestionable, however, is the effect of the improvements in the producers' goods sector in reducing the costs and prices of manufactured goods and thereby expanding markets and releasing innovation elsewhere in the system. The labor savings have been mentioned already; literally without exception the cost of materials declined as a proportion of the value of product in the manufacturing industries between 1880 and 1890. In the following period, as agricultural prices and minerals prices rose, the cost of materials ratios increased slightly; but in only one case, the nonferrous metals, was the change sufficient to wipe off the technical gains of the previous decade.

The development of capital in agriculture is an essential part of this story. We have already discussed the role of the investment created by the shift of population into the undeveloped West North Central region. Without a great deal of mechanization, however, the shift to more fertile areas would not have been sufficient to release workers to industry and to keep down the prices of food products in the face of the demand pressures of industrialization and immigration in the last third of the century. Actually, agricultural prices came down over the period in almost exactly the same degree as all commodity prices. Manufactured goods and mine products had a greater price decline than the average for the whole system, and construction prices came down hardly at all, actually rising in the last two decades. The two decades between 1859 and 1879, and especially the ten years after the War, were the period of greatest increase in farm improvements and introduction of capital equipment. This timing, in addition to its importance in preventing the Ricardian pressures from inhibiting the growth of industry, is extremely important for subsequent farm history because of its coincidence with the timing of peak farm prices. Farmers are both encouraged and enabled to make capital purchases in periods of high agricultural prices; the mortgage burden is felt later—in this case, in the long deflation that came after the war decade of the sixties.

Finally, it is necessary to consider the changes in the organizational structure of industry and in the capital markets that accompanied and reinforced the changes in technology and composition that we have outlined. Recall that, in Schumpeterian terms, the importance of capitalist enterprise is primary; without entrepreneurial innovation, inventions count for nothing. Furthermore, he argued, entrepreneurship requires a governmental atmosphere of *laissez faire*, if not open support. In the analysis of Professor Gerschenkron, the development of entrepreneurial abilities and the complicity (in some cases the innovational drive) of the government are both essential first steps, if not prerequisites of the initial spurts of growth. In the United States, the acquisitive instincts reached full flower in the nineteenth century, and the last third of the century carried the development of social Darwinism to its extreme. For twenty years after the Civil War, the government—either through an honest conviction that unfettered competition promised the greatest social advance or through outright corruption during such scandals as the Gold Corner panic of 1869 or the Crédit Mobilier affair three years later—maintained a remarkable "anything goes" atmosphere in the business community. The first reform administration, Grover Cleveland's, succeeded in withdrawing government operations from the underworld. But he failed to deal effectively with the surplus problem and with the silver forces and the protectionists. The century ended with the Dingley tariff, the rescue operations of J. P. Morgan, and the final victory of the sound-money forces and the gold standard. Schumpeter called the second Kondratieff, whose upswing contains the first and the beginning of the second surge we have described, the bourgeois Kondratieff. The third Kondratieff wave, which began with the spurt of income growth at the end of the century, he called the *neomercantilist*. Whether or not we agree that mercantilism, in the sense that focuses economic policy in the needs of the state, characterized the first quarter of this century, it must be agreed that Theodore Roosevelt and Woodrow Wilson represent a rebirth of government after the familiar history of social irresponsibility in the last third of the nineteenth century. The laissez-faire posture of that period is all the more remarkable when it is contrasted with the role of the government in financing and promoting railroads and disposing of public lands before and to some extent in the years immediately following the Civil War.

If the state was guilty of few crimes of commission—that is, of outright interference with entrepreneurial activity—it must nevertheless answer for its omissions in the monetary sector. In the persistent, misguided effort to stay out of the money market, to abide by the letter and the spirit of the Independent Treasury legislation, the government added to the confusion and missed the opportunity to contribute to maturity in the capital markets. This is not to say that change did not take place, but simply to argue that what changes came about were almost all made *in spite of* the Treasury. The monetary sector adapted sufficiently to the needs of industry so that in the course of the last third of the century the ratio of money to income rose from 0.18 to 0.45. (The ratio in 1955 was 0.59.) It is of more interest as an indication of the availability of credit and the extent to which expansion was financed by borrowing (as opposed to retained earnings) that the ratio of primary securities to national income rose from 1.23 in 1860 to 2.13 in 1870 to 3.24 in 1900.

During the last decade of the century, three innovations in the securities markets changed the nature of industrial financing. The first was the introduction of "trust" certificates and industrial preferred stock, which were traded at the stockholder level. The second, coincidental with the merger promotions, was the expansion of the market for new securities to include direct public sale. The next step, the Morgan stage, was the growth of underwriting at the turn of the century.

The economy approached industrial maturity in this period with the shaky assistance of a hectic but slowly maturing financial community. The seasonal concentration of funds in New York and the willingness of the banks to employ short-term funds for long-term uses were the most dangerous elements of immaturity, apart from the fundamental inadequacy of the national banking system's "control." Between 1850 and 1900, the assets of financial intermediaries—the banking system, including savings and insurance institutions, investment companies, and government financial institutions—rose from $75 per head of population to $494 (in dollars of 1929). This development facilitated the growth of income, of course. But the booms and speculative bursts that unregulated banking fostered also contributed to the severity of the letdowns after each burst of real investment. That is another story.

To recapitulate, the two bursts of income growth in the last third of the nineteenth century appear to have been closely associated with two major structural changes. One was a wave of railway building that constituted per se a tremendous demand for capital. In addition, railroad development released a chain of other innovations, economies of scale, and reorganizations that closed a development block and changed the nature of American industry. Second, by the end of the century, two new capital-intensive industries had appeared, electric utilities and street railways, and a set of institutional changes in the scale of enterprise and the organization of the capital markets made possible another spurt of growth. In the period since then, income has grown at a declining rate until the most recent war and postwar era. Capital-output ratios have been declining, and the capital-labor ratios have similarly been falling, until the burst of investment made necessary by the war. The increase in leisure, which does not figure in the net national product index, has continued and may be accelerating. It is extremely difficult to distinguish the results of technological change, in the sense of shifts in the production function, from the results of the increased use of capital. However, a recent experiment with aggregate production functions by Professor Solow attributes seven-eighths of the doubling of output per man-hour to technical change since 1909. These developments should probably stand as the characteristic features of the rate of growth in the last half-century.

. . . . .

VI

CONCLUSION

This [Selection] has attempted to explain the growth of national income in the nineteenth century by applying a simple capital-adjustment theory of growth to the three spurts of growth that marked the period. There are several assumptions implicit in this procedure; the most important follow. First, it has been assumed that industrialization took place in the United States in a series of clearly defined forward surges —specifically, in the period between the depression of 1837 and the Civil War, the decade and a half following the end of the War, and the decade centered on the turn of the century. Second, it has been assumed that the changing values in a multiplier-accelerator model could be used to explain the changes in the rate of growth of the economy. Third, it has been assumed that structural changes that increase directly or facilitate the rate of accumulation of capital will provide the driving force behind the surges of income development. It was observed that, in each of the rapid-growth periods, there was a change in the composition of activity that increased the importance of industries which, because of their position in the network of interdependence of production, were especially powerful in creating chains of demand for manufacturers and closing structural blocks elsewhere in the system. The major of these technical breakthroughs were, in the first two cases, carried forward by the railroad development and, in the last case, by institutional developments in the capital markets. Agriculture, in most respects the losing sector, maintained or supported the pace of industrial development by a series of technological improvements and geographical relocations that released the growing labor force for industry and made possible the feeding of the growing urban work force at steadily declining prices.

While the first quickening of growth, in the forties and fifties, may be labeled the industrial revolution by virtue of its precedence, it makes more sense to speak of a continuing revolution. In the first upward surge, there was a great shift from consumers' to producers' goods in the composition of output; the economy lost its essentially commercial focus, turning toward industry. After the Civil War, on the second railroad wave, the nature of agriculture changed, and a series of reverberations back from the heavy-goods needs of the railroad opened the way for innovations in heavy industry and, in turn, in the sectors dependent on metals for equipment and materials. In this period and until the late nineties, the interruptions to growth developed in the extremely unstable capital market, an area of structural tension. By contrast to European experience, especially among the imitators of English industrialization, the government contributed only by taking a stiff laissez-faire posture toward the more extravagant promotional behavior of the last third of the century and by imposing a series of protective tariffs. The tariffs, by adding to the fiscal surplus, may have caused more harm than good.

There had been a revolution by the end of the century, a bourgeois revolution whose dimensions it would take the Karl Marx of the *Communist Manifesto* properly to celebrate. The greatest "approach to delicacy" in history had been achieved. In the period that followed, the neomercantilist revival, the rate of income growth declined, and the state moved in to close some of the structural gaps and tensions that were part of the legacy of industrialization.[1]

---

[1] I wish to thank the Harvard Economic Research Project for permitting me time to complete this study and the Department of Economics, Ford Foundation Research Fund, for editorial assistance. I am especially grateful to Stanley Lebergott and to Professor Alexander Gerschenkron and the following members of his Seminar: Paul David, Albert Fishlow, and Professor Barry Supple, all of whom patiently and helpfully discussed with me an early version of the present chapter. Neither they, the Project, nor the Department necessarily agree with the assertions or conclusions in the chapter.

[*Editorial note:* In the foregoing chapter the detailed footnotes, which were present in the original, were omitted in order to conserve space. In their place, the following list of some of the principal secondary sources mentioned by Professor Conrad is printed: Erik Dahmén, "Entrepreneurial Activity in Swedish Industry in the Period 1919–1939," reviewed by Alexander Gerschenkron in *Review of Economics and Statistics*, XXXIX, 4 (November, 1957); James S. Duesenberry, *Business Cycles and Economic Growth* (New York, 1958), and "Some Aspects of the Theory of Economic Development," *Explorations in Entrepreneurial History*, III, 2 (1950); Alexander Gerschenkron, "Economic Backwardness in Historical Perspective," in Bert F. Hoselitz (ed.), *Progress of Underdeveloped Areas* (Chicago, Ill., 1952), "Notes on the Rate of Industrial Growth in Italy, 1881–1913," *Journal of Economic History*, XV, 4 (December, 1955), and "Reflections on the Concept of 'Prerequisites' of Modern Industrialization," *L'Industria*, II (1957); Raymond A. Goldsmith, statement before Joint Economic Committee, 82d Congress, 1st Session: *Employment, Growth, and Price Levels*, Part 2, "Historical and Comparative Rates of Production, Productivity and Prices"; Simon Kuznets, "Long-Term changes in the National Income of the United States of America Since 1870," in *Income and Wealth, Series II: Income and Wealth of the United States—Trends and Structures* (Cambridge, Eng., 1952), and "Quantitative Aspects of the Economic Growth of Nations: Levels and Variability of Rates of Growth," in *Economic Growth and Cultural Change*, V, 1 (1954); Robert F. Martin, "National Income in the United States, 1799–1938," *National Industrial Conference Board Studies*, 241 (New York, 1939); W. W. Rostow, "The Take-Off into Self-Sustained Growth," *The Economic Journal*, LXVI, 261 (March, 1956); Joseph A. Schumpeter, *The Theory of Economic Development* (Cambridge, Mass., 1934), and *Business Cycles* (New York, 1939); Robert M. Solow, "Technological Change and the Aggregate Production Function," *Review of Economics and Statistics*, XXXIX, 3 (August, 1957); Melville J. Ulmer, "Trends and Cycles in Capital Formation by United States Railroads, 1870–1950," *Studies in Capital Formation and Financing*, Occasional Paper 43, National Bureau of Economic Research (New York, 1954); and three studies from National Bureau of Economic Research, Conference on Research in Income and Wealth, *Trends in the American Economy in the Nineteenth Century* (Studies in Income and Wealth, XXIV, Princeton, N. J., 1960): Robert E. Gallman, "Commodity Output, 1839–1899," Douglass C. North, "The United States Balance of Payments, 1790–1860," and William N. Parker and Franklee Whartenby, "The Growth of Output Before 1840."]

14

From Wildcatting to Monopoly,
1850-1914

by

FRANK THISTLETHWAITE

The old nations of the earth creep on at a snail's pace; the Republic thunders past with the rush of the express.
—ANDREW CARNEGIE, *Triumphant Democracy* (1886)

In 1816 a Committee of the United State Senate reported that it was as cheap to bring goods three thousand miles from Britain as to carry them thirty miles overland: "A coalmine may exist in the United States not more than ten miles from valuable ores of iron and other materials, and both of them be useless until a canal is established between them, as the price of land carriage is too great to be borne by either." When coal from Virginia had difficulty in competing with coal from South Wales, it was little wonder that Americans relied on the iron, machinery and hardware of Birmingham and Sheffield. Until bulky raw materials could be hauled cheaply overland, seaborne commerce helped to preserve the agrarian character of American life. Only when canals and railways had knit together a single market out of local communities scattered over half a continent did heavy industry migrate across the Atlantic. In particular, it was the railway—itself the product of iron, coal and steam—which provided the prime force behind America's unprecedented industrial growth.

Until mid-century Americans drew their raw materials principally from forest, soil and ocean. Their houses, ships, even roads, were made of pine, oak or chestnut; their rooms were warmed by wood-burning stoves and lit by candles or lamps, the tallow or oil for which came from whales; their wagons and machinery were greased by vegetable fats and harnessed with leather and hemp rope; the wheels of their grist mills were turned by water. The mining of coal, iron and lead was still a parochial business. Coal was carried by canal barge from the Alleghenies to heat the homes of Philadelphia and from Philadelphia, by schooner to New York; but the cost of its freight still prohibited the use of steam in most of New England's cotton mills. Small, up-country furnaces continued to smelt bog ore into wrought iron for rural blacksmiths by means of charcoal burnt in the bountiful forest.

The railway of the 1850s, however, demanded iron, copper and coal; and by bringing iron ore to coal and enabling manufactures to be concentrated in towns, increased America's industrial potential. Anthracite and then coke, carried by rail from the Allegheny fields, fired the furnaces of Pennsylvania. In 1849, an Indian named Majigigig led prospectors to the literally named "Iron Mountain" in the wilderness of northern Michigan. Ten years later, railway tracks to the shores of Lakes Michigan and Superior made it possible to bring richer ores from the new mines of Marquette and Menominie nearly a thousand miles by steamer across the Great Lakes to the Erie ports and thence by rail to the western gateway of the Appalachian coalfields at Pittsburgh which became the center of the iron trade. This iron ore "frontier" took another leap westwards in the 1890s beyond the furthermost reach of Lake Superior to northern Minnesota. Here, on the fabulous Mesabi Range, ore was, and is, obtained not by arduous underground mining but by using steam shovels to scoop the rich iron-earth into freight cars bound for lake steamers at Duluth. Superior ores—80 per cent of America's total in 1913—were responsible for a tenfold increase in production in the thirty years after 1875 and encouraged the U.S. Steel Corporation in 1907 to build a new steel manufacturing town at Gary, on Lake Michigan, five hundred miles west of its Pittsburgh headquarters. The copper-mining "frontier" moved even farther west. New England shipwrights got their copper sheathing from small, local deposits until in the mid-'40s railways created a copper-mining boom in Michigan. By the time of the Civil War, copper from the Calumet mine, delivered by rail and ship to the smelters of Bridgeport, Connecticut, and later of Cleveland on Lake Erie, provided copper and brass for the castings, piping and wire of the young engineering industry. Twenty years later the building of the

Northern and Southern Pacific railways made possible large-scale copper mining in Montana and Arizona, and copper production jumped from 30,000 tons to 130,000 tons in ten years.

When in the 1850s Americans began to feel the lack of cheaper illuminants and lubricants than the products of the whale, petroleum oil was a quack Indian remedy. But in the summer of 1859, a certain Colonel Drake drilled an adapted salt-boring rod through the oil-saturated earth at Titusville in the Pennsylvania mountains to a lake of subterranean petroleum. The resulting fountain of oil was the signal for a new and most gruelling race for the prizes of industrial wealth. Within three years a flock of "wildcatters," fighting for claims and risking a hideous death from explosion, had made of Pithole Creek a grotesque forest of derricks and had started a wild oil boom on the Philadelphia exchange. But getting oil out of the ground was one thing; marketing it was another. To cart barrels over mountain roads or to float them down the Allegheny River was tedious and expensive. Not until branch railway lines had connected the oil region with trunk railways at Pittsburgh and Erie was the refining of oil possible on an extensive scale. The oil industry was the creature of the railway. The cost of pumping and refining was negligible beside that of transporting the bulky, heavy liquid, even by the newly invented tank car, over the long distances from well to refinery and from refinery to consumer. Favorable railway rates were vital to oil refiners; and the lower rates which Cleveland could command, owing to the competition of two railways and lake shipping, enabled that lake-side city to wrest the leadership in refining from Pittsburgh which was at the mercy of a single railway.

The oil frontier also began to push westwards. So quickly were the early oil reservoirs exhausted that Pithole City which, at the height of the boom, had a bigger postal business than any other Pennsylvania city except Philadelphia, reverted to an open wheat field. In 1891, over 31 million barrels of oil were pumped from the Pennsylvania mountains; but thereafter the pace was set by new fields farther west: by Ohio in 1895, and then, about the turn of the century, by far-off California which increased its production to 73 million barrels in 1910. Still later, oil from newer fields in Texas, Oklahoma, Louisiana and Illinois entered the nation's pipeline in response to a revolutionary demand for petrol for motor-cars which came just when, through the growing use of electricity, urban oil lighting declined. This development strengthened in a new way the uniquely close connection between oil and transport in American life. . . . Before 1910, apart from what went into machine oil and axle grease, most of the annual 200 million barrels or so of oil from American wells was consumed in homes where cheap oil fuel was a boon. In prairie farmhouses kerosene stoves warmed kitchens and cooked the food and kerosene lamps provided for the first time an adequate pool of light for evening reading round the family table.

At this time, it was said, many of the whalers of New Bedford, Massachusetts, with generations of seafaring blood in their veins, sold their ships and gear and invested the proceeds in the oil wells of Pennsylvania. At the same call, two English immigrants, Maurice Clark and Samuel Andrews, with experience in refining vegetable oils, formed a partnership in 1863 with a twenty-six year old commission dealer in Cleveland called Rockefeller to enter the refining business. Within a decade, oil manufactured by the Rockefeller firm was lighting English homes and lubricating English locomotives. Once again, with important results for both sides of the Atlantic, the pull of the continent proved stronger than that of the ocean in the careers of Yankees and Englishmen.

The exploitation of the continent's mineral wealth made possible the migration of heavy industry across the Atlantic. . . . the first machine-driven, factory-housed industry to be established on the western shores of the Atlantic was cotton. By 1850 the American textile industries had passed far beyond the "colonial" stage, although wool lagged behind cotton. From early days British machinery had been improved upon and superseded by important native inventions such as ring spinning, which was already beginning to make Lancashire mill-owners take notice. The factory system of Waltham, Massachusetts, was more integrated than that of Oldham, Lancashire, and skilled artisans from the Pennines were now less conspicuous. The industry, which consumed something like a quarter of the cotton crop, supplied the home market with most of its coarser cloths.

American machine shops were beginning to turn out articles which impressed the world with their ingenuity. At the Great Exhibition of 1851 British manufacturers were impressed by the McCormick reaper and the Singer sewing machine. These two inventions were the first ambassadors of a characteristically American technique which was in time to transform the industrial productivity of the western world. "Already," wrote Professor Clapham, "the well-informed knew that an American was more likely than an Englishman to get tiresome and expensive handicraft operations done for him by machinery."[1] In the 1850s the manufacture of standard articles by means of interchangeable parts, invented by Eli Whitney, perfected by Samuel Colt, and extended from small arms to clocks and watches at one end of the scale and farm machinery at the other, made possible also the sewing machine

---

[1] Sir John Clapham, *An Economic History of Modern Britain* (Cambridge, 1952), vol. II, p. 12.

which, in turn, revolutionized the making of clothing and boots and shoes. And experience in making the accurate gauges, calipers and cutting tools involved created that vital prerequisite to modern engineering, a machine-tool industry.

But until the Civil War these advances were limited. It is true that the twin influence of the railway, marrying coal to iron ore and demanding iron for rails and rolling stock, greatly expanded the iron trade. More up-to-date methods crossed the Atlantic. The immigrant David Thomas had brought the technique of anthracite smelting from South Wales to Pennsylvania in 1839 and his example encouraged hundreds of his fellow-countrymen to bring their skills and talent for choral singing to Scranton and Wilkes-Barre. As a result furnaces and rolling mills began to turn out the heavier iron needed for railways ten times as fast as the old charcoal furnaces and foundries had done; and in the '6os the production of pig-iron more than doubled. But domestic production was not cheap enough to choke off the flow of railway iron from Britain which in spite of the high tariff of 1862, continued to play a prominent part in railway construction for another twenty years. In 1860 the iron trade ranked only sixth among American industries, being less important than timber and flour milling; and industry as a whole occupied the energies of only a minority of Americans, of whom sixty per cent were still engaged in agriculture and a high proportion of the rest in commerce and transport. The industrial advance of the '5os was a mere portent of what was to come.

The Civil War marks a new departure. It was not simply that war demands were a tonic for engineers, ironmasters, canners, boot, shoe and clothing men who found themselves, after Appomattox, with capital and plant ready to capture new markets in West and South. The triumph of the Republican Party gave the manufacturer his chance in American public life. Secession meant the final eclipse of those mercantile interests which had hitherto dominated commerce and politics. The cotton Whigs of New York, committed to an Atlantic trade based on the southern staple and the continental distribution of imported manufactures, found themselves crowded off the stage by a thrusting class of industrialists, determined to use their capital and "know-how," not to trade, but to manufacture and sell. These gentry were obsessed, not with the Atlantic, but with the continent and its wealth of raw materials and 30 million consumers. Through spokesmen like Simon Cameron, the wealthy ironmaster-politician of Pennsylvania who became Lincoln's first Secretary of War, this class wrote a new and radical version of the American system into the program of the Republican Party. The Pacific Railway Act of 1862, reaffirming in a new guise the old national policy of internal improvements, set the framework for completing the continent's transport system. The National Bank Act of the following year, by substituting Federally-chartered for State-chartered banks, provided a more stable network of credit. In 1864 a contract labor law, counteracting the safety-valve mechanism of the Homestead Act, encouraged industrialists to make use of cheap, immigrant labor, by permitting them to import European and Chinese workers under contract to work at what often amounted to sweated wages, a practice reminiscent of indentured service. Although the Morrill Tariff of 1861 was designed merely to provide the Government with war funds, the influence of manufacturers' lobbies so increased duties on imported manufactures that by 1865 the average rate had doubled and some commodities were taxed at as much as 100 per cent of their value. With the return of peace, such was the mood of impatient optimism, so great were the prizes of industrial enterprise and so tempting the bribes which seeped into Washington from business profits, that for a generation the politician became virtually the servant of the business man.

After Appomattox a new surge of westward expansion gave increased momentum to the economy. The central factor in that expansion was the railway. It was the demand of the railway for rails, bridging, locomotives and rolling stock which was to transform the modest iron trade of 1860 into the great steel industry of 1900; and it was steel which, in the ramifications of this chain reaction, was to industrialize American society.

When in 1864 young Andrew Carnegie, son of an immigrant Scots handloom weaver, returned from wartime railway duties in Washington he decided to leave the Pennsylvania Railroad, in which he had risen from telegraphist to divisional superintendent, in order to join one of the Pennsylvania's engineers in the building of iron bridges. With his railway connections Carnegie was soon manufacturing bridges and rails for the Pennsylvania and other lines. Carnegie was an upstart ironmaster in an established industry; but his rapid rise was symptomatic of the close relation of iron and railways. During the first post-bellum railway boom, which culminated in the collapse of 1873, the demand for railway iron seemed insatiable. In the four years ending in 1873, 25,000 miles of new track were laid, considerably more than half the entire mileage in 1868. As a result, pig-iron production more than trebled between 1860 and 1873 when it approached three million tons, of which more than half went into railways.

But iron was only a first step. In spite of the tariff and domestic production, the import of British rails increased over seven times in the five years after the War. One reason was that most of these rails were made of steel. In 1873, Andrew Carnegie, when selling American railway bonds in England, was impressed by the record of a steel rail in use at Camden Town Station after wear which had broken down seventeen iron rails, and decided to take advantage of the Schenck Tariff of 1871 to turn over to steel. Carnegie was a laggard in this, believing that "pioneering doesn't pay." The principle of making steel cheap enough, not merely for needles and sword blades but rails, had been worked out by an American ironmaster, William Kelly; but conditions were not ripe for its development. The wartime desire to convert the Union's ironclad monitors to steel armor led to the introduction from England of the superior Bessemer process which manufactured steel by subjecting molten pig-iron to a blast of hot air. The new accessibility of Lake Superior ores, which had the necessary low phosphorous content, enabled a number of firms to begin making steel and by 1873 American Bessemer "converters" were turning out some 140,000 tons of steel a year, 85 per cent in the form of rails. Even the long depression of the mid-'70s failed to stunt the industry's growth; and in the subsequent prosperity the half-million tons of 1877 were dwarfed by the two and a half million of 1886 when, only twenty years after the erection of the first pilot plant, the United States replaced Great Britain as the greatest steel producer in the world. By the turn of the century the Carnegie Steel Company alone produced four-fifths as much steel as the entire British industry.

. . . . .

. . . . American business men had conquered a multitude of problems in their own fashion. An expanding continental market encouraged them to "think big," and to invest their profits in building even larger blast furnaces, more up-to-date rolling mills. Carnegie had a new steel mill dismantled and rebuilt because his lieutenant, Charles Schwab, had learnt from its construction a way of saving a dollar, instead of the fifty cents, per ton on the output of the original design. . . . Better equipment and a ruthless drive increased the output per man of American blast furnaces thirty times between 1850 and 1919, and the price of steel rails fell from 160 dollars a ton in 1875 to 17 dollars in 1898. An American furnace produced twice as much as the equivalent furnace on Tyneside [in England]. At a dinner of British manufacturers in the '90s, Carnegie, in response to a complacent speech about the excellence of British equipment, told British ironmasters what he thought to be amiss with their steel trade: "Most British equipment is in use twenty years after it should have been scrapped. It is because you keep this used-up machinery that the U.S. is making you a back number." The best American steelmen had, indeed, made their mills, in Kitson's words, "models of arrangement and efficiency." The old shortage of skilled craftsmen had become a blessing in disguise. It had forced American ingenuity to devise labor-saving machinery and rationalized lay-outs which permitted the employment, at low wages, of those unskilled immigrants from Eastern Europe whom America's industrial prosperity had attracted to the United States. Machine methods also, in time, created a new cadre of machine-minded operators even more valuable than the old-fashioned craftsman. As Kitson put it: "The high standard . . . especially of technical education . . . undoubtedly is much to their advantage."

The most spectacular example of transatlantic migration was tinplate. American manufacturers of tin cans for the petroleum and food-processing industries imported their tinplate from South Wales where the method of tinning steel plates had been perfected. Taking advantage of the McKinley Tariff of 1890, the can manufacturers determined to make their own tinplate, importing for the purpose Welsh technicians. The experiment prospered so well that within two years over three million pounds of tinplate was being manufactured by nineteen works. The marriage of cheap domestic steel with an expanding market for canned goods was consummated. The McKinley Tariff and the low cost achieved by American producers through superior manufacturing techniques, in spite of a far heavier wages bill, had a devastating effect on the industry in South Wales where old-fashioned craft methods were employed to make tinplate largely for the American market. American imports rapidly died out and the Welsh industry was badly hit. Several Welsh tinplate firms moved across the Atlantic taking with them hundreds of immigrant Welsh tin-platers. Thus basic, heavy industry was attracted to the United States and another stage in the expansion of Europe into North America was complete.

Meanwhile, the furnaces and rolling mills which darkened the skies and grimed the hilly streets of Pittsburgh were turning out iron and steel so cheap as to invite a multitude of new uses. Orders for rails might be reduced to those needed for replacements; but the Baldwin and other companies did not lack orders for ever heavier locomotives and rolling stock which, along with such varied components as boilers, steel shafting and armor plating, immensely expanded the heavy engineering industry. When in 1888 the Carnegie Company acquired the giant steel works at Homestead the new plant was entirely converted from the production of rails to that of structural shapes for bridges and buildings. Iron and steel came to the aid of the now densely populated cities in the form of standardized iron girders for that wonder of the New World, the Brooklyn Bridge, and for the elevated railways and six-story buildings of New York. But conventional buildings of six stories were dwarfed in Chicago by the erection in 1891 of a towering structure of steel girders, the cantilevered framework of the new twenty-story Masonic Temple. The skyscraper revolutionized urban building and made it possible to house, in busy "downtown" areas of great cities, the inflated office staffs which transacted the expanding business of America by means of telephones and typewriters, inventions which themselves were the product of pressed steel, copper wire, electricity and the principle of interchangeable parts. When Taft became President in 1909 the railway had ceased to be the chief impulse in American economic life and the ramifications of iron and steel were lost in an acceleration of industrial change brought about by a multiplicity of interacting factors from electricity and machine production on the one hand to capital aggregations and the appetites of an increasingly urban people on the other.

Overnight, it seemed, this nation of farmers and horse traders had mastered the intricate mysteries of a technical civilization. During the twenty years after 1870 the United States experienced the most rapid rate of industrial growth the world had seen. By 1900 the greatest producer of raw materials and foodstuffs had also become the greatest manufacturer. In the 1870s farming contributed 20 per cent, mining and manufacturing only 14 per cent, to the national income; but thirty years later the farming contribution, reduced to 16 per cent, was equalled by that of finance and surpassed by the contribution of 21 per cent from mining and manufacturing. The American people multiplied from 40 million in 1870 to 92 million in 1910. Although of this teeming increase many an Ohio farmer or Swedish immigrant tried his hand at pioneering in the new West, many more farmers from Vermont or New Jersey or immigrants from Poland or Wales moved into the industrial centers of the East and the Middle West. In 1860 sixty per cent of the Americans who worked were on farms and only 26 per cent in industry and transport; whereas in 1900 only 37 per cent were on farms and some 46 per cent in industry and transport. There also grew up a new order of industrial centers like the coalmining towns of West Virginia, the iron towns of Pennsylvania or the light engineering towns of New England. The population of the great cities was swollen by a new influx of workers employed, for instance, in the clothing trades and machine shops of New York, the copper works of Cleveland or the steel mills of Chicago. In the last forty years of the nineteenth century the towns and cities of the United States grew more than twice as fast as the nation as a whole and in 1900 they housed about a third of the American people. . . . and already in 1890 four out of every five persons in Massachusetts were townsfolk. Of the great metropolitan cities, New York, Chicago and Philadelphia, each had over a million citizens. Brightly lit shops, restaurants and theaters dazzled the farmer in from the country. Electric trams, overhead railways and the underground—copied by Boston from London and Budapest—carried office workers down town to the ten- and twenty-storied buildings where, with ticker tape and telephone, they transacted the business of an entire continent. . . . By the turn of the present century the farmer had become a somewhat forlorn figure in American life. The new romance of business had dispelled the old romantic ideal of the American countryman. Once the unique object of Jeffersonian aspiration, the farmer had become little more than a "hick," "hayseed," a figure of music-hall fun. His place in American folklore had been usurped by a new stereotype: the white-collared business man.

The cult of business owed its power to the example of the tycoon. Before the Civil War there were few really rich men and the fortunes of these were, on the whole, modest. Of the hundred or so millionaires, most of whom had made their money in foreign trade or land speculation, only a handful could even approach the twenty million dollars fortune, made in furs and multiplied in Manhattan property, which John Jacob Astor bequeathed to his children in 1848. Fifty years later a new social order of wealth had been created out of the exploited resources of the continent. Fortunes made in real estate, like Marshall Field's in Chicago; in timber, like the Weyerhaeuysers'; in milling, like the Pillsburys'; in meat-packing like the Armours'; in mining or simply in speculating in the wheat pit, brought an aristocracy of *nouveaux riches* to the Gold Coast of Chicago or San Francisco's Nob Hill. Still greater riches from railways, steel, copper or oil proved an irresistible weapon in the hands of the *arrivistes* who clamored for admission to the glittering society of New York's Four Hundred or the summer season at Newport. Here the princely families of industry vied with each other in conspicuous display the like of which had never been seen before, even at Versailles or St. Petersburg. . . . The wealth of these magnates was in effect untold, since it was impossible to capitalize accurately the true extent of their holdings; and the power they exerted over American life was revolutionary. Their position was the result of concentration of capital inherent in the process of industrial growth.

The story of that concentration begins in the little court off Lombard Street in the City of London where, in 1837, George Peabody had started that merchandising business which was to be the foundation of his career as a merchant banker, financing Anglo-American trade and selling American railway bonds. In 1864 the firm passed into the hands of another Yankee dry-goods trader, Junius S. Morgan, who brought it new power and authority in 1870 by successfully underwriting a formidable French government loan. A year later Morgan's clever, mathematically-minded son, John Pierpont, who had been sent to represent the firm in New York, organized there the banking house of Drexel, Morgan and Co. American business still depended on British capital for its expanding activities. British funds were forcing the pace of railway building with all that this meant for the migration of heavy industry across the Atlantic, and for settling the Greater West whence the movement of crops was, in turn, financed by British credits. By 1910 some 6,000 million dollars of foreign capital was invested in American enterprise, well over half of it British. The migration of capital across the Atlantic was a basic, formative condition of the industrial transformation of the United States; and it is hardly surprising that we should turn to Lombard Street for the original impulse to that capital concentration which was ultimately to release Wall Street from the Old World's leading strings. Pierpont Morgan's powerful London connection gave the start to a career which was to end in domination of the American money market.

Within a few years the Morgan combination, by successfully refunding the U.S. Government's Civil War debt, reopened this American market to British investors. Morgan thereupon turned his forceful talents to American railways. In 1879 he rescued William Vanderbilt by secretly disposing of a quarter of a million of his New York Central shares to British clients of Junius Morgan; and he soon followed this first venture by more active intervention. . . . the generation of Gould, Huntington and Russell Sage, always speculators, not operators, had played ducks and drakes with the American railway system. Competing lines bled each other white in ruinous rate wars. Even where the volume of traffic justified the heavy investment, profiteering from stock manipulation ruined sound roads and sometimes almost brought traffic to a standstill. Most railway stock was heavily watered, and in the panic of 1893 more than half of the country's railway mileage went into receivership. The good name in London of the House of Morgan, resting as it did on the gleaming prospects of America, was in jeopardy. For, in John Moody's words, the Morgans had always been "bulls on America."[2] Therefore, to protect the investments of his British and other clients, "Jupiter" Morgan took on his broad shoulders the affairs of railway after railway, reorganizing their finances and management, raising new capital, buying up competing lines and consolidating each group he handled into a single, economic unit exercising effective and often monopolistic control over a growing traffic region. What began as a means to an end became an end in itself. By acquiring blocks of voting shares Morgan emerged in the '90s as the august controller of a continent-wide network of railways which included such giants as the Northern Pacific, the Erie and the Southern. In addi-

---

[2] See J. Moody, *Masters of Capital* (New Haven, 1919), p. 29.

tion he had a powerful voice in the affairs of the New York Central, the Baltimore and Ohio and other lines.

Morgan was not, however, the only banker to build an empire by reorganizing moribund railways. Another New Yorker, Edward H. Harriman, after pocketing the votes of an important group of Dutch stockholders, insinuated himself into the direction of the Illinois Central and with a mortgage on this revived company annexed the bankrupt Union Pacific to a network which began to reach across the continent. At this point he met his match in another railway chieftain, James J. Hill, who, to the north, was building up a parallel satrapy from the Pacific to the Mississippi. Hill started, not as a banker, but as a railroader. Canadian-born, he joined two British adventurers, George Stephen and Donald Alexander Smith, in building the Great Northern from Duluth to Seattle. From the profits of his well-run railway Hill acquired important interests in New York's First National Bank and in Morgan's Northern Pacific which flanked his route to the south. Whereupon in 1900 Harriman, after a vain attempt to come to terms with Hill over a joint monopoly of railway traffic in the Greater West, set about defeating his rival by quietly buying up Northern Pacific stock in the open market, an operation which meant finding between eighty and a hundred million dollars in cash. It was a battle of titans. James Hill, who learnt from the ticker tape of the gyrations of his Northern Pacific stock while railroading in the Pacific North-west, cleared the line for his private train, which broke the record between Seattle and the Mississippi on the way to New York. Here his fight with Harriman to buy up stock created a wild boom on the exchange which brought its nemesis in a spectacular panic. Only a last-minute truce between the two averted the ruin of the entire banking and broking structure of Wall Street. . . .

Harriman's fight with Hill had been financed by the City Bank of New York; and behind the City Bank lurked the great and swelling resources of the Standard Oil Company. For the drive to combination was by no means confined to the pull of banking towards industry. The reverse process also operated. The accumulation of capital from profits in the new industries impelled the emerging tycoons, not merely to strive towards monopoly within their own industry, but, by launching into banking, to extend their power into further reaches of the economy.

Fifteen years after starting his first refinery at Cleveland, John D. Rockefeller commanded a virtual monopoly of the sale of oil. Rockefeller's achievement is a tribute to his long, if narrow, vision, his book-keeping mind, his ruthless pursuit of money power, his horror of waste and respect for order. But it had to be someone's achievement. The wildcatting conditions of early days could not continue. Where a hundred and one producers with primitive equipment faced sudden death, physical and financial, to market oil at wildly fluctuating prices, only the toughest survived. Rockefeller, perceiving that the refinery, not the well, was the nodal point of the industry, and that the man with the extra reserve of capital would emerge stronger from each successive market slump, forced his wife to wear last year's bonnet so that he could put every cent of profit into more and better refineries. This put him in a position to exploit the one overriding condition which determined the sale of oil. The greatest element in its price was the cost of transport. Oil was also valuable freight to railways. Since Rockefeller could guarantee a larger and steadier flow of oil traffic, the railways operating out of Cleveland granted him secret rebates which enabled him to undersell his rivals. Such is the simple secret of Standard Oil's initial success. By exploiting its strong position to improve its product, by using lake steamers, by building pipe lines, Standard emerged in 1879 as the controller of over 90 per cent of refined oil, able to dictate its own terms to the railways. Thenceforward for a generation, in one legal form or another, Standard Oil exercised a virtual monopoly over the sale of oil both at home and abroad. The Company's earnings were so gigantic that, in spite of the voracious needs of the oil business, they spilled over into a multitude of enterprises—in railways, in copper, in iron ore, in public utilities. So dominant on Wall Street were the "Standard Oil crowd," where their National City Bank alone came to dwarf all other banks in the country, that for a time they rivaled the power of the great Morgan himself.

In steel, too, the pace of concentration was equally forced. Exploiting his talent for cultivating influential connections and for picking partners, Andrew Carnegie forged ahead, sinking the profits from his simple partnership into more efficient plant than his competitors. Already the leading producer of basic iron and steel, he began in the 1880s to extend his control over all departments of this complex industry. His partnership with Frick brought him coalmines, coking plants and railways. He bought ore fields in Michigan and, finally, after a tussle with Rockefeller, leased the great Mesabi Range in Minnesota. He built a fleet of ore boats on the Great Lakes; a new port, Conneaut, on Lake Erie; and, finally to be free from the Erie Railroad, a private line of his own from the lake to Pittsburgh. Carnegie was, however, faced with powerful combinations of manufacturers of steel wire, tubes, tinplate and similar products who were in a position to bargain about the price of his steel. In some of these combinations was to be discerned the hidden hand of Morgan; and in the end Carnegie came face to face with that massive banking power. For some time Carnegie had wished to retire and devote himself to philanthropy. After rejecting offers from various syndicates to buy out the Carnegie Company, including one from Rockefeller, Carnegie determined to force the financial world to buy him out on his own terms. Believing that combination was the only solution for the steel industry and that he was in a stronger position than his rivals, he proceeded in 1900 to announce a series of expansion programs aimed directly at the independents. The threat of this war of attrition served its purpose. At this time Carnegie was making a quarter of the Bessemer steel and half the structural steel and armor plate in the country and, having built his empire entirely on his own resources, his financial position was impregnable. Wall Street and the steel trade were in a panic. Even his partner, Schwab, believed that Carnegie's day, which was that of a one-man business, was done and that he should go. In the upshot Schwab and Gates, one of the threatened independents, persuaded Morgan that he alone could command the resources to buy Carnegie out. In a memorable interview with Morgan, Carnegie named his price—$450,000,000 dollars—which Morgan accepted without demur. To raise the money he gathered together all the important steel interests, including the Rockefeller group, to launch the greatest company the world had seen. The United States Steel Corporation of 1901, with a capitalization of over a thousand million dollars, controlled seventy per cent of the American iron and steel industry.

· · · · ·

In the first decade of the present century, Morgan applied his talents to the creation of "trusts" in other fields such as that of agricultural machinery. Morgan and Standard Oil were by no means the only powerful groups on Wall Street engaged in such activities. But when in 1907 the less happy activities of smaller men led to another disastrous panic it was Morgan who, mobilizing his own resources with those of other giants such as Rockefeller, Harriman and Frick, preserved intact the immense structure they had created. Wall Street had become one of the great money markets of the world.

When, at the outbreak of war in 1914, the stock markets of half the world closed, the blood of Wall Street brokers ran cold at the thought that foreign investors would try to dispose overnight of their four thousand million dollars' worth of American securities in the United States. The Exchange closed its doors; and it seemed as though Wall Street were still financially dependent on Lombard Street. But when four months later the Exchange timidly reopened, the unexpected occurred. Stocks not only remained firm, but boomed. The American capital market proved resilient enough to take the strain of a world at war. In 1915 an Anglo-French purchasing commission arrived in New

York seeking a loan to finance their American supplies. The sum proposed was unprecedented; but a loan of 500 million dollars was successfully underwritten by the House of Morgan who also undertook to handle Allied purchases of food and materials, while at the same time the American steel industry, under Charles Schwab, geared itself to turn out overwhelming quantities of armaments and ships.

Under the stress of war, the centuries-old flow of capital and manufactures from the Old World to the New was dramatically reversed: once, Junius Morgan in London had supplied credits and British rails for American railways, whereas now his son Pierpont, in New York, was raising vast sums to supply Britain and France with the armaments of war. It was the beginning of a new age.

15

Variations in the Rate of Economic Growth in the U. S. A., 1869-1939

by

BERNARD WEBER

and

S. J. HANDFIELD-JONES[1]

1. The object of this paper is to examine the changing rate at which the American economy has grown and expanded in a period of approximately 70 years, to offer some observations on the movement of real wages, and to point to some of the forces which help to account for both.

Our primary interest is the long fluctuations in secular growth as evident in various series of real income and output. We are not concerned with the familiar fluctuations in prices and interest rates although we recognize their relationship to the process of economic growth. No more are we concerned with the short-period business cycle, for we wish to concentrate on the progressing performance of factors in use and not on the varying degrees to which existing factors are employed, degrees which tend to average out in the longer run. Both these classes

Reprinted from *Oxford Economic Papers*, VI, 2 (June, 1954), pp. 101–32, with omissions, by permission of the editors, The Clarendon Press, and the authors.

[1] We are greatly indebted to Professor E. H. Phelps Brown for encouragement and valuable comment, while at the London School of Economics, where most of the statistical work embodied in this paper was carried out, and thereafter. Thanks are also due to Professor Kuznets for reading the manuscript and supplying comment.

of fluctuation have received a good deal of attention from economists and economic historians, but the movements referred to have until recently been relatively neglected. Yet they can equally claim to be a characteristic feature of economic growth.

Apart from its intrinsic interest, the study of the uneven course of progress in the U.S.A. is useful for comparison with some recent work of a similar nature relating to the United Kingdom. In particular, two recent papers have explored the check to real wages and real income a head[2] which occurred in the British economy some time in the 1890's and lasted until 1914. It was shown that the check to real wages can to some extent be explained by a distributive change,[3] but that the major cause of the check to both, real wages and real income a head, must be sought in a check to productivity, statistical evidence for which was supplied.[4]

A comparison with the U.S. data in the period 1890–1914 is of interest therefore if only to establish whether and to what extent the check to productivity which occurred in the United Kingdom and probably also in other countries of western Europe had a counterpart in the U.S.A. It is only by the use of the comparative method that we may hope to establish whether or not such phenomena as the "climacteric" in the United Kingdom and the causes giving rise to it are peculiar to that country alone or are of more general significance. No less interesting than the comparison of movements of real income a head and productivity is the comparison of the course of real wages relative to other incomes.

. . . . .

2. Except for the downswings associated with the trade cycle, there is no check, in the sense of actual decline (or failure to advance), to the growth of real income a head in the U.S.A. until the 1930's, but there are significant variations in the rate of secular growth.

These variations are strongly evident in S. Kuznets's estimates of real national product. The estimates are given in the form of averages calculated for decades[5] and the fluctuations cannot therefore be ascribed to the peculiarities of individual business cycles. Percentage changes from decade to overlapping decade show that three periods of relatively

---

[2] Real income is expressed per head of the gainfully occupied population throughout this paper.

[3] E. H. Phelps Brown and P. Hart, "The Share of Wages in National Income," *Economic Journal*, vol. lxii, June 1952, p. 253.

[4] E. H. Phelps Brown and S. J. Handfield-Jones, "The Climacteric of the 1890's: A Study in the Expanding Economy," *Oxford Economic Papers* (N.S.), vol. iv, No. 3, Oct. 1952, p. 266. [See above, Selection 10—*Ed.*]

[5] S. Kuznets, *National Product since 1869*, N.B.E.R., 1946, p. 118.

faster growth can be distinguished: the decades covered under 1874–83 and 1879–88; 1894–1903 and 1899–1908; and finally 1914–23 and 1919–28. In the intervening periods, it appears, economic progress as measured by real income a head, could advance only at a slower rate. S. Kuznets himself noted such long swings in the rates of growth of national income (measured net or gross), some of its components, population and income *per capita*, with population lagging fairly consistently behind. He located the peaks in approximately the late 1870's, the early 1900's, and the mid-1920's, and the troughs in the early 1890's, about 1910–12, and the mid-1930's. The duration of these swings is thus just over 20 years. . . .

The rates of change in real income a head as well as in real wages are set out in Table 1, and Fig. 1 illustrates the movement of real income a head as expressed by percentage deviations from its linear trend.

3. There are a number of factors on which the growth of real income a head depends: efficiency in production; changes in the relative importance of sectors of different efficiency; income from abroad and changes in the terms of trade.

TABLE 1

U.S.A.: RATES OF INCREASE IN REAL INCOME A HEAD AND REAL WAGES FROM DECADE TO OVERLAPPING DECADE, 1869–1938. COLS. (1) AND (2) IN 1929 PRICES

	(1) S. Kuznets's Net National Product (Bill $)	(2) Col. (1) per Head of the Gainfully Occupied Population ($)	(3) Rates of Change in Col. (2) (%)	(4) Rates of Change in Real Wages (%)
1869–78	9.3	642	..	..
1874–83	13.6	813	+26.7[a]	+2.0
1879–88	17.9	920	+13.1	+9.5
1884–93	21.0	936	+1.8	+4.7
1889–98	24.2	955	+2.0	−0.7
1894–1903	29.8	1,056	+10.6	+1.9
1899–1908	37.3	1,167	+10.4	+3.5
1904–13	45.0	1,246	+6.8	+2.9
1909–18	50.6	1,293	+3.8	+1.2
1914–23	57.3	1,375	+6.4	+8.8
1919–28	69.0	1,545	+12.3	+13.1
1924–33	73.3	1,531	−0.9	+7.5
1929–38	72.0	1,440	−5.9	+9.3

[a] The extremely high rate of change is in part due to an understatement in the 1869 Census of Manufactures. S. Kuznets estimates that a maximum upward adjustment of 5 per cent for 1869–78 and successively less for subsequent decades is called for (*National Product since 1869*, p. 61). This would, however, only slightly affect the rate of change in 1874–83 which appears excessive.

Income from abroad and foreign trade contribute only a small proportion to national income in the U.S., and even large changes in these
factors are unlikely to affect the course of national income in a substantial way. We have therefore not attempted to make the statistical
adjustments which would illustrate the course of national income under
the assumption of unchanging terms of trade and in the absence of
income from abroad.

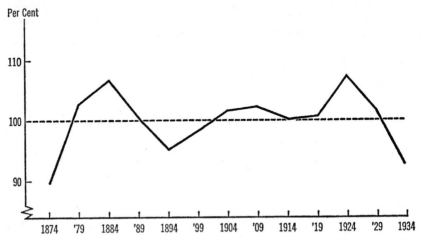

FIG. 1.   U.S.A.: Net National Product (1929 prices) per Head of the
Occupied Population, 1874–1934. Per Cent Deviations from Linear Trend.

The effect of changes in the relative importance of sectors with
different outputs a head is of much greater consequence, particularly
in economies undergoing rapid transformation. If, for instance, in the
course of industrialization, there is a transfer of resources from agriculture to manufacturing and if output a head in the latter is greater
than in the former, the real income of the community may be considerably increased without any changes in productivity in either sector.

We have estimated the effect of such changes in the U.S.A. in 1870–
1930 by taking into account the changing distribution of the labor
force and by assuming that output a head in each of the major sectors
of the economy, such as Agriculture, Manufacturing, Trade, etc., remained throughout as it stood in 1900. The result of the calculation
suggests that in the absence of changes in productivity there would
have been an overall rise of approximately 30 per cent in real income
a head by 1930, a rise which is in large part to be accounted for by a
relative shift away from agriculture towards manufacturing, trade, and
the services.

Decennial percentage increases in real income a head arising from intersector shifts (as distinct from increases due to the advance of productivity in each sector) do not, with the possible exception of the period 1910–30, suggest a relationship with the fluctuations in secular growth noted in section 2. For figures see Table 2. The low entry in 1880 is largely explained by the absence in the 1870's of a shift away from agriculture.[6]

TABLE 2

U.S.A.: Increase in Real Income per Head of the Gainfully Occupied Population due to Inter-Sector Shifts

	1870 %	1880 %	1890 %	1900 %	1910 %	1920 %	1930 %
Base: 1870	—	0.9	7.5	12.2	17.8	21.8	29.9
Base: Preceding decades	—	0.9	6.5	4.4	5.0	3.4	6.6

4. Having noted inter-sector shifts we must now turn to what is the most important element in the growth of real income a head, namely productivity itself.

We have examined the course of productivity in the following sectors of the United States economy: Agriculture; Construction; Manufacturing; Mining, and Transport and Communications. For the period from 1870 to the First World War we have calculated our own productivity indexes by making use of physical output data and Census estimates of persons gainfully occupied in the respective sectors. From 1900 onwards various other productivity indexes become available and these have been used to indicate the course of output a head in the period 1917–39, as well as to check our results in years before 1917. Comparison with our own work shows, on the whole, good agreement, but cannot in every case be expected to be too close in view of variations in coverage of both the output and input indicators. Our indexes, for instance, are calculated per head of persons occupied (and include therefore employed and unemployed), while some of the other indexes are corrected for unemployment. Productivity indexes which allow for unemployment are more satisfactory for some purposes, but we are here concerned with trend and may assume that the latter is not significantly affected by cyclical changes in employment. Table 3 illustrates the "productivity history" of [four of] the five sectors. Construction apart, each sector shows remarkable progress. The frequent ups and downs are those of the trade cycle and need not concern us here, but there are also longer variations in the rates of growth which are of interest and must be examined.

---

[6] The percentage of persons occupied in agriculture, forestry, and the fisheries was 50.2 per cent. in 1870 and 50.0 per cent in 1880. By 1890 it had fallen to 42.8 per cent.

Three periods of faster growth alternating with three periods of deceleration, similar to those found by Kuznets in his national product data, can be distinguished, but the actual turning-points can be identified only approximately. Rather than locating them from changes in the slope of 9-year moving averages, as was done by Kuznets, we have preferred to select for turning-points peaks or troughs of the trade cycle nearest to significant changes in trend. If 1870, the first year covered by our indexes, can be assumed to mark the trough of the first period of faster growth, and 1938 the trough of the last period of slower growth, we can trace three complete swings, similar in timing and duration to those found in Kuznets's national product data, as follows:

	Trough	UPSWING	Peak	DOWNSWING	Trough
I	1870	[late 1870's]	1882	[early 1890's]	1894
II	1894	[early 1900's]	1907	[1910-12]	1919
III	1919	[mid-1920's]	1929	[mid-1930's]	1938

The figures in brackets are Kuznets's dates on which the swings in national product are centered.

The two later swings are strongly evident in the Manufacturing,[7] Mining, and Transport and Communications sectors . . . (Table 3). One qualification only is required. Output a head estimates for transport are available after 1914 for a few odd years only and cannot be analyzed in comparable form, but the estimates for individual years point to a cumulative rise throughout the period between the two wars. This trend may or may not be confirmed by an annual series, but it is certain that a most important element in this sector is the growth of efficiency due to fuller utilization of systems and the growing length of haul.

A similar pattern can be traced in Agriculture, although the upward lift after 1894 is broken during 1898–1902, and in the 1930's the sector diverges from Manufacturing and Mining by continuing the progress of the 1920's, although at not quite so fast a rate.

Productivity in Construction follows a pattern of its own. It is dominated by the "Building Cycle," a type of fluctuation similar in duration, though not, except for the inter-war years and the immediate pre-1917 period, in chronological timing. It is a fluctuation which is best separately analyzed in terms of supply and demand for houseroom and more specifically in terms of population growth and migration.

The outcome of our productivity analysis must now be related to the movement of real income a head. Table 3 gives, in a comparable form, the rates of growth of productivity in four sectors and of real in-

---

[7] In Manufacturing the upswing after 1894 seems to have reversed some time between 1900 and 1905, rather earlier than in the other two sectors.

TABLE 3

RATE OF GROWTH IN REAL INCOME PER HEAD OF THE GAINFULLY OCCUPIED
POPULATION AND IN OUTPUT A HEAD IN FOUR SECTORS OF THE
UNITED STATES ECONOMY, 1869–1938

	(1) Real Income per Head of the Gainfully Occupied Population (%)	(2) Manufacturing. Output a Head (%)	(3) Transport and Communications. Output a Head (%)	(4) Mining. Output a Head (%)	Agriculture. Output a Head (%)
1869–78	..	..		..	..
1874–83	+26.7	+3.5	+4.0	+18.6	+9.6
1879–88	+13.1	+9.8	+8.4	+21.8	+6.9
1884–93	+1.8	+5.3	+7.1	+16.0	+3.6
1889–98	+2.0	+5.1	+2.8	+6.5	+5.3
1894–1903	+10.6	+12.7	+7.5	+11.1	+7.6
1899–1908	+10.4	+13.8	+12.3	+21.5	+7.4
1904–13	+6.8	+6.9	+6.7	+14.5	+13.9 +12.1	+4.2
1908–18	+3.8		+9.9	..	+11.5	
1914–23	+6.4		+7.6	..	+6.3	+5.6
1919–28	+12.3		+14.0	..	+19.4	+9.7
1924–33	−0.9		+14.8	..	+9.6	+10.2
1929–38	−5.9		−3.6	..	+0.7	+6.3

come a head. Fluctuations in the latter are closely confirmed by similar fluctuations in the former, a confirmation which is highly encouraging in view of the independence of the two sets of data. A pattern of growth characterized by alternating periods of faster and slower growth seems to be firmly established for a large section of the economy. However, it must be remembered that not all sectors studied display this pattern (i.e. Construction) and that some sectors are not included in our analysis (i.e. Trade, Services, etc.). Nevertheless the fluctuations in the four sectors are large and powerful enough to account for the pattern of the similar fluctuations in real income a head.

5. Changes in productivity can be further examined by calculating indexes of output a head in a number of industries for which data of both output and manpower are available. Such indexes are not, in each case, as reliable as those calculated for the aggregate sectors of the economy, largely on account of difficulties encountered in estimating, in consistent and comparable form, the number of persons occupied. . . .

Our indexes do not extend to years later than 1914 and we have not attempted to survey the trends for the 1870's and 1880's in view of the paucity and possible unreliability of the data. But our analysis of the period 1890–1914 brings out a few points of interest.

A most striking fact to emerge is the fast advance of the iron and steel complex of industries, an advance which must largely be accounted for by such innovations as the opening of the Mesabi range; the supersession of the Bessemer method by the open-hearth process, with its advantages in permitting the use of a wider range of raw materials, including scrap; the increasing size of furnaces, and technical integration and mergers.

But the trend of output a head advanced, if at a slower pace, in

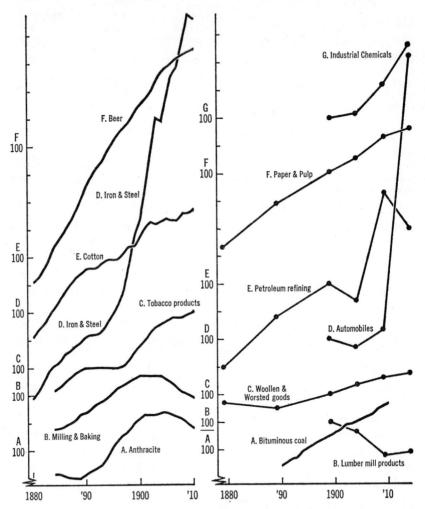

FIG. 2. U.S.A. Indexes of Output per Head in Some Industries, 1879–1914.

9-year moving averages.
1890–9 = 100.
One vertical division = 10 points.
1899 = 100.

A: 9-year moving average 1890–9
= 100.
One vertical division = 20 points.

most industries (examined) during the 1890's and until 1900–5, thus confirming the upswing in the aggregate manufacturing sector. The slowing down in the rate of growth after the turning-point is similarly confirmed by some individual industries, but the pattern is considerably more varied. If general advance was the keynote before 1900–5, each industry went its own way thereafter.

A selection of the industries examined is graphed in Fig. 2.

It would be folly to lay undue stress on generalizations derived from the amount and nature of the data assembled here, but three tendencies of a general validity suggest themselves. First, the similarity of the movement of output a head before 1900–5, already referred to; the subsequent

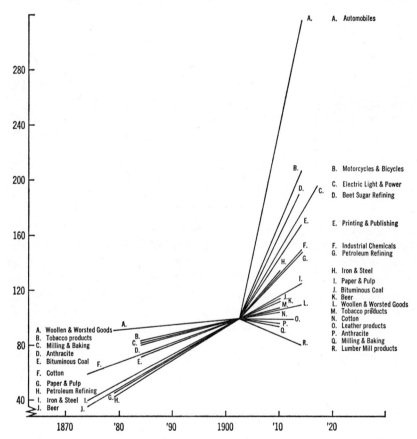

FIG. 3. U.S.A.: Indexes of Output per Person Occupied or Employed in Some Industries, 1874–1917.

9-year moving averages except Fabricant indexes and index for Electric Light and Power. 1900–4 = 100; Fabricant indexes 1899–1904 = 100; Electric Light and Power 1902 = 100.

"splaying out," with some industries continuing their advance while others decelerated or suffered decline; and finally the divergent history of "old" and "new" industries after 1900–5.

These points are best illustrated by means of a diagram. In Fig. 3 output a head indexes are represented by two sets of lines, the first connecting the beginning of the various indexes with the base period, taken to center on 1899–1904; and the second connecting the base with the last years for which output a head was available. The "splaying out" is forcibly brought out, and it is equally evident that the industries which drive upwards after 1900 are the "new" industries such as automobiles, motor cycles, electricity, industrial chemicals, etc, while the old industries slacken or at the best continue as before. But it is the traditional industries which dominate the pattern of development for they are fully grown; the newer industries and techniques, rich in promise for the future, were in this period of only limited application and importance. But their fast advance at a time when other industries, associated with older techniques, were decelerating is of interest for the light it sheds on the process of economic growth itself.

6. The purpose of this section is to explore the relationship between capital accumulation, innovation, and the fluctuations in the growth of real income a head, noted in sections 2, 4, and 5. For that we rely largely on the capital coefficient or ratio of the stock of capital to the flow of income, each measured in real terms.

. . . . .

Through 1894–1939 the long-run trend of the capital coefficient, based on capital formation data, is best summarized as horizontal, but if the lower values in 1879, 1884, and 1889 are included it could equally be regarded as moderately rising (Fig. 4). Interpreted in less formal terms, a stable capital coefficient implies constant returns per unit of physical capital while a rising coefficient would mean diminishing returns. A tendency to diminishing returns is likely to set in at some stage as a result of successive applications of capital, of a given type, per unit of labor. On the other hand, such a tendency will be counteracted by improvements and innovations, and these appear to have been powerful enough to maintain in the long run a stable capital coefficient in both the United Kingdom and the U.S.A.

We do not intend to place much emphasis on the trend of the coefficient over the whole time range of the series. Its movements in the short run are no less significant, and we look to them for illumination on the changes in the rate of progress. A single generalization describes these short-run trends: the capital coefficient rose in the periods of slow growth in real income a head, and it fell in the periods

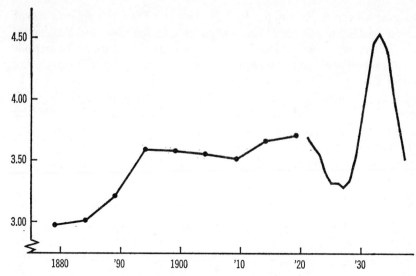

FIG. 4.   U.S.A.: Capital Coefficient (Ratio of Capital Stock to Flow of Income), 1879–1939.

5-year moving averages in 1921–37.

of more rapid growth. In the 1930's the unusually heavy depression strongly affected the trend so that it is difficult to verify this correlation, but it is clearly the case in the 1920's when the coefficient fell quite sharply and real income a head made rapid strides. Prior to 1919, the capital coefficient is only available at 5-year intervals, and the years for which it could be calculated do not in each case tally with the turning-points in the swings in real income; furthermore, the estimates for mid-decade years (1884, 1894, etc.) are less reliable than those relating to the last year in each decade. However, in 1884–94, a period of slower growth in real income a head, the coefficient rose; in 1894 to 1909 the coefficient fell while real income a head advanced rapidly; and in 1909–19, another period of slower growth, the coefficient rose once more. The movements are well defined except perhaps for the fall after 1894 which is so small as to be well within the margin of error. On the other hand, the break in trend in 1894 is very strongly marked and the coefficient for that year is almost certainly too low. Moreover, pronounced movements in trend are likely to be exceptional since both annual investment and the annual increment in the growth of income form only a small proportion of total capital stock and total annual real income. . . .

   This relationship between the course of the capital coefficient and changes in the rate of growth of economic progress measured by real income a head is not unique to the economy of the U.S.A. In a recent paper relating to the U.K.[8] three phases in the movement of the capital coefficient were distinguished, and these phases correspond to periods of more and less rapid economic progress. In 1880–95 real income grew faster than capital stock and the capital coefficient fell; from 1895 to 1913 real income hardly rose at all while capital rose by much the same extent as before and thus the coefficient increased; and finally the coefficient fell again in 1924–38, when real income again rose substantially faster than the stock of capital. Rarely does one find a relation occurring as unexceptionally as this in the records of complex and dynamic economies.

The capital coefficient is, of course, the inverse of the average productivity of capital, measured over the whole range of the economy, to which the concept of real income a head, or the average productivity of the labor force, is symmetrical. It follows that the movement of each can be predicted if any specific production function for the economy as a whole is specified. The simplest case is a function unchanged through time by changes in technique or other innovations. An increase in the stock of capital available to a given labor force will then result in an increase in output and thus an increase in output per head; but the increase in output will be less than proportional to the increase in the stock of capital, so the capital coefficient will rise. If accumulation was proceeding more rapidly than usual in certain periods of time, real income per head would rise more rapidly and so would the capital coefficient. Since the coefficient is observed to fall in periods of rapid growth of real income a head, the varying rates of economic progress cannot be explained by varying rates of accumulation.

In some periods, such as 1884–94 and 1909–19, when the capital coefficient rose while real income a head also increased, if relatively slowly, this simple model of accumulation is not unreasonable. But the observed developments in the other periods for which the coefficient has been calculated, and the consequent stability of the coefficient over the whole span of years, can only be explained by processes of innovation, so transforming production functions that the tendency towards diminishing returns was halted or reversed.

Innovation in this context must be conceived in the broad Schumpeterian sense. It includes not only technical changes in production processes and equipment but also the discovery of new resources, the development of new types of organization, and new methods of management.

---

[8] E. H. Phelps Brown and B. Weber, "Accumulation, Productivity and Distribution in the British Economy, 1870–1938," *Economic Journal*, vol. lxiii, June 1953, p. 263.

And the links between innovations, accumulation, and progress are therefore tenuous. Rapid progress may be experienced due to innovation when the capital stock is increasing no faster than the labor force, as in the United Kingdom between 1924 and 1938; innovation and progress may occur and yet not affect the capital equipment used; and what is more important, a good deal of innovation can be carried into effect in the course of capital replacement out of depreciation funds. On the other hand, periods of rapid expansion in the growth of real income a head are normally periods of accelerated capital formation, implying that innovation generally stimulates an increase in the proportion of capital to labor. If accumulation rather than innovation appeared to be the primary determinant of the expansion in progress, a complex analysis of the demand and supply of capital would be required; but since the capital coefficient tends to fall rather than rise at such times, the emphasis must be placed on innovation.

The evidence arising from our capital coefficient analysis requires, however, cautious handling and is not of a kind which permits emphatic conclusions until more refined methods and statistics are available for verification. Quite apart from the difficulties relating to the adequacy and reliability of the statistical materials, there are difficulties of a conceptual kind which must be kept in mind.

The growth of real income is a function not only of accumulation and capital-requiring innovations but also of such factors as the structure and organization of the labor force, management, etc. Changes in any of these may be reflected in the capital coefficient irrespective of what happens to capital stock. Hence the validity of the capital coefficient as a tool of analysis of the kind employed here depends in part on the relative role capital *cum* innovation plays in economic progress.

It may be objected that variations in the rate of growth of real income a head may arise as much from the varying degree to which the capital stock is utilized as from new capital. In other words, a falling capital coefficient may be due not to innovation but to greater utilization of existing capacity and a rising coefficient may merely reflect greater waste of resources. However, fluctuations in the use of capacity are largely a phenomenon associated with the trade cycle and need not concern us here since they tend to average out in the longer run. Nor would a persistent trend towards increasing excess capacity, even if established, seriously affect the argument. Only variations in the use of capacity similar to the swings in economic progress noted might affect our results, and we know of no evidence to postulate such movements.

Capital coefficients may therefore, we maintain, usefully be employed to illuminate some of the key relationships in economic progress, as indeed the empirical findings confirm. They might prove even more profitable if they were to be based not on aggregate capital stocks and outputs but on stocks in individual industries and sectors of the economy. In addition average coefficients might with advantage be supplemented by marginal coefficients, and some technical measures of capital efficiency might prove illuminating.

7. It is natural to think first of the processes of innovation as an aggregate of many unrelated inventions and improvements, each by itself insignificant but of importance *en masse*. While such gradual continuous improvement is always occurring, the pattern of technical progress as a whole appears to have been dominated not so much by this kind of gradual advance as by discontinuous and massive innovation. There are at any time a small number of basic factors which are technically fundamental to large groups of industries or indeed to the whole area of productive activity. Such factors include the source of power or the type of prime mover, the methods of transportation, the property of materials, and such fundamental techniques as the interchangeability of parts, automatic control systems, and high-temperature technology. One or two inventions and discoveries of this kind can transform the common technical foundation in a large sector of the economy and may revolutionize production functions all round. Steam combined with steel produced a second industrial revolution of this character, and electricity, the internal combustion engine, and industrial chemistry brought about a third. And perhaps a fourth is now in preparation.

It is to discontinuities in such basic innovations that we look for an explanation of the uneven rate of progress in the U.S.A. Periods of rapid advance are periods of widespread application of new methods and materials in many fields, infinitely complicated by chains of consequential innovation and the possibilities of each benefiting from the changes occurring everywhere else. As the new possibilities are gradually losing scope the pace will slacken; compared with the substitution of a steel steamship for several sailing-ships, the addition of further steamships to the transformed fleet cannot be expected to make much difference, even though they may be of improved design. During these ensuing periods of relative technological stability, preparations for the next advance will likely be under way. But the delay between invention and massive innovation may be prolonged, and a good deal of expenditure may have to be incurred with little or no immediate return. Funds must be found for the costs of research, for early and perhaps unsuccessful experiment, for pilot plants, and finally heavy investment may be required to make the new product generally available. At the same time, alternative claims for resources for a host of other purposes, such as war and rearmament drives, unproductive capital exports, building booms, or gold-rushes, may delay or interrupt the application of technical invention[9] and may thus slow down the pace of economic advance.

8. We may now briefly indicate some of the major specific innovations which are associated with the upswings in the rate of growth of economic progress in the U.S.A. The innovations mentioned cannot, of course, pretend to be comprehensive, but may serve as a tentative indication of the nature of the changes involved.

Thus the expansion of the 1870's may be associated primarily with steam power. It was in the 1870's that steam became more important than water as a source of power in manufacturing, measured by both the number of units in which it was employed and by the total power generated. Even more important was the opening of the interior and the development of new resources which was made possible by the application of steam to transport. The trend of railway building was sharply upward from the mid-1860's to the all-time peak in the mid-1880's. Thereafter it reversed, and although it continued at a high level through 1885–1917, the most productive lines as regards effect on real national income were completed in the earlier period. What remained was more in the nature of supplement and extension rather than breaking new ground.

By the early 1880's the most productive lines were completed and the post civil-war spurt was losing scope. Further extension could not produce the same effect and the rate of advance could not be maintained. Were it not for the invigorating stimulus of the railways on a country rich in undeveloped resources, a stimulus perhaps not as potent in the 1880's as it was in the 1870's but nevertheless powerful, the setback to the rate of growth might have been even greater.

Similarly, the expansion of 1894–1907 may be ascribed to a large extent to innovation by way of discovery and development of new resources and to the widespread exploitation of the innovations made possible by steam in combination with steel. Steel in the form of machinery, rails, ships, and building was indeed the fabric of expansion. Output of steel ingots and castings rose from 4.4 million tons in 1894 to 23.4 million tons in 1907; even so, its contribution to national productivity is enormously understated and cannot, of course, be measured directly by output or productivity in the steel industry, no more than the effect of railway development can be summarized by mileage of lines laid or by some measure of efficiency of freights or passengers carried. The magnitude of the contribution of these innovations must

---

[9] For an exposition, as regards the U.K., of the thesis that investment alternated between productive and unproductive (or relatively more and less productive) outlays, see W. W. Rostow, *British Economy in the 19th Century*, 1948, ch. 1. [See above, Selection 9—Ed.]

be estimated in terms of the consequences, immediate and remote, of their massive application throughout the economy.

Closely connected with the progress in the iron and steel industry were developments in mining where perhaps the most important individual development was the opening up on a large scale of the Mesabi range from which came the rich and abundant ore used in the manufacture of iron and steel. The exploration of oil became important and new sources of base metals were exploited. If advance in this sector was due in large part to a better transport system and to developments elsewhere, its importance in its own right as a class of innovation particularly significant in the economic progress of the U.S.A. is unchallengeable.

By 1907, however, the major force of these basic innovations appears to have spent itself. Opportunities for further massive extension were gradually being exhausted and once again the economy could progress only at a slower rate of growth. Retardation was, however, not universal. New techniques were being developed and new industries forged ahead and if, as yet, relatively insignificant in their effect on the economy as a whole, they were nevertheless a pointer to the future.

Finally, the fast advance of the 1920's can be linked to the maturing of "new" industries and techniques—such as electricity, the internal combustion engine, ferrous alloys, industrial chemicals, etc.

9. That the swings in the rate of growth of real income are a real phenomenon and not a statistical illusion we take to be reasonably established. . . . But granted that we accept the statistical findings, there still remains the problem of determining whether the fluctuations discussed form part of a long-period cycle or whether the various ups and downs reflect no more than distinct historical events.

The argument in favor of thinking there is a cycle is the comparative regularity of the undulation revealed.

The case against it is that economic progress, as measured by real income a head, must follow one of the following courses:

1. Constant rate of progress.
2. Continually falling rate of progress.
3. Continually rising rate of progress.
4. Rate of progress sometimes higher and sometimes lower.

But only the last of these is probable. Yet if this is the course of advance, then it is in the nature of any trend we fit to throw up deviations on either side of the trend alternatively, and this in itself can hardly be regarded as a cycle.

The case against is further strengthened in that only three swings have been observed, a number of events which would appear altogether insufficient for emphatic judgment in favor of a cycle no matter how regular. Moreover, the first and third swings are associated with recovery from civil war and world war respectively. Only the swing from the mid-1890's to 1914 is relatively free from the upheaval of war.

For these reasons we should perhaps avoid the term "cycle." Perhaps we are nearest the truth if we say that fluctuations in the rate of growth of economic progress are to be expected from time to time in the expanding economy but may occur at irregular intervals and be of varying intensity.

· · · · ·

10. [This section considers the course of real wages in the United States. Real wages were affected by shifts in the distribution of income which were favorable to labor in the interwar period and adverse to it in the 1870's and in 1885–1917. The latter check is particularly striking, and is discussed in terms of the immigration of unskilled labor; the relative inflexibility of wage rates; and the growth of monopolistic combinations and practices.—Ed.]

11. We may conclude with a brief comparison of development in the U.S.A. and the United Kingdom in the 20 years or so before the First World War.

By way of a counterpart to the British climacteric which came in the 1890's and lasted until 1914[10] we can find nothing in the U.S.A. beyond some retardation in the rate of growth. Moreover, the check in the United Kingdom lasted considerably longer and was accompanied until 1907 not by retardation but by a major expansion in the U.S.A. Far from the two economies following a pattern of growth sympathetic in direction they are in the late nineteenth century nearer to exhibiting a rhythm of growth opposite to each other. This is the case in 1894–1907 when the rate of growth is rising in the U.S.A. while the United Kingdom suffers almost a standstill, but it does not apply in 1907–14 when the U.S. reversed its trend to resemble more closely United Kingdom experience. Unlike the United Kingdom, however, the U.S.A. did not cease its advance but merely slowed down its pace. The different rhythm of growth in the U.S. and the United Kingdom cannot be gone into here, and it is at any rate discussed elsewhere.[11] For our purposes it must be sufficient to point to the existence and alternation in both

---

[10] [See above, Selection 10.—Ed.]

[11] A comparison of secular fluctuations in the growth of real income for the two countries over the whole period 1869–1938 is made by Professor Brinley Thomas in his article on "Migration and the Rhythm of Economic Growth, 1830–1913," *The Manchester School of Economic and Social Studies*, vol. xix, No. 3, Sept. 1951.

countries of fluctuations in secular growth, set in motion by similar forces, and to note, in particular, the divergence in intensity and duration in the 20 years or so before the First World War.

Comparison of the movements of real wage rates shows a check in both countries. In the United Kingdom real wages actually declined from the late 1890's while in the U.S.A. the increase in the 30 years from 1885 to 1916 amounted to no more than 7 per cent. The fact that real income a head was rising rapidly in the U.S.A. at this time is a clear indication of the distributive character of the check. In contrast, the decline of real wages in the United Kingdom can only in part be attributed to distributive factors. The main emphasis there must be placed on the check to national productivity which depressed other incomes as well as wages. Even had labor maintained its relative position, real wages would only have remained stable.

PART
· V ·

INCOMPLETE
DEVELOPMENT:
FRANCE AND ITALY

INTRODUCTION

The emerging industrial system of the nineteenth century did not transform to the same degree every country which was touched by it. This Part offers three illustrations of the types of approach which historians have adopted to the development of two economies, France and Italy, which enjoyed only partial success. Two points, however, must be borne in mind at the outset. The first is that France and Italy have been selected for illustrative purposes only: there were other countries which also failed to attain anything like the level of development which characterized the British and American economies. The second point is that French and Italian economic growth prior to the First World War can be judged "unsatisfactory" only when compared with the leading economies of the nineteenth century. Relative to their own previous experience the period was one of quite significant advance and far-reaching economic change. Although available measures of long-run expansion are still somewhat rudimentary, they give a fair idea of the magnitudes involved. Thus, one estimate for the national product of France between the 1840's and the first decade of this century gives an average rate of growth per decade of 18.6 per cent for the economy as a whole and 16.3 per cent on a per capita basis. Comparable data for Italy between 1862 and the First World War are 15.7 per cent and 8.1 per cent. These figures may be usefully contrasted with average decennial rates of growth of national product for other countries:[1]

		Total (%)	Per Capita (%)
United Kingdom	1860/9–1905/14	25.0	12.5
Russia	1870–1913	27.7	10.4
Denmark	1870/8–1904/13	32.7	19.3
Sweden	1861/8–1904/13	34.8	26.2
Germany	1860/9–1905/14	35.6	21.6
Canada	1870/9–1905/13	47.1	24.7
Japan	1878/87–1903/12	49.2	33.7
U.S.A.	1869/78–1904/13	56.0	27.5

In the case of France two contrasting essays are reprinted. That by Professor Rondo E. Cameron of the University of Wisconsin (Selection 16) presents material which was subsequently incorporated with other results of his research in a wider-ranging study, *France and the Economic Development of Europe, 1800–1914* (Princeton, N. J., 1961). To Professor Cameron the causes of France's relative economic retardation seem to lie in such factors as inappropriate raw material endowments (to this extent it might suitably be compared with Professor Baykov's analysis of Russia's development in Selection 21) and misguided government policies. On the other hand, in Selection 17, Professor David S. Landes of the University of California at Berkeley concentrates far more attention on the pattern and outlook of entrepreneurship—on those social and cultural factors which conditioned the behavior of businessmen and which, Professor Landes argues, were the major (although not the only) reasons for France's poor showing. Although no two studies can be entirely representative of a large body of literature, those by Professors Cameron and Landes are good examples of the two principal types of hypothesis concerning this particular subject.[2]

The overall performance of the Italian economy in the late nine-

---

[1] Simon Kuznets, "Quantitative Aspects of the Economic Growth of Nations. I. Levels and Variability of Rates of Growth," *Economic Development and Cultural Change*, V, 1 (October, 1956), 13. On this subject also see Tables 1 and 2 in Selection 2.

[2] For other references to the controversies surrounding this subject, see the Selected Bibliography.

teenth and early twentieth centuries was also disappointing.[3] One index implies an annual average rate of industrialization (i.e., growth in manufacturing, *not* total product) of 3.8 per cent between 1881 and 1913—characterized by only two relatively brief subperiods of rapid expansion in 1881–88 (4.6 per cent per annum) and 1896–1908 (6.7 per cent per annum). And even in the latter period "industrial growth . . . seems to have proceeded in a less uniform and more jerky fashion [than in other countries], denoting perhaps a more delicate state of public confidence and greater entrepreneurial uncertainties and hesitations."[4] As explanations of this situation (particularly in contrast with the situation in such countries as Russia and Japan) Professor Gerschenkron suggests an inappropriate tariff policy (which did not protect the crucial growth-inducing industries); the relatively low level of railroad construction, which thereby denied to the economy one of its main potential driving forces; an unstable political environment joined to widespread labor unrest; and "the absence of any strong ideological basis to industrialization."

On the other hand, even if the overall performance of the Italian economy had been much more impressive, it is still most probable that it would have featured the contrast which has been evident in the economic history of the country for the last hundred years—the contrast between the poverty of the South and the relative prosperity of the North. For the fact is that, relative to the economy as a whole, the southern regions have always been underdeveloped. This aspect of Italian economic growth is the subject of Selection 18, in which Professors Shepard B. Clough of Columbia University and Carlo Livi of the University of Venice indicate the economic contrasts involved, and investigate the economic and social forces which lie behind them. Their analysis seems particularly relevant to the 1960's—when the lack of balance between regional rates of growth is a problem for advanced countries as well as for economies in the initial stages of development.

---

[3] For a scholarly view of Italian industrialization in this period, see Alexander Gerschenkron, "Notes on the Rate of Industrial Growth in Italy, 1881–1913," *Journal of Economic History*, XV, 4 (December, 1955), 360–75.

[4] *Ibid.*, pp. 362–66.

16

Economic Growth and Stagnation
in France, 1815-1914[1]

by

RONDO E. CAMERON

———————————————————————————————

I

Throughout the first half of the nineteenth century and probably as late as 1860 France was the world's wealthiest nation. Its agricultural resources were the greatest in Europe at a time when agriculture was the occupation of the major part of the population even of Europe. It held second place in world industrial production, after Britain. It had the largest population of any Western nation except Russia before being surpassed by the United States in 1869. Yet by 1914 France ranked behind the United States, Russia, Germany, Austria-Hungary, and

Reprinted from *The Journal of Modern History*, XXX, 1 (March, 1958) (pp. 1–13, with omissions), permission of The University of Chicago Press and the author. Copyright 1958 by The University of Chicago.

[1] A paper prepared for discussion at the first Newberry Library Conference on French History, May 11, 1957. The author expresses his appreciation to Dr. Stanley Pargellis, librarian and host to the conference; to Professor Henry Bertram Hill for suggesting both the conference and the topic; and to the participants in the conference, from whose comments and criticisms the author, if not the paper, has benefited in no small degree. A report of the conference is in the *Newberry Library Bulletin*, IV, No. 7 (December 1957). . . .

Great Britain in total population and was seriously challenged by Italy among Western nations. In total industrial production France had fallen behind the United States and Germany as well as Great Britain. In the production of per capita real income—the best single measure of economic welfare—France had been surpassed not only by the three latter nations (with the possible exception of Germany) but probably by Switzerland, Belgium, the Netherlands, one or more Scandinavian countries, and several commonwealths of the British Empire.

The general pattern of growth in France resembled that of other Western nations, except that in periods of prosperity the peaks were lower—with one notable exception—and in periods of depression the troughs were deeper. Statistics of national income, industrial production, capital formation, and other measures of economic growth, while subject to wide margins of error, will perhaps permit the following rough characterizations. The years from 1815 to 1846 in France constituted a period of slow, steady growth in total income (averaging 2 or 3 per cent per annum), punctuated by minor fluctuations and terminated by the severe economic and political crisis of 1847–51. There followed, from 1852 to 1857, a brief period of very rapid growth, surpassing that of any other nation in the same decade but ending abruptly in another deep depression in 1857–59. From 1860 to 1882 the economy grew once again at a rate close to that of the period 1815–48, although interrupted by the catastrophic Franco-Prussian War and its economic consequences. From 1882 to 1896 the rate of growth was very low or possibly even negative, but the century ended with another reprise, 1897–1913, comparable with that of 1815–48. Taking the century as a whole, it is quite clear that the rate of growth of all relevant variables was substantially below that of other Western industrial nations; growth in the period 1883–96 was so slow as to justify the term "stagnation." Indeed, in comparison with rates of growth in several countries—notably Germany and the United States—the entire period from 1871 to 1914 appears to be one of *relative* stagnation. In part the comparison is illusory, as a result of the extremely low rate of growth of the French population: when all other growth rates are reduced to a per capita basis, the comparison is by no means so unfavorable to France. Even so, it still indicates that France grew more slowly than its neighbors.

This disappointing performance becomes more puzzling when one reflects upon some of the advantages that France possessed in the first half of the century. Not only was France a wealthy nation; it was also a leader in technology. In both pure and applied science the contributions of Frenchmen rivaled those of any other nation. French engineering schools were the acknowledged leaders in their field. France possessed an ample supply of skilled labor in both industry and agriculture. French businessmen, whose numbers were swelled and spirits quickened by recruits of other nationalities, were energetic, alert, and intelligent. French textile manufacturers lost no time in adopting the new techniques of spinning and weaving that had been developed in England, even when that meant stealing them from the enemy during the Napoleonic wars. French ironmasters were among the first on the Continent to replace charcoal with coke in the smelting process, despite substantial geographical and geological handicaps and high tariff protection for charcoal iron. French bankers made insurance an industry of the first order under the Restoration; they pioneered the field of investment banking and developed the techniques for managing large-scale enterprise under the July Monarchy and the Second Empire. Yet, in spite of its great relative wealth, its advanced technology, its skilled labor force, and its ambitious and intelligent scientists, engineers, and businessmen, the fact remains that France fell well behind most other Western nations in industrial development in the second half of the period under consideration.

Many authors have offered explanations of this phenomenon (some even before it was clearly visible) and many factors—geographic, political, social, and cultural, as well as "purely economic"—have been cited as contributing to it. Whatever the factors on which they lay greatest emphasis, however, all responsible scholars agree on the mechanism—or lack of one—by which these factors affected the growth rate of the French economy: the failure to invest in domestic industry. This paper offers no "new" explanation of the phenomenon; it seeks, rather, to group and analyze all possible factors in order to separate those which were fundamental and determining from those which were merely contributory or incidental. In so doing, it will employ those familiar twin pillars of economic theory, supply and demand.

II

The most distinguishing social characteristic of modern France has been its low rate of demographic increase. The facts of this situation are too well known to bear repeating in detail. Suffice it to say that, whereas population grew by more than 1,000 per cent in the United States during 1815–1914, by about 167 per cent in the United Kingdom and Germany, and by similar magnitudes in most other Western nations, the French population increased by only 35 per cent in the same period.

The effect of a stationary or slowly growing population on the demand for final goods and services scarcely needs emphasis. Without customers there are no markets; without new customers there is no extension of the market, with its concomitant increases in specialization and the division of labor, except insofar as rising incomes and new foreign outlets result in larger expenditures. There is general agreement among students of population that

> . . . when population is growing rapidly, an expansionist and aggressive spirit tends to animate entrepreneurs and the economic community. For, since each sees his market expanding, there is expectation that augmenting sales opportunities will rapidly relieve transient gluts and seeming overcapacity, and there is less pressure than otherwise, therefore, to introduce monopolistic restrictions. This optimistic state of expectations is fed, moreover, by the conditions that obtain in the investment goods industries when population growth is conjoined with an availability of resources. When population is not growing, or is declining in number, a less optimistic state of expectation may, but perhaps need not necessarily, prevail. There is a presumption, however, that cessation of population growth contributes to the rigidification of the economic structure of a society.[2]

Professor Kuznets, in the most comprehensive recent international survey of economic growth, finds: "In general, there is a positive association between rates of growth of population and of total product. All the coefficients of rank correlation . . . are positive and substantial; and the tests indicate that most of them are significant at the 1 per cent level."[3]

Two important qualifications need to be made to these statements of the relationship of population to economic activity. First, there are cases in which a large population can be a deterrent rather than a stimulant to economic growth. Countries with a high initial ratio of population to capital and exploitable natural resources (among which are many of today's "undeveloped" countries) fall into this category. To some extent this may have been the case in France. At the beginning of the nineteenth century its population density was somewhat greater than most of its neighbors and to that extent may have constituted a larger "hump" to overcome in the initial stage of industrialization. But in view of the rapid extension of technological possibilities in the West and the relative abundance of capital in France, it seems unlikely that this was a very significant influence.

In the second place, population growth is—or may be—in part a consequence, as well as a cause, of economic growth. The chain of causation running in this direction was undoubtedly a factor in the extremely low rate of population growth in the second half of the century, in

---

[2] J. J. Spengler, "Anthropologie et demographie: Generalitiés," in IX° Congrès International des Sciences Historiques, *Rapports* (Paris, 1950), I, 24–25.

[3] Simon Kuznets, "Quantitative aspects of the economic growth of nations. I. Levels and variability of rates of growth." *Economic development and cultural change*, V (1956), 28.

particular. On the other hand, the rate of growth of French population in the first half of the century was already quite low, although
the rate of growth as well as the level of income was relatively satisfactory. Considering the important social, psychological, and political
factors affecting the French birth rate which had little or nothing to
do with economics, it is reasonable to conclude that population growth
was more important as a cause than as an effect of economic growth
in nineteenth-century France.

Population and per capita real income are the most important determinants of aggregate demand. However, the distribution of income
as well as its magnitude likewise plays an important role in the
demand for final products. Other things being equal, the greater the
degree of inequality in incomes, the smaller the proportion that will be
spent on consumption goods. Owing to the relatively large proportion
of small proprietors in the total population, many investigators have
concluded that wealth and income were unusually widely distributed in
France. This appears, however, to be an erroneous notion. At the beginning of the twentieth century, one-third of the adult population
owned no income-producing property at all. Of the two-thirds of the
nation classed as *proprietaires*, 85 per cent owned but 13 per cent of all
property. The maximum income that could be obtained from an average
holding in this category was but 320 francs—scarcely enough to support a family without additional income from labor, even though the
francs were gold. In fact, the majority of the proprietors in this group
derived less than 80 francs a year from their property. The remaining
87 per cent of the wealth was held by only 10 per cent of the adult
population, and more than half of this was in the hands of the few
thousands who constituted less than one-half of 1 per cent of the adult
population. No doubt income was more widely distributed than wealth,
but there is no reason to suppose that either was more widely distributed
—at least by any significant margin—than in other Western nations.

The unequal distribution of wealth and income contributed to lowering the proportion of income spent on current consumptions; but other
influences worked in the same direction. French frugality is proverbial
the world over. All classes of the French population, including even
unskilled workers, exhibited a high propensity to save, but this trait
was especially characteristic of the numerous peasants and *petits
bourgeois*. Because of its peculiar demographic pattern, France had a
significantly higher proportion of its population in the middle and older
age groups than any other country. These are precisely the groups that
have both the greatest incentive and the greatest ability to save. The
small size of the typical French family, the desire to elevate one's self
or one's children in the social structure through the accumulation of

a modest fortune, the ideal life of the *rentier*, the large proportion of peasants living away from the blandishments of the cities and harboring dreams of acquiring more land as they nursed the growing hoards in their *bas de laine*—all these factors contributed to raising the average propensity to save.

One might suppose that the high average propensity to save would have encouraged economic growth by facilitating capital formation. However, French saving did not always take a socially productive form. From 1850 to 1914 between one-third and one-half of all French savings were channeled abroad in the form of foreign investments. While these investments yielded a higher return, on the average, than equivalent investments in France and thus increased, in the short run, the national income over what it would otherwise have been, they did in one sense of the word deprive French industry of capital, and set the stage for future capital losses through inflation and repudiation. Even more damaging to the cause of French industrial growth was the large demand for capital by government. Approximately 25 per cent of all French savings in the period were invested in the securities of central and local governmental units. Although viewed as wealth by the private owners, these securities can scarcely be regarded as such from the point of view of national income accounting. The funds thus acquired by government either were used for the most part to cover current operating deficits or were immobilized in such politically inspired and economically unproductive monuments as the local-interest railways. If one calculates the average propensity to save after first deducting from savings the current budget deficit, it is by no means so impressive as otherwise. Finally, the *bas de laine* was no mere household expression. In spite of its large foreign investments and, after 1875, its unfavorable balance of trade, France continued to accumulate gold throughout the century. But much of this gold failed to lubricate the wheels of industry, serving instead to swell the sterile hoards in woolen socks.

The decision to save or spend is one aspect of consumer tastes or preferences. In still other respects, the habits of French consumers militated against the development of modern industry. To foreigners, especially Americans, the most striking feature of French consumption patterns is the large proportion of expenditures devoted to products of the soil, on the one hand, and to artistic and luxury goods (including domestic service and leisure), on the other. Budget studies for both the nineteenth and twentieth centuries indicate that Frenchmen spent—and spend—a far higher proportion of their incomes for agricultural products—principally food and wine—than any other Western nation. To be sure, the distribution of consumption expenditures is a function of the level and distribution of income and of the relative prices of all consumable goods and services, as well as of "preferences." But even after adjustment for differences in income, the proportion of expenditure devoted to primary products in France is well above the average of other Western nations.

III

. . . . .

The most crucial determinant of the industrial potential of France lay with the supplies of industrial raw materials, including fuel. France possessed great wealth in its agricultural resources (for which it demonstrated its solicitude by excessive tariff protection), but it was poor indeed in fuel, useful minerals (except iron ore), and other industrial raw materials. Between 1870 and 1914 industrial raw materials constituted 60 per cent by value, of total French imports; for Germany the figure was less than 50 per cent and for England less than 40 per cent. (To be sure, England imported a much larger percentage of foodstuffs than France did, but this did not enter directly into the cost of production of industrial products.) Of the major industrial nations before 1914, only the United States had a net export balance in foodstuffs and raw materials; all others had to pay for imported raw materials and foodstuffs by exporting manufactured goods and such "invisible" exports as shipping, insurance, and financial services. Three-fourths of England's manufactured exports sufficed to pay for all imported raw materials; Germany's imports of raw materials were, on the average, roughly balanced by equivalent exports of manufactured items; but the value of France's imported raw materials exceeded manufactured exports by 25–35 per cent, despite the predominance of manufactures in French exports.

The most critical of industrial raw materials was coal. By the end of the nineteenth century virtually every industrial process involved the use of coal, which also constituted the principal source of domestic heat and light. In France the manufacture of iron and steel absorbed more than one-sixth of the total consumption (domestic production plus net imports) of coal in the period 1880–1912. (Only in Belgium did the ferrous metals industries take a larger proportion of total coal consumption.) In 1912 the railways and the manufacture of gas took, respectively, 15 and 7 per cent of the total. The engineering, chemical, textile, nonferrous metals, glass, and paper industries also consumed important quantities, as did the production of electricity.

Only France, among the major industrial nations, had to rely on imported coal to meet its total fuel requirements—and that despite the fact that the ratio of exploitation to reserves was considerably higher than in other countries. In 1913 the United States produced more than 500 million tons of coal; the United Kingdom, 290 million; Germany, 279 million; France, only 41 million. But at those rates of exploitation the total probable and possible reserves of the United States, as estimated by experts of the International Geological Congress would last for 4,000 years; of Germany, for 2,200 years; of the United Kingdom, 650 years; of France, only 400 years. Between 1830 and 1910 French coal imports ranged from a low of 25 per cent of total consumption (in 1830) to a high of 45 per cent (in 1857); from 1870 onward, imports averaged one-third of total consumption, or one-half of total domestic production. France made up the deficit in her domestic production by purchasing from its principal industrial rivals, the United Kingdom, Belgium, and Germany. Pit-head prices of coal in France averaged twice as much as in the United States, about 50 per cent more than in the United Kingdom, and about 20 per cent more than in Germany. Yet, as between France and her European neighbors, there were no appreciable differences in methods of exploitation.

Iron ore is the only important industrial raw material possessed in abundance by France, but in the years before World War I even this was of restricted value. Just prior to the Franco-Prussian War, Lorraine already produced almost 50 per cent of all French ore, but the Treaty of Frankfurt of 1871 ceded most of the producing mines to Germany. The invention of the basic process of steelmaking in 1878 enhanced the value of the vast beds of minette ores and stimulated new explorations in French Lorraine; after challenging new technical problems had been solved, the Briey basin was brought into production by 1894 and in 1910 produced more than two-thirds of all French iron ore. But the absence of suitable fuel in the immediate vicinity, plus the fact that Saar coal came to be employed largely for smelting ore from German Lorraine, continued to serve as a damper on the development of the French iron industry.

Copper, lead, zinc, and tin were the only other metals of major economic significance before World War I. French scientists and engineers made important contributions to the technology of copper and zinc, in particular: and French capital was employed in copper, lead, and zinc mines in Belgium, Germany, Spain, Italy, Sweden, and the United States. But no important resources of any of them existed in France, which was almost wholly dependent upon imports of these metals.

French industry was hampered not only by the short supply and high costs of mining coal but also by the costs of transporting it and other raw materials, whether produced domestically or imported. Unlike the situation in Germany, Belgium, and England, few of the major French mining centers were located in or near industrial centers or centers of population. In 1831 the noted engineer Auguste Perdonnet, in explaining the difficulties encountered by French ironmasters wishing to adopt coke smelting, pointed out that transportation costs on coke-smelted iron frequently amounted to between one-third and one-half the total cost of manufacture. As transportation facilities improved, these fantastic proportions were reduced, but the differential in favor of foreign producers was never entirely eliminated.

In the early 1840's the several gas works located in Paris consumed approximately 65,000 tons of coal per year. The entire amount came from Belgium because French coal was either unsatisfactory for the production of gas or too expensive or even more distant. The pit-head price of the coal in Belgium was 17 francs per ton, but the cost to the gas companies was 44 francs: customs duties amounted to 6 francs, and the transportation added 20 more.

. . . . .

IV

The low rate of urbanization in France has been referred to in another connection, but the "peasant problem" was primarily a political and social rather than a purely economic problem. Its roots antedate the revolution of 1789. Whereas in eighteenth-century England the process of agricultural enclosure set in train a movement out of agriculture that was intensified by the positive attraction of new industries, a contrary tendency—the *morcellement* of territory—took place in France and reached a climax when the Revolutionary land settlement confirmed large numbers of peasants in the ownership of the land they occupied. *Morcellement* was further encouraged by the Revolutionary law on inheritances: in the hundred years following the Revolution the number of agricultural proprietors doubled, while the population as a whole increased by less than 50 per cent and the agricultural population remained virtually stationary. The widespread peasant proprietorship not only resulted in underemployment of manpower in agriculture but also prevented a growth in the size of the unit of cultivation and inhibited the utilization of the most advanced techniques.

A similar consequence flowed from the policy of commercial protection by slowing the transfer of resources, both labor and capital, from areas of low to areas of high productivity. Agricultural protection was especially costly in the three decades before World War I, when improved means of transportation brought large quantities of cheap foodstuffs to Europe from newly opened overseas countries. But even under the Restoration and July Monarchy agricultural protection hindered the industrial development of the nation.

The protection accorded to industry was at least as damaging. Few proponents of industrial protection used the argument that protective duties would stimulate the introduction and development of new industries; fewer still were the industries introduced as a result of protection. (The one notable exception to that statement, sugar, ruined France's leading colonial industry in the process.) Instead, the prevalent attitude among the advocates of high tariffs was *sauve qui peut*. The coal tariff of 1816 and the prohibitive duties on ironwares under the Restoration and July Monarchy hindered the introduction of coke smelting and the puddling process; after the new techniques won the field in spite of the duties and other obstacles, the ironmasters demanded continued protection to offset the higher cost of domestic coal and the expense of importing fuel; but this artificial advantage was, in turn, countered by the duties on coal and coke, despite the obvious dependence of France on external supplies of this essential fuel. The engineering, machinery, and other industries using large quantities of iron, steel, and coal, which could have competed in the world market had they been allowed to purchase raw materials at world prices, were thus penalized—and with them the nation as a whole—for the benefit of a few uneconomical but strategically placed industries.

Many other aspects of governmental policy and administration could be singled out for their adverse effects on economic growth. Per capita taxation in France was the highest in the world for most of the century. Moreover, approximately three-fourths of all government revenues—a larger proportion than in any other Western nation—came from indirect taxes, the most inimical to economic growth of all forms of taxation. The high absolute and relative levels of taxation might have been justified if the government had used the resources for purposes of positive economic development, but such was rarely the case. Costs of collection consumed a disproportionately large share of each year's receipts. Military expenditures (including service on war-induced debt) absorbed about half of the total budget, or rather more than 5 per cent of the national income. On January 1, 1913 the total number of *fonctionnaires* (state, departments, communes, etc., but excluding *militaires*) exceeded one million—more than 2½ per cent of the total population and about 5 per cent of the labor force. One of the principal results of maintaining this army of bureaucrats was the withdrawal of personnel from productive occupations in order that they might interfere with the production of wealth by those who remained in industry. Take, for example, the administration of the mining laws. The costly and complicated process, dating from the first Napoleon, that had to be followed in order to bring a new mine into exploitation stands in marked contrast to the exceedingly liberal mining law adopted by Prussia in 1865 and was responsible as much as any single factor for the long delay in activating the Briey iron-ore basin. Other examples could be cited. On the whole, it appears that government activity, both promotional and regulatory, retarded more often than it assisted economic growth.

V

The causes of the disappointing performance of the French economy in the period 1815–1914, in the second half of that period in particular, did not lie—originally, at least—in a shortage of capital or of technical skill and knowledge; on the contrary, these essentials of economic growth existed in relative abundance. Nor are the causes to be found *directly* in the capacities, habits, and attitudes of the French people, including, of course, the entrepreneurial groups. Instead, the deficiency of aggregate demand for the products of industry, on the one hand, and higher average costs of production in certain key industries than prevailed elsewhere constituted the major obstacles to industrial development. The deficiency of demand stemmed from the low rate of population growth, the unequal distribution of wealth and income, and consumer preferences expressed in relatively strong propensities to save, to enjoy leisure time, and to consume the products of agricultural and artistic industries. (But it must be remembered that consumer preferences reflected in part an adjustment to conditions of supply.) On the supply side, the salient characteristic and perhaps the most important single difficulty in the problems facing the French economy was the relative scarcity and consequent high cost of industrial raw materials and fuel, especially coal. This obstacle was magnified by difficult locational problems entailing expensive transportation and by unwise policies and inept administration by government.

. . . . .

In its attempts to help the industrialists overcome their problems, the government with few exceptions did more to hinder than to promote economic growth. What the situation called for throughout the century was less, not more, governmental action.[4] Even if the essence of the problem had been clearly perceived—which it was not—demographic movements are notoriously unresponsive to government policy, and no amount of legislation will create coal deposits where they do not exist. With regard to her economic capabilities, France produced *too much* rather than too little food and coal. The same may be true of iron and steel as well, although, in the absence of the coal tariff, production of

---

[4] It should be clearly understood that I refer here to action intended for the purpose of promoting economic growth. Other types of legislation—for example, protective social welfare measures—no doubt influenced the rate of growth of wealth and income, but they must be judged by other criteria as well; in any case, there was precious little legislation of that type in nineteenth-century France.

those items might have been economically pushed to greater lengths. In any case, French consumers and most other French industries paid the price of protection for agriculture, coal, iron, and steel. Had it not been for the artificial encouragements of commercial policy, more resources would have been utilized in pursuits where they were economically more efficient,[5] such as fine fabrics, porcelain, crystal, glassware, machinery and engineering products, watches, paper products, etc. The fact that it was with these commodities that France was able to compete in international markets lends weight to the argument that it was not merely tradition or love of luxury that caused French producers to specialize in commodities requiring large proportions of skill, design, and individuality relative to the value of raw materials but that it was rational on strictly economic grounds. Cobden, in commenting on the results of the Crystal Palace Exhibition of 1851, noted:

> England was unrivalled in those manufactures which owed their merit to great facilities of production, and Americans excelled in every effort where a daring mechanical genius could be rendered subservient to purposes of general utility; but there was one country which, in articles requiring the most delicate manipulation, the purest taste, and the most skillful application of the laws of chemistry and the rules of art to manufacturing was by universal consent allowed to hold the first rank; that country was France.

The great technological innovations of the late eighteenth and nineteenth centuries that transformed economic and social life, built great cities, and bound mankind closer together for good or evil relied primarily on mineral fuels and the basic metals. These were precisely the resources in which France had the least natural advantage. In her long history France has known many eras of greatness, but the age of steam and steel was not one of them. Or, since no time is inherently good or bad but only a time of opportunity, true greatness for France in the nineteenth century would have consisted in producing those commodities for which her resources were best suited and in using her great cultural and intellectual influence for pacific and humanitarian ends, including the progressive liberalization of international commerce and communications. That is exactly what many French investors, engineers, and entrepreneurs did in their private capacities in the great task of world economic development and industrialization. Unfortunately for France and Europe, their actions did not always mirror the policies of their government.

---

[5] I stress the word "economically," because there is no reason to believe that in the technical sense French industries were, on the average, any less efficient than those of other countries. In some respects—e.g., in the utilization of fuel—they may have been *more* efficient technically because of cost considerations.

17

French Entrepreneurship and Industrial

Growth in the Nineteenth Century

by

DAVID S. LANDES

<hr/>

I

The study of French enterprise and entrepreneurship is rewarding
for two major reasons. In the first place, anything that will help explain
the present weakness of French industry and commerce throws light in
turn on one of the most important political phenomena of the last 150
years: the fall of France from hegemony under Napoleon to the position
she holds today. Secondly, the history of French business and businessmen is significant precisely because of France's relatively minor place
in the economic world. If we are to weigh the validity of the recent
emphasis of theorists on the role of the entrepreneur qua se in the
over-all process of economic change—on the contribution of the personal element to the impersonal operation of the system—we must consider not only the more "modern" nations but those less industrialized
as well. It will not suffice to study the progress of American or German
business and deduce therefrom impressive theories on the importance
of the businessman. The converse must also be examined: To what

Reprinted from *The Journal of Economic History*, IX, 1 (May, 1949) (pp. 45–61,
with omissions), by permission of the Ecomomic History Association and the author.

extent are certain attitudes and values inimical to the development of enterprise? Or concretely in the case of France, to what extent have the character and mentality of the French financier, industrialist, or merchant been responsible for the relatively retarded status of the country's economy?

Unfortunately, owing to certain inhibiting factors, some of them the temporary reflection of postwar instability and impoverishment, others the semipermanent result of outdated academic traditions and an unfavorable social milieu, French scholars have not only neglected the subject almost entirely but are unlikely to give it much attention for a long time to come. This, of course, makes the problem of research that much more difficult—the historian must in effect start from scratch. But at the same time it renders all the more urgent, in so far as scholarly needs may be termed "urgent," a provisional synthesis that will introduce the question and furnish a solid foundation for future specialized effort. This article does not quite pretend to be such a synthesis. It is meant more as a suggestive outline, directed especially at other students of entrepreneurship in the hope of arousing, first, interest and, second, criticism.

For the study of French entrepreneurship, the years from about 1815 to 1870 are undoubtedly the most important.[1] This was the period of France's industrial revolution, the critical era of change and growth that in large measure fixed the economic structure of the country. It is precisely during this time of decision, therefore, that the influence of the individual may be expected to have been paramount. Furthermore, from a purely practical standpoint, the researcher is best off in the nineteenth century. The student of entrepreneurship obviously needs private archives, family records, and the papers of various firms. Such materials are almost nonexistent for the prerevolutionary period, and after 1789 their inaccessibility varies directly with their contemporaneity. In a country where every businessman fears the fisc and every bourgeois worships privacy, it would be utter presumption to ask for documents of recent date. Even those of a century ago are rarely opened to outsiders, as the rebuffs of many a French scholar will testify.

II

What, then, was the French entrepreneur of the industrial revolution like? Here a word of caution is in order. As one writer put it: France is diversity. It is astonishing to note the geological, climatic, ethnographic, cultural, and other variety found in an area smaller than

---

[1] For the purpose of this article, the entrepreneur is not only the "innovator" as such but the adapter and manager as well. In other words, the entrepreneur is the businessman who makes the decisions.

the state of Texas. In one sense, therefore, there is no such thing as *the* French businessman. On the other hand, the development of a single, conscious nation with its implications for economic, social, and spiritual unity has inevitably shaped the individual more or less to the common mold. In spite of nuances and exceptions, there are definitely certain characteristics of entrepreneurship during this period generalized enough to constitute a type.

To begin with, the average French entrepreneur was a small business-man acting for himself or at most on behalf of a handful of partners. This was especially true in 1815. To take the two most important in-dustries, in textiles he was still at that time the "undertaker," the little capitalist who furnished the raw material to scattered spinners and weavers and then collected the finished goods for market, and in metal-lurgy he was the isolated *maître de forges*, with his furnace built along some country stream in the neighborhood of iron deposits and forests. Transportation in those days was provided by a multitude of *maîtres de poste*, haulers, boatmen, and, especially for local shipments, peasants exploiting their livestock in the quiet season. Foreign trade was in the hands of small commission and shipping firms, some of them with perhaps one or two coasting vessels, others with as many as half a dozen ocean-going sailers, while retail trade continued in the small, cluttered shops of the eighteenth century. Finally, such credit as was available came from private lenders or from small local banks, many of them built on profits made in commerce and industry and most of them restricting their clientele to an intimate circle of trusted friends and relatives. The corporation, to all intents and purposes, did not exist.

Naturally, the years that followed changed this picture in many im-portant respects. Certain districts, notably Alsace, the Nord, and Nor-mandy, saw the rise of impressively large cotton factories. If the woolen industry, owing to slower mechanical progress, cannot show develop-ments of comparable magnitude, companies like Paturle-Seydoux at Câteau-Cambrésis and Holden at Reims nevertheless represented im-portant concentrations of capital and labor. In the manufacture of iron and steel, where a more important outlay of capital was required, the Schneider plant at Le Creusot and the De Wendel mills at Hayange and Stiring were only the best known of the larger units. During these years, the railroad, which necessitated an unprecedented accumulation of private capital, completely transformed land transport. Foreign trade was similarly affected, though to a lesser degree, by the steamship. It was during this period also that retail commerce made its first significant departure from the tradition of centuries with the introduction of fixed prices and the creation under the Second Empire of the first successful department stores and branch outlets. As for finance, it required the boom psychology of the 1850's and 1860's to launch the first corporative investment and deposit banks.

Nevertheless, a survey of French business in 1870 quite clearly shows that these new concentrations of economic strength were still the exception. In land transport the change was complete; the very nature of the new technique imposed regional monopolies and large corporations. But in the other primary economic sectors, the small entrepreneur remained the norm, even in those areas where the factory system had come to prevail.

In the second place, the French businessman was a fundamentally conservative man, with a firm distaste for the new and unknown. Security was his first concern, and it was generally felt that the quickest road to success was the slow but sure one. The main thing was to watch the sous; the francs would take care of themselves. Thus enterprise was generally characterized on the one hand by a high rate of book amortization—also intended incidentally to conceal the size of profits— and on the other by slow turnover of equipment. The average French producer was reluctant to buy machines to begin with; when he bought them, he wanted them to last. How much this emphasis on caution and thrift was due to the influence of the peasant mentality it is hard to say. Suffice it to point out that even today the visitor to France is struck by the passion for conservation of the most trivial objects, even *la ficelle* of Maupassant.

A third major characteristic of the French entrepreneur was his independence: the typical firm was pretty much self-sufficient. Since the cost of expansion usually came out of company revenues and, if necessary, the pockets of the owner or his relatives and friends, the goal of enterprise was the highest possible *rate* of profit. Naturally, all were not equally successful in this endeavor, but the fact remains that most French industrial growth in this period was financed precisely in this manner. To choose merely one striking example among many, the unusually prolific and prosperous Motte textile interests of Roubaix, who were said to purchase or build a new mill every time a Motte was born, never found it necessary to request outside credit or funds of any sort.

It is fairly obvious, however, that cautious management, obsolescent plants, and high profits are not a combination designed to flourish in a world of cutthroat competition. As stated above, the French entrepreneur prized security above all, and a secure market meant one well protected from foreign inroads. For all but the last few years of this period, therefore, French industry and commerce were protected by a series of impassable duties and prohibitions, which for most businessmen came to represent as much a permanent element of the environment as the ground on which their factories stood.

Nevertheless, the elimination of foreign competition was not in itself sufficient to guarantee the prosperity of any and all producers. This was, after all, a period of technological change, and certain firms inevitably fell behind in capacity and efficiency. Theoretically, the competition between these marginal units and the more progressive firms should have been enough in itself to eliminate the laggards and hasten modernization. In many cases it did have this effect. Yet the fact remains that backward forms of production and distribution remained widespread in France for a surprisingly long period side by side with far more efficient techniques. In part, of course, this was due to the cost of transportation, which made it difficult, especially in the heavy industries, to compete far from the base of operations. But there are far too many cases where this explanation will not suffice, and there it would seem that the usual mechanism of competition was not operative. It is not easy to find concrete examples owing to the inaccessibility of records of business costs and prices, but the data available in the many government tariff inquiries and similar sources would seem to show quite definitely that the more efficient French producer was not inclined to push his advantage. In most cases he preferred a healthy amount of what Joseph Schumpeter has called "entrepreneurial profit" to the elimination of rivals and a consequent rapid expansion of capacity. The latter involved much more effort to begin with, and might well have necessitated appeals to outside credit.

Furthermore, this dependence on high tariffs was only one aspect of a general reliance on the aid and protection of the government. Under the old regime the French manufacturer had been more a functionary than an independent entrepreneur; industry had been in large measure a sort of hothouse growth, nurtured by and derived from the central administration. The Napoleonic period, if anything, strengthened these characteristics. It is not surprising, therefore, that the businessman came to look on the government as a sort of father in whose arms he could always find shelter and consolation. This fundamentally infantile attitude, which must be distinguished from the predatory outlook not uncommon in the United States, was carried in this period to remarkable lengths and characterized businessmen from one end of the scale to the other. There is essentially no difference between the request of a wheelchair maker of Belleville that the state purchase twelve of his devices for donation to various hospitals and the petition in 1848 of three of France's biggest iron firms, Schneider, Boigues, and Bougueret-Martenot, that the government take over the defaulting Paris-Lyons Railroad and make good on four million dollars owed for delivery of rails.

To be sure, there were important exceptions to this widespread conservatism and timidity. Contrary to popular assumption, France has had her share of pioneers, and indeed the French rather pride themselves on their imagination and ingenuity. The powerful innovating influence of the Saint-Simoniens comes perhaps first to mind. These disciples of a utopian reformer, many of them trained engineers, combined keen business instincts with the vision of a new economic world, and their role in the French industrial revolution, especially in the fields of transport and banking, cannot be overestimated. Or take retail trade, where Boucicaut established the world's first successful department store, the Bon Marché, Potin produced the first packaged foods for sale through branch outlets, and Révillon revolutionized the French and, on occasion, the world fur business.

Nevertheless, the influence of these and other innovators was considerably dampened by certain characteristics of French enterprise. In this connection, one factor is worthy of special consideration: the difficulty for the *novus homo* of obtaining funds. Under the old regime, the shortage of business capital in France had been just about chronic. Such money as was available went by preference to the various government *charges* or into landed property. During the nineteenth century the situation was apparently much improved. Superficially, at least, the demand for capital was satisfied by reinvestment of profits and the loans of relatives and friends. But this condition was obviously not calculated to facilitate the advent of those newcomers whose only assets were their talent and imagination. Moreover, these difficulties were accentuated by the relatively limited role of the corporation in the French industrial revolution. The unprecedented potentialities of this new business form lay not only in its ability to concentrate thousands of anonymous petty fortunes, the aspect most often emphasized, but in its use as a vehicle for the penniless innovator. In France, however, this use was sharply circumscribed for various reasons, not least among them the red tape and legal difficulties involved and the keen distaste of the saving public for aleatory business investments.[2] It is easy to show that even in those fields where the *société anonyme* predominated, the new form of organization served more to consolidate the position of established financial interests than to open the way for new men. The railroads are an excellent example.

This shortage of risk capital serves to explain in turn, at least in part, why France has so often failed to appreciate its own inventors. From

---

[2] It was not until 1867 that the formation of a firm with completely limited liability and transferable ownership was permitted by the mere act of registration. On the complications and obstacles imposed by the previous regime, see C. Coquelin, "Des Sociétés commerciales en France et en Angleterre," *Revue des Deux-Mondes* (N.S.), XIII, iii (1843), 397–437.

Lebon's discovery of gas lighting at the turn of the eighteenth century, through Girard's spinning machine, Sauvage's screw propellor, and Verguin's accomplishments in artificial dyes, to Tellier's refrigerator and beyond, the list of innovations which originated in France only to find their quickest and greatest development abroad is quite impressive.

Finally, even in those cases where newcomers succeeded in imposing themselves, they usually did so only at the expense of important concessions to the *status quo*. It is no coincidence that so many of the self-made pioneers should appear in the field of retail trade where the scattered shops already in existence were in no position to resist, or that among the Saint-Simoniens, the Péreire brothers, who insisted on carrying the fight to the vested interests, were eventually broken, while an entrepreneur like Talabot, who withdrew from competition with Schneider and the other big ironmasters when warned of the possible consequences, died with his fortune intact. France has been prolific of talent and genius, but she also has had an effective way of putting innovators in their place.

III

It is not within the scope of a short article to discuss and evaluate the many factors that undoubtedly concurred to make the French businessman of the industrial revolution what he was. Nevertheless, certain of these seem more important than others, particularly the structure of French society and the traditions on which it rested.

In discussing the typical firm of this period, one important feature, its family character, was deliberately omitted in order to differentiate clearly between the economic and social aspects of the problem. With rare exceptions, French enterprise was organized on a family basis and the entrepreneur conceived of his business, whatever its nature, not as a mechanism for the production or distribution of goods nor a means to indefinite wealth and power but as a sort of fief that maintained and enhanced the position of the family, just as the produce of the manor and the men-at-arms it could muster were the *material* basis of medieval status. If the family was inclined to remain in business, there was always room for future generations. Thus some firms, like the Japy hardware and watchmaking company, had careful rules regulating the right of each partner to introduce a son or son-in-law into the organization. And if, as was only too often the case, the family was looking forward to "higher" things, a good business was always a steppingstone to a career in the government service, possibly even to ennoblement or marriage into the aristocracy. In either case, the *affaire* was never an end in itself, but the means to an end. The obsession of the entrepreneur with the enterprise as such, which Sombart finds so common in America and Germany, to all intents and purposes did not exist in France.[3]

This fact in turn helps to explain some of the other characteristics of French enterprise already discussed. A family firm is first and foremost a private affair, which accounts in large measure for the self-imposed goal of financial self-sufficiency and the slow adoption of the corporative form. In this respect, the extravagant lengths to which the French businessman has carried what is known as *le secret de l'affaire* are worthy of note. When in 1908 the De Wendel interests felt compelled for the first time in their history to call in outside capital, they preferred to pay 4.5 per cent to German investors rather than borrow at 4 per cent on the French market and publish statutes and statements as required by law. It is truly astonishing to follow the evolution of some of these industrial fiefs, which start as simple private firms, take in generation after generation of children and in-laws, and remain through changes in name and legal status, through wars and depressions, in the control of what one writer has called the *dynasties bourgeoises*.

Furthermore, a family firm is necessarily a cautious firm. It is easy to speculate with the money of others; it is sometimes even easy to gamble with one's own funds. But it is somewhat harder to take chances when every question must be approved by a keenly critical circle of relatives primarily interested in the conservation of the patrimony. And in France at least as much attention has always been given to the preservation as to the creation of wealth.

This characteristic also explains in part the paradox of entrepreneurial dependence on government aid and the undeclared war between business and the state which is so often shocking to the foreign observer. If the administration has always been the tutor of French commerce and industry, it has also been the bureaucratic overseer and prying fisc, half meddler, half thief. Moreover, in France the government has come to be a relatively transitory phenomenon. Rulers come and go, republics rise and fall, but the family goes on. No wonder that taxes are and always have been evaded with a clear conscience. . . .

Although the fundamental business unit was the family, these families were in turn parts of the larger whole, and their outlook was inevitably colored by the prevailing mores, traditions, and attitudes of French society. In every society there exists a hierarchy of status based in part on function, in part on customary values. This hierachy is in effect a scale of social approval and consideration and is unquestionably a primary factor in channeling the aspirations and activities of the group.

---

[3] W. Sombart, *Quintessence of Capitalism* (London: T. F. Unwin, Ltd., 1915), 172–75.

Moreover, this scale is especially susceptible to "cultural lag" and represents an essentially conservative force.

In the French social structure the businessman had always held an inferior place. Three major forces conduced to this result. In the first place, he was detested from the start by the nobility, which rightly saw in him a subversive element. The aristocracy, its military and administrative functions slowly but surely ossifying in a new world of gunpowder and mercenaries, centralization and bureaucracy, turned at bay on its bourgeois adversaries and wreaked revenge with the strongest weapon it had left, prestige. Unable to compete with the driving spirit of these ambitious newcomers, unable to defeat them on their chosen ground of business with their chosen weapon, money, the nobility deliberately turned its back and tilted its nose. Against the practical, materialistic values of the businessman it set the consciously impractical, unmaterialistic values of the gentleman. Against the restless ambition of the parvenu, it placed the prestige of birth; against the mercurial efficacy of money, the solid stability of land; against the virtues of diligence and austerity, the dignity of leisure and the splendor of pomp and circumstance.

If anything, the revolutions of 1789 and 1830 strengthened this attitude. Those few nobles who under the old regime had been active as ironmasters, glass manufacturers, and so on, or had followed the Colbertist tradition of encouragement of and investment in industry, were now for the most part impoverished. To be sure, many of the new generation, especially those whose titles were of recent vintage, were to lend their names and prestige to entrepreneurial efforts and place their capital in railroads, insurance, and other corporative enterprises. But the aristocracy as a group had hardened its heart. The early years of the July Monarchy saw a marked reaction against the new way and the consecration of the myth of noble superiority, social, spiritual, and even physical. One has only to read the flood of scornful literature that followed the Revolution of 1830 to feel the bitterness approaching revulsion on the part of the dispossessed toward anything smacking of bourgeois business and money.

That the entrepreneur was considerably influenced by the prestige of this "superior" group is obvious from his continued efforts to rise into its ranks, either directly or through marriage. For the same reasons, the businessman was rare who did not acquire sooner or later a landed estate, considered the safest of investments and an important criterion of social status. Obviously, most of these new gentry were simply absentee landlords. In some districts like Bordeaux the practice was just about unanimous, and there shippers and merchants were at least as well known for their vineyards and vintages as for their commercial activities. It is impossible to say with any precision how much of the national wealth was diverted from business enterprise on this account, but most writers are agreed that, whether made as a form of conspicuous consumption or for more serious reasons, such investments by business-men and nonbusinessmen were a significant obstacle to industrialization.

The hostility of the aristocracy would not have been enough in it-self, however, had it not been for the acceptance of this concept by the nonbusiness elements of the *bourgeoisie*. This heterogeneous group, which is more easily defined negatively than positively since it includes almost everyone not falling into the small category of nobility or the large mass of the people, had developed in the course of centuries of slow ascension a scale of status heavily weighted with the prejudices of an aristocratic society. Of the multitude of professional groups that composed the *bourgeoisie*, the businessmen were generally relegated to the bottom of the ladder, other things being equal. In the last an-alysis, this social inferiority was what made possible the system of *charges* under the old regime, which by conferring on the *nouveaux riches* the prestige, security, and sometimes ennoblement of public office further depreciated the entrepreneurial classes and intensified their efforts to rise up and out of their "sordid" occupations.

These prejudices by no means died with the Revolution. Instead, the older *bourgeoisie*, dominated by civil servants and the liberal pro-fessions, tended to stress their prestige in the face of rising capitalist elements. In this they were, generally speaking, quite successful, and the invidious distinction between the two groups has continued right up to the present, though with considerably less force since the economic and monetary disasters due to World War I. Considerations of status, moreover, were strengthened by such factors as the security of official or professional positions and the character of the French educational system, a primary force for social conservatism. For these reasons, the best talents in France almost invariably turned to the traditional honorific careers such as law, medicine, or government. This was true even of the children of businessmen. To be sure, the important entre-preneurs were succeeded by their own offspring, but here the importance of conserving the family heritage was a vital consideration, and, besides, great wealth has always excused many a fault. The average businessman was not so fortunate. Apparently, this "curse of *fonctionnarisme*" and the rush toward the liberal professions created in turn a certain perni-cious instability on the lower entrepreneurial levels. One observer, struck by the age of the Flavigny wool firm of Elbeuf, was moved to write: "This inheritance of ownership in industry is something very rarely found in France; the designation 'and son,' so common in Eng-land, is almost unknown in France. Is it the fault of our legislation or of our fickle character?"

The forces of aristocratic snobbery and bourgeois aspiration were significantly assisted by a third, the pressure of literary and artistic opinion. The war between bourgeois and intellectual in France is of long standing, and the progress of the industrial revolution, which coincided with the surge of romanticism, only embittered the quarrel. For the bourgeois, especially the businessman, the intellectuals were suspect if only for their nonconformity. For the intellectual, the genus *épicier*, which included any and all moneymakers, was the essence of crass, hypocritical Philistinism. And if in this fight the Philistine held the purse strings, the pen and brush proved at least as effective. The novels of Balzac, the comedies of Scribe and Augier, and the caricatures of Daumier perpetuated the tradition of Molière and Lesage and fixed as never before the unflattering picture. MM. Jourdain, Turcaret, Poirier, and Robert Macaire are all members of the same family.

The effect of these forces was a general atmosphere that can best be termed anticapitalistic. The medieval concept of production for use and not for profit, of a static as opposed to a dynamic society, never lost its validity. The vitality of the guild idea in France right up to the present day bears witness to this. This current of thought was by no means an insignificant feature of the economic environment and was directly reflected, to choose only one example, in the hostility often encountered by French business at the hands of officials and in the national and local legislatures. The most spectacular cases were perhaps the attacks in the Chamber on private railroad corporations during the 1830's and 1840's and Napoleon III's temporary prohibition on new stock issue in 1856, but these were less discouraging in the long run than the persistent, silent opposition of an unfriendly bureaucracy. Furthermore, it is in the light of this spirit of antagonism toward the new world of industry and commerce that the historian must assess such important phenomena as the traditional French emphasis on quality as against quantity, the preference for handwork over machine work, the keen distaste for anything smacking of speculation or easy money, the frequent praise of agriculture and the land as opposed to business and the city, and so on.

Nor was the entrepreneurial community itself immune to this pervasive sentiment. It is surprising how many of the attacks on the new capitalism came from businessmen, who if generally opposed more from interest than principle, nevertheless made use of and reinforced the traditional conservative arguments. Even the more progressive entrepreneurs, those naturally most favorable to the economic revolution, were affected. The student of French industry, impressed by the social-security systems, technical schools, housing projects, canteens, churches, and other philanthropies characteristic of almost every firm of any size, cannot help feeling that the businessman was often leaning over backward to appease public opinion. Moreover, how else explain the fact that the majority of the more important manufacturers and merchants personally undertook, even sought, the responsibility of what were frequently minor administrative functions at the expense of business duties? Not for the political influence—entrepreneurs have never lacked for instruments to this end. Nor for the negligible prestige of the mayoralty of a provincial village. The desire to show that the businessman was more than a moneygrubbing egoist, that he too could be civic minded, was undoubtedly a factor.

The discussion of the anticapitalist stream of sentiment brings us to the important question of religion as a factor in entrepreneurship. Long before Weber observers had noted that the more advanced industrial and commercial populations of Europe were predominantly Protestant. The rough congruence of capitalism and Reform seemed to indicate a mutual compatibility and reciprocal stimulation of the Calvinist ethic and those qualities which go to make a good businessman.

The proponents of this thesis have found much in French history to support their contention. From the seventeenth century on, the role of Protestant bankers, merchants, and industrialists has been utterly, almost astonishingly, out of proportion to their place in the total population. In the period we are studying, the leading financial houses of France, the so-called Haute Banque, were for the most part Calvinist; so were many, if not most, of the leading shipping and commission houses, especially in Le Havre, Bordeaux, and Montpellier-Sète; and in industry, the remarkable prosperity of the cotton manufacturers of Mulhouse was only the most striking example of Protestant accomplishment.

Obviously this was more than coincidence. Whether, however, the very nature and ethic of the Calvinist faith shaped its adherents for business success, as Weber maintained, is something else again. It is quite clear that in the beginning the Reform found recruits among all classes and that, if, owing in part to requirements of moral discipline and the literacy imposed by individual Bible reading, Protestant members of the working class tended to rise in the social scale, the new ethic nevertheless proved just as favorable to the constitution of a prosperous and zealous peasantry as to the creation of capitalists.

French scholars have been inclined instead to emphasize the minority character of the French Calvinists, with all that such a position implies in the way of effort, determination, and cohesion. As members of a group that had long been openly or tacitly persecuted, the dissenters of the nineteenth century were in a sense the products of a *passé de sélection sociale*. Moreover, from a purely practical standpoint, the Protestants were long more or less excluded from precisely those honorific professional and official careers that attracted the best of their Catholic compatriots. In a way, the capable and ambitious Protestant was almost forced into business.

But, and here Weber's stress on the Calvinist ethic is relevant, the success of Protestant entrepreneurship was not simply a negative phenomenon, a success sought and accepted for want of anything better. It was unquestionably bound up with the very nature and origin of the new faith, with that very quality expressed in the name, "Protestantism." The essential thing is not that the French Calvinists were diligent, thriftly, honest, and so on (they certainly had no monopoly of these virtues) but that they were revolutionaries, not only against Rome, but against the whole medieval-Catholic tradition. For them it was no disgrace to do business; rather it was a disgrace to be idle. Where the Catholic entrepreneur felt keenly the slights of an aristocratic social hierarchy, the dissenter, fortified by the consciousness of his election, was impervious to the sharpest shafts of genteel scorn. His concepts of social value and levels of aspiration were almost diametrically opposed to those of the Catholic majority. There is all the difference in the world between a family like the Seillière, perhaps the most important Catholic representatives of the Haute Banque, who, once ennobled under the First Empire, never again married with commoners, and the competing Protestant houses, the Mallet, Hottinguer, Odier, Vernes, Mirabeau, Neuflize, and others, who never dispersed their fortunes in glorious but unremunerative alliances and intermarried with one another until their lines have become almost inextricable.

On the other hand, the matter is not so simple as all that. Certain Catholic circles, notably the textile manufacturers of the Nord and of Lyons, have shown precisely the same tendencies: the intense, almost exclusive, concentration on the pursuit of gain, the pride in business activities and the firm, scorn of the idle no matter how high-born and how highly placed, and intermarriage with other business families. And these groups, especially the spinners and weavers of Lille, Roubaix, and Tourcoing, are among the pillars of the Roman church in France.

Furthermore, there is good reason to believe that the Reform, while favorable to sustained and self-respecting entrepreneurial effort, nevertheless tended as time went on to dull the spirit of innovation. The puritan virtues, which suited ideally the steady, unspectacular enterprise of the seventeenth and eighteenth centuries, were not so well adapted to the daring and imagination required by the fast pace of modern business. When to this is added the vested nature of much French Calvinist enterprise (by 1848 most of the Protestant entrepreneurial dynasties were already firmly established and more concerned with maintaining their position than in taking chances), it is not surprising that the actual pioneers of the French industrial revolution were for the most part non-Protestant. At the same time, it should be noted that these same qualities of sane, steady, and concentrated effort were perhaps those best adapted to the economic structure of the country; the Protestant businessman was in one sense simply a bigger and better edition of the average enterpriser already described. Many of the radicals have come and gone. The *haute société Protestante* is as powerful as ever.

IV

It is obviously impossible in a short paper to cover every factor directly or indirectly conditioning French entrepreneurship. For this reason I have not specifically discussed such less fundamental considerations as the political, fiscal, or legal environments. Nor have I attempted to weigh the importance of the business mind as one of the major forces shaping France's over-all economic development. Even if it is true that the average French enterpriser has lacked drive, initiative, and imagination—and the evidence indicates that he has—the question still remains of to what extent this failing is attributable to the entrepreneur qua se and to what extent it reflects severe, external handicaps with which he has been unable to cope. Which is the greater factor in the stagnation of a given French steel firm: the timidity of the directors or the cost of coal? It is a nice point, and one that can only too rarely be decided with any precision.

This much may be said: Questions of ultimate causality aside, ideas once formed are as powerful as the strongest material forces, the two types of phenomena continuously interact; and the influence of French entrepreneurial psychology on her general economic structure has been and is extremely important. It is so important that many observers of the present day, from the impatiently chauvinistic American tourist to the leading figures of French commerce and industry, are inclined to give it first priority on the list of France's economic problems. As Lucien Febvre put it: "We shall buy machines, fine machines, when we have acquired from top to bottom a mechanical mentality. We shall organize production effectively when we have freed ourselves of a certain Louis-Philippic petty-bourgeois psychology. Think first. Act afterwards. Then, yes, France, regenerated, will be able to resume a role of leadership in the world. Then yes, the mortgage will be lifted, the heavy mortgage placed on our country by its cult of old ideas, its serene but stubborn museum-piece traditionalism."[4]

---

[4] L. Febvre, in Introduction to C. Morazé, *La France bourgeoise, XVIII*e*-XX*e *siècles* (Paris: A. Colin, 1946), p. ix.

18

Economic Growth in Italy: An Analysis of the Uneven Development of North and South

by

SHEPARD B. CLOUGH

and

CARLO LIVI

If problems of historical study are to be chosen on the basis of their importance in affecting the course of human affairs through time, no phase of life in Western culture during the century and a half after 1800 is more worthy of study than that of economic development. During these one hundred and fifty years there was an increment of total production within western Europe of an estimated 1,500 per cent and an increase of output per capita of some 500 per cent. At no time in history had an equal advance been made at such a rapid pace.

For a great number of reasons, some of which are to be investigated here, all parts of western Europe, to say nothing of the rest of the world, did not share equally in this economic growth. Consequently there came into being great discrepancies in the economic well-being and in the political-military power of different states and of different regions within states—between the so-called economically developed and the underdeveloped areas of the earth. In the course of time, people in

Reprinted from *The Journal of Economic History*, XVI, 3 (September, 1956) (pp. 334–49, with omissions), by permission of the Economic History Association and the authors.

underdeveloped areas, particularly those within national states where certain districts had experienced economic growth, came to want material status equal to that of their conationals and to demand assistance from state funds for raising their level of economic activity. Then, at about the same time, people in more advanced economic districts came to believe, especially in countries where services of the "welfare state" had become extensive, that economic growth of backward areas within their nation would reduce the financial support which they had to give to their cocitizens. They began to think, also, that it was not only their duty to improve the material well-being of the less fortunate, but that they would be better off if the "poor were richer" so that they could do business with them.

Because of such considerations a movement for regional economic equality took root and grew—a movement that was nourished by such economic factors as the presence in backward areas of raw materials, of cheap labor, and of an effective market demand for at least some of the staples of consumption. This movement has led to a spate of speculation about the causes of, and cures for, regional economic differences and to a myriad of plans for the development of economically underdeveloped areas.

Of all the cases of uneven economic growth in any one nation, one of the most striking and one which is particularly pregnant with lessons of economic development is to be found in Italy. Here the South, the *Mezzogiorno*, has fallen economically far behind the Center and North, particularly the latter.[1] Although the South contains 41 per cent of the land area of Italy and has 37 per cent of the population, it accounted in 1953 for but 19.6 or 21.2 per cent of the country's national income, depending upon whose estimate is used. As a consequence, national income per capita in the South was in the same year only some 41 per cent of that of the rest of the nation.

Although we do not have statistical evidence of a strictly comparable character for Italy of a century ago, it would seem that the differences between the South and the rest of the nation have grown greater rather than less. Local taxes, which have not been fundamentally altered in character since 1861 and which today produce revenue on a regional basis in direct proportion to national income, indicate a widening of the

---

[1] The South comprises the provinces of Abruzzi and Molise, Campania, Puglia, Basilicata, Calabria, Sicily, and Sardinia. The Center includes Tuscany, Umbria, Marche, and Lazio. The North is composed of Piedmont, Liguria, Lombardy, Trentino and Upper Adige, Venetia, Venetia Julia, and Emilia. The territory actually contained in the three sections has changed through time because of frontier alterations. For a detailed description of the regions and changes effected since unification in 1861, see *Statistiche sul Mezzogiorno d'Italia, 1861—1953* (Rome: Svimez, 1954), p. xi.

gap. In fact, in the decade 1871-1880 the South accounted for about a third of all the local tax revenue of the nation and a per capita revenue about 75 per cent that of the rest of the Kingdom.

The drastic economic differences between the North and the South are accentuated not only by the fact that they have increased, but also by the fact that they exist between two regions which nourish resentments of each other and which are so far apart that there cannot be intimate contacts of large numbers of their populations. The fact that Piedmont and Lombardy are removed from Sicily by some thousand miles and that Sardinia is in a real sense cut off from the mainland by the sea has not confirmed the old proverb that "distance lends enchantment." Quite the contrary. Northerners have traditionally regarded the South, which they usually have not known from firsthand observation, as being peopled with inferior human beings, and Southerners have looked upon the North, with which they have been ill acquainted, as inhabited by selfish individuals who somehow or other have exploited them. Only in recent times have serious efforts been made to overcome such prejudices and to raise the level of economic activity in the South. And only in the last few years have scholars sought critically to analyze the reasons for unequal growth between North and South.

As a first step in any such investigation, it is necessary to determine what sectors of the economy, whether agriculture, industry, or services, are lagging behind the others and what parts of these main sectors of economic activity are particularly backward. In following such a procedure one finds that in 1952, although 41 per cent of Italy's gross national income came from industry, the South, which had, as we have seen, 37 per cent of the national population, accounted for only 18.2 per cent of industrial income; that although 25.6 per cent of national income came from agriculture, the South was responsible for but 32.8 per cent of total agricultural income; and that although the remaining 33.4 per cent of national income came from other activities, the South accounted for only 13.3 per cent, a proportion that, small as it was, was inflated by income from "public administration," which was paid for in part by taxpayers from other regions of the nation.

Apparently these proportions had in a rough way been similar for a long time. In 1876 the South had but 17 per cent of the industrial workers of the Kingdom, 16 per cent of the steam boilers, 15.4 per cent of the concessions for water power, and a correspondingly small percentage of mechanical looms in the cotton textile industry. In agriculture, on the other hand, the South produced in the early years of the 1870's, 53 per cent of Italy's wheat, 32 per cent of its potatoes, and accounted for enough of the other products of the soil to indicate that its total agricultural output was in line with its percentage of the territory of the Italian state. In transportation the South was at the time of unification definitely behind the rest of the country, having in 1861 only one fifth as much railway and one third as much roadway mileage per capita, and one seventh as much railway and one third as much roadway mileage per square kilometer of territory, as the rest of the country. This weakness in transportation facilities suggests but a slight division of labor, which is a prerequisite of economic growth, and indicates that the "services" sector of the economy was weak, whereas in all advanced economies it is found to be strong.

The above data bear witness to the economic inferiority of the South in respect to the rest of Italy at the time of unification and to an increase of this inferiority over time. They suggest, moreover, that a historical inquiry into the reasons for the South's economic backwardness must be concerned primarily with the industrial and services segments of the economy.[2] This was to have been expected, for the greatest advances in production per operative have been realized in these branches of activity—indeed, output per worker in industry and in services in Italy is at the present time about twice that of workers in agriculture.

The question why the North has experienced greater industrialization than the South has for a long time been the subject of bitter debate among Italian economists and economic historians. Southerners have tended to explain the difference in political terms, contending that the South was neglected by the statesmen of the North who led the movement for the unification of Italy and who wielded power in the new state in the first years after 1861. They have maintained that industrial growth in the South was stunted because Southern industries were suddenly faced with the competition of Northern ones, were deprived of adequate tariff protection when the low rates of the Kingdom of Sardinia were extended to the entire peninsula, and were discriminated against when Italian tariff rates were pushed up at the end of the century. They have claimed that governmental expenditures for public works were much greater in the North than in the South; that all the good positions in public administration went to Northerners; and that Northern tax laws, particularly the "grist tax," which were adopted by Italy, worked a hardship on the South. In short, they have maintained that responsibility for the economic inferiority of the South is to be laid at the door of the North.

In some quarters, especially in the North, this more or less standard account has been seriously questioned. Critics have endeavored to

---

[2] In the sixty years prior to World War II, world manufacturing increased sevenfold. In this period Italy's share of world manufacturing remained fairly steady at about 2.5 per cent of the total. League of Nations, *Industrialization and World Trade* (Princeton, 1945), p. 13.

demonstrate that marked differences existed between the two regions at the time of unification, and they have maintained that the continuing difference cannot be accounted for on the ground of political action, because state intervention was neither of a magnitude nor of an intensity sufficient to change the course of economic development. . . .

Any adequate investigation of why industry and services developed more rapidly in the North of Italy than in the South entails, in the opinion of the authors of the present article, a study both of cultural diffusion and economic growth. It is a study in diffusion because most of the new industrial technology, many of the business practices, and some of the capital for the "industrial revolution" originated in a triangle with apexes in England, northern France, and western Germany and thence spread to other places. And it is a study in economic growth because the seeds of industrialization sown by diffusion would have amounted to little had they not fallen in places where conditions were favorable to their development and would be of little interest in the present context if they had not borne some fruit.

The double task before us is furthermore complicated by the circumstance that some of the factors with which we shall be dealing and much of the evidence which can be marshaled concerning them are so intertwined that from one point of view they appear as "causes" and from another as "effects" of change. In other words, we are involved here, as so frequently in the social sciences, in trying to determine which came first the hen or the egg, or, for that matter, the rooster, and have to take refuge in the principle of necessary concomitance.

From out the maze of data that have been amassed on the subject of industrial diffusion, it is possible to derive two broad generalizations which can serve as points of departure for the present investigation. One of these is that industrial techniques, mechanized transportation, and new business institutions usually moved first to those places where cultural ideologies, economic conditions, and technological knowledge were most similar to, and where communications were the most active with, the early industrialized districts. As can be seen from Table 1, manufacturing spread first to those places within Western culture that were closest to England geographically, or culturally as in the case of North America, and only subsequently to profoundly different cultures. Furthermore, within areas thus circumscribed, industry was attracted to localities that had coal and iron deposits, water power, cheap transportation facilities, and a relatively high agricultural output or active commerce per capita of the population. Therefore, we may well ask at the outset whether these conditions for "pulling" industry to underdeveloped areas were more powerful in Northern or Southern Italy.

If these factors in diffusion are dealt with in the reverse order to

TABLE 1

Percentage Distribution of the World's Manufacturing[a] Production

Period	United States	Germany	United Kingdom	France	Russia	Italy	Canada	Belgium	Sweden	Finland	Japan	India	Other Countries	World
1870	23.3	13.2	31.8	10.3	3.7	2.4	1.0	2.9	0.4	—		11.0		100.00
1881–85	28.9	13.9	26.6	8.6	3.4	2.4	1.3	2.5	0.6	0.1		12.0		100.00
1896–1900	30.1	16.6	19.5	7.1	5.0	2.7	1.4	2.2	1.1	0.3	0.6	1.1	12.3	100.00
1906–10	35.3	15.9	14.7	6.4	5.0	3.1	2.0	2.0	1.1	0.3	1.0	1.2	12.0	100.00
1913	35.8	15.7	14.0	6.4	5.5	2.7	2.3	2.1	1.0	0.3	1.2	1.1	11.9	100.00
1913 [b]	35.8	14.3	14.1	7.0	4.4[c]	2.7	2.3	2.1	1.0	0.3	1.2	1.1	13.7	100.00
1926–29	42.2	11.6	9.4	6.6	4.3[c]	3.3	2.4	1.9	1.0	0.4	2.5	1.2	13.2	100.00
1936–38	32.2	10.7	9.2	4.5	18.5[c]	2.7	2.0	1.3	1.3	0.5	3.5	1.4	12.2	100.00

Source: *League of Nations, Industrialization and World Trade* (1945), p. 13.
[a] Includes finished products, semimanufactures, like unworked metals, pulp, coke, fertilizers, and cement, as well as manufactured foodstuffs, like flour, canned goods, and sugar.
[b] The second line for 1913 represents distribution according to frontiers established after World War I.
[c] U.S.S.R.

which they have been listed above, for the very good reason of following an ascending scale of complexity, attention may first be drawn to those endowments of nature given to the two parts of the Italian peninsula. Niggardly as Italy seems to have been treated in the distribution of the great natural resources which played so important a role in the early development of mechanized industry, there is no doubt but that the North fared much better at the hands of nature than did the South. As regards fertile land, the North certainly had the advantage, for the Po Valley is superior to any area of similar size in the South. Here at least, agricultural output per capita was great enough to permit some savings for investment and to allow the diversion of some labor from agriculture to other kinds of economic activity. As regards mineral deposits, neither region had large supplies of all-important coal, but otherwise the North had distinct advantages. It had iron ore around Lake Como, in the Val d'Aosta, on the Island of Elba, and at Terni in Umbria, which accounted for the establishment in each of these localities, except on the Island of Elba, of smelting and metalworking industries, whereas the South had principally sulphur, lead, and zinc, which were not important enough to change radically the regions in which they were found. As regards water power, the North had the fast and steady-flowing Alpine streams, fed by glaciers and a vast system of lakes, which attracted the cotton and woolen textile industries to them, whereas the South had practically no rivers of commercial importance, and those that did exist were usually dry in the summer. Finally, although both North and South had many good ports, the North had the Po and its tributaries for inland water transportation, to say nothing of canals dug in the flat Po Plain, whereas the South had no inland waterways whatsoever.

Thus, although the natural resource pattern of Italy, could not by any stretch of the imagination be described as remarkable, nature had given the North enough of an advantage over the South so that the former rather than the latter region attracted manufacturing in the early industrial development of the country. This was of great importance for subsequent growth, for the tendency of industries to draw satellite industries to them worked in favor of that area which started first. Thus, the machine industry became located in the North, especially around Turin and Milan, because of the availability of iron and steel and because the chief users of machines, that is, the textile industries, were nearby; the railway equipment industry became established at Genoa, Turin, and Milan because of the supply of metal, proximity to the early market, and local supplies of capital; and the rubber industry was founded at Milan because of the industrial demand for rubber products.

Another advantage which the North had over the South in the process of industrialization was that it had closer and more abundant communications with the earlier-industrialized regions of Europe. Englishmen and Frenchmen who took the "grand tour" to Italy seldom got below Rome, and if they did reach Naples, they usually found it the "very negation of God" in its primitiveness. The French, during the Revolution and Napoleonic period, had much closer relations with the North than with the South, doing much to break down those ideological, political, and hence economic growth. Indeed, they did something to foster the economic development of the North, the Continental System being designed to be of advantage to the Napoleonic Kingdom of Italy as well as to France.

After the restoration effected by the Congress of Vienna, communications between Piedmont and France and England continued to be particularly active. The fact that the Kingdom of Sardinia included a large French-speaking area north of the Alpine passes and along the coast to Nice meant that Piedmontese leaders knew French, kept abreast of what went on in France, and looked to France for leadership in all aspects of life. It was not strange that some of the first railways in Piedmont were built to connect Turin with Paris and that the first great Alpine tunnel, that of the Monte Cenis (1871), was constructed to facilitate rail traffic between the two capitals.

With England, too, the Kingdom of Sardinia had an active exchange of ideas and persons. Not only did many Italian political exiles, like Mazzini, seek refuge in England, but the Piedmontese followed closely the work of English economists and engineers. They received Richard Cobden with warmth on the occasion of his Italian trip; they usually included England when they went on their own "grand tour" of western Europe; and they employed many Englishmen in their industrial enterprises.

For their part, Lombardy and Venetia, which were under Austrian domination, respectively, until 1860 and 1866, had close relations with economically more advanced areas, especially with Switzerland and Germany. Swiss entrepreneurs were so numerous at Bergamo that they formed a kind of colony, which exists even to the present time; the Falcks, who entered the metallurgical industry in the Como region, came from the Rhineland; and foreign names are scattered through the annals of the economic life of Lombardy and Venice. Both provinces had, in fact, a whole coterie of intellectuals who followed the economic and technical literature of England and France and who were anxious to introduce new techniques and economic institutions to their territories.

Not only, however, did the North have an advantage over the South in matters of natural resources and communications with already indus-trialized regions, but also it had a more favorable ideological climate than the South for the acceptance of new methods of production— it had more of a desire to improve the material well-being of the people by increasing production per operative. In the North the medieval and Renaissance economic achievements of Venice, Genoa, Milan, and Florence were glorified and were recognized as having been a necessary condition for the great cultural accomplishments of these cities. Here the acquisition of wealth through trade and industry was not, in general, considered socially degrading, and the members of many noble families, of whom Count Cavour is an excellent example, invested capital in in-dustrial enterprises. In the South the owners of great estates maintained the traditional scorn of the medieval landed nobility for trade and manu-facturing, put their agricultural earnings largely into farming or into living the life of great seigneurs, and rarely turned to the somewhat hu-miliating callings of commerce and industry. Members of other classes had little capital to invest, were hostile to new business methods and attitudes, and had many characteristic modes of behavior which were not conducive to economic growth.

These differences find peculiar support from information pertaining to the joint-stock form of business organization. A detailed study of corporate companies shows, as can be seen from Tables 2, 3, and 4, that the North had relative to its proportion of the population many more incorporated businesses than the South, a great deal more in corporate investments, and more corporate capital per industrial worker than the South. From the extensive use of an institution that was, at the time under consideration, an entrepreneurial innovation, especially in in-dustry, the North, it seems fair to assume, had more of an urge than the South to effect economic progress and more of a penchant for in-dustrial development.

The data contained in the tables suggest that still another factor con-ducive to the drawing of industry and to economic growth generally,

TABLE 2

JOINT-STOCK COMPANIES IN ITALY,
INCLUDING RAILWAYS
(Millions of Lire)

Year	Number with Home Office in South	Number in Kingdom	Nominal Capital South	Nominal Capital Kingdom	Paid-in Capital South	Paid-in Capital Kingdom
1863	50	372	171	1,298	not available	
1867	43	291	99	1,528	83	1,192
1872	59	585	198	2,377	127	1,562
1876	95	622	217	1,974	164	1,341
1887	503	1,568	378	2,900	272	2,135

that of saving out of current income in order to invest in producers' goods, was stronger in the North than in the South. This conclusion seems to be confirmed by such direct evidence as savings bank accounts, of which the South had in 1877 only 7.1 per cent; by data pertaining to bank discounts, of which the banks of issue in the South accounted for

TABLE 3

PAID-IN CAPITAL OF JOINT-STOCK COMPANIES
BY IMPORTANT SECTORS OF THE ECONOMY, 1876
(Thousands of Lire)

Segments of Economy	South	Kingdom	Percentage of South
Banks	81,471	505,399	16.1
Insurance	12,718	80,747	15.8
Mining	34,500	80,770	42.7
Manufacturing	9,804	132,058	7.4
Building—Housing	7,133	81,732	8.7
Railways	——	366,079	—
Other	18,342	94,034	19.5
Total	163,968	1,340,819	12.2

TABLE 4

CAPITAL OF FOREIGN JOINT-STOCK COMPANIES
OPERATING IN ITALY
(Thousands of Lire)

Year	South	Kingdom	Percentage of South	Percentage of Foreign Capital to Total Capital South	Kingdom
1863	125,000	318,620	39.2	73.1	17.2
1867	30,000	78,397	38.3	36.0	4.4
1872	46,875	120,974	38.7	36.9	5.2
1876	56,486	173,019	32.6	34.4	9.9
1887	97,395	426,725	22.8	35.8	17.7

27.5 per cent in 1878; by statistics on bank loans other than governmental, of which the South had 5.5 per cent; by the fact that the South had only 16 per cent of joint-stock banks in 1876; and by findings which indicate that the South had only 12 per cent of the capital in corporations in 1887. In the ensuing years these proportions increased only moderately. In 1952, current and savings accounts in the South were 20 per cent of the nation's totals, bank loans were 17 per cent, and discounts, 20 per cent. Moreover, in this same year the South accounted for only 12.3 per cent of private investments, although public investments brought the percentage of all investments in the South up to 20 per cent of the Republic's total.

One of the reasons advanced to explain the lower rate of savings in the South than in the North has been that the rate of natural growth of population in the former region has been much higher in relation to economic growth than in the latter. Italian experience supports the general observation that as population approaches the limit of food resources and other production potentials, the rate of savings becomes exceedingly low. Demographic phenomena have, indeed, played an important role in the uneven economic development of North and South.

For most of the period for which adequate statistical information is available, Southern Italy has had a much higher birth rate than the North, and in spite of a greater rate of emigration, a higher rate of natural increase.

TABLE 5

NUMBER OF BIRTHS PER 1,000 INHABITANTS

	1881–1885	1896–1900	1936–1940	1950–1951
North	36.1	33.3	20.2	15.4
South	40.5	35.8	29.1	25.5

TABLE 6

NATURAL INCREASE PER 1,000 INHABITANTS

	1881–1885	1896–1900	1936–1940	1950–1951
North	9.9	11.5	7.4	5.5
South	11.7	10.7	13.5	15.7

TABLE 7

OUT-MIGRANTS (−) AND IN-MIGRANTS (+) AS PER CENT OF NATURAL INCREASE

	1901–1911	1931–1936	1936–1951
North	−31.9	+ 4.5	+ 6.2
South	−62.2	−36.0	−20.7

Such demographic behavior had two consequences which were particularly relevant to economic growth. One was that the South tended to have a larger percentage of its population than the North at unproductive ages, especially at the early ones when dependency is the greatest. The second was that emigration, which is usually regarded in overpopulated areas as a highly desirable thing, was, in fact, an economic drain, for most emigrants are at the early productive ages, and the cost of raising these people falls largely as a net economic burden on the economy whence they come. Estimates of what this burden has been for Italy as a whole, and especially for the South, reach staggering sums— sums which might have been saved and invested.

Not only, however, have a high rate of natural increase, a large per-

TABLE 8

POPULATION BY AGE GROUPS

(Percentages)

Ages	Regions	1871	1901	1921	1936
0–14	North	32.5	34.0	30.1	28.3
	South	32.5	34.9	32.6	35.0
15–39	North	38.9	36.9	40.0	45.8
	South	38.7	35.9	36.9	41.9
40–59	North	19.9	19.4	19.4	18.5
	South	19.9	19.7	18.7	16.0
60 and over	North	8.7	9.7	10.1	7.4
	South	8.9	9.5	11.0	7.4
Unknown	North			0.4	
	South			0.8	

TABLE 9

OCCUPATIONAL DISTRIBUTION OF THE ACTIVE POPULATION, 1952

(Percentages)

	North	South
Agriculture	36.6	52.3
Industry, transportation, commerce	40.2	28.3
Other	23.2	19.4

centage of children in the population, and a high out-migration tended to have unfortunate economic consequences for the South, but the labor force in the South has been used less effectively than that of the North. Occupational distribution in the South has been such that a larger proportion of workers has been kept in the low-income earning segments of the economy, such as agriculture, than in the North. Furthermore, the labor force in the South has not been able, because of extensive illiteracy and lack of technical education, to develop skills, at least from early ages, at the same rate as in the North. In 1871 the number of illiterates per 100 inhabitants over six years of age was 59 in the North and 84.1 in the South, while in 1948 the corresponding numbers were, respectively, 5 and 24. In 1949—1950, the North and center accounted for 70 per cent of all school children in technical or professional upper middle schools, that is, for young people from approximately the ages of thirteen to eighteen, while the South accounted for the other 30 per cent. Even the public health of the North has been superior to that of the South, if we may judge by the fact that the expectation of life at birth in the years 1936/1937 was 60 years in the North and 54.2 in the South and that expectations of life in the two regions were not the same until the ages of 20–30 were reached.

A final aspect of the differences between North and South that affected their receptivity to mechanized industry and their general economic growth was the much greater social flexibility in the North than in the South—a less rigid socioeconomic class structure, a more fluid pattern of ideologies, and a more pliant attitude toward productive techniques. As has been observed by many students of social change, the breaking down of rigidities by some great movement of "reform," whether Protestantism, Marxism, or the French Revolution, prepares the way for the adoption of innovations in various segments of society. In the case of Italy, social rigidities were not only more thoroughly destroyed in the North than in the South during the turbulent years of the French Revolution and of Napoleon, but many of them continued to come under more severe attack in the North than in the South during the entire period of the Risorgimento and well into the history of united Italy. The "revival" of Italy was essentially a Northern movement, with Northern leaders and Northern troops, and was virtually imposed on the South. Nor, as has been maintained by some Southern historians, was the South "exploited" by the North after unification, for the South paid a smaller share of taxes to the national treasury than it paid to provincial and local taxes, and it received a greater amount of governmental expenditures for public works in proportion to its national tax payments than the North. Indeed, the state's effort to improve conditions in the more backward part of the nation is illustrated by the fact that whereas the South had only 7.2 per cent of the railway mileage of the country in 1861, it had 32 per cent of it in 1875.

In all respects the North appears to have had advantages over the South for receiving elements essential to economic growth in the great process of diffusion and subsequently for sustaining economic growth. Throughout the history of united Italy the range of opportunities for alternative decisions regarding the use of economic resources of every description has been greater in the North than in the South. The early industrial spurt of the North had a stimulating effect which increased the economic differences between the two parts of the nation. Only recently, particularly since World War II, have earnest policies been initiated to raise the economic level of the South to a point somewhere near that of the North. This means, as is evident from the Vanoni Plan for Italy's economic development during the next ten years, a deepening of investment, primarily for the making of jobs for the most backward part of the country. Here is an interesting experiment in economic growth of a backward area that has few locational advantages for the establishment of the high-income earning segments of the economy, especially industry.

PART
· VI ·
TWO LATECOMERS:
JAPAN AND RUSSIA

INTRODUCTION

The general case of economic growth in Japan and Russia has already been touched on (see Part I, pp. 10, 41–42). There follow four studies of particular aspects of economic expansion in those two countries. Once again the principal (although not the exclusive) emphasis is on the pre-1914 experience of the economies under consideration, since it was then that the decisive transformations began—and began, in both cases, in the discontinuous manner which gives such a spectacular appearance to the beginnings of economic growth (see Selections 3 and 22). As is evident from the table in the introduction to Part V (p. 326), the average growth rate per decade of national product between roughly, the 1870's and the First World War, was, for Japan, 49 per cent (34 per cent per capita), and for Russia, 28 per cent (10 per cent per capita).

To give as broad a view as possible of the nature and background of Japanese economic growth before 1914, Selection 19 reprints, almost in its entirety, the introductory chapter of Professor William W. Lockwood's standard work on the economic development of Japan from 1868 to 1938. Since this is largely a summary chapter, those readers who wish to follow up any particular aspect should obviously turn to the original and informative pages of this substantial book. Yet even in a summary some of the most important characteristics of Japanese growth stand out. For example, the importance of nationalism, and therefore of politics, is clear: the conscious drive for modernization (in non-economic as well as economic fields) was obviously a function of the new vision of Japan and its destiny, and the new social and political arrangements of the country, after 1868. And by the same token, at least in the initial stages of industrialization, the direct role of the state, both as entrepreneur and stimulant, was crucial. (It was the more important in that war and armaments figured prominently in the activities of the government: by 1913 almost 50 per cent of the budget and over half the outstanding debt were devoted to military uses.) As Professor Lockwood shows, the direct influence of government was principally felt in the heavy industrial sector.

On the other hand, enterprising and effective private action was no less significant for Japanese economic progress—and this was true not only of the quasi-aristocratic industrial dynasties which helped create large-scale enterprise (and took over many of the government-built units when the state withdrew), but also of the thousands of small-scale entrepreneurs, in agriculture as well as industry, who were responsible for such impressive advances in output and productivity. Further, as so often happens in backward countries, where so large a proportion of existing production and assets is concentrated in the primary-producing sector, it was on agriculture that a large part of the immediate burden of industrialization fell (particularly since foreign capital was relatively unimportant in Japan until immediately before the First World War). Starting from this point, Professor Gustav Ranis, of Yale University, examines the financing of Japanese economic development (Selection 20) within a theoretical framework which enables him to derive conclusions which range further than the particular case study involved.

In considering the growth of the Russian economy it seemed appropriate to start with a general survey, by Professor Alexander Baykov of the University of Birmingham, of some of the strategic factors in the country's long-run development. As Professor Baykov points out, while no one would deny the importance of social and institutional factors in economic change, historians may sometimes have paid too little attention to those physical characteristics of a country (its topography, its size, and its natural resources) which literally and figuratively underlie its productive capabilities. In Selection 21 he provides us with a concise survey of the physical bases for a good part of Russia's economic history, and goes on to consider some aspects of the post-1917 period. (The student might find it interesting to compare this approach with that of Professor Cameron, in Selection 16, to French development in the nineteenth century.)

The second essay on the Russian experience, by Professor Alexander Gerschenkron of Harvard University, largely concentrates on the crucial period of the late nineteenth and very early twentieth centuries. In an earlier article[1] Professor Gerschenkron concluded that the great reforms of the 1860's (notably the abolition of serfdom in 1861, but also extensive judicial and administrative reforms), while undoubtedly significant for the future, "did not immediately usher in a period of very rapid industrial progress." He found that this latter only became noticeable during and after the 1880's, his index of Russian industrial production growing at an average annual rate of just under 6 per cent between 1885 and 1913 (with a peak of 8 per cent in the 1890's). In the late nineteenth century, while Russian society produced a significant number of active and purposeful entrepreneurs, it was the state which appeared to take the lead in stimulating the rise of industry—partly by tariffs (which were the highest in Europe), partly by direct and indirect subsidies, but perhaps principally by an intensive program of railroad construction: some 15,000 miles of road were built in the 1890's and by 1900 the state controlled about 75 per cent of total railroad investment. This burst of construction was important not only because of its consequences for transportation costs, but also because of the conscious stimulus it gave to the industries supplying goods to the railroads. The financial role of the government was also striking: by levying heavy taxes on low-income groups, it not only increased revenues, but also restricted consumption, thus keeping the domestic price of grain low and the level of crucial grain exports high.

The results of all this in terms of industrial growth were undoubtedly impressive in the last decade of the nineteenth century. Subsequently, dislocation in the first years of this century was followed by a renewed forward thrust of the economy (by now less dependent on state action) in the years immediately before 1914. In Selection 22 Professor Gerschenkron summarizes the most important aspects of this early phase of Russian industrialization within a broader framework for the study of economic growth. He then turns, logically, to consider some alternative ways of viewing the course of Russia's economic evolution, and ends the chapter with a stimulating appraisal of Professor Rostow's hypotheses (see Selection 3) in the light of his own studies of European economic growth in the nineteenth century.

---

[1] "The Rate of Industrial Growth in Russia Since 1885," *The Journal of Economic History*, Supplement VII (1947), 144–74.

19

Foundations of
Japanese Industrialism

by

WILLIAM W. LOCKWOOD

THE RESTORATION BACKGROUND

The speed with which Japan emerged from quasi feudalism to become a modern state with a large sector of its economy organized along industrial, capitalistic lines is in striking contrast to the centuries of evolutionary growth characterizing the process in the West.

In Europe capitalistic production had its origins in the late Middle Ages. In England, for example, it can be traced back to the growth of exports of wool and wool manufactures as early as the thirteenth and fourteenth centuries. Foreign trade stimulated the rise of the merchant-employer system of industry under the leadership of merchant guilds. Gradually there developed in Western Europe new modes of economic organization, e.g., wholesale trade, improvements in banking and transport, commercial accounting, the domestic system of manufacture and later the factory. These interrelated changes were associated with other

Reprinted by permission from *The Economic Development of Japan: Growth and Structural Change. 1868–1938*, by William W. Lockwood (pp. 3–34, with omissions), copyright © 1954 by Princeton University Press.

expansive influences which slowly undermined the old, localistic order. Of primary importance was the widening of markets for staple manufactures. The growing requirements of armies and navies, the spread of colonization and conquest, the growth of population and cities—all played their part. So, too, did the progress of mechanical invention, especially in the utilization of iron and new sources of power. By the nineteenth century the factory, with its organization of labor and power machinery in a single coordinated process, was firmly established in England. More slowly it spread across the continent, fostered by the growing power of the merchant-industrialist class allied with the new national states in their competitive struggle for supremacy.

By comparison, Japan as recently as the early nineteenth century remained in a stage of economic development hardly more advanced than that of Western Europe in the late Middle Ages. Of her 28 to 30 million people the overwhelming majority were unfree, poverty-stricken peasants. They lived mostly in self-sufficient rural villages. The foundation of the economy and chief source of wealth was the cultivation of rice, carried on by primitive methods little changed over the centuries.

This agrarian base supported an aristocratic ruling hierarchy of some 270 territorial lords (*daimyō*) and the warrior class (*samurai*). The former had long held feudal sway in their territorial fiefs, while acknowledging nominal allegiance to the emperor in Kyoto. Since 1603, however, they had been actually under the dominance of one of the great military families, the Tokugawa, at Edo (Tokyo). Some 40% or more of the peasants' produce was annually appropriated by the *daimyō* and the shogun (the hereditary Tokugawa dictator) for the support of themselves and a vast army of vassals and retainers numbering upwards of 2 million. The remainder barely sufficed to sustain the population at its existing level. An earlier growth in numbers, associated with an expansion of the cultivated area in the seventeenth century, had been arrested, despite the persistence of high fertility patterns. Thereafter a precarious equilibrium between population and food supply was maintained only by famine, disease, abortion, infanticide, i.e., by operation of all the Malthusian checks save war.

Accompanying the growth of cities in the seventeenth and eighteenth centuries, and fostered by the peace and unity of Tokugawa rule, was a considerable development of manufacturing, mining, and interregional trade. The home industry of farm households came to be supplemented by workshop production organized under clan monopolies or craft guilds. But industrial output continued to be essentially handicraft in character. And the artisans and tradesmen remained an inferior class without political rights or social status. Manufacturing was dispersed through rural villages or concentrated in castle towns and centers like Edo and Osaka where it served the wants of the aristocrats. Trade was predominantly a movement of rice from country to city, mostly in payment of feudal dues. There was only limited exchange of industrial products. Mainly these were luxury items. Commerce remained crippled by manifold political restrictions and regulations, including an almost complete ban on foreign intercourse.[1] Through strict controls over travel and trade, as well as over freedom of occupation and enterprise, the Tokugawa regime sought to suppress the growth of any new forces which might threaten the feudal-agrarian foundations of the state.

. . . Significantly, nevertheless, [feudalism] served only to stunt and not to stifle the advances in technology and commerce which had received their first sharp impulse in the turbulent fifteenth and sixteenth centuries. Already by 1750 and even earlier the institutions of agrarian feudalism were heavily qualified. The economic disorder of the next 100 years itself testifies to this fact. Much of it can be attributed simply to the ineptness of an archaic military dictatorship in dealing with the resulting problems of population growth, currency, debt, and taxation. Only when Japan's industrialization in the twentieth century is seen as a projection of these earlier trends, now accelerated by the opening of the country to Western influence, can its speed and its technical achievements be understood.

The Decay of Feudalism. The modernization of Japan after 1868 has been likened to the bursting of a dam. It was the more violent because it brought the release of long-pent-up forces.

In part these pressures were economic in character. The latter half of the Tokugawa period, from the early eighteenth century onwards, resembled in certain respects the situation which had recurred periodically in the long history of Japan and other Oriental countries. Consumption requirements expanded beyond the inelastic limits of a backward and exploitative agrarian society, as a result of population growth and the insatiable demands of a parasitic ruling caste. Production and distribution within the traditional framework also became subject to violent disturbances arising from the mismanagement of public finance. From 1750 on the Shogunate was in almost constant financial difficulty. It sought escape by heavier taxes, borrowing, and disorderly debasements of the currency. In lesser degree this was true of many *daimyō*, who tried in turn to solve their problems at the expense of the

---

[1] In 1640 all foreign trade and foreign contacts were excluded from Japan except at Nagasaki, where a few Dutchmen and Chinese were allowed to remain under rigid supervision. The death penalty was prescribed for any Japanese attempting to leave or return to his country, and the construction of ocean-going vessels (i.e., those of more than 500-*koku* capacity) was forbidden. . . .

samurai and peasantry. These circumstances sharpened the struggle among contending classes to either maintain or improve their positions. Alone they might have led to nothing more than a redistribution of political power along traditional lines. This time, however, new and revolutionary forces were at work within the country. The traditional institutions of Japanese feudalism were progressively undermined at the foundations by the slow growth of a commercial economy, and the rise of a new and ambitious class of merchants and townspeople.

As in Europe, the old self-contained barter economy, and the rigid pattern of class relations associated with it, gradually crumbled under these mercantile influences. The *samurai*, a *rentier* caste, became progressively impoverished and indebted to the merchants (*chōnin*) as their rice stipends proved inadequate to meet increasing money requirements. Attempts to extract larger revenues from the peasants only intensified the difficulties of the latter, who likewise found themselves exposed to the insecurity of a growing money economy. Currency debasement and crop variations brought wide fluctuations in the price of rice, the one crop that was the precarious base of the economy. To these uncertainties the manipulations of merchant speculators further contributed, now injuring the farmer and now the city consumer.

The *chōnin*, though expanding their wealth and influence at the expense of the *samurai*, chafed under multifarious feudal restrictions on initiative and opportunity. These included restrictions on the transfer of land, on foreign trade, on improvements in internal transport, and on the manufacture of certain goods. Most irksome was the subordinate social status to which they were confined by an arrogant military aristocracy. Progressive clans also sought to expand their revenues through promotion of new manufactures and of trade. Here developed a new breeding ground for mercantilist ambition. The energetic young *samurai*-bureaucrats who pioneered this development began to display a new spirit of capitalistic enterprise which could only find full expression through a break with the *ancien régime*.

To these difficulties and discontents were added a series of famines and natural disasters in the latter Tokugawa years. The misery of the peasants in certain areas drove increasing numbers off the land in flight to the cities. After 1750 the strain on the traditional structure was reflected at the base in a series of peasant rebellions. At the top there was a steady decay of the power of the Shogunate, and increasing defiance of its authority by the more independent clans. The whole process culminated in a crisis of public finance in the nineteenth century, reminiscent of that of Louis XVI on the eve of the French Revolution. All the authority of the *Bakufu* (the Shogunal regime), with its highly developed system of espionage and military repression, was unable finally to stave off collapse after 1850.[2]

Economic discontent was reinforced in turn by other factors in the last decades of the Tokugawas. Some were literary and religious in character. An intellectual renaissance led to a rediscovery of national traditions and a revival of Shintoism, with its glorification of the emperor, whose traditional prerogatives had been usurped by the shogun. Such movements were eagerly supported by dissident clans restive under the autocratic rule of Edo. It was the arrival of Western gunboats and traders, however, coinciding with the virtual bankruptcy of the Shogunate, which precipitated the crisis. The expansion of Russia in the north, the encroachments of Britain and other powers in China, finally the "apparition of Perry" and his warships—all these were watched with rising apprehension in Japan. They revived and intensified memories of European ambitions and predatory rivalries dating back to the sixteenth century, before the exclusionist edicts of Tokugawa Ieyasu and his successors. This time the conviction spread that a policy of passive isolation could lead only to disaster.

Effective power within the feudal clans had now passed largely from the control of the effete *daimyō* . . . into the hands of able young *samurai* of inferior rank. By various means these men had steadily acquired a growing knowledge of Western military science, practical arts, and history. In the new learning, and in expanding intercourse with the West, the more farsighted saw fresh possibilities for national rejuvenation under the aegis of the emperor, as well as new scope for personal enterprise and power. More and more it seemed that only through such a course of action was national survival possible. The obstacle was the Shogunate, which now found itself caught between the

---

[2] There are also parallels and common elements in the process of financial disorder and agrarian decay as it appeared in both China and Japan after 1800. However, the extent of economic deterioration in China seems to have been more serious than in Japan, and in any case the firm grip of the ruling class in the island empire precluded anything like the Taiping Rebellion.

Moreover, there seems to have been a basic difference in the nature of the disorders attacking the foundations of the State. The revolutionary change which took place in Japan after 1850, while equally stimulated by the intrusion of the West, was partly a response to expansive forces already latent within the Japanese economy. These were economically progressive in that they fostered the growth of industrial production, trade, and commercial capital, but their full expression required a reorganization of political institutions. In China the nineteenth century witnessed the reappearance of the familiar cycle of economic decline and dynastic upheaval. Except for disruptive influences from the West, this might have left unchallenged the basic pattern of an agrarian bureaucratic state. Japan seems to have been headed for some radical change in her institutions in any event. Only the tight seclusion policy of the Tokugawas prevented it from appearing some time before it did. This difference had a good deal to do, no doubt, with the contrasting response of the two societies to the impact of the West in the nineteenth century.

insistent demands of the foreign powers and the growing assertiveness of rebellious clans grouped around the throne.

Intense indignation was aroused in Kyoto circles by the treaties of the 1850's. In these the Shogun was forced to grant such privileges as limitation of customs duties and extraterritorial rights to the "hairy foreigners." No less rankling were the indemnities subsequently exacted in reprisal for incidents. The luckless *Bakufu* was now attacked as the betrayer of national interests and usurper of imperial prerogatives, as well as the cause of mounting economic distress. Already weakened by internal decay and financial ineptitude, which had brought it to the verge of insolvency, it was unable to stem the rising tide of revolt. In the early 1860's the forced residence of the *daimyō* at Edo, a powerful device of political control in earlier years, was abolished. "Like wild birds from an opened cage," they fled with all their retainers in the space of a week. Other reforms followed, but they were too little and too late. In 1867–68, after a brief military struggle, the western clans emerged victorious; the Shogunate fell. With it collapsed the whole structure of centralized feudalism.

Restoration and Reform. Supported by the triumphant clansmen, a new boy emperor assumed the throne in 1868. In his Charter Oath he promised a series of reforms, including the famous pledge that "intellect and learning would be sought for throughout the world, in order to establish the foundations of Empire."

During the next decade sweeping reforms were undertaken by the new clan bureaucrats around the throne. Their central purpose was to strengthen and consolidate the new regime. In 1869 the clans were induced to surrender their land registers; in 1871 came the abolition of fiefs. A new structure of national administration and taxation arose on the ruins of the old territorial organization. As in France after 1789, feudal proprietary rights were swept away by decree. In Japan, however, government pensions (later commuted to national bonds) were issued to the feudal nobility in return for the surrender of their revenues. In addition the government assumed the debts of the *daimyō* to the merchants. This minimized resistance to the new regime and enabled many of the more enterprising aristocrats to metamorphose themselves into leading financiers of the new Japan.

Restrictions were abolished on freedom of movement and internal trade, freedom of cropping and property rights in land, and freedom of entry into new occupations. The land tax reform of 1873 created a unified revenue system in the form of a fixed money tax collected from landowners in proportion to the newly assessed value of their land. Through this device the State financed itself through the early, critical years. The result, however, was to fasten fresh burdens on the peasant which largely nullified his "emancipation" and threatened at times to bring on widespread rebellion. Other reforms, based on foreign study and the advice of foreign experts, were introduced in the Army and Navy; in education, law, and public health; and in police and civil administration. In industry and finance the Meiji statesmen assumed the lead in pioneering the new technology. They created a new fiscal system, banks and insurance companies, railways, steam shipping, postal and telegraph services, and factories. With driving energy the new regime bent itself to the task of building new foundations of national power which would be secure against opposition at home and potential threats from abroad.

The lead in the Restoration and subsequent reforms was taken by a group of able young *samurai*-bureaucrats. These came mainly from the powerful western clans—Choshu, Satsuma, Tosa, and Hizen. Their motives were a mixture of patriotism, fired by the dangers of the international situation, and ambition for personal advancement. They were supported by a few of the court nobles and by the Osaka and Kyoto merchants, whose financial aid in the revolt against the Shogun proved indispensable. By 1850, indeed, the line between the *chōnin* and the *samurai* had become increasingly blurred, both socially and economically, as the former acquired aristocratic privilege and the latter were driven into commercial pursuits. As a class, however, the merchants were still weak and politically dependent. Many were tied to the Shogun and the more conservative elements of the aristocracy by monopolistic privileges of trade and finance. Popular hostility toward the *ancien régime* was in fact directed partly at these exclusive privileges, which restricted the economic opportunity of independent journeymen, traders, and *samurai*.

In the transition to Meiji Japan, comparatively few of the wealthy *chōnin* had the enterprise and flexibility to adapt themselves to changed circumstances. The new industrialists, landlords, financiers, and public officials who emerged after 1868 to share political power with the military bureaucrats were largely recruited also from *samurai* ranks, as well as from the more prosperous farmers and petty tradesmen. Thus the Meiji "Revolution" was not the story of a rising business class, which burst the bonds of feudalism to establish its supremacy in a mercantile state. Still less was it a democratic revolt transferring political power to representatives of the mass of peasants and workers.

The great Prince Hirobumi Ito, framer of the Constitution of 1889, later said of his task: "It was not the people who forcibly wrested constitutional privileges from the Crown as in other countries, but the new regime was to be conferred upon them as a voluntary gift for the sake of their future prosperity." This statement is rather euphemistic in its implications, both as to the role of the "people" in earlier revolutions of the West, and the power of the emperor in Japan. The French Revolution, for example, despite its slogans, was hardly what we would today call a democratic revolution in either its inception or its outcome. Its actual consequence was to complete the emancipation from feudal serfdom, to establish a unified nation-state, and to proclaim a new legal freedom and equality under the ascendant power of the middle class. So in Japan a political unification and legal emancipation now took place. Here, in contrast to France, the leadership came largely from the more able and independent members of the former ruling caste, who revived the ancient symbols of the throne as a weapon of power. Joined by similar elements from merchant and commoner ranks, they combined to form a new oligarchy securely in control of the apparatus of the modern state and armed with the techniques and resources of a developing capitalism.

Despite the shifts in the balance of forces within this oligarchy, which in later decades were considerable, and despite the underlying trend toward democracy which manifested itself particularly in the decade 1920–30, this constitution of power remained basically unaltered in prewar Japan.

With this dramatic series of events, Japan was now opened to the first tides of the Industrial Revolution, and the attendant growth of modern capitalism. But the development which followed was more than simply the absorption by the Japanese of the material drives and technology of the West. Its tempo reflected the release of indigenous forces long latent in Japan. Similarly, its progress continued to be shaped by national characteristics deeply rooted in Japan's ancient culture. It gave new expression to the traditional eagerness of this island people for foreign ideas, especially in the applied arts. It gained momentum from their traditional industry and skills, built up in the exacting tasks of rice culture and peasant handicrafts. It found cohesive strength in the amenability of the Japanese to disciplined organization under acknowledged leaders—beyond the family. "To work in a group is second nature to him," says Emil Lederer. Recalling the experience of other peoples, one also remarks with what comparative ease in Japan the old caste distinctions and guild controls of feudal days broke down in favor of a more rational organization of economic life within the national framework. Again, the imprint of centralized dictatorship under the Tokugawas, together with the smallness and cultural unity of the country, helped to spare the Japanese that long struggle to overcome town and territorial localisms which intervened in Europe between the breakup of feudalism and the formation of national states. . . .

The very speed of the transition in Japan, however, and the manner of its accomplishment, gave a twist, a special emphasis, to what followed. Especially evident is the persistence of family patterns even in industrial organizations employing the most advanced technology; the firm grip of the ruling group directing national development toward the ends of state power and military expansion; and the formation, within this oligarchy, of great financial combines inheriting the traditions of clan and guild monopoly and dominating large-scale industry, trade, and finance from the very beginning. The liberalizing tendencies which elsewhere accompanied the growth of a broad middle class and an urban proletariat have not been absent in Japan. But they have labored under exceptional disabilities traceable to the peculiarities of Japan's historical development. Only in a general and imprecise fashion can one speak of the rise of capitalism in Japan, in the Western sense, and then only with reference to certain sectors and aspects of Japanese society.

THE MEIJI FRAMEWORK

With the opening of the Meiji era there set in a feverish process of modernization. Japan was now exposed to a rising tide of Western influence. Foreign trade more than doubled in volume in the first decade after 1868. Young Japanese by the score went abroad to study Western science and technology, political institutions and economic organization. Foreign experts and foreign merchants arrived in increasing numbers. The young *samurai*-bureaucrats of the new Imperial regime embarked on a program of sweeping and autocratic national reforms. The dream of men like Okubo, Kido, Iwakura, and others was first to consolidate the power and authority of the new government against internal opposition; second, to build a strong national state able to defend and assert itself in the arena of world politics. These ambitions set the framework and tempo of national development during the next quarter century. They formed the natural basis for a close mercantilist alliance between the bureaucrats and the nascent class of financiers and industrialists.

Both the Meiji Restoration and the reforms which crowded in its wake showed the remarkable capacity of the Japanese at critical points to produce vigorous leaders able to map out a long-term program and then to move decisively to put it in action. As H. F. MacNair once observed, Japanese history is replete with examples of this trait of leadership: the will to power, the plan, the patient wait for the strategic moment, then the bold, swift stroke. It appears in Ieyasu's ruthless measures after 1600 to stabilize the Tokugawa Shogunate on enduring foundations. It reappears in the cool calculation and decisive action of the Western clans when the moment came to overthrow the Shogun. It now led to an eager, discerning acceptance of the West by the young *samurai* reformers, which contrasted so strongly with the inertia and obscurantism of the scholar-bureaucrats of contemporary China when faced with the same challenge. Coupled with this trait of leadership is the *judō*-like tactic of biding time, bowing when necessary to superior force, and calculating the strategic moment for driving at a weak point in an opponent's armor. These qualities in combination have featured Japan's foreign policy through the modern period—most recently in the decision to plunge into war in 1941 and the philosophic acceptance of defeat and occupation in 1945.

In the early Meiji years the new government proceeded resolutely to demolish the crumbling structure of feudalism and assert its authority throughout the country. With the suppression of the Satsuma Rebellion in 1877, its political supremacy was finally established over the dissident clans. Political conflict, however, led to acute financial disorder through the seventies. Governmental expenditure far outran revenue, owing to heavy military outlays and the burden assumed when the clan debts were taken over and pensions were awarded the old aristocracy in return for cancellation of their feudal dues. Issues of government paper money invited currency depreciation. The latter was further aggravated, beginning in 1877, by the note issues of the new national banks. These banks had been formed largely by ex-aristocrats with little banking experience but now possessed of capital in the form of national bonds turned over to them by the government when their pensions were commuted.

As in France a century earlier, large currency issues thus resulted from the financial demands upon the new regime and its inexperience in money matters. But here the parallel ends. The French upheaval and ensuing wars led to the total repudiation of the *assignats* in 1797. In Japan the disorder was checked before it got out of hand. After 1881 the government finances and the currency of the country were put on a stable basis under the skillful guidance of the new finance minister, Count Matsukata. The depreciated paper of the preceding years was progressively retired in favor of convertible notes issued by the Bank of Japan, established in 1882. The banking system was reorganized, the national debt stabilized and refunded. Additional sources of revenue were developed to supplement the land tax. As a result the new financial regime was able to weather the Sino-Japanese war of 1894–95 with little difficulty. Following the abandonment of silver in favor of a gold standard in 1897, Japan's credit standing had improved to the point where she could borrow advantageously in foreign capital markets. . . .

Pioneering of Industry and Trade. Meanwhile energetic steps were taken by the government to modernize the Army and Navy, to improve transport and communications, and to establish new industries. The first railroad was constructed from Tokyo to Yokohama with the aid of a small British loan in 1870–72. The first steamship built by the Japanese was the 104-ft., 60-h.p. *Chiyodagata*, completed in 1866 after four years of effort. Steamer service was inaugurated shortly thereafter between Yokohama and Nagasaki. It was rapidly extended with government subsidies and encouragement. By 1893 Japan had acquired her first 2,000 miles of operating railway, her first 100,000 tons of steam vessels (mostly purchased abroad), her first 4,000 miles of telegraph lines. Shipyards, arsenals, foundries, machine shops, and technical schools were established or modernized with the aid of imported equipment and the advice of foreign technicians. Also under state patronage, the first modern silk filature was opened in 1870 with a French expert as superintendent. Cotton spinning mills were built or reequipped with imported machinery, largely from England. Experimental factories were set up to produce cement, sugar, beer, glass, chemicals, and a variety of Western-type goods.[3] The mining of copper, coal, and precious metals was also energetically promoted. Mineral production increased sevenfold from 1876 to 1896; in the latter year the consumption of coal reached 3.6 million tons. Nearly half of the coal was consumed in factories, which already numbered 7,640 and employed 435,000 operatives.

The government itself financed and operated many of these new ventures in the early years. Especially was this true of transport, mining, and engineering industries, where military needs were important. Later, as private initiative and experience developed, as the profits of government undertakings proved meager, and as the State needed funds for armament, it disposed of most of its industrial properties, often at bargain prices. It thus assisted in founding a number of the great financial and industrial fortunes of later years. Strategic industries like iron and steel remained under close official supervision, however. They were sheltered from competition by tariffs and subsidies. In addition, the State retained a powerful voice in the over-all direction of industrial development through the activities of the official and semiofficial banks, and more indirectly through the close affiliations of the bureaucracy with big business.

The growth of foreign trade after 1868 was both a cause and a result of these expansionist influences. Imports in the early years consisted largely of Western manufactures, chiefly textiles, machinery and equip-

---

[3] "It can be said with truth that there was scarcely any important Japanese industry of the Western type during the latter decades of the nineteenth century which did not owe its establishment to State initiative." G. C. Allen, *A Short Economic History of Japan*, London, 1946, p. 30.

ment, and other metal products. Factory-made yarn and cloth tended to displace handicraft products of domestic origin. This added to the distress already occasioned by the decline of town markets which had followed upon the loss of feudal income by the nobility and their retainers. As a result large numbers of artisans in traditional trades lost their livelihood. Only gradually were Western techniques assimilated in such industries as cotton manufacture and sugar refining to the point where domestic producers could withstand foreign competition. On the other hand, an increasing share of imports represented Western-type goods serving new wants—e.g., ships, petroleum products, woolen goods, railway equipment, munitions, and machinery. In the early years about half of the total came from Great Britain, whose nationals also predominated in the handling of trade. Import requirements, together with remittances for shipping, banking, and commercial services performed by foreign firms, imposed a heavy strain on Japan's balance of payments. From 1872 to 1881 gold and silver were exported (net) to the amount of 71 million yen. (The yen averaged U.S. $0.94 in exchange value between 1874 and 1881.)

Among merchandise exports, raw silk occupied the leading position from the beginning of the Meiji era. A foreign demand also developed for Japanese tea, rice, copper, coal, marine products, and miscellaneous handicrafts such as pottery, paper, lacquer, and bronze. It was silk, however, which dominated the export trade from the outset. Production of raw silk expanded from 2.3 million pounds in 1868 to 10.2 million pounds in 1893. Exports of silk and silk manufactures constituted the bulk of this production. They accounted for as much as 42% of Japan's total exports abroad during this whole period. Under the stimulus of foreign demand, cocoon raising was improved, and the reeling process began to be taken out of the peasant household to be organized in workshops and factories employing mechanical power. Throughout the modern history of Japan this single raw material played a unique role. Until as late as 1930 it continued to be the chief source of foreign exchange to finance Japan's industrialization, as well as the chief source of rural income supplementing the proceeds of rice cultivation. . . .

The Formative Stage. The dramatic character of events in Japan in the quarter century after 1868 often leads to an overestimate of the speed of her economic transformation. First steps are important, to be sure. It was during this formative stage that the foundations were laid for the building of the defense industries and for the steady expansion of the civilian economy in subsequent decades. New wants came into being, new techniques were slowly assimilated, and a new framework of government institutions and policy was established. As industry, trade, and finance assumed more capitalistic forms, the economy as a whole also began to display the cyclical alternation of expansion and contraction which characterized the capitalist economies of the West. The vagaries of currency and fiscal policy, coupled with variations in the foreign trade balance, brought an expansionist boom from 1877 to 1881, followed by a period of deflation and retrenchment in the eighties. This gave way in turn to a revival of prosperity at the end of the decade, which was further intensified by the Sino-Japanese war in 1894–95.

As the nineteenth century drew to a close, Japan's business and political leaders were gripped by a fever of industrialization. Her commercial expansion was also beginning to attract the attention of the outside world. Robert P. Porter, an American economist who visited the islands on behalf of the U.S. National Association of Manufacturers, was struck with the soaring industrial ambitions voiced by Japanese leaders in all walks of life. "Among public speakers are found not only officials whose special province is trade and agriculture, but even a naval officer of high rank has considered it not beneath his dignity to tell his countrymen that they can only become a great nation by development of trade, and that trade is as worthy of their best efforts as war."

Actually, however, the basic economic occupations and mode of life of the common people remained substantially unchanged through the first twenty-five years of the Meiji era. Foreign trade did not expand beyond modest proportions in relation to the economy as a whole. Its importance lay mainly in the realm of technological borrowing—i.e., as a highroad for the introduction of new influences. . . . Exports consisted almost wholly of agricultural, fishing, and mineral produce, supplemented by the handicraft wares of traditional industries. Modern-style factories were still limited in number and small in scale. In 1886, for example, the steam power used for industrial purposes totalled only 4,094 h.p., distributed through 217 plants. Inland transport was still largely by hand-drawn cart and pack horse. Wide price disparities between interior regions reflected the continuing self-sufficiency of village life. The land tax, a heavy burden on small peasants, furnished over 90% of State tax revenues in the early seventies. Twenty years later it still accounted for as much as 60%. Together with exorbitant rents and usurious debt charges, it continued for another generation or more to sluice off large amounts of agricultural income for the support of State enterprise and industrial investment.

Probably the most substantial additions to real national income during this period did not result directly from the growth of factory industry and foreign trade. They grew mainly out of general improvements in agriculture, handicrafts, and internal commerce following the removal of feudal restrictions and the unification of the country under a strong, central government. Freedom of movement and occupation, the abolition of clan tariff barriers and tolls, free transfer of property rights in land, the unification of the monetary and banking systems, the growth of population, steady improvements in agricultural methods, better transport—such new conditions and new forces brought a slow expansion of the internal market and a rise in productivity. For example, with little change in production techniques the cultivated area in rice is reported to have increased 7% from 1878–82 to 1888-92 while the average yield rose 21%. This resulted in a significant increase even in the rice crop, long the great staple of Japanese farming. A similar growth appeared in other agricultural output, in the extension of fishing activities, and in the mushrooming of numerous small handicraft industries scattered through the countryside. Capital accumulated from land rents and from small-scale trade and banking formed a growing pool of funds for the financing of land improvements, and of workshops, trading ventures, and the like.

The framework of large-scale enterprise was being laid in the seventies and eighties; but the bulk of the new economic activity in this gestation period was along more traditional lines which required no sharp break with the past. The continuing rural character of Japan is shown in the fact that places of under 10,000 population still accounted for an estimated 82% of the people in 1898. The new growth in population at this time was still being absorbed mainly in rural areas. The redistribution of people toward the cities in new industrial and commercial occupations was only setting in at the turn of the century.

RISE OF MODERN INDUSTRY AND TRADE

The decade of the 1890's marked a turning point in the evolution of the Japanese economy. On the foundations laid in earlier Meiji years the outlines of an industrial system now began to take shape. The assimilation of machine technology, the accumulation of banking and industrial capital, the expansive influences of world prosperity and rising prices—all facilitated a rapid rise of industrial output. Especially was this true for textiles and other consumer goods. Two victorious wars, at an interval of a decade, gave additional impetus to the development of transport, banking, and strategic industries under the leadership of the State and the nascent *zaibatsu*. By 1914 Japanese industrial capitalism was still weak and rudimentary by comparison with the advanced economies of the West. But it had now emerged from its formative stage. The basic patterns were established which were to characterize it for the next quarter century.

War and Economic Expansion. The first war with China, 1894–95, grew out of the designs of Japan's military bureaucrats upon Korea; also, it is said, from their need at home for a "forward" foreign policy to distract and disperse the rising tide of parliamentary obstruction which had emerged under the Constitution of 1889. Politically the war reinforced the power and prestige of the oligarchy for another generation, winning unified support for Japan's aggressive entry into the arena of Far East imperialism. Economically, it exerted a stimulus no less immediate and far-reaching in its consequences. Arms expenditures accelerated the upswing in prices already under way. New banks and small industrial and trading concerns mushroomed under the recently promulgated Commercial and Banking Acts, of 1890 and 1893. Military requirements doubled the merchant marine in two years. A boom developed in a number of industries producing war supplies.

The brief military campaign resulted in a resounding victory on land and sea over the forces of the corrupt and decadent Manchu regime. From this Japan proceeded to wrest important advantages, despite the intervention of Russia, Germany, and France to prevent her from retaining the principal prize, the Liaotung Peninsula, which the luckless Li Hung-chang had been forced to cede in the peace negotiations. Under the treaty of Shimonoseki (and the subsequent convention retroceding the Liaotung Peninsula) an indemnity of £38.1 million was exacted from China. This provided Japan with a gold and sterling reserve with which she made the important shift to the gold standard in 1897. By virtue of her newly won prestige she was also able to terminate the humiliating treaties of 1858 with the Western Powers. The new treaties ended extraterritorial privileges for foreigners in Japan. They also freed her from the limitation of her tariff to a 5% level under an agreement of 1866.

Achieving independence at home, Japan's leaders now embarked forthwith on a career of imperialist expansion in Asia. The familiar slogans of markets, national security, and imperial destiny found an immediate response in the quickened national consciousness and the commercial ambitions aroused by Japan's first triumph on the stage of world politics. The initial step, following the victory in China, was the acquisition of Formosa and the Pescadores, and of trading, navigation, and industrial rights in China. Obtaining these strategic assets, and redoubling her armament program, Japan now prepared in turn for the challenge to Russia in 1904. From the second conflict she again emerged with swollen territorial and strategic gains. She had won a paramount position in Korea and succeeded to czarist rights in South Manchuria. These commitments to empire assumed during the critical decade from 1895 to 1905, together with the political prestige and authority conferred upon the armed forces by victories in the field, were destined to exert a profound influence upon the subsequent course of Japan's development. They cast the mold for her domestic politics, as well as her relations with the rest of the world.

The economic impetus afforded by the Sino-Japanese War likewise carried over into the next decade. Now it was reinforced by similar stimuli on a larger scale during the war with Russia. Again a conflict of limited duration, fought on foreign soil, hastened the development of financial institutions, marine transport, and industrial technology, without itself imposing an insupportable drain on Japan's still meager reserves. The necessary financial resources were mobilized with the aid of an improved banking system, and at the price of continued, heavy taxation. The special banks of an official or semiofficial character set up in previous years now proved their value, for political as well as economic ends. This time, too, Japan was able to supplement domestic loans and expanding tax receipts with substantial foreign borrowings. Basically, however, it was the steady underlying expansion of national productivity and wealth which made it possible for her to extend rapidly her military and overseas commitments during this period. Economic growth thus lent support to rising political ambitions.

Reliable over-all measures of this economic growth are lacking for the period before World War I. Data . . . suggest that total production and real income in Japan, allowing for the rise in prices, may have increased by 80 to 100% in the quarter century ending in 1914. . . . Whatever the details, certainly the growth was substantial, and pervasive. Manufacturing, mining, and large-scale transportation advanced by leaps and bounds, agriculture and many of the service industries at a slower rate. Yet even farming and fishing expanded sufficiently to supply food for a 25% gain in population from 1894 to 1914, with some rise in dietary standards and only minor imports of foodstuffs. This growth seems to have been achieved with little or no increase in the number of workers in these primary occupations. Virtually the entire increase in the number of gainfully employed was absorbed in industry, commerce, and the other services. As a result it appears that by 1914 no more than three out of five families in Japan were still earning their living mainly in farming, and a third of them had some supplementary occupation. By comparison, the proportion runs above this in China, India, and most other Far Eastern countries even today.

It is important to observe, however, that the shift of employment to manufacturing and the service trades was able to proceed as it did only because primary production also expanded. Agriculture, fishing, and forestry provided the new industries with domestic raw materials and markets. They also furnished exports with which to pay for industrial materials and machinery. And they made it unnecessary to import large quantities of food to support growing city populations. Even the production of rice, staple crop for centuries, is estimated to have increased 30% from 1890–94 to 1910–14. It reached 249 million bushels a year in the latter period. Net imports also increased nearly fourfold, but still amounted to only 5.5% of total consumption.

More and more the Japanese people were now specializing their economic activities to produce surpluses for sale in the commercial market. For example, mining and manufacturing (excluding tiny family workshops) expanded until they employed over 2 million workers in 1913. These mines and factories produced commodities mainly for the growing home market, but also to a lesser extent for sale abroad. Allowing roughly for price changes, both Japan's imports and exports approximately doubled from 1889–93 to 1899–1903. They doubled again in the ensuing decade. The expansion of exports provided foreign exchange which, supplemented by borrowings abroad, made it possible for Japan to buy a growing volume of foreign machinery, equipment, and raw materials to meet her industrial and military requirements. One index of industrial activity, coal consumption in industry and transport, rose from 2 million tons in 1893 to 15 million tons in 1913. Railway mileage more than tripled, while freight ton-mileage increased seventeenfold. Japan was still a third-rate industrial nation by world standards. But she was well embarked by this time on an industrial revolution, with substantial gains already apparent in national income and power.

Founding of Large-Scale Industry. This development presented two aspects, in part supplementary, in part antagonistic, to each other. One was the forced-draft expansion of large-scale banking, shipping, heavy industry, and colonial enterprise. The other was the more diversified and pervasive modernization of agriculture and traditional industries, and the appearance of Western-style factories producing consumer goods like textiles.

The first grew largely out of government initiative, subsidy, and protection. Here the aims of State policy joined with the interests of private financiers to build up enterprises essential to military preparedness and colonial development. The second likewise benefited immensely from various types of governmental aid in such fields as technical education, crop improvement, reclamation, bank credit, transport and other public utilities. These benefits, however, were more indirect and more diffused throughout the economy (though in the case of technical education they accrued in the largest measure to the financier-industrialist-trader class, especially its more powerful members).[4] Here the

---

[4] The incidence of government policy on the distribution of income is of course a complex field of inquiry. In addition to a preoccupation with strategic industries, it may be noted here simply that State policy in Japan reflected a consistent bias

expansion of output and trade grew out of the development of special-ization, of more modern techniques, of new circuits of exchange. It came about through the response of tens of thousands of entrepreneurs to new economic opportunities at home and abroad. . . .

This latter sector of the economy was in the main competitive and small-scale in organization. Its production processes were technically simple; its capital requirements limited. By contrast the mining and metallurgical industries, shipping, and colonial enterprises like the sugar industry of Formosa were dominated from their inception by compara-tively large financial groups. They worked in close association with the government and were most of them dependent on official support. Typically these industries required advanced industrial techniques and were capital-intensive in character.

Of the large-scale, State-sponsored industries established in the years before World War I the most successful perhaps was the merchant marine. Japan had an ancient tradition of maritime enterprise, inter-rupted only by the exclusionist policy of the seventeenth and eighteenth centuries. The Meiji regime early recognized the strategic importance of shipping and ship construction. From 1870 on it extended official support. Progress was rapid after the fillip given by the Sino-Japanese War, which required the purchase and charter of a considerable amount of foreign tonnage. In 1896 the government undertook a general sub-sidy of ocean shipping. It thus abandoned its earlier, more selective favors to particular firms like the Nippon Yusen Kaisha, formed in 1885 through a merger of government and private interests and with a government-guaranteed dividend of 8%. In 1899 a differential subsidy in favor of Japanese-built ships was introduced to stimulate domestic con-struction.

As a result the Japanese merchant fleet (steam vessels) expanded to 1,500,000 tons in 1913. This represented a threefold increase over 1896. Half of Japan's overseas trade was now carried in Japanese bottoms, as against less than 10% before the war with China. The large Japanese firms were now in an increasingly strong bargaining position in the shipping conferences of the Far East. Within two generations they were to rise to a commanding position in the carrying trade of the region. By contrast, Japanese shipyards had yet acquired only limited capabilities. And they were still largely dependent on imported mate-rials. But with the help of construction subsidies they were now turning out ships at an average rate (1909–13) of about 100 steam vessels

---

(1) in favor of industry as against agriculture, (2) in favor of exports to finance Japan's external requirements, and (3) in favor of large propertied interests and employers, as reflected in discriminatory tax policy, hostility to trade unions, and the absence of protective legislation for factory workers. . . .

totalling 50,000 tons a year, in addition to the smaller types of warships. Overseas shipping, and the larger shipyards, remained in the hands of a few big companies. These continued to receive, after 1909, government support under the Ocean Service Subvention Act of that year. Government subsidies supplied most of the profits of the ocean shipping trade throughout this period. . . .

Equally strategic in character, but more difficult to establish in Japan, were the metallurgical industries. Steps were taken early in the Meiji era to modernize and expand the mining industry. But the lack of mineral resources confined subsequent developments to small proportions except in two fields: copper and coal. Copper production expanded through the World War years; subsequently, here as in the case of oil, Japan became increasingly dependent on imports. Though a variety of other minerals registered large relative advances in output, the actual amounts remained small except in the case of coal. In 1913, in fact, coal accounted for 71 million yen, half the total value of mineral production. Imports of foreign ores, metals (including semi-manufactures), and other minerals already amounted to about 100 million yen, reflecting the growing demands of the machinery, equipment, and construction industries.

The principal requirement of the metal-working industries was of course iron and steel. Of total metal and mineral imports in 1913, pig iron constituted 10% and finished steel about one half. A Japanese iron and steel industry had been launched in 1901 when the government-owned Yawata Iron Works commenced operations. Several smaller plants were also built by private interests during the next decade. But severe handicaps were encountered in the technical difficulties of the process and the inadequacy of domestic supplies of ore and coking coal. By 1913 pig iron output had been pushed up to 243,000 tons and steel output to 255,000 tons. Yet the former still represented only one half and the latter one third of domestic consumption. The rest was supplied by imports. Costs were high, and the industry achieved even this limited development only by State sponsorship and subsidy. It is interesting to note, nevertheless, that growing production plus imports now provided steel supplies for domestic use at an annual rate of about 740,000 tons during the years 1911–13.

In the machinery and equipment industries the modest success of the shipbuilding trade was fairly typical. After the nationalization of railways in 1906, the manufacture of railway equipment increased in response to government orders. The electrical equipment industry also advanced in the 1900's as new thermal and hydroelectric generating plants were built. On the whole, however, Japan remained dependent throughout this period on imports of vehicles, scientific instruments, and machinery, as well as finished steel. Had it not been for war and armament expenditures, and a national policy dedicated to the encouragement of strategic industries, this dependence would have been even greater.

Agriculture and the Traditional Industries. The founding of large-scale industry in Japan, because of its political support, its strategic implications, and the striking contrast it offered with traditional Japan, attracted a good deal of attention from the outside world. But it was the expansion of Japan's basic economy—agriculture and small-scale industry built on traditional foundations—which accounted for most of the growth of national productivity and income during this period.

Here and there a domestic occupation gave way to foreign competition as the Japanese economy became more closely linked with the outside world. One striking case was the decline of raw cotton production after 1887, despite the growing demands of Japanese spinners. With the removal of the duty on cotton in 1896 Japan accepted dependence on imports of Indian (and later, American) cotton. Cotton imports were handled by a few big importing firms, which maintained close relations with the spinners. The future growth of the cotton textile industry proceeded on this basis, and cotton virtually disappeared as a domestic crop. In the main, however, the history of different sectors of Japan's economy at this time is one of differential rates of expansion, with varying degrees of modernization in traditional occupations.

The growth of food production has already been noted. Probably it approached a 35–40% increase over the period 1894 to 1914. This growth is highly significant in view of the basic importance of agriculture in the national economy and the likelihood that the farm population increased little during this period. . . . In part it represented a slow increase in the cultivated area. In part it resulted from more fertilizer, better credit facilities, double cropping and other more intensive methods of farming, paralleled by corresponding changes in coastal fishing. The basic organization of agriculture remained little altered. Some 55% of the cultivated area was still devoted to rice, produced chiefly by the hand labor of farm households on tiny plots of ground. Japan's 5.4 million farm families still cultivated farms averaging only 2.6 acres apiece. Many had a good deal less.

Land ownership was also dispersed in small holdings, except for the holdings of a few big proprietors. The commercialization of agriculture, however, and the burden of high taxes and interest charges on the small peasant, had brought a large increase in tenantry in the earlier Meiji years. Some 39% of the cultivating farmers owned no land by 1910. About 45% of farm acreage was tenanted. Tenants typically paid rents in kind, fixed by oral agreement and amounting to 45 to 60%

of the crop on rice land. In addition they usually had to furnish their own farm implements, seed, and fertilizer.

The crowding of people on a limited land area resulted in high rents and land values; it also perpetuated the low productivity of hand cultivation. Farm machinery was virtually unknown, of course. Over half the land was cropped without even the help of draft animals. Improvements in the lot of the small farmer were further limited by the shortage of credit. Interest rates still ran to 20% or more in the villages. Taxes likewise remained a heavy burden. Even with the introduction of business and income taxes to supplement the land tax in meeting the rising level of armament expenditures, the agricultural class continued to furnish the principal source of government revenue. In 1908 it was estimated that the farmer paid land, income, and business taxes amounting to 28% of his income, by comparison with 14% in the case of the merchant and industrialist. Low farm income from all these causes impelled people toward the cities in search of better economic opportunity. There they exerted a persistent drag on wage levels in nonagricultural occupations. Despite the advances recorded above, P. Mayet's dictum of 1878 was to remain true for a long time to come: "The principal and most needed improvement in the system of Japan's National Economy is to be found in the direction of agriculture."

Rice and other food crops continued to provide the principal means of farm livelihood. To an increasing degree, however, agriculture was now being supplemented by alternative sources of income from industry and ancillary services. This came about in a variety of ways. One, of course, was the migration of members of farm families to the cities in search of jobs—as in the case of recruiting of farm girls by the spinning mills. Another was the spread of new industrial demands and employment opportunities to small towns and through the countryside, especially in the vicinity of the larger cities. . . . In some cases there developed an expanding domestic or foreign market for traditional Japanese handicrafts—native-style paper, pottery, luxury fabrics, etc.—with little resulting change in production techniques. In others, new industries were introduced, e.g., those producing Western-style paper, beer, bicycles, and cement. Or a substantial change took place in traditional methods, such as the introduction of power looms in the export branch of the textile trades.

Growth of the Textile Trades. The rise of the silk industry was the most conspicuous instance of the adaptation and growth of a traditional industry in response to foreign demand. World silk demand continued to expand in the years before World War I. Japan rapidly acquired a dominant position in the market. Her output of raw silk grew from 7.5 million pounds annually in 1889–93 to 27.9 million pounds in

1909–13. Exporting three quarters of this product in the latter period, Japan had already passed China and her European competitors. She was now supplying half the requirements of the United States, the world's principal consumer. In addition, a small trade in silk fabrics was maintained. This languished after 1898 in the face of rising tariffs in the United States and elsewhere, but exports of silk fabrics (mainly habutai) still led cotton cloth exports until 1913.

The expansion of silk production and improvement in quality were accomplished through technical advances in both cocoon raising and the reeling industry. In cocoon production one half the gain in output through these two decades resulted from the spread of double cropping —the introduction of a summer-autumn crop. More scientific methods of egg production and silkworm feeding also improved and standardized the quality of cocoons. This period, moreover, witnessed a growth in the average size of filatures, and the extensive replacement of hand reeling by machine methods. By 1913, 76% of the raw silk produced was fila-ture silk; the hand reel persisted mainly in the supply of silk to domestic weavers.

The silk industry as a whole, however, continued to be essentially small-scale and rural in character, except for the larger filatures and big export houses. Nearly one third of the farm households of the country derived some supplementary income from the raising of co-coons. In 1913 there were still 284,869 hand-reeling establishments in the countryside, in addition to 4,701 machine-reeling filatures. Weaving likewise remained a peasant occupation to a large extent. The chief element in production costs, from silkworm to fabric, was labor. Much of the capital even was accumulated from local sources, though in-creasingly the working capital of the filatures and commission merchants came to be provided directly or indirectly by large exporters and city banks.

The second large industry to develop during this period, cotton textiles, was likewise built on traditional foundations. In this case, however, the technical transformation under the impact of Western influence was more radical, especially in the spinning branch.

It is a familiar fact that the cotton textile industry has been the pioneer of the industrial revolution the world around. Japan was no exception. The factors which led to its rapid assimilation and growth in Japan were no different than those which have operated elsewhere, notably in Asia: a large consumer market ready at hand; the adaptability of handicraft skills and of unskilled, low-wage labor to the operation of power machinery for weaving and spinning; the limited capital require-ments of textile mills; the availability of cheap raw cotton; and a climate sufficiently humid for spinning. The twenty years before World War I saw the firm establishment of the factory system in cotton textiles in Japan. By 1913 the Japanese industry was securely in control of the home market. In addition, it had already commenced that overseas expansion which was to raise it to a front rank position in the world's cotton goods trade during the next generation.

Like other Japanese industries, the cotton mill industry achieved its first substantial growth after 1890. Prior to this time machine-spun yarns from abroad had made heavy inroads in the Japanese market, traditionally supplied by the coarse hand-spun product of peasant households. Meanwhile the introduction of factory spinning in Japan proceeded only slowly despite government patronage. In the nineties progress was accelerated. By 1899 the industry boasted some eighty-three mills with 1,170,000 spindles and an output of 355 million pounds of yarn. The larger firms, organized in the Japan Cotton Spinners' Association, had also begun to modernize the weaving industry with power looms imported for use in specialized weaving sheds attached to their spinning mills.

Domestic factory yarn now rapidly replaced Indian yarn in the Japanese market. Aided by an epidemic in Bombay, which temporarily disrupted Indian exports in 1896, the Japanese spinners also gained a substantial foothold in the China market for coarse yarns. India's textile industry, however, still greatly exceeded that of Japan in size. The Chinese industry was yet in its infancy, though beginning to embark on a similar process of growth. For many years China, together with India, was to remain the principal international market for cotton goods from Lancashire and its newer competitors. In all three countries the process of spinning was modernized far more swiftly than weaving. The latter continued mainly on a workshop, hand-loom basis.

The Japanese spinning industry continued its expansion through the 1900's. By 1913 it had doubled again, with capacity now at 2.4 million spindles and a yarn production of 672 million pounds. Along with this growth in production had come an increase in the size of plants, and a slow improvement in their ability to spin finer yarns. Their competitive position abroad was further improved by the better marketing and credit facilities and the closer integration of the industry, especially in its export branch. Capital costs, including the costs of imported British machinery, were still relatively high, but were offset by day-and-night operation in two shifts. Output per spindle was therefore two or three times as large as in Western countries. Concurrently the weaving trades also increased the scale and efficiency of their operations as the power loom and factory system slowly made their way. From 1894 to 1913 the number of weavers and weaving establishments declined by one third; yet the production of fabrics woven from cotton, silk, hemp, and other fibers approximately doubled. However, weaving remained essentially a cottage industry. At the end of this period there were still nearly 400,000 independent and piecework establishments. They averaged only 1.5 workers per plant. Even in cotton weaving, where the big cotton spinners extended their activities, the number of power looms did not exceed 50,000.

In Japan as elsewhere the textile industries relied mainly on low-wage female labor. In the weaving sheds and silk filatures, largely rural industries, nine out of ten workers were women. Even in the cotton spinning mills over 80% of the operatives were females. One out of four was under sixteen years of age. These girls were recruited on contract from peasant homes, often reluctantly. They were housed and fed in company dormitories which blended the factory system of the West with the paternalism and strict discipline of traditional Japan. Wages were low, even by Japanese standards. Labor efficiency was equally so. Japanese spinning and weaving mills required about four times as many operatives as American mills of similar size and equipment. There were no factory laws. Any organization of workers to bargain collectively or strike was effectively forbidden under the Police Regulations of 1900. Except in a few model mills, conditions of life and work generally exhibited the poverty, the crowding, the lack of worker protection which characterized the introduction of the industrial system in the West early in the nineteenth century. In Japan as in England the factory system in its first stages relied mainly on the labor of women, who were more amenable to the discipline of factory work and also less able to protect themselves from industrial abuses.

The coming of age of the Japanese cotton industry is reflected in its growing strength in international competition during this period. Imports of both cotton yarn and piece goods into Japan no longer figured significantly in the domestic market. Exports grew steadily. At first they consisted mainly of coarse cotton yarns (20-count and below), sold in China and to a lesser extent in Korea for hand-loom weaving. By 1913 Japan already supplied a quarter of the world exports of yarn, sharing the large Chinese market with India. China still imported two thirds of her yarn requirements, though her own spinning industry was now becoming mechanized and re-established as a factory industry. By 1913 she too had nearly a million spindles, a quarter of them owned by Japanese companies. A growing share of Japanese exports now began to take the form of cotton cloth. It was mainly gray shirtings and sheetings, drills, and other coarse and heavy goods. Totalling 412 million linear yards in 1913, these likewise found their principal market in China. Here they had largely ousted American exporters from the field, as noted above. They also offered increasing competition to the products of Lancashire, long dominant in the China import trade.

By 1913 Japan was already exporting to foreign countries and Korea about half of the cotton processed by her cotton mills. Some 30% of the output of her spindles was exported directly as yarn, as compared with over 40% in 1900. The remainder was processed by the Japanese weaving trade. But perhaps as much as 20% (by value) was subsequently sold abroad as cotton cloth. Another 10% was exported in the form of knit goods and other manufactures. A rough comparison of 1913 with 1900 yields the following conclusions: spinning mill output rose 150%—from 268 to 672 million pounds; something over one half of this increase represented an increase in exports of yarn and cloth; less than 10% went into replacing former imports into Japan; the balance, about one third, apparently reflected a net expansion of the domestic market for cotton yarn and its manufactures. (Hand-spun yarn had virtually disappeared from the market by the turn of the century.)

Thus the early growth of the cotton industry took place in response to an expansion of the market at home as well as abroad. It was in the export branch of the industry that technical progress was most rapid. But the importance of the foreign market in the rise of the industry, great as it was, appears to have been less than is often supposed.

In cotton consumption Japan now ranked sixth in the world. Some 60% of her raw cotton came from India in the years 1910–13, another 25% from the United States. Though the Japanese industry could still boast only one third the spindleage of Indian mills, it was now forging ahead more rapidly. Together with India, Japan had ousted Britain from the yarn market of China. In addition, she was already supplying about 15% of China's imports of cotton piece goods, having captured much of the market for coarse goods from American exporters.

Yet the widespread expansion of Japanese goods to more distant markets still seems remote. Exports of broad goods (20's and over) were still confined to a few coarse and heavy types. Sixty per cent of Japan's yarns were 20's or less. The finishing industry was undeveloped. Reliance on British machinery made costs of mill construction relatively great, while labor costs were much higher than wage comparisons suggest. As yet Japan still presented no serious challenge to Lancashire in world markets. The latter's exports of cotton cloth were nearly thirty times those of Japan in 1910–13, and still constituted two thirds of world trade in this field.

Within Japan, however, the cotton industry ranked second only to silk in importance. These two far overshadowed other industries, both in employment and value of output. Woolen, hemp, and muslin manufactures had also developed on a modest scale, but they remained largely dependent on Army orders and government protection. The structure of Japanese industry at this time was probably about as follows: In all manufacturing industries (excluding construction) there were something over 3.5 million persons occupied wholly or part-time in 1913. This was still less than one seventh of the country's total labor force. Probably one in three such persons was a small employer, or an independent who engaged neither hired nor family labor in significant amounts. Excluding these proprietors would leave 2.0–2.5 million wage and family workers. According to S. Uyehara, who puts the number at about 2 million, textiles alone employed 40% of these workers, largely women and girls.

Most of the remaining industrial employment was found in traditional trades even less affected by modernization. For example, three occupations—the making of Japanese paper, braids, and mats—accounted for another 40%. About half of the total of 2 million employees were in factories with less than five operatives. The newer, larger-scale industries like the metallurgical, machinery, and chemical still contributed only a small fraction of industrial income and employment. Japanese industry remained at this time predominantly small-scale in organization, its roots in the traditional skills of old Japan, its markets mainly the consumer needs of people still living close to the traditional poverty line of the Orient.

The preponderance of the cotton and silk industries is almost equally striking in Japan's foreign trade. As already noted, both imports and exports expanded rapidly throughout the Meiji era, playing a key role in the whole process of economic development. For the most part this was trade with foreign countries, not Japan's own colonies. Even in 1913 exports to Formosa and Korea were only 13% of other exports; imports from them only 9%. Of total shipments overseas, raw silk constituted 30% and silk manufactures another 7%. Cotton goods of all types added a further 20%. Thus silk and cotton together provided nearly three fifths of Japan's exports.

This textile trade was highly specialized by regions. China (with Hongkong and the Kwantung Leased Territory) took three quarters of Japan's cotton goods exports to all countries, including Korea. The United States took two thirds of her raw silk. On the import side, raw cotton from India and the United States accounted for a third of the value of all foreign purchases. Another third was divided evenly between foodstuffs, and metals and manufactures. The remainder represented miscellaneous raw materials and equipment for Japanese industries, purchased in a wide range of markets. Already well established, in short, was the pattern of Japanese trade which was to persist for another twenty years, until, in the thirties, dislocations set in motion by the world depression and the war in China brought radical changes.

It was this underlying growth of Japan's agriculture and other basic industries, most of the consumer goods industries built on ancient foundations, which enabled the island empire to support her growing population and expanding political commitments during this period. Through a steady process of modernization they produced the rising national income which supported large State budgets for armament and colonial development. They provided the exports to pay for much of the heavy import of munitions, machinery, and other essentials for strategic industries. Despite these charges upon the national dividend, they were the means by which Japan carried herself through the first stages of economic development and emerged from her agrarian-feudal background to take on the aspects of a modern industrial power.

What actual improvements came about in the material well-being of the Japanese population during this early period is difficult to determine. Some advance in living standards is evidenced in the decline of mortality rates, in increased per capita consumption of food and clothing supplies, and in the growth of public services of various kinds —especially in the cities. Most of the rise in total national income, however, seems to have been absorbed in supporting the growing population. Capital formation and arms expenditure absorbed additional amounts of the increment. Kokichi Morimoto, on the basis of fragmentary family budget studies in 1913, concludes as follows: "The mode of living—housing, food, clothing, and other factors of living—has not made noteworthy improvement. The mass of the people live in just the same way as they did during the feudal régime." This verdict appears to be too sweeping. . . . But it points to the formidable obstacles, both social and technological, which stood in the way of real improvements in the lot of the peasant and worker, despite the notable growth in the scale and productivity of the Japanese economy. . . .

20

The Financing of
Japanese Economic Development

by

GUSTAV RANIS

An economy which is able to achieve only subsistence levels of income by means of a full and optimum utilization of its resources is in
serious difficulties. Unless it can count on extensive credit from abroad,
it may be properly identified as "doomed" rather than "underdeveloped." Domestic capital formation must carry the heaviest burden in
any developmental effort, and there is very little which can be squeezed
out at near-subsistence levels of income and consumption. Happily, most
of the world's low income areas are not "doomed" in this sense.
Reserves of productivity usually do exist somewhere in the underdeveloped economy; the prime problem of development is to gather
them in and utilize them efficiently. It is the purpose of this paper to
demonstrate the existence and successful utilization of such reserves
in the Japanese economy during the nineteenth century "break-out"
phase of her development. We intend to analyze the use of fiscal and
monetary policies in the effort to preserve a maximum pool of savings

Reprinted from *The Economic History Review*, 2d series, XI, 3 (April, 1959) (pp.
440–54, with omissions), by permission of the Economic History Society and the
author.

at each subsequent higher level of income, either by a direct siphoning off into government coffers or, through interference with the distribution of income, by channelling it into other "dependable" hands.

I

"Taking up the slack" in any economy means making potential increments of productivity socially available, largely by means of re-shuffling resources with a minimum need for additional investment. In the case of Japan, "slack" was in evidence mainly in the form of excess labor on the land and reserves of productivity in the land.

The ability to withdraw labor hours from one sector of the economy and apply them elsewhere without suffering a loss of output in the former represents perhaps the purest form of such "slack." This represents the employment of the "disguised rural underemployed," the squatting uncles and cousins who have become proverbial in the literature. The Japanese rural working population fell from 14.74 million in 1878–82 to 14.19 million in 1928–32, an absolute decline of 3.7 per cent during a period when total population was increasing at a rate of more than 1 per cent annually. This transfer, moreover, is understated since the shift of marginal working hours from agricultural to non-agricultural pursuits in the absence of any physical relocation is un-accounted for.

A second and closely related form of reserve productive capacity becomes evident when we consider reorganization and the limited addition of capital in the agricultural sector. This, in Japan, includes the adoption of a wide variety of new techniques, improved crop selection, breeding and rotation, winter draining permitting the double-cropping of rice and barley, the more intelligent and intensive use of fertilizer. The unit size under cultivation did not change; nevertheless, yields per acre as well as per man increased substantially. A small investment in the improvement of simple tools and techniques led to a large increase in productive capacity. Every investment which breaks through a bottleneck and results in higher levels of income should not, of course, be considered in the same vein; the only pragmatically useful distinguishing feature of this process of "slack" recovery is the extremely high marginal productivity of the first and insignificant injection of capital. Over the same 1878–82 to 1928–32 time-span, agricultural output increased by more than 153 per cent, . . . raising the productivity of those remaining on the land by 163 per cent.

· · · · ·

. . . The bulk of this increase in agricultural productivity occurred during the last twenty years of the nineteenth century; the rural work-

TABLE 1

GOVERNMENT SUBSIDIES
(1,000 Current Yen)

Year	AGRICULTURE AND FORESTRY			INDUSTRY			COMMERCE (Inc. Exp., Imp., Transp.)			GENERAL			TOTAL	
	Cur.ᵃ	Realᵇ	Per Cent of Total	Cur.ᵃ	Realᵇ	Per Cent of Total	Cur.ᵃ	Realᵇ	Per Cent of Total	Cur.ᵃ	Realᵇ	Per Cent of Total	Cur.ᵃ	Realᵇ
1880	—	—	—	410	830	20.4	255	515	12.6	1348	2723	66.9	2013	4067
1882	2	4	—	796	1595	34.0	125	250	5.3	1422	2850	60.7	2345	4699
1890	—	—	—	2328	5734	58.7	131	323	3.3	1500	3695	38.0	3959	9751
1895	—	—	—	2910	7098	46.4	1375	3354	22.0	1976	4820	31.6	6261	15271
1900	358	644	1.5	12018	21615	52.0	6636	11935	28.7	4131	7428	17.8	23143	41624
1905	228	355	1.1	11588	18050	55.2	5929	9235	28.2	3242	5050	15.5	20987	32690
1910	328	494	.8	15322	23075	38.0	12472	18783	30.9	12213	18393	30.3	40335	60746
1915	2083	2950	4.7	15920	22550	35.7	12296	17416	27.6	14215	20135	31.9	44514	63051
1920	551	291	.6	19976	10230	19.6	32409	17111	32.8	46560	24583	47.0	18896	52215
1925	6865	4661	4.3	71198	48335	44.4	23077	15667	14.5	59048	40087	36.8	160188	108749
1929	21421	17660	10.8	79868	65843	40.2	21645	17844	10.9	75571	62301	38.1	198515	163647
1932	28267	33061	11.2	43583	50974	17.3	27446	32101	10.9	152271	178095	60.5	251567	294231
1935	37596	36679	17.8	23151	22586	10.9	20778	20271	9.9	129469	126311	61.4	210994	205847
1938	78167	57140	20.0	42066	30750	10.8	159665	116714	40.9	110780	80980	28.3	390678	285584

ᵃ *Nihon Keizai no Kōzō Bunseki* (Analysis of Japanese Economic Structure), Ichiro Nakayama, editor, Toyo Keizai (1954), Chapter IX, part 2.
ᵇ Using Ohkawa's general price deflator, 1928–32 = 100, developed at the Hitotsubashi Economic Research Institute.

ing population declined by 2.1 per cent, output increased by 72.3 per cent and agricultural labor productivity by 73.3 per cent.[1] This is also the period, as seen in Table 1, for which the introduction of public capital into agriculture was at a much lower level than in later years; smaller returns in labor productivity concurrent with a larger investment effort leads us to conclude that the considerable reserves of productivity in the Japanese economy were running out after the turn of the century.

The successful gathering in of existing reserves of productivity does not, of course, guarantee that anything but fuller stomachs, or more of them, will result. In a low-income economy there invariably exist powerful pressures for consuming the gains which can be made to accrue. To withstand the extremes of such pressures—even more than the need to enhance people's willingness and ability to work—is a central problem of economic growth. If "slack" which constitutes, so to speak, a once-and-for-all bargain is dissipated, development becomes once again extremely painful or impossible. Pressures against the investible surplus of an economy at each and every stage of development derive from population growth and increases of per capita consumption. It is the purpose of the following section to review the means by which such pressures were contained and high savings propensities achieved.

II

Japan experienced a substantial increase in numbers, from 34 million in 1870 to 44 million in 1900 and 64 million in 1930. There, as elsewhere, increased economic activity was associated with increased numbers. History shows this to be inevitable. A developing economy must either be able to accommodate such increase, or cease growing.

Accepting the inevitability of devoting a share of the potential savings fund to the feeding of additional mouths, the economy must marshal its forces to resist the influences tending to increase per capita consumption. It is, of course, neither possible nor desirable to keep the door against increased consumption levels hermetically shut; nevertheless, it is the size of the attainable margin above the maintenance of an existing capital stock and a growing population which tells the story between successful and unsuccessful attempts at development.

An economy's siphonable savings are composed of the voluntary and involuntary contributions of its people; an economy breaking away from low levels of income and consumption must rely heavily on maintaining a high marginal propensity to save out of new and higher levels of income. In Japan, a severely regressive tax structure, coupled with favorable savings propensities among the upper income groups, served

---

[1] In the twenty years after 1900 productivity increased by only 42.2 per cent.

to siphon off, for purposes of development, much of the increment in income accruing during the "break-out" period. Dissipation of resources in consumption on non-productive investment was minimized.

The Land Tax. The peasant traditionally has carried the heaviest burdens in Japanese society. Before 1868 he supported the feudal ruling classes in the court cities; after the Restoration he became the prime source of developmental capital. Good returns to be obtained from the soil—through his labor—were gathered up by means of high rents and the tax on land.

Table 2 indicates that the land tax alone provided more than 70 per cent of central government revenues during the first decades after the Restoration; local governments, for which no revenue breakdown was available, acquired a similarly large proportion of their income from the land. Taxing away the agricultural *produit net* represented the dominant source of government revenue, at least until the turn of the century when the agricultural "slack" was becoming exhausted and increasing returns in secondary production provided an alternative tax base.

The effects of the land tax on incentives and income distribution in agriculture are of prime importance. The initial burden of the 1873 levy was not appreciably different from that imposed during the preceding Tokugawa period. But the resulting pressures were different and gave rise to a seemingly contradictory economic behavior pattern: increased productivity and a reduction of the real tax burden, accompanied by increases in tenancy. The real burden on the individual cultivator of a lump sum tax liability was substantially reduced over time, not only by the increases in agricultural productivity cited above but also by secular increases in the price of rice. In fact, as we shall see, this lower real tax burden benefited only the larger landowners while small cultivators found themselves under increasing pressures to sell out. The result . . . was a persistent increase in the proportion of cultivated land under tenancy [which rose from 37.0% in 1883 to 47.7% in 1930].

The apparent contradiction here can be cleared up by emphasizing the severe cyclical price fluctuations to which the small peasant-owner fell victim. Unlike the large landlord, he was not in a position to choose his time of tax payment and was forced to dump large amounts of produce on a market over which the former had considerable control. Regardless of volume, the value of the produce marketed could easily fall below the average assumed as a tax base by the original valuation procedure. The only alternative might well be to go into debt and, since the only credit available, short term and high rate, was offered by the same landlord in his rôle of usurer, the end result was

TABLE 2

Composition of Central Government Tax Take[a]
(Current Million Yen)

Year	Land Tax	Per Cent of Total	Excise Taxes[b]	Per Cent of Total	Sub-Total (Land Tax & Excises)	Per Cent of Total	Income Tax	Per Cent of Total	Business Taxes[c]	Per Cent of Total	Customs Duties	Per Cent of Total	Miscellaneous	Per Cent of Total	Total
1870	11.3	73.9	—	—	11.3	73.9	—	—	—	—	1.1	7.1	2.9	18.9	15.3
1880	42.3	72.9	5.8	10.0	48.1	82.9	—	—	—	—	2.6	4.5	7.3	12.6	58.0
1890	40.1	51.7	16.9	21.8	57.0	73.5	1.1	1.4	.3	.4	4.4	5.7	14.8	19.1	77.6
1900	46.7	24.6	54.4	28.6	101.1	53.2	6.4	3.4	7.3	3.8	17.0	8.9	58.2	30.6	190.1
1910	76.3	15.9	89.6	18.7	165.9	34.6	31.7	6.6	32.5	6.8	39.9	8.3	208.9	43.6	478.9
1920	73.9	6.2	375.4	31.6	449.3	37.8	190.3	16.0	116.7	9.8	69.4	5.8	361.4	30.5	1187.1
1930	68.0	4.8	529.0	37.4	597.0	42.2	200.6	14.2	112.1	7.9	105.4	7.4	401.2	28.4	1416.3

[a] Japan, Department of Finance, *Financial and Economic Annual of Japan*.

[b] Including tax on sake, tobacco, sugar, soya, textile fabrics, as well as profits from camphor, salt and tobacco monopolies (where applicable).

[c] Including business tax, succession tax, tax on bonuses, capital interest tax, business profits tax, war profits tax, and special profits tax (where applicable).

clear. The reduced real burden of the land tax benefited only a limited group.

. . . . .

The Japanese landlord of the Meiji era presents a sharp contrast to Ricardo's wastrel type. From the outset he devoted himself to improvements, promoted societies for the discussion of agricultural techniques, introduced winter drainage and helped sponsor the growth of superior rice strains. The topographical dictates of Japanese rice culture (except possibly in the northern island of Hokkaido), as well as the high level of rents, contributed to the preservation of the small unit of cultivation and the avoidance of "capitalistic" forms of agricultural management. There is no evidence of any sizeable diversion of the landlords' respectable surpluses to high living or speculation. A large share of these surpluses as well as of the Land Tax proceeds was invested outside of the primary sector. In terms of making funds available for an over-all development programme, the residual rent, the interest on the rural debt, as well as the Land Tax proper must be included.

Other Fiscal Measures. The fiscal system as a whole—rather than single effective levies such as the Land Tax—must, of course, bear the burden of preserving a maximum proportion of the increased real output accruing as the result of developmental activity. Japanese taxes were heavy in an absolute and severely regressive in a relative sense. The total direct tax revenue allocatable to agriculture and non-agriculture as a percentage of the net income in each sector is presented in Table 3. The heavy burden on agriculture becomes even more evident when we recall (see Table 1 above) that government subsidies in this sector represented only a very small proportion of the total during the nineteenth century. Even in subsequent decades, when non-agricultural income was growing at a faster rate and had reached higher absolute levels, the tax burden on agriculture remained relatively more severe. The absolute burden on the economy as a whole was, however, considerably reduced at the conclusion of the nineteenth-century "take-off" period.

Regressiveness in the tax structure cut across sectoral lines. The dependability of profit receivers in the burgeoning secondary sector left fiscal policy here essentially free to disregard the dangers of potential luxury spending, speculation, or non-productive investment, and to concentrate on containing the broad base of consumption. Following Engel's Law, excise taxes on food and clothing are likely to be most effective in this effort in the low-income area. Moreover, as such an economy grows, the pressure for consuming the increments in income which accrue in the course of development are bound to change direction. An awareness

TABLE 3

ALLOCATION OF DIRECT TAX BURDEN

Year (Annual Average)	Direct Tax Allocatable to Agriculture[a] (Cur. Mil. Yen)	Net Income of Agriculture[b] (Cur. Mil. Yen)	Tax Burden on Agriculture (Per Cent)	Direct Tax Allocable to Non-Agriculture[a] (Cur. Mil. Yen)	Net Income of Non-Agriculture[b] (Cur. Mil. Yen)	Tax Burden on Non-Agriculture (Per Cent)
1878–1882	63.6	376	16.9	6.3	283	2.2
1884–1887	63.6	287	22.1	9.5	313	3.0
1888–1892	58.5	377	15.5	9.8	420	2.3
1894–1897	65.6	531	12.4	13.2	660	2.0
1898–1902	99.1	816	12.1	35.4	1106	3.2
1903–1907	113.6	1015	11.2	79.3	1467	5.4
1908–1912	153.4	1222	12.6	132.2	2077	6.4
1913–1917	167.7	1422	11.8	145.4	3216	4.5
1918–1922	295.7	3205	9.2	431.1	7967	5.4
1923–1927	304.2	2892	10.5	506.2	9706	5.2
1928–1932	205.5	2117	9.7	421.3	9723	4.3
1933–1937	197.3	2539	7.8	559.2	13159	4.2

[a] Tax figures are from an unpublished manuscript by Mr. Seiji Tsunematsu of the Agricultural Research Institute of the Japanese Department of Agriculture and Forestry. It is intended to be a part of an as yet unpublished volume, "Nihon Keizai to Nōgyō" (Japanese Economics and Agriculture).

[b] Income figures from the worksheets of the Economic Research Institute at Hitotsubashi University.

of the specificity of demand at one time and of such shifts over time is essential if the tax structure is to be flexible enough to trap a good share of the increases in per capita income not voluntarily freed for investment.

Excise taxes held a place of prominence, second only to that of the Land Tax, in the Japanese fiscal system. [See Table 3.] The levy on sake alone amounted to about 20 per cent of total tax revenue around the turn of the century. Selective excises on soya, sugar, textiles, and government monopoly profits in tobacco, camphor and salt—really only another form of indirect taxation—constituted the rest. Changes over time in the array of consumer goods subject to tax (e.g. from soya to tobacco) and in the schedule of rates (e.g. selective increases in 1875 and 1882) are evidence that the revenue system was kept flexible in order effectively to block consumption in the course of a shifting pattern of demand.

Government policy called for heavy taxes on both peasant and consumer and a lighter burden for the landlord and industrial-merchant classes. The income tax did not appear until 1887 and then at the low flat rate of 3 per cent. Table 2 shows that proceeds from this source were negligible before 1900; the definition of the tax base, moreover, rendering all interest on government and other savings bonds, all life insurance premia and forty per cent of all dividend receipts deductible, transformed it into a severely regressive levy.

A so-called business tax, equivalent to a proportional corporate income tax, went into effect only in 1896. It was levied on commercial and industrial enterprises, proportional to a formula using the amount of capital involved, the rental value of the plant and the number of employees. The highest rates (5-6 per cent on the rental value of the premises) were reserved for such luxuries as restaurants and hotels. Transportation and engineering enterprises, on the other hand, enjoyed rates of from 0.1 to 1 per cent. Progressive levies, i.e. the Capital Interest Tax and the Business Profits Tax were not enacted until 1926. Even more significant are vaguely defined exemptions granted to "the iron foundry business" and areas "producing certain important goods." Needless to add, benefits which could not be bestowed in the law itself could be granted in its administration.

Incentives for reinvestment and the accumulation of productive wealth were further strengthened by the absence of inheritance and real estate taxes before 1905, and the prevalence of very low rates thereafter. In combination with the predominance of primogeniture in the Japanese family such policies guaranteed the transfer of industrial fortunes virtually intact from generation to generation. Negative taxes or subsidies could, of course, supplement tax exemptions where necessary.[2] On the expenditure side also, as we have seen, industry and commerce were favored at the expense of agriculture and the workshops.[3]

The strongly oligopolistic trend in Japanese industry leading to the establishment of conglomerate enterprises reaching into every area of industrial activity made its own contribution to this redistribution of the income shares. The Zaibatsu and Zaibatsu-linked enterprises served, in a sense, as an arm of the national treasury; concessions exacted from the small producer in sub-contracted domestic industry can be viewed as a fiscal levy; monopoly prices on the consumer side can be viewed as an indirect tax. In a situation where it is assured that profits will not lie idle or, more importantly, be misused, the old question as to whether a competitive or monopolistic market configuration is better suited to growth seems to resolve itself.

All efforts were directed at siphoning off increments in income which had accrued to undependable would-be consumers, while preferential treatment was accorded those with whom only the ability, never the willingness, to reinvest was at issue. A blatantly regressive tax-expenditure structure is favorable to development only if the potentially investing classes are naturally disposed in that direction, or are subject to the discipline of an intervening state.

The largest contribution of the landlord-industrialist group came through the direct reinvestment of profits; moreover, this group subscribed to a large share of the banking capital and was instrumental in the flotation of the domestic debt. The fact that they abstained from diverting resources to non-developmental purposes is evidence of a degree of cooperation—or discipline—which makes it difficult to ascertain where the public sector ended and the private began.

· · · · ·

The lion's share of voluntary savings was of the "retained" rather than the "transferred" variety. In agriculture some direct accumulation took place in the form of agricultural improvements—by the deployment of an additional fraction of a peasant's time to road construction

[2] Especially in areas where the need for additional protection was felt, since the Unequal Treaty System deprived Japan of the tariff as a tool for development. The shipping trade, for example, was almost wholly dominated by the American Pacific Mail Company from the early Meiji days. The Mitsubishi Steamship Company was encouraged by the government, guaranteed against losses until the American company could be brought to its knees, and received an 8 per cent yearly dividend thereafter.

[3] Subsidies were, moreover, employed as a fine instrument for channelling investment. To relieve the balance of payments pressure, for example, ocean-going navigation, preferably in Japanese-built bottoms, was encouraged. A subsidy of 1.2 yen per ton was offered for ships in excess of 1000 tons. If the engines were a Japanese product as well, an additional payment of 5 yen per unit of horsepower was allowed for.

or fence mending. In small-scale domestic industry a similar expansion or improvement of the workshop during spare hours helped mobilize reserve productive capacity directly. But such contributions are not significant in relation to the cumulative reinvestment of profits in the large industrial enterprises.

Landowners and industrialists provided the bulk of "transferred" voluntary savings. They subscribed to a major portion of the banking capital, and there is evidence that a limited amount of government debt found a market outside of the banking system. Some loans floated during the nineteenth century were partly subscribed to by "individuals" and "companies" in what appears to be a normal savings operation. But the public market remained very narrow; 12.47 million of the 12.50 million yen New Loan of 1878, for example, was placed with the Mitsui family. The private equity market was also narrowly based. Most industry employed the closed corporate system, controlled by either the Zaibatsu, the government, or some form of coalition of the two. Attempts at broadening participation were by no means lacking. The government issued pamphlets explaining the joint stock company structure to the public, established advisory "commercial bureaus," clearing houses on the London model and a Tokyo Stock Exchange in 1878. To the present day, however, there has been little evidence of a wide-spread willingness or ability to adopt the more advanced financial techniques of this type.

Surprising, however, is the fact that the lower income groups, discriminated against by heavy taxes and an imperfect credit market, nevertheless managed to increase their rate of voluntary savings. The relative success of institutional patterns of savings, in spite of high taxes and moderate inflation, attest to proverbial Japanese thriftiness. Moral suasion from the top of the hierarchical structure was effectively employed in the effort to strengthen such tendencies. Imperial edicts had a considerable impact after the so-called Restoration of the Emperor to secular power. "Let us avoid all luxuries," to quote a typical one, "so that we can keep up with the world; truly the development of our national productive strength has its roots in reverent obedience. . . . May you, our people, take these, our wishes, to heart."

Savings banks, of which some 460 were in operation by the end of the nineteenth century, became the most popular vehicle in the effort to strengthen such habits among the lower income groups. The Japanese evidenced a definite affinity for an institutionalized regulated savings mechanism, as characterized also by the postal savings system, mutual aid associations and cooperative societies. In terms of real magnitudes, however, total voluntary savings, by direct investment on the farm and in the household, and by indirect investment through financial intermediaries, were small compared with the reinvestment of business surpluses, and the use of tax-financed public funds.

Inflation-Forced Savings. It would seem ideal to be able to plan development as follows: initially exploit available reserves with a minimum of investment; tax these funds away and employ them to clear bottlenecks in other sectors, with resulting secondary increases in income; a suitable tax structure can then be expected to yield the capital needed for further expansion. Unfortunately, this is an unrealistic pattern. Development does not proceed by neat stages; long gestation-period investments in social overhead and capital goods industries are usually required even in the early days of a logically consistent developmental effort. As a result, voluntary plus taxation-forced savings may prove inadequate in terms of the anticipated addition to the capital stock, and the *ex post* savings-investment equality is re-established through inflation.

In spite of the very favorable propensities and policies described above, Japan was forced to resort to credit creation in order to accommodate the total projected investment activity in the course of development. The amount of over-all credit creation[4] is difficult to establish. Agriculture and small-scale industry were faced with a highly centralized money market and did not receive substantial amounts of long-term credit. The considerable overlap between Zaibatsu enterprises and the banking system makes it impossible to obtain meaningful estimates of business debt. The government itself, initially handicapped by the absence of a dependable market for its bonds, resorted to deficit financing on a considerable scale.

Japan's national debt is presented in Table 4; on the average, it amounted to nearly 30 per cent of the national income during the nineteenth century. A variety of guises for outright credit creation was employed. Old Tokugawa feudal debts were funded by means of a 23 million yen bond issue; in 1876 samurai pension claims were commuted into instruments of credit. In neither case was there an exchange for previously existing purchasing power. The entire domestic debt outstanding in 1878 was credit-financed. The 12½ million yen Public Works Loan of that year, however, initiated efforts to place a portion of the debt with the public. A precise breakdown is not available; but a closer examination of the 1883 twenty million yen Nakasendo Railway Loan, for instance, yields the interesting fact that it was "oversubscribed" to the extent of 18 million yen; "individuals" applied for 30 per cent, "banks and companies" for 68 per cent of the total. Since

---

[4] It is understood that net credit creation by the private sector may be offset by the public sector and that government deficits may merely serve to mobilize hoards of an equivalent amount.

profit receivers participated as "individuals" and plowed back their profits as "companies," we can assume that banks accounted for the lion's share of the latter. Probably 50 per cent of the national debt incurred during the nineteenth century resulted in the creation of new purchasing power.

It should not be surprising that all available indices record price increases for these decades; what is surprising is that these increases were not more substantial. Tsuru's figures show an increase in the wholesale price level of 138 per cent from 1868 to 1900, an increase in the cost of living of 148 per cent from 1873 to the turn of the century.[5] Yamada obtains a 77 per cent advance in wholesale prices from 1875 to 1900[6] and Ohkawa's widely-quoted index shows a similar, more modest increase.[7] A moderate amount of inflation may, of course, serve a useful purpose in "shaking up" an economy, loosening old moorings and providing fresh incentives. In Japan, credit creation resulted simply in moderate price increases and additional forced savings without culminating in spiralling transfers of resources from savings and production to speculation and hoarding.[8]

Except for the years preceding the Satsuma Rebellion the banking system exercised restraint and made a significant contribution to stability. The Bank of Japan assumed all power of note issue in 1882 and succeeded in recalling the bulk of earlier wild-cat issues. Selective credit controls were used to ensure the deployment of credit to bottleneck areas where it might do the most good. The extent of specialization within the powerful quasi-official banking institutions may be cited here. The Yokohama Species Bank (1880) was set up to serve the foreign trade sector; the Hypothec Bank (1896)—working through prefectural Agricultural and Industrial Banks—to make long-term loans on the security of immovable property to agriculture and small-scale industry; the Industrial Bank of Japan (1900) to service the needs of manufacturing establishments. Most of the "private" banks were in the hands of the Zaibatsu whose close links with the government have been alluded to above. Firm control over the alternative sources of

---

[5] Shigeto Tsuru, "The Development of Capitalism and Business Cycles in Japan, 1868–1899," an unpublished doctoral thesis, Harvard University, 1940, Appendix.

[6] Yuzo Yamada, "Nippon Kokumin Shotoku Suikei Shiro" (Estimated Japanese National Income), *Oriental Economist* (Tokyo, 1951), p. 57.

[7] From working papers at the Hitotsubashi University, Tokyo, Japan.

[8] Attempts to develop beyond one's means need not, of course, result in domestic inflation, if the foreign balance can serve to cushion the effects of the extra demand created. Nineteenth-century Japan was, however, neither willing nor able to make extensive use of other people's savings to supplement her own. Prior to the adoption of the Gold Standard in 1899 only two long-term loans totalling less than 17 million yen were floated abroad. The bulk of the inflationary pressure remained at home.

finance by the government and "dependable" groups outside the government assured the effectiveness of credit rationing in realizing any established hierarchy of investment priorities.

TABLE 4

OUTSTANDING NATIONAL DEBT OF JAPAN
(Million Yen)

Year	Domestic	Per Cent of Total	Foreign	Per Cent of Total	Total
1877	213	94	13	6	226
1897	399	100	0	0	399
1907	1088	48	1165	52	2254
1914	991	40	514	60	2506
1924	3356	69	1506	31	4863
1930	4476	75	1479	25	5955

Source: From Yasuzo Horie, "Japan's Balance of International Payments in the Early Meiji Period," *Kyoto University Economic Review* (April, 1954).

Nevertheless, the basic explanation for the avoidance of cumulative inflation must be sought in the fact that Japan was able to put such a large share of her programme on a pay-as-you-go basis. If the excess of purchasing power over real resources at any one period of time can be contained, primary pressures are reduced; and if there are favorable anticipations based on confidence and culturally-conditioned obedience —as well as an absence of union pressures and escalator clauses—the impact of such presures as do result is minimized. Small capital expenditure called forth increases in output sufficiently quickly to absorb unavoidable pressures for increased consumption, and sufficiently large to free resources for an over-all development effort. The major responsibility for enabling Japan to avoid the hard choice between stability and development must be assigned to the fiscal policies she pursued.

21

The Economic Development
of Russia

by

ALEXANDER BAYKOV

<hr />

I

The main difference in economic development as between Russia
and the West European countries, from the middle of the eighteenth
century to the second quarter of the twentieth century, was that Russia's
industrial development was much slower, while the growth of her
population was much more rapid than in the West; a difference which
found its reflection in the standard of life of the population of Russia.
The population of Russia increased from 14 million in 1722 to 129
million in 1897. Even if we exclude the population of the new territories
which were incorporated into the Russian State during this period, the
population increased from 13 million to 65 million in the basic territory.
In reality, the increase here was even greater, because several millions
migrated from the older parts of Russia to newly-conquered territories.
Population thus increased much more rapidly in Russia than in the
West European countries, and this growth of the population took place

Reprinted from *The Economic History Review*, 2d series, VII, 2 (December, 1954)
(pp. 137–49, with omissions), by permission of the Economic History Society and
the author.

on an agricultural basis. The total urban population during the nine-teenth century only increased from approximately 1½ million at the beginning of the century to 16½ million at the end; whereas total population in the meantime increased by 97 million.

The Russian urban population in 1800 was only approximately 3½ per cent of the whole—one-half of the ratio of urban to total popula-tion of France—not to mention England, in which, already by 1800, more than one-fifth of the population lived in towns. During the nineteenth century, this difference in the degree of urbanization con-stantly increased, and, at the end of the nineteenth century, Russia with 12.8 per cent urban population, as against over 40 per cent in France and Germany and over 70 per cent in England, was the most rural of the main European countries.

This prevalence of rural population in Russia was so striking that it is no wonder that most of the explanations for the retardation of Russia's economic development have been centered on the analysis of agricultural processes. The most generally accepted explanation is that Russia's economic retardation, especially the slow development of industry, was due, first, to Tatar invasion and the long maintenance of serfdom and, after its long-overdue abolition, to the preservation of certain features of a serf economy up to the beginning of the twentieth century. Among these factors were the continued system of repartitional tenure; the trammels of the village commune; the continued restrictions on civil and economic rights and on freedom of movement by the peasantry; the preservation of the strong social and political position of estate-owners; the continued government by autocracy together with an administration based on the land-owning class without the partici-pation of other classes. They also included the intervention of State power in economic activities to a much greater degree than in other countries (with its tendency to sponsor non-competitive enterprises, by the creation of primitive monopolies, by bulk government purchases of certain industrial supplies for the Army and Navy at high assured prices and by the protectionist policy of excessive tariffs). These and other similar *institutional* explanations of the causes of economic retarda-tion of Russia have now become generally current.

It would be foolish to deny the influence of Tatar invasion or of the long duration of serfdom or the influence of other institutional factors on the economic development of Russia. However, the importance of these institutional causes of the retardation of Russia's economic de-velopment is largely overstated. For example, the existence of serfdom cannot answer such problems as why England, where serfdom had to all intents and purposes ended as early as in the fourteenth century, and which had abundant iron and coal deposits, produced less cast iron than

Russia in the eighteenth century, and even imported it (along with linen) from Russia and Sweden, while in the second half of the nineteenth century, when serfdom had been abolished in Russia, Russia produced much less coal and iron than England and imported both from England. Why, in the eighteenth century, when serfdom in Russia had been strengthened in comparison with the previous period, when the serf-owning classes were the actual rulers of the country, when the autocratic rule of the State was more prominent than before, was not Russia even further behind the leading European nations than in fact she was? For at that time in some branches of industrial production such as in iron and linen, Russia was ahead of England, France and Germany. In 1740 Russia produced 31,975 metric tons of cast iron, England 20,017, France 25,979 and Germany only 17,691 m. tons. It was only from 1805 that Russia, in the production of cast iron, fell behind England, from 1828 behind France and the United States and from 1855 behind Austria and Germany. Why, also, in the second half of the nineteenth century, when serfdom had been abolished, did Russia fall more and more behind the leading West European countries in industrial and, to some extent, agricultural development? It is asserted that this was caused by the maintenance of serfdom up to 1861, as a consequence of which industry suffered from a shortage of labor and capital for its development. However, all available evidence points out that the shortage of labor (and even of hired labor) was not the limiting factor in the development of industry. In industries which had economic possibilities for development, the amount of labor employed during the first half of the nineteenth century increased very rapidly, and *hired* labor was predominant in most of them. Besides, the serf population *itself* cannot be treated as a homogeneous group. Only as regards estate-owned serfs can we speak of "serfs" in the proper meaning of the term, but these comprised only a quarter of the total population on the eve of the abolition of serfdom. Even if we take all the varieties of serf status, we find that, on the eve of the abolition of serfdom, they only accounted for just a little over half the total population (57.7 per cent). In 1858 out of the total population of 74 million, they amounted to 42,717,000. Thus, even on the eve of the abolition of serfdom there were in the country nearly 32 million people free of any kind of serf status, a non-serf population greater than the total population of contemporary England or France. Why was it not possible for 32 million free people to accumulate capital and participate in the development of industry to the same degree in Russia as in the other European countries?

For these and many other reasons it is not possible to accept institutional theories as the main explanations of the economic backwardness of Russia. Historians traditionally pay much attention to the institutional framework, to political institutions, social structure and social-philosophical views of society, to religious institutions, to relations with other States, and so on. Economic historians, too, mostly concentrate on forms of economic organization, on the institutions of production, distribution and finance. Much less attention has been paid to, and very little research has been done to examine, the influence of natural resources, including transport, in their inter-relations with the population-trends and changes in technique. Research in this direction might necessitate the correction of many accepted explanations of economic development of different countries.

In this field one stock assumption, uncritically accepted as a working concept, has done much harm to realistic research into the causes of Russia's economic retardation, i.e. the assumption that Russia is a "very rich country" as regards natural resources. But in reality European Russia viewed in historical perspective was worse endowed in natural resources than most of the leading West European countries. In order to utilize Russia's natural resources, the Russian people had to overcome more handicaps than the populations of most of the leading West European countries.

Up to the beginning of the eighteenth century the Russian State developed on a territory the European part of which was very poorly endowed with natural resources and transport possibilities. The soil of Moscow and the adjacent regions is very poor in comparison with that of most of the land in France, Germany and England proper. Climatic conditions presented greater difficulties for the introduction of proper crop rotation, for the breeding of livestock and the full utilization of labor in agricultural occupations than in West European countries. Given the same level of agricultural technique, the Russian peasant of Central and North European Russian regions had to overcome more natural handicaps than his counterpart in West European countries.

The agricultural resources of European Russia on the territory of the Russian State within the frontiers of 1700 were very limited, and if the Russian State had continued to develop on this territory alone it would soon have suffered from agrarian over-population, and its population would have been unable to grow at the pace at which it actually grew during the eighteenth and nineteenth centuries. In the same territories, during the eighteenth century, the Russian population increased by approximately 70 per cent, but, during the nineteenth century it increased approximately three times. Such an expansion was possible only because the population of the older territory of the Russian State of the eighteenth century received a great deal of their agricultural supplies from the newly-conquered territories of Southern Russia. As early as the end of the eighteenth century, most of Central and North European Russia (especially Moscow and the areas around Moscow) became consuming regions with deficiencies in the balance of agricultural production and consumption. At the same time this territory had no industrial resources which could be compared with the industrial resources of the West European countries. The Central and North-Western regions of Russia have only very poor deposits of iron-ore, and these could only be worked by primitive methods of production, and were uneconomic to work with more advanced techniques of smelting. When Peter the Great initiated a new drive for expanding the production of iron, these old Russian regions could not provide sufficient supplies of ore, and it was necessary to go over to the mountains of the Urals—1000 miles away from the historical centers of the population, from possible sources of labor supply and from the established centers of administration and trade of the country. It is enough to compare the location of Urals iron ore in relation to the historically established distribution of the population in Russia with the location of iron-ore deposits and the distribution of the population in England, Germany and France, and with corresponding transport possibilities, to understand why Russia was handicapped in this respect too. In addition the Urals lack deposits of coking coal conveniently located near to iron-ore. In England, coal found near the surface was used as a fuel as early as the sixteenth century. Experiments in the use of coal for smelting iron-ore started as early as 1612 and coal was finally adopted for industrial use by 1735. But Russia had only poor deposits of brown coal (not suitable for coking and not easily accessible) in the Moscow region. Coal of very poor quality which would not burn without an admixture of charcoal and was not suitable for coking, was discovered in the Urals only in 1797. Even then its mining was not undertaken because it was found uneconomical.

It would therefore be no exaggeration to say that it was the invention of smelting iron-ore with coke that gave England (and afterwards the other West European countries) the power rapidly to develop their iron production. This invention could not have been made in Russia, whatever institutional framework had existed at that time, because neither in the old center of Russian metallurgy in the central regions and Olonetsk region nor in the Urals were there available together the raw materials needed (i.e. iron ore and coking coal). This invention could not be industrially used in Russia until the second half of the nineteenth century. Only then did it become possible economically to interconnect old centers of Russian population in the central regions with the deposits of iron ore in Krivoi Rog and coking coal in the Donets Basin. This invention allowed England immediately to increase the production of iron by leaps and bounds, while Russia, with only one region with iron-ore deposits which was unprovided with coking coal, needed sixty years (from the middle of the eighteenth century to the first quarter of the nineteenth century) to double her production of iron. England was able, in the same period, to increase her production of iron more than thirty times.

Until the invention of the coke-smelting of iron was realized the Urals iron industry had some initial advantage. The region had easily-mined, rich iron ore, an abundant supply of wood for charcoal, supplies of water-power and cheap serf labor. However, its industry suffered from a very high, and constantly increasing, cost of transport, of charcoal from areas farther and farther away, and the high cost of transport of finished goods from the Urals to the markets. Besides, smelting on charcoal imposed certain limitations on the size of furnaces and on their productive cycle. The initial advantages of the Urals put Russia in the forefront of all West European countries as producers of cast iron in the eighteenth century, but after the application of coke-smelting, Urals iron could not compete in cost with European, especially English production. It was the absence of suitably-located coking coal and the high cost of transport that was the main cause of the slow development of iron-production in the Urals—not difficulty in obtaining labor.

It should also be remembered that territory on which the Krivoi Rog iron-ore basin (i.e. the main iron-ore basin of European Russia) was situated was conquered by Russia from Turkey as late as 1733–74 and part of the Donets basin territory in 1739, i.e. at the time when, in England, the Industrial Revolution was already being launched. These regions to the south of the Donets and the Dnieper rivers had been the stage for centuries of struggle between the centralized Russian State, the Tatars, Turkey and Poland and were consequently very sparsely populated. Catherine II went so far as to promote the colonization of these regions with Germans, Bulgarians and Greeks, and many thousands of them actually settled there. It was economically impossible to connect these two basins, Krivoi Rog and the Donets, with the historically evolved main centers of population of the Russian State until railway connections were built. The Urals, in spite of their enormous distance from the Moscow and Petersburg regions, were connected with these markets by a system of rivers and canals; but often it still required two navigational seasons to bring a load from the Urals to Petersburg with intermediate wintering in Tver. In certain favorable water and weather conditions, it was possible to reduce transport time to six months, but it is very interesting to note that, owing to nearly double costs of hiring horses and labor for towing, loading and unloading operations in the summer months compared with those of winter, the famous Demidov firm of ironmasters often preferred to spread navigation over two seasons rather than shoulder the higher costs of transportation within a single season. On the other hand Krivoi Rog and the Donets basin could not be linked with the Central region (distance from Krivoi Rog to Makeevka in the Donets region 463 km. and to Moscow over 1000 km.) by the river system because, unfortunately, the rivers of that region flow in the wrong direction, and could not economically be connected by canals owing to great technical difficulties of construction. It was because Russian rivers flowed in the wrong directions that, up to the end of the eighteenth century, Russia had at her disposal only the Volga river system and Northern Dvina water system. This played an enormous part in determining the direction and development of Russian trade and also (in the early period of Russian history) of her cultural development. Had the Krivoi Rog iron-ore basin and the Donets coal basin been located in the Moscow region, and the Volga flowed from the Moscow region to the Black Sea instead of the Caspian, the history of Russia's economy, and her political and cultural history, would have been very different from what they in fact were.

II

Many more well-known facts support the thesis that historically Russia was much handicapped by a deficiency in the location of her natural resources. Owing to the location of natural resources and lines of communication, until railways could be built, it was only possible to develop agricultural production in the southern regions of Russia and to use it for supplying food to the central and northern regions of Russia and (later on) for export. When railways began to be built, the Urals industry could not even provide sufficient iron and steel, not to speak of engines and rolling-stock. Between 1870 and 1879 Russia imported more than half (59 per cent) of the iron and steel she consumed, and even in 1890–9, by which time the southern regions were supplying more iron than the Urals, Russia still imported more than a quarter (27 per cent) of her consumption of iron and steel. The cause of this was that, up to the middle of the nineteenth century, Russia produced practically no coal. Until it became possible to develop the Donets and Krivoi Rog basin coal and iron ore, the Russian economy was built on grain and timber as its main natural resources. Even at the end of the nineteenth century, in 1886–90, with a total consumption of coal still very low in comparison with West European countries, Russia imported a quarter of her coal consumption; and, up to the Revolution of 1917, the industry of the Petersburg region depended on imported English coal, which was cheaper (owing to lower transport costs) than coal brought from the Donets basin.

The turning-point in Russian industrial history came when, for the first time in her history, it was possible to join the coal of the Donets basin and the iron ore of Krivoi Rog with the old central regions of Russia. But the cost of building this new basis for the future develop- ment of Russian industry was borne, in the main, by the peasantry. In the last analysis, it was the Russian peasantry who paid for the foreign loans contracted for the building of the Russian railway system and for the foreign investments in mining and the iron and steel industries of the southern regions. Of the fifty-three years from 1860 to 1913, Russia had only twelve years with a negative balance of trade, and over this period taken as a whole, her exports were 6½ billion (6,593,843,000) rubles higher than her imports, and all this export surplus was swallowed by the service on loans and payments for other invisible imports. At the outbreak of the Great War in 1914, Russia's total indebtedness (public and private) amounted to 7½ billion rubles or about 3,750 million dollars. Throughout the period 1860–1913, over three-quarters of Russia's exports were agricultural exports. It was in this period that Russia was nicknamed "the granary of Europe" and the Russian Finance Minister Vyshnegradsky coined the phrase, "Let us eat less, and export."

Yet Russia was a poor granary. Her sown area and her livestock grew very slowly. The standard of living of her peasantry was much below that of the farmers of the countries to which Russian exports went. She was a granary which, at the beginning of the twentieth cen- tury, suffered an agrarian over-population to the extent of about 20 million.

III

If we turn now to the Soviet period, we see two distinct processes: a very rapid trend of increase in industrial output and a very uneven and slow development of agricultural production. The main results of Soviet economic development are well known. In spite of some disagreements among West European scholars as regards Soviet methods of statistical measurement, and consequently about actual rates of growth of indus- trial output and the extent of fluctuations in agricultural production, all agree that in the last twenty peaceful years in the Soviet Union a tempo of development of industrial production unprecedented in Russian history has been achieved. I shall not attempt here to summarize the well-known facts of industrial and agricultural developments in the Soviet Union, but shall try to suggest some explanations of why such developments became possible and, in fact, took place.

In the first place, I shall put here the temporary influence of the Soviet economic policy aimed at the concentration of the economic activity on raising the productive capacity of the national economy and

not on increasing consumption. By planned distribution of the total consumers' goods produced in the country it was possible, during the
thirteen years from 1926 to 1939, not only to absorb 23½ million of
the natural increase of the population into the towns but to turn an
additional 6.1 million rural inhabitants into urban-dwellers. In this way
for the first time in Russian history, the natural increase in population
was absorbed by the towns. This permitted an increase in the numbers
of workers employed in the national economy (excluding agriculture)
by nearly 20 millions between 1928 and 1940 as well as an increase in
the technical qualifications and general educational level of town-
dwellers as a whole. This in its turn not only made it possible to devote
additional labor to the expansion of the productive capacity of industry
in the southern regions (in the development of whose resources only a
start had been made in the last twenty-five years before the Revolution), but also made possible the building of a new metallurgical and
coal base for the further development of industry in the Urals and
Siberia—Magnitogorsk, Kuznetsk, the Karaganda coal-iron combines—
and the development of non-ferrous metallurgy in Kazakhstan, especially copper-production. It would be no exaggeration to say that, when
the coal of Kuznetsk and Karaganda was linked with the iron-ore of the
Urals, and when the copper of Dzhezkazgan and Kounrad in Kazakhstan was linked (by the newly built Turkestan-Siberian railway) with the
engineering industry of the Moscow region, a new stage in Russian
industrial history began. This application of the labor force also permitted the creation of a modern engineering industry. Thereby Soviet
industry, for the first time in the history of Russia, was able to build
machines which make other machines. This maturer stage of industrial
development had been the weakest link in Russian industry in pre-
Revolutionary times.

The application of modern technique has made it possible to overcome many of the handicaps imposed by the location of Russian natural
resources.[1] In general it is very improbable that private enterprise would
have undertaken to build a Volga-Don Canal or a Urals-Kuznetsk-
Karaganda combine, even at the present level of technique, since it
would have required not only enormous capital investment but the
co-ordination of the interests of investors in many branches of economic
activity. Even in the United States, the Tennessee Valley project was
carried out by the Government and not by private enterprise. In order
to link the Urals iron-ore with Central Russia, Peter the Great was forced

---

[1] For example, the linking of Kuznets coal with Magnitogorsk iron ore, the use
of peat for production of electricity, the utilization of hydraulic energy of the
Dnieper and the Volga, became possible only by the application of the most modern
technique.

to take this task into the hands of the State and to impose certain hardships on the Russian peasantry and even to extend serfdom to industry. In order to create the Russian railway system and connect the iron-ore and coal of Southern Russia with Central Russia it was necessary "to eat less, and to export," to use a protective tariff policy and to force the peasantry to bear the main cost of the investment.

The building of a modern industry, and the possibilities of further development were again paid for in the main by the peasantry. In this lay the cause of the slowness and the difficulties in the development of agricultural production.

This time, the industrial development was achieved on, so to speak, an internal basis. Foreign investment played no part, foreign trade played a much smaller role than in the pre-Revolutionary period, and agricultural exports in all the years of the Soviet period did not reach even half of the level of pre-Revolutionary exports. The exertions of the Russian peasantry this time made possible a rapid growth of industrial labor and of labor employed in the education, welfare and cultural services and the administration of the country; a growth which has been reflected in the growth of the town population.

IV

What light do these past economic tendencies of Russian development throw on the economic prospects of Soviet Russia? Will the Soviet Union find it possible to continue this rapid industrial development? Will it be possible simultaneously to increase agricultural production so as not only to provide the same standard of living for an increased population, but even to raise it? Will it be possible to achieve further increase in the town population and in the numbers of the industrial population on the basis of internal industrial and agricultural resources—or will Russia follow the path of the West European countries in the development of her industry and in the growth of the town population—the path of great increases in foreign trade?[2]

In attempting to consider these questions, in the light of historical experience it is impossible to do more than to enumerate the problems to which a final answer cannot yet be given. Thus, as regards fuel and power resources, it is probable that they would impose no limit on the development of industry in the near future. The Soviet Union has potential deposits of coal and water-power resources which can for a long time serve as a basis for much greater industrial development than at present. But four-fifths of the potential coal deposits are located

---

[2] The magnitude of this problem can be realized if we remember that in the next twenty years the net increase of the population of the U.S.S.R. might amount to some 60 million. . . .

in Asiatic Russia. Five-sixths of her resources of water-power are also in the Asiatic part of the Soviet Union. On the other hand most of the known iron-ore deposits are in the Urals, and in Central and Southern Russia. It must, however, be remembered that our information is based on 1936 data when only 60 per cent of Soviet territory had been geologically mapped—and only very superficially prospected. Many discoveries have been made since, but no information is available. All the main discoveries of non-ferrous metals have been made during the Soviet period, for before the Revolution Russia was considered a country poorly endowed with non-ferrous metals. Now it is thought that with the exception of tin, tungsten, molybdenum, cobalt and some other rare metals, the Soviet Union has already discovered deposits adequate to meet the requirements of her industrial production for a long time ahead. But here again, most of these deposits are located in the Asiatic part of the Soviet Union and in the Urals, as well as some in the Caucasian region. European Russia has practically no deposits of non-ferrous metals. So, although in general it can be said that neither fuel nor minerals will be a limiting factor on the development of Soviet industry, the overcoming of economic obstacles to the exploitation of fuel and power and mineral resources would be necessary owing to the character of their location. In 1939, for example, the average length of a haul of coal on the railways was 709 km. as against 485 km. in 1913, i.e. the length of haul was increased by nearly a half. Britain used only one-third as high a proportion of its fuel and power for railway transportation, and the United States and Canada only two-thirds as high a proportion as the Soviet Union. Russia cannot economically afford to go on increasing the length of haul of fuel and raw materials. The location of resources therefore necessitates an eastward movement of Russian industry. This movement has been initiated in the last 25 years, and will have to be continued in the future.

As regards food resources, great expansion (i.e. increasing the area under crops) is also possible only in the Asiatic part of the Soviet Union. It has been estimated by a very competent agricultural economist (Prasolov) that the Soviet Union has approximately 80 million hectares of land suitable for agriculture which could be added to the arable area, i.e. the present arable area could be increased by some 40 per cent. But this land is situated in zones climatically less favorable than the existing regions and, consequently, its cultivation will require more effort. Very recently the Soviet Government initiated a campaign for bringing into cultivation 13 million hectares of unused land in the Kazakh Republic, in Western Siberia, in the Urals, the Volga region, and to some extent in the North Caucasus. But in regions more remote from the present centers of the population and industry, the development of new land would become possible only if local markets could be developed. And this would necessitate a simultaneous increase in both agricultural cultivation and industrial urban growth in new regions.

Very considerable untapped fish reserves are available in the Siberian rivers, in the Arctic Sea and on the Far Eastern seaboard, but their use is limited by the productive capacity of the canning industry, and by refrigeration and transport facilities. This, again, indicates the necessity for an eastward tendency in the future development of industry. As regards more intensive use of land, in the European part of the Soviet Union there are possibilities for much greater increases in the productivity of land, in yields and in the ratio of livestock to land. The work recently started on afforestation and irrigation of the southern regions affected by drought should make possible the more intensive use of land over a large area. But the results of some of these measures will be forthcoming only in twenty to thirty years.

Thus the possibility of substantially increasing agricultural production in the near future depends on a more and more intensive use of agricultural resources already in exploitation. This intensification will become possible only on the condition that investment in agriculture proceeds at a higher tempo than hitherto, and will depend on the extent to which the standard of living of the rural population is improved. This means that more industrial production would have to be allocated for capital investment in agriculture and for the supply of rural population, which still represents a majority of the inhabitants of the Soviet Union. Without some such policy, it is very doubtful whether a great increase in the productivity of agriculture can take place.

There are indications that the Soviet Government is aware of this problem and has started to introduce corresponding measures. Probably this need to increase the supply of capital and consumers' goods to the agricultural sector of the national economy plus the need to increase the supply of consumers' goods to the town population would slow down temporarily the tempo of investment in heavy industry. Perhaps a temporary limitation of the supply of labor might also slow down the tempo of industrial development, because the main reserves created by agrarian over-population have already been absorbed in the earlier period, during which the rate of growth of the town population has been nearly twice as high as the natural increase. On the other hand, the greatly increased and constantly improving ratio of equipment to labor in industry and the constant improvement in the skill of labor should reduce the need for high annual additions to the labor force.

As far as markets for the increased industrial production are concerned, I consider that for our generation, at any rate, the Soviet Union's problem will be more that of an unsatisfied demand than of a search for external markets. The development of the transport system has been behind the development of the national economy in the last twenty-five years. Great investments will be needed to expand and improve the Soviet rail, coastal, sea, river and road transport systems. The living standards of the masses of the population, as regards dwellings and amenities in the towns and per capita consumption of industrial goods, are still much behind that of the leading industrial countries. Besides, apart from current consumption, accumulated stocks of durable consumers' goods in the possession of the population are very low compared with those in the West European countries. In the Western countries, stocks of durable consumers' goods represent the main obstacles for sales of current production. In the Soviet Union (for this generation in any case) all goods of good quality should find their own demand.

To sum up, the foreseeable development of Soviet policy and the present distribution of potential resources justify the expectation that industrial development in the Soviet Union could still go on for say the next twenty years at a greater speed than in the West European countries, but perhaps with some slowing down of the rate of development of heavy industry, accompanied by a speeding up in the output of consumers' goods as compared with the preceding twenty-five years. The increase in the town population would continue, but at a lesser rate than in the period 1929–39. This development is feasible on basically internal industrial and agricultural resources. Moreover, further increases in agricultural production in the next twenty years will probably be sufficient only to cover the natural increase in the population. It is very doubtful whether a substantial improvement in the supply of basic agricultural products per head of the population can be achieved and no return to agricultural exports of pre-Revolutionary magnitude can be expected.

22

The Early Phases of Industrialization in Russia and Their Relationship to the Historical Study of Economic Growth

by

ALEXANDER GERSCHENKRON

The following pages do not purport to cast the topic in a new mold. My views on the course of European industrialization in the nineteenth century in general and on that of Russia in particular have been laid down in a number of essays published within the span of the last ten or twelve years.[1] This circumstance, however, should cause no dis-

A paper presented to the International Economic Association's Conference on the Economics of the Take-Off into Sustained Growth, September 2–11, 1960, at Konstanz. Reprinted by permission of the International Economic Association and the author. The Association plans to publish the proceedings of this Conference late in 1962.

[1] The most relevant among those essays may be listed as follows: "The Rate of Industrial Growth in Russia since 1885," *The Journal of Economic History*, Supplement VII, 1947; "Economic Backwardness in Historical Perspective," in *The Progress of Underdeveloped Countries*, edited by B. Hoselitz, Chicago, 1952; "The Problem of Economic Development in Russian Intellectual History of the Nineteenth Century," in *Continuity and Change in Russian and Soviet Thought*, edited by E. Simmons, Cambridge, Mass., 1955; "Review," *ibid.*; "Notes on the Rate of Industrial Growth in Italy, 1881–1913," *Journal of Economic History*, December 1955; "Reflections on the Concept of 'Prerequisites' of Modern Industrialization," *L'Industria*, 1957, no. 2; "Caratteri e problemi dello sviluppo economico Russo," *Rivista Storica Italiana*, 71, no. 2, 1959; "Rosario Romeo e l'accumulazione primitiva del capitale," *Rivista Storica Italiana*, 71, no. 4, 1959.

appointment to the members of this conference. A paper on an assigned topic resembles the proverbial gift horse in that no reasonable person will expect too much from it. Still, it need not be entirely toothless, and it is possible that a confrontation of my views with those of Professor Rostow might yield one or two additional insights; at the very least, it may draw sharper contours around the methodological problems involved.

I. A SUMMARY VIEW OF RUSSIAN INDUSTRIALIZATION, 1885–1914

Something more will be said presently on the crucial question of appropriate spatial and temporal limitations in historical studies. Suffice it to say here that my research has been confined to the European industrialization of the nineteenth century. My basic observation, used as a point of departure, is as simple as are the propositions to be derived from it. It may be formulated as follows: During the period under review the map of Europe offered a motley picture of areas varying very considerably among themselves with regard to the degree of their economic backwardness; in the course of the same period, processes of rapid industrialization began in several of those areas from very different levels of economic backwardness.[2] This, however, was of crucial significance for the nature of the subsequent development. Depending on a given country's relative economic backwardness on the eve of its industrialization, the course and character of the latter tended to vary in a number of important respects. Those variations may be summarized in the form of a few brief propositions.

1. The more backward a country's economy, the more likely its industrialization was to start discontinuously as a sudden great spurt proceeding at a relatively high rate of growth of manufacturing output.

2. The more backward was a country's economy, the more pronounced in its industrialization was the stress on bigness of both plant and enterprise.

---

[2] There is no need at this moment to justify the identification of the *economic area* with a politically bounded country; nor to explain how the concept of the degree of economic backwardness can be rendered measurable beyond saying that in actual historical fact the differences in the level of economic development among the countries of Europe were sufficiently discrete so that application of various conceivably appropriate criteria yields very similar results with regard to the ordinal array of the countries concerned; accordingly, for the purposes at hand, the degree of backwardness in the given historical circumstances may be regarded as an operationally usable concept.

3. The more backward was a country's economy, the more pronounced in its industrialization was the stress on producers' goods as against consumer's goods.

4. The more backward was a country's economy, the heavier was the pressure in the course of its industrialization upon the levels of consumption of its population.

5. The more backward was a country's economy, the greater was the part played in its industrialization by special institutional factors designed to increase the supply of capital to the nascent industry and, in addition, to provide it with less decentralized and better informed entrepreneurial guidance; the more backward the country, the more pronounced was the coerciveness and comprehensiveness of those factors.

6. The more backward the country, the less likely was its agriculture to play any active role in the process of industrialization by offering to nascent industry the advantages of a growing internal market based in turn on growing productivity of agricultural labor.

Russia's place in the concert of European countries seated according to the respective rank of economic backwardness was hardly in doubt. When, in 1910, E. V. Tarlé surprised the Russian public by stating his fantastic thesis that Russia in the last quarter of the eighteenth century was not a backward country if compared with Western Europe, he stirred up a controversy which still has not quite found its well-deserved rest.[3] No such claims have confused the students of Russian economic history in the second half of the nineteenth century. It was not doubted that Russia in, say, 1875 was burdened with the most backward economy among the major countries in Europe. Remaining within the Continent, one had to cross the Pyrenees or the Balkans in order to find economically even less advanced states of any size.[4]

The story of Russian industrialization in the last fifteen years or so of the past century would seem to conform very well to the general propositions set forth in the preceding. There was a sudden and considerable acceleration in the rate of growth of Russian industrial output in the second half of the 1880's. During the decade of the 1890's the rate of growth kept rising, reaching an average level of about 8 per

---

[3] E. V. Tarlé, "Byla li Yekaterininskaya Rossiya otstaloy stranoy?" (Was Russia under Catherine [II] a Backward Country?), reprinted in E. V. Tarlé, *Sochineniya*, Vol. IV, Moscow, 1958, pp. 441–68.

[4] Cf. in this connection my forthcoming paper on "Some Aspects of Industrialization in Bulgaria, 1878–1939."

cent a year for the decade. It is worth noting that the process was still gathering further momentum in the last few years before 1900 when the upsurge, or at least its first act, was terminated by the onslaught of the general crisis in Central and Eastern Europe. It is, of course, true that interspatial and intertemporal comparisons of industrial growth, particularly in periods of rapid advance, must be treated with great caution.[5] Yet, when all is said and done, the Russian rate of growth in the 1890's appears to be a good deal above the annual average rates of growth achieved during periods of rapid industrialization in, say, Germany (while the German rates in turn exceeded comparable rates that had been still earlier attained in England).

Similarly, the relative top-heaviness of the Russian industrial structure as well as its relative concentration upon producers' goods strongly impress themselves on any observer of Russian economic history of the period. Furthermore, during the years of industrial upsurge in Russia the economic wellbeing of the Russian peasantry was subject to extraordinary pressures. Those pressures have since been belittled by the Soviet government's policy of superindustrialization and wholesale collectivization in the 1930's. There is no doubt, however, that in no Western country did the periods of "industrial revolutions" exact sacrifices from the populations comparable to those made in Russia in the closing years of the last century. In fact, the peasant unrest in the early years of the century, culminating in the great wave of peasant rebellions during the revolution of 1905, may be seen as the direct consequence of the burdens which the industrialization of the 1890's had imposed upon a rural population which had been eking out a miserable existence from a barbarously primitive agriculture.

Nor can there be any doubt that all the basic features of an indusrialization that had begun in conditions of extreme backwardness were powerfully reinforced and accentuated by deliberate action on the part of the government. Using a panoply of measures ranging from the high protective tariff via subsidies, profit guarantees, tax reductions, and tax exemptions accorded to industrial enterprises, to manifold laxities in enforcing bothersome laws and ordinances and police and military help in case of labor conflicts, and culminating in huge government orders at extremely high prices, the Russian state furthered the growth of domestic industries. In pursuing those policies, the State, or more concretely the Ministry of Finance, was characteristically interested in those branches of industry which in later usage began to be circumscribed as "heavy industry"; at the same time, it was the large-scale

---

[5] Cf. my illustration of the formidable quantitative significance of the index number problem in Alexander Gerschenkron, *A Dollar Index of Soviet Machinery Output*, Santa Monica, Calif., 1951.

enterprises which established and ran large-scale plants that received help and encouragement. In these important respects, the policies of the Russian government essentially reproduced the policies of the so-called "investment banks" in a number of Central European and West European countries. But the differences in degree were clearly noticeable; for the Russian government's discrimination against "light industries" and against small enterprises in any branch of industry was applied with even greater consistency and ruthlessness.

The several years of stagnation which came in the wake of the crisis of 1900 tended to obscure the results of the great spurt. To a sharp-eyed American tourist who visited the country in 1901, "ten or fifteen years of violent stimulus seemed resulting in nothing."[6] But Henry Adams was wrong. He failed to grasp the extent of the transformation that had taken place within the industrial structure of the economy, to say nothing of the quantitative expansion of that structure. A far-reaching modernization had occurred with regard to technology, modes of entrepreneurial behavior, managerial practices, and aptitudes of the labor force.

This brief summary of the golden period of modern industrialization in Imperial Russia must suffice here. What matters is not a full story of the great spurt of the nineties. For that the reader must be referred to the essays mentioned in [the first footnote to this paper], and beyond them to a body of literature quoted or cited in those essays. The interest at this point lies in the methodological implications. In general, the quality of an historical approach can be gauged most clearly from a scrutiny of the limits beyond which it cannot be pushed, and by its confrontation with the results of alternative views of the same subject matter. Thereby a firmer basis may be laid for a discussion of Professor Rostow's views.

It is only the inveterate tendency of historians to prefix the definite article to every generalization about the course of historical events that calls for the trivial observation that the view of Russian industrial history as summarized in the foregoing is only one of several possible and plausible views. An illustration can be easily provided. Instead of viewing the Russian industrialization as a special case of an all-European pattern varying along the gradient of economic backwardness, and instead of regarding the Russian government as merely casting into bolder relief certain intrinsic features of industrialization in conditions of backwardness, it is quite possible to turn the problem round and to view the government and its *political* interest as primarily determining the course of Russian industrialization. It is then easy to

---

[6] *The Education of Henry Adams, an Autobiography,* Boston and New York, 1918, p. 444.

order the historical material in such a way as to put the main weight of emphasis upon the role of the State. The result may be regarded as the "traditional" pattern of spurts of economic development in Russia. For the first indications of such a pattern would go back beyond the days of Peter the Great into the depth of the pre-Petersburg Russia of the sixteenth century. Every spurt appears then as a recurring complex of several unfolding sequences. At their origin stood a fundamental conflict: the political tasks of Russian states were quite "modern" in the sense that they had to match wits, policies, and power with the advanced nations of the time, while the economy that should have given sustenance to the political effort was hopelessly backward. Hence economic development became a function of diplomatic and military pressures. When the latter rose there were sudden attempts at economic modernization, designed to raise the economic potential as quickly as possible to a level more consonant with political needs. In their very nature, those violent spurts inevitably imposed heavy obligations upon the population; this in turn required extraordinary—and quite un-modern—means of coercion and repression in order to make the population accept the burdens. The government's interest in continuing the spurt might pass with the passing of military and political conditions that had provoked the spasm of economic activities. But often the spurt continued until the exhaustion of the population's ability to suffer and to endure forced a change of pace and policy upon the government, letting the country relapse once more into a protracted state of stagnation.

The differences between the two approaches are obvious. Partly, they comprise variations in the course of events, but partly also variations in the interpretation of identical events. Industrialization of Russia involved the country's westernization under any circumstances. But in the "traditional" pattern the very attempt to imitate the West with regard to modes, techniques, and levels of production required moving further away from the West in some other equally momentous respects. To the extent that the peasantry was reduced to serfdom in order to force it to bear the cost of economic progress, westernization of the economy seemed to be inseparably connected with its "orientalization." Moreover, the "traditional" pattern with its built-in period of stagnation following the spurt implied a more or less prolonged "post-spurt" period during which the economic backwardness of the country was again on the increase. Finally, the injection into the body social of "oriental" elements tended eventually to reinforce the tendency towards stagnation. If serfdom was originally introduced in order to promote economic development, it became one of the major obstacles to further progress. Thus a curious zigzag course was an integral part of the "traditional" pattern. By contrast, the "all-European" pattern of growth may indeed involve eventual decelerations, but specific obstructions of economic development are not assumed to be created in the very process of growth.

At the same time, elements which are common to both patterns call for different explanations according to the pattern chosen. As a rule, simple political interpretations in the "traditional" pattern are paralleled by more complex economic sequences in the "all-European" pattern. For in the former the government policy alone is the *explicandum*. Thus in the former the urgency of military plans, be they aggressive or defensive, serve as a sufficient reason to explain first the start and then both the speed and the extent of the effort at economic development. A smashing military defeat, suddenly revealing the weaknesses of a system is then regarded as having caused the change in government policy. On the other hand, if governmental action is viewed as merely accentuating and reinforcing causal sequences that are inherent in the economic situation of the country concerned, political explanations will prove inadequate. Then, in order to explain the *beginning* of the great spurt, i.e., the kink in the curve, one may wish to regard the situation preceding the outburst as one of tension between the potential advantages of industrialization and the actual stagnant state of affairs. In such a situation, further increase of tension—be it by a technological innovation abroad that is particularly suitable to the conditions of backwardness, or through removal of some considerable obstacle or obstacles to industrial progress by government action— may move the country across the critical line beyond which all the accumulated and as yet unutilized opportunities suddenly come to life. It is precisely because industrialization had been so slow in coming that the existing opportunities extend over wide ranges, making possible simultaneous growth along a broad front so as to permit additional advantages stemming from creation of circuits of reciprocal demand, generous mutual transmittals of external economies, and unimpeded scope for indivisibilities. These are some of the factors that make for increased tension in the pre-spurt period; they must be taken into account in interpreting the meaning of Propositions (1) and (2) as set forth [at the beginning of this paper].

Similarly, in terms of the "traditional" pattern the concentration on producers' goods is an obvious result of the nature of the government's demand. If, however, the interpretation is in terms of the "all-European" pattern, the stress on producers' goods must be related to different factors.[7] One of them is the fortuitous circumstance that in

---

[7] It is true, of course, that for the world as a whole industrialization implies an increase in the share of capital goods in total output. But for each individual country the existence of opportunities to import machinery and equipment from abroad provides, in principle, for widely disparate types of industrialization with regard to the relative rates of growth of consumers' and producers' goods.

the second half of the nineteenth century technological progress happened to be a good deal faster in the area of producers' goods than in that of consumer's goods. The latter in the century was the occurrence of the great spurt of industrialization, the more pronounced was the differential between the rates of technological innovations in the two areas. Furthermore, the more backward was an area, the greater was the role played in its industrialization by borrowed technology and the greater, therefore, the *propensity* to concentrate on those branches of output within which recent technological progress had been most pronounced. At the same time, however, in the given conditions of the nineteenth century technological progress went hand in hand with, and in fact presupposed, increases in the scale of industrial plants. Thus technological factors go far to explain the relationships summarized in Proposition (3) above; as they also serve to cast further light on Proposition (2) in which bigness of plant is related to a country's degree of backwardness. For technology, producers' goods, large scale of plant, and high rate of growth—all these are closely interrelated. In particular, it has been often observed that producers' goods allow of wider and more complex complementaries than consumers' goods. To use Professor Dahmén's term, producers' goods make for larger and more effective *development blocs*, and the more backward a country the more the success of its industrialization may depend on the existence of a hierarchy of well-adjusted development blocs.[8]

Let us return now to the industrialization of Russia at the end of the nineteenth century and try to ascertain the applicability to it of what has been called the "traditional" pattern of Russian economic development. Clearly, our instruments of perception are not fine enough to separate conjoint motivations and to gauge their relative importance and influence. Yet to look for the elements of "traditionality" in the great spurt of the 1890's is not necessarily a useless enterprise, and may yield a few additional insights into the nature of the transformation that was taking place.

No one studying the course of economic change in Russia during the period under review can fail to be impressed with the extent and intensity of the government's intervention. Military pressures, grand designs in the field of foreign policy, old fears and new resentments visibly hovered over Russian policies of industrialization. After the defeat in the Crimean War it was believed that the abolition of serfdom, construction of railroads with imported materials and equipment, and comprehensive judicial and administrative reforms would suffice to change Russia's military position in the world. The ease with which Disraeli deprived Russia of many of the fruits of her victory over the

---

[8] [See Editorial note at end of Selection 13, above.—*Ed.*]

Turks and Prince Gorchakov's helplessness at the Congress of Berlin (1878) demonstrated to Russian statesmen that further and more positive action in the economic field was called for, if the balance of power was to be redressed. True, the diplomatic defeat at Berlin was not immediately followed by rapid industrialization. It took several years to draw the necessary inferences and to overcome the traditional aversion from industrialization. But the connection between the two phenomena is undeniable.[9] Nor can it be gainsaid that the government's interest in railroad building and in industries serving railroad construction was clearly co-determined by considerations of military strategy and the desire to assure for the army and the navy more efficient and more plentiful supplies of products of domestic industries. Finally, the period of stagnation that came after 1900 showed clearly that the patience of the peasantry was exhausted; as such it was an all too familiar epilogue to a period of rapid growth. Those were unmistakable elements of the "traditional" pattern.

On the other hand, the incompleteness of the traditional pattern in the 1890's must not be overlooked. Most of all, one would look in vain, during the spurt of the 1890's, for any serious institutional device that would be "oriental" in nature and still would be designed to make the continuation of the spurt possible.[10] More important is another, although not unconnected point. To appreciate fully the nature of the great spurt of the nineties one has to look beyond it, across the years of industrial stagnation from 1900 to 1906 to the resumption of industrial activity that began in 1907 and continued until the outbreak of the first World War. In comparing the period just mentioned with the years 1885–1900, certain differences stand out clearly and can be summarized as follows:

1. The rate of industrial growth, exceeding as it did six per cent per year on an average, was somewhat lower in 1907–14 than in 1885–1900, but still quite high.

---

[9] This is not the place to supply qualification and reservations. The connection between military interests and industrialization is never a simple one. There is always the reproduction of the classic Colbert-Louvois conflict between long-term plan and concern with immediate needs. There is furthermore the traditional concern with agriculture as the source of manpower—*rusticorum mascula militum proles*—and of draft power for the army. There is, finally, the fear of the military leadership and of the social groups from which it springs that industrialization while increasing the military potential of the country will reduce the weight of the army within the state. All these were present in Russia of the period.

[10] Neither the establishment of strong representatives of the central government equipped with sweeping powers over the self-governing institutions of the peasantry (1889), nor the attempt to provide additional protection to the field-commune (1893) can possibly vitiate the statement made in the text. Those measures were neither important enough nor retrogressive enough to be so considered.

2. The Russian government, concerned with healing the wounds in the Russian budget which had been inflicted by the war with Japan and the revolution, did not resume the policy of encouragement of industrial growth to any comparable extent.

3. As a result, some of the industrial enterprises which had been established under the tutelage of the state during the earlier period found themselves standing on their own feet and continuing their development in conditions of independence, while others came under the financial protection of banks which for the first time began to supply long-term credits to industrial enterprises and in general to mold their policies upon the pattern of investment banks in other European countries.

4. With regard to bigness of plant and enterprise and to the preference for producers' goods as against consumers' goods the banks continued the policy previously pursued by the Russian government; there is furthermore no doubt that the banks in many ways encouraged the cartelization and merger movement which became very conspicuous in the years preceding the outbreak of World War I, causing the scale of enterprise to grow even faster than the scale of plant.

5. Finally, the years 1907–14, unlike those of the earlier period, were marked by some relaxation of the pressures upon the levels of consumption of the masses of the population. Certain improvements, however modest, were undeniable.

It remains only to draw the inescapable conclusion. If one regards the great spurt of 1885–1900 in isolation, the applicability of the "traditional" pattern along with the "all-European" pattern is a very defensible proposition. If, on the other hand, one regards the whole period 1885–1907 as an—articulated—unity, a somewhat broader and perhaps more interesting view tends to emerge. Then indeed it becomes possible to see the great spurt of those years as one during which the features of the "traditional" pattern appear not only in an incomplete, but also in a valedictory fashion. Most important in this respect is that the period of stagnation after 1900 was greatly foreshortened in comparison with its historical antecedents and lasted only for a few years. After 1907 none of the "traditional" features seem to be clearly discernible in the process of continuing industrial growth. In other words, while during the early part of the period "traditional" and "all-European" features compete for the attention of the student and for preference in his emphasis, in the later part of the period it is easy to interpret Russia as partaking in a general process of industrial development in conditions of diminishing economic backwardness. Another way of describing the change would be to say that while in previous spurts of economic growth quantitative westernization in terms of levels of output had been purchased at the price of institutional sacrifices, on the threshold of the new century both quantitative and institutional patterns of industrialization were integrated and became, as it were, "homodromic."

This cursory view of nearly three decades of Russian industrialization before World War I may be conveniently terminated at this point and with this conclusion. For elaborations and reservations relating specifically to Russia, the interested reader may refer to the previously cited articles. On the other hand, to the extent that what has been said about Russia is only a segment within this writer's general approach to the problems of European industrialization, a critical evaluation of that approach may be profitably presented against the background of Professor Rostow's views.

II. APPROACHES TO MODERN INDUSTRIAL HISTORY

If one looks back upon the skeleton of an approach to industrialization as summarized in the six propositions offered at the beginning of the preceding section, some of the similarities to, and the differences from, Professor Rostow's approach become apparent at once. As to the former, the most important—and from this writer's point of view, the most welcome—similarity between the two schemes is the stress on the discontinuous character of the development. The idea that there "is" a "beginning" of industrialization which can be ascertained in an operational fashion by an increase in measurable quantities of crucially significant magnitudes is common to both approaches. But at this very point of quantitative operationality the differences begin and then expand to other areas. Some of them refer to the mode of measurement; others are conceptual in nature.

As one reads through the pages of *The Stages of Economic Growth*,[11] one is surprised by the emphasis Professor Rostow places upon the rate of growth of national income and the share of investment therein. He discusses them as though reliable information on such magnitudes were readily available. While it is true that we know at least something about the *composition* of historical incomes at current prices at given points of time, it should be clearly understood that the work done so far on the rate of growth of national income in the nineteenth century is altogether inadequate—with two or three significant exceptions—

---

[11] W. W. Rostow, *The Stages of Economic Growth, A Non-Communist Manifesto*, Cambridge, 1960. [See above, Selection 3—*Ed.*]

to serve as a basis for any serious generalization about long-term changes in the rate of growth. The highly uncertain, if not adventurous, way in which in many cases the component series have been constructed is not necessarily the most critical deficiency of historical computations of national income. Worse, much worse, is the way in which data at current prices are converted into constant prices. The procedures used for this purpose—whenever not modestly concealed—would seem to be unbelievably crude. As a result, the statistical data yielded by the various deflating operations often tend to defy interpretation. It would seem that the first task facing students of long-term changes in the volume of national income should be to decide to forego the use of price indices that have been prepared for very different purposes (such as the study of price fluctuations) and to construct appropriately weighted series specifically adjusted to the requirements of the deflating procedure.[12]

As long as this is not done, one perhaps might be able to measure the rate of overall change in national income over long periods of, say, 75 or 100 years, as has been done, e.g. in the studies of François Perroux and Walther Hoffmann, but it would seem quite illusory to expect to isolate the relatively short and strategically significant periods of rapid growth. It may be noted that those deficiencies are merely technical in nature and antedate as it were the posing of the index number problem which likewise will have to be faced, once the elementary crudities and inadequacies have been removed. It is my belief, therefore, that to the extent that Professor Rostow's generalizations are derived from existing long-term national income statistics, their empirical anchorage is not as firm as it should be, the two or three exceptions to the contrary notwithstanding. This is particularly true in the case of Russia. For the time being, there are simply no reliable estimates of national income in Russia, be it at current or constant prices for the periods before 1900, and what is available for the years 1900–1913 is much too thin, much too short, and much too unreliable for any useful inference.

The deficiency of the data and their processing, however, is not the whole story. Even if complete and reliable data were available, it would still be very questionable whether national income figures can be expected to reveal the *inception* of new processes of growth. By and large, it was true in Europe that the more backward a country on the eve of its great spurt of economic development, the higher was the percentage of the population gainfully employed in agriculture and the stronger was the concentration of growth upon a relatively very small

---

[12] Cf. Alexander Gerschenkron, "Problems in Measuring Long Term Growth in Income and Wealth," *Journal of the American Statistical Association*, Vol. 52, December 1957, pp. 450–57.

area outside of agriculture. Under these conditions, a good deal of time must elapse before even a very rapid growth in the small area can affect national income as a whole and become distinguishable as a separate factor from the violent crop fluctuations which tend to dominate national income in countries where agriculture is backward and extensive in nature. Therefore, to concentrate on national income data very often may lead to errors in timing of periods of growth which in turn may lead to errors in causal imputation and general interpretation. For these reasons, the general approach to European industrial history and the special case of Russian industrial history as sketched out in [Section I] of this paper are based on quantitative evidence referring to the growth of manufacturing and mining rather than national income as a whole. Needless to add that while series on industrial output are more readily available, much more reliable, and much more meaningful than those on national income, considerable care must be exercised in using them and, in particular, whenever possible, appropriate tests must be made to gauge the quantitative significance of the index number problem involved.[13]

There is, however, a further difference between the approach as presented here and Professor Rostow's approach. It lies in what to my mind is a certain rigidity or absoluteness with which Professor Rostow treats the concept of the "beginning." It should be understood, of course, that any attempt to draw a starting line across the flow of time is of necessity conventional; that it makes sense only in terms of the criteria applied by the historian, and that it must be judged solely in terms of these criteria. The present writer found that on the whole the presence of two distinguishing features was sufficient for his purpose in recognizing a "great spurt" of industrial growth: (a) a fairly resolute kink in the curve of industrial output, indicating a sudden and substantial rise in the rate of growth, and (b) a continuation of the spurt across a period of international depression without any conspicuous diminution in the rate of growth. This is not very dissimilar from Professor Rostow's second criterion for the "take-off" which consists of a "high rate of growth of manufacturing"; for reasons mentioned above, his first criterion referring to national income is difficult to accept; while his third criterion referring to institutional changes in the course of the take-off touches on the problem of prerequisites or preconditions and must be treated separately below.[14] The trouble, however, is that situations depictable in terms of such criteria are, or at least can be, seen as recurring. Professor Rostow assures his readers that the Russian

---

[13] Cf. the forthcoming study: Alexander Gerschenkron, *Index Number Problem in Indices of Industrial Output: A Quantitative Appraisal*, RAND Corporation.
[14] W. W. Rostow, *The Stages of Economic Growth*, p. 39.

Five Year Plans "are to be understood not as a take-off, but as a drive to maturity."[15] It must be so, because he is the best judge of what his terms mean. Still it is awkward that the three criteria for the "take-off" listed by Professor Rostow without any doubt fit the Soviet case. In fact, given space, it could be shown that they fit it much better than they do the period 1885–1914. It is true, of course, that after having described a previous experience as a "take-off," one is caught in the vice of a suggestive or at least auto-suggestive simile, is forced to view the "take-off" as a unique experience, and accordingly is precluded from regarding the Soviet experience as still another "take-off." To do so would pervert the concept or at least subvert the metaphor. From the point of view of the present writer's approach as presented in the foregoing, rigidly formulated assertions of this kind are neither necessary nor, perhaps, desirable. First because what one may choose to regard as a "great spurt" need be neither the first nor the last phenomenon of the kind. From a different point of view, it may prove very useful to consider what happened in Petrine Russia of the early eighteenth century as a "great spurt" of industrial development. And one may wish to go on rediscovering "great spurts" whenever the specific situation of "tension" has reproduced itself. To speak of an "initial" great spurt can make sense only within a given spatial and historical framework. It is as important to place one's model within a clearly specified historical period as it is imperative not to overlook—still less to disguise—the arbitrary and very relative nature of our choices in this respect. Clearly, such choices tend to predetermine the results or at least the interpretation of the results of research. An explicit justification is, therefore, very much in order. World War I and the Revolution that followed it need not, but very profitably can, be seen as having created a break in the historical flow, quite apart from the fact that by the end of the twenties Russia no doubt was more backward in relation to advanced countries than it had been in 1914, thus making for new "tensions." Instead of regarding Russian economic development in the 1930's as something altogether different from the 1885–1914 experience, it might be said with some explanatory force that it was precisely the tragedy of the Russian situation that as a result of violent historical convulsions and by the will of a ruthless dictatorial government, the country was forced to act as though it had not had its "initial" great spurt of modern industrialization and in fact to revert even further back into the depth of Russian history by reproducing a much more complete replica of what has been called in the preceding "the traditional pattern" of Russian economic growth.

---

[15] *Ibid.*, p. 66.

This paper being concerned primarily with the early phases of industrialization in Russia, there is no need to go into Professor Rostow's attempt to present the whole flow of Russian economic development as conforming well to his general scheme of growth through a series of more or less distinguishable stages. But a few brief remarks may be in order because they may serve to point up the same methodological problem of choice and emphasis. Professor Rostow's contention that "in its broad shape and timing . . . there is nothing about the Russian sequence . . . that does not fall within the general pattern"[16] is interesting but can cause no surprise. In historical analysis of this kind, the basic methodological precept, of course, is that everybody finds what he is seeking. Those who seek uniformity can find uniformity and those who seek diversity can find diversity. It all depends on how broad the student chooses his shape and his timing to be. If a very broad and long view is taken, most differences tend to come out in the historical wash. This is satisfying, but the pleasure is obtained and maintained at some little cost. If one concentrates on the results of growth some of the problems faced in the process of growth inevitably disappear. To give an example, from the point of view of the approach as presented in [Section I] of this paper, one might distinguish advanced areas, areas of medium backwardness, and areas of very considerable backwardness. In terms of sources of capital supply to, entrepreneurial guidance in, and organizational independence of, industrial enterprises England's industry enjoyed the maximum of independence. In an intermediate area such as Germany a period of industrial development under the tutelage of the banks (before, say, 1900) was followed by a period in which the independence of industrial enterprises markedly increased. In an area of very considerable backwardness such as Russia, tutelage by the state was followed by tutelage by the banks while signs of industrial enterprises that were unsheltered and unguided either by the government or by the banks were just beginning to appear in the years preceding World War I. Thus in the end—of the historical period considered—everything seemed to lead to the same goal. In this sense, the case of Russia— seen *in latum et in longum*—"is" the general case. But to say this is to debar oneself from perceiving the industrialization *in the making*, that is to say, from comprehending the industrial development of Europe as a case of unity in diversity.[17] If the latter is desirable, Russia would still

---

[16] *Ibid.*

[17] It must be admitted, however, that the very broad view has the advantage of being somewhat less dependent upon accuracy of fact or figure. It is, for instance, incorrect to say that the "traditional society" in Russia was "shocked by Napoleon" (Rostow, *op. cit.*, p. 65); the contrary is true and the Napoleonic invasion and Napoleon's defeat tended to strengthen the existing regime; the period of reforms dur-

appear as subsumable under the "general case"; this is done, however, not by neglecting the peculiarities of the Russian development or just mentioning them as being "unique" or exceptional, but by seeing them as deviations that can be systematized and thus brought within the purview of a general approach; of a pattern, that is, arranged along a scale of gradations of economic backwardness. Thus, while the two approaches ostensibly deal with very similar matters, in reality the direction of the exploratory interest and, as a result, also the subject matter in each case tend to differ a good deal.

This should become particularly clear when attention is focused upon the conception of prerequisites or preconditions of industrial development. There has been a good deal of confusion with regard to that concept. Sometimes it is interpreted in an unduly strict fashion as "necessary and sufficient" conditions to be fulfilled before economic development and industrialization can begin.[18] Unfortunately, economic historians have no operational method at their disposal to determine either the "necessity" or the "sufficiency" of individual prerequisites, except by inferring from the occurrence of an event that it has been necessarily and sufficiently pre-conditioned, which is probably as correct as it is unexciting.[19] At the same time, it is also clear that much of what passes in modern discussion under the name of "preconditions" (such as the emergence of entrepreneurs, investment in fixed and working capital, or employment of hired labor) is not in the nature of *pre*conditions at all, but the very stuff economic development or industrialization is made of.[20] The refuge from the double curse of non-operational con-

---

ing the reign of Alexander I preceded rather than followed the War of 1812; nor, to give another example, is there much foundation for saying that the "Russian take-off was aided by the rise in grain prices and the export demand for grain which occurred in the mid-1890's, for it was this rise that made attractive the laying of vast railway nets . . ." (*op. cit.*, p. 66). By the time Russian grain prices started rising significantly, the peak of railroad construction was over. But Professor Rostow's scheme is so broadly constructed and so thoroughly permeated by a delightful *pressappochismo* that errors of this type cannot seriously detract from its value. Nor does the fact that while Russia is credited with having gone through its "take-off" before World War I, the Austrian-Hungarian Monarchy which in the beginning of the century by any conceivable standards was a good deal more advanced than Russia is said to have been in "an early preconditions state" (*op. cit.*, p. 118). It is possible, incidentally, that correcting the last-mentioned point might even give Professor Rostow the opportunity of connecting Austria's not entirely passive role in bringing about World War I with a specific "post-take-off" situation of choices in that country.

[18] Thus Professor Rostow asserts that "in the late eighteenth century . . . only in Britain were the necessary and sufficient conditions fulfilled for a take-off," *op. cit.*, p. 31. The twin concept reappears on p. 37.

[19] As is mentioned below, even the correctness of this way of predicting in reverse is questionable once the concept of "prerequisites" or rather the possible useful concepts of "prerequisites" are subject to closer investigation.

[20] It is therefore not surprising to see Professor Rostow at one point (*op. cit.*, p. 49) mix *pre-conditions* and *conditions* of growth very freely.

ceptualization and useless tautology seems to lie in the listing of a number of empirically obtained factors to which in the industrial history of one or several countries it appears reasonable to impute the subsequent industrial development. Such factors then are regarded as preconditions of economic growth. Abolition of an archaic framework in agricultural organization and/or increase in productivity of agriculture, or creation of an influential modern elite which is materially or ideally interested in economic development, or the provision of what is called social overhead capital in physical form and/or "original accumulation" of capital in the sense of previously established claims on current national income—all these are cases in point and, in one form or another, are very properly mentioned by Professor Rostow.[21] Beyond that, some reference to the multifarious forms in which the prerequisites are fulfilled in the individual areas is designed to take care of the "unique" factors in development. This is a procedure that is well in line with the broadly generalizing spirit of Professor Rostow's schemata, and as such unexceptionable within his framework.

The approach as presented in [Section I] of this paper, however, calls for a different procedure. It may be briefly summarized as follows: If the list of factors to which industrialization appears reasonably imputable in a very advanced country is applied to countries whose economic development has been delayed, two things will forcibly impress themselves upon the observer: (1) Some of the factors that had served as prerequisites in the advanced country either were not present at all, or at best were present to a very small extent, in the more backward countries. (2) The great spurt of industrial development occurred despite the lack of these "prerequisites." The value of posing the problem in this fashion lies in the fact that it inevitably directs research towards a further question, to wit, in what way and through what devices did backward countries substitute for the missing "prerequisites"? It may appear then that some of the alleged "prerequisites" are not needed at all in industrializations proceeding under different conditions. But the positive result of raising the question is more important. For, almost at once a series of various substitutions becomes visible which can be readily organized in a meaningful pattern along the lines of increasing economic backwardness.

Then, to give one example, the previously discussed role of the banks in Germany can be regarded as a specific substitute for the inadequate "original accumulation of capital" in that area of medium backwardness, while the budgetary policies of the Russian government under Count Witte may be seen both as a substitute for insufficient "original

---

[21] Cf. *op. cit.*, pp. 22–6.

accumulation" and as a substitute for policies of credit creation by investment banks for which conditions in Russia were not yet ripe. And, to give another, no less significant, example, the Russian government's purchases at generous prices of industrial goods from the nascent industries may be seen as a substitute for a non-existent "internal market" of Russian peasantry, while the government's high pressure taxation policies were to a considerable extent a substitute for the very inadequate increase in the productive capabilities of Russian agriculture. Perhaps nothing can emphasize more strongly the limitations of an unduly simplified and excessively generalized approach than the comparison between the respective historical *loci* of the enclosure movement in England and in Russia. It may indeed make sense to espouse the traditional view of the English eighteenth century enclosures and to regard them as assuring increases in the supply of agricultural produce and being therefore in the nature of a prerequisite for the "industrial revolution" in England. But the great spurt of Russian industrialization had long passed its peak and had entered into its second and much calmer stage when as a result of Stolypin's legislation the traditional framework of the village commune—even more archaic than the open-field system in England—began to be demolished and the road to output-raising enclosures was at length opened.[22] Thus the English "prerequisite" when translated into Russian, tended to become —*sit venia verbo*—a "postrequisite."[23]

---

[22] Even so, Professor Rostow's statement (*op. cit.*, p. 115) that "Russia . . . slowly completed its preconditions and moved, from the 1890's forward into a take-off . . ." may be operationally obscure, but it is not incorrect provided that the term precondition—to use the Reverend Doctor Folliott's apt phrase—is "taken in its utmost latitude of interpretation." Indeed, railroads had been built and the serfs emancipated; besides, we are very properly in the healthy habit of thinking that any effect has been wholly and sufficiently caused. Yet we may also wish to go beyond the obvious. Assuming that the function of a concept of this kind is to serve as a programme for research and using the term prerequisite within the meaning suggested in the text, one could argue that in a very backward country, such as Russia, where the eruptive character of the great spurt is particularly marked, one would expect industrialization to "start" *without completing* what in other and more fortunate countries went under the name of "prerequisites." Seen in this way, even the retrorse inference from the fact of subsequent growth becomes less cogent logically and less plausible historically.

[23] Cf. the forthcoming study by the present writer: "Agrarian Policies and Industrialization in Russia, 1861–1914." Delayed as the agrarian reform was, it hardly would have occurred if there had been a greater shift away from the traditional institutional framework. Stolypin, the servant of the autocracy, dared attack the traditional system of communal land tenure. If men like Miliukov or Maklakov—the outstanding representatives of Russian political liberalism—had come to power, the agrarian reform most likely would have consisted in expropriating the estates of the gentry *in favor* of village communes. In conditions of considerable backwardness, the problem of "political and social prerequisites" defies simple solutions and generalizations as much as does that of "economic prerequisites."

These are important relationships. They deepen and enrich the value of an approach which pivots around the concept of relative backwardness. A study of these relationships in the course of past industrializations creates certain sets of expectations with which one may approach the exploration of yet unstudied conditions both in the past and in the present. But the expectations may or may not justify themselves. It would be deceptive therefore to try to elevate them to the rank of predictions. In the past, much originality was displayed by backward countries in creating substitution patterns for "missing prerequisites" of industrial growth. And there is no reason to assume that the creative sources will spring forth less richly in future. Still, it makes good sense to try to explain the new as a deviation from the old on the assumption that the deviations can be ultimately organized into a still fuller whole. To do this is both the task of the economic historian and his hope. But the task will be frustrated and the hope perverted should the economic historian forget that in constructing his various approaches and in his very attempts to improve them, he also pushes towards the limits of their applicability, to the point that is, at which the approach has fulfilled its exploratory function and must recede before a different method of looking at processes of economic change. This writer at least has increasingly felt that after having spent some time and thought in exploring the growing advantages of backwardness, it may be in order to devote attention to such difficulties and obstacles to economic development as accumulate with the increase in the degree of economic backwardness. Such a shift in interest may well reveal some specific "missed opportunities" in the course of Russian economic history and may lead to a more general concept of "nodal points" at which the advantages of backwardness reach optimal levels and beyond which lies at least a limited period of declining promise and growing disability. But this should be the topic of another paper.

Selected Bibliography

▼▼

PART I. INTRODUCTION: ECONOMIC HISTORY, ECONOMIC THEORY, AND ECONOMIC GROWTH

Aitken, H. G. J., "On the Present State of Economic History," *Canadian Journal of Economics and Political Science*, XXVI, 1 (February, 1960).

Clapham, J. H., "Economic History as a Discipline," *Encyclopaedia of the Social Sciences*, V, 327–30, reprinted in F. C. Lane and Jelle C. Riemersma (eds.), *Enterprise and Secular Change* (Homewood, Ill., 1953).

Heckscher, E. F., "A Plea for Theory in Economic History," in F. C. Lane and Jelle C. Riemersma (eds.), *Enterprise and Secular Change* (Homewood, Ill., 1953).

Journal of Economic History, XVII, 4 (December, 1957), articles on "The Integration of Economic Theory and Economic History."

Sombart, Werner, "Economic Theory and Economic History," *Economic History Review*, II, 1 (January, 1929).

Texts and Readings

Agarwala, A. N., and Singh, S. P. (eds.), *The Economics of Underdevelopment: A Series of Articles and Papers* (New York, 1958).

Higgins, Benjamin, *Economic Development: Principles, Problems, and Policies* (New York, 1959).

Lewis, W. A., *The Theory of Economic Growth* (London, 1955).

Meier, Gerald M., and Baldwin, Robert E., *Economic Development: Theory, History, Policy* (New York, 1957).

Okun, Bernard, and Richardson, Richard W. (eds.), *Studies in Economic Development* (New York, 1961).

Pepelasis, Adamantios, Mears, Leon, and Adelman, Irma (eds.), *Economic Development: Analysis and Case Studies* (New York, 1961).

Special Topics

Arndt, H. W., "External Economies in Economic Growth," *Economic Record*, XXXI, 61 (November, 1955).

Baldwin, Robert E., "Patterns of Development in Newly Settled Areas," *The Manchester School*, XXIV, 2 (May, 1956).

Bauer, P. T., *Economic Analysis and Policy in Underdeveloped Countries* (Durham, N.C., 1957).

—— and Yamey, B. S., *The Economics of Under-Developed Countries* (Cambridge, Eng., 1957).

Berrill, K., "International Trade and the Rate of Economic Growth," *Economic History Review*, 2d series, XII, 3 (April, 1960).

Cairncross, A. K., "International Trade and Economic Development," *Kyklos*, XIII, 4 (October, 1960).

Capital Formation and Economic Growth (Universities-National Bureau Committee for Economic Research, Princeton, N.J., 1955).

Clemence, R. V., and Doody, F. S., *The Schumpeterian System* (Cambridge, Mass., 1950).

Domar, Evsey, *Essays in the Theory of Economic Growth* (New York, 1957).

Duesenberry, James S., *Business Cycles and Economic Growth* (New York, 1958).

——, "Some Aspects of the Theory of Economic Development," *Explorations in Entrepreneurial History*, III, 2 (December, 1950).

Dupriez, Leon H. (ed.), *Economic Progress* (Louvain, 1955).

Fellner, William, *Trends and Cycles in Economic Activity* (New York, 1956).

Galenson, Walter, and Leibenstein, Harvey, "Investment Criteria, Productivity, and Economic Development," *Quarterly Journal of Economics*, LXIX, 3 (August, 1955).

Harrod, R. F., *Towards a Dynamic Economics* (London, 1948).

Hirschman, Albert O., *The Strategy of Economic Development* (New Haven, Conn., 1958).

Hoselitz, Bert F., *Sociological Aspects of Economic Growth* (Glencoe, Ill., 1960).

—— (ed.), *The Progress of Underdeveloped Areas* (Chicago, Ill., 1952).

—— (ed.), *Theories of Economic Growth* (Glencoe, Ill., 1960).

Kahn, A. E., "Investment Criteria in Development," *Quarterly Journal of Economics,* LXV, 1 (February, 1951).

Kuznets, Simon (ed.), *Problems in the Study of Economic Growth* (National Bureau of Economic Research, New York, 1949).

Leibenstein, Harvey, *Economic Backwardness and Economic Growth* (New York, 1957).

Myrdal, Gunnar, *Economic Theory and Underdeveloped Regions* (London, 1957).

Nurkse, Ragnar, *Patterns of Trade and Development* (Stockholm, 1959).

———, *Problems of Capital Formation in Underdeveloped Countries* (Oxford, 1953).

Rostow, W. W., *The Process of Economic Growth* (New York, 1952).

Schultz, Theodore W., *The Economic Organization of Agriculture* (New York, 1953).

Schumpeter, Joseph A., *Business Cycles* (New York, 1939).

———, *The Theory of Economic Development* (Cambridge, Mass., 1934).

Singer, H. W., "The Distribution of Gains between Investing and Borrowing Countries," *American Economic Review,* XL, 2, *Papers and Proceedings* (May, 1950).

Spengler, J. J., "Economic Factors in Economic Development," *American Economic Review,* XLVII, 2, *Papers and Proceedings* (May, 1957).

Sweezy, Paul, *The Theory of Capitalist Development* (New York, 1942).

United Nations, *Measures for the Economic Development of Under-Developed Countries* (New York, 1951).

Viner, Jacob, *International Trade and Economic Development* (London, 1953).

PART II. INTERNATIONAL COMPARISONS AND THE LESSONS OF HISTORY

Aitken, H. G. J. (ed.), *The State and Economic Growth* (New York, 1959).

Ashworth, W., *A Short History of the International Economy, 1850–1950* (London, 1952).

Clark, Colin, *The Conditions of Economic Progress* (London, 1951).

Coleman, D. C., "Industrial Growth and the Industrial Revolution," *Economica,* N.S., XXIII, 89 (February, 1956).

Easterbrook, W. T., "Long-Period Comparative Study," *Journal of Economic History,* XVII, 4 (December, 1957).

Economic Development and Cultural Change, IX, 3 (April, 1961), "Essays in the Quantitative Study of Economic Growth Presented to Simon Kuznets."

Feis, H., *Europe, the World's Banker, 1870–1914* (New Haven, Conn., 1930).

Gerschenkron, Alexander, "Economic Backwardness in Historical Perspective," in Bert F. Hoselitz (ed.), *The Progress of Underdeveloped Areas* (Chicago, Ill., 1952).

———, "Reflections on the Concept of 'Prerequisites' of Modern Industrialization," *L'Industria,* 2 (1957).

———, "Social Attitudes, Entrepreneurship, and Economic Development," *Explorations in Entrepreneurial History,* VI, 1 (October, 1953).

Goldsmith, Raymond W., "Financial Structure and Economic Growth in Advanced Countries," in Universities-National Bureau Committee for Economic Research, *Capital Formation and Economic Growth* (Princeton, N.J., 1955).

Habakkuk, H. J., "The Historical Experience on the Basic Conditions of Economic Progress," in Leon H. Dupriez (ed.), *Economic Progress* (Louvain, 1955).

Hilgerdt, F., *Industrialization and Foreign Trade* (League of Nations, Geneva, 1945).

Hoffman, W., *The Growth of Industrial Economies* (Manchester, 1958).

Hoselitz, Bert F., *Sociological Aspects of Economic Growth* (Glencoe, Ill., 1960).

International Economic Association, Conference on the Economics of the Take-Off into Sustained Growth, 1960. Papers to be published late in 1962.

Journal of Economic History, Supplement VII, *Tasks of Economic History* (1947), articles on "Economic Growth."

———, Supplement X, *The Tasks of Economic History* (1950), "The Role of Government and Business Enterprise in the Promotion of Economic Development."

Kuznets, Simon, "International Differences in Capital Formation and Financing," in Universities-National Bureau Committee for Economic Research, *Capital Formation and Economic Growth* (Princeton, N.J., 1955).

———, "International Differences in Income Levels," reprinted in *Economic Change* (New York, 1953) and in Bernard Okun and Richard W. Richardson (eds.), *Studies in Economic Development* (New York, 1961).

———, "Notes on the Take-Off," in volume on the economics of the take-off, to be published by the International Economic Association in 1962.

——, "Quantitative Aspects of the Economic Growth of Nations," in various issues of *Economic Development and Cultural Change:*

"Levels and Variability of Rates of Growth," V, 1 (October, 1956).
"Industrial Distribution of National Product and Labor Force," V, 4, Supplement (July, 1957).
"Industrial Distribution of National Income and Labor Force by States, United States, 1919–21 to 1955," VI, 4, Part II (July, 1958).
"Distribution of National Income by Factor Shares," VII, 3, Part II (April, 1959).
"Capital Formation Proportions: International Comparisons for Recent Years," VIII, 4, Part II (July, 1960).
"Long-Term Trends in Capital Formation Proportions," IX, 4, Part II (July, 1960).
"The Share and Structure of Consumption," X, 2, Part II (January, 1962).

——, *Six Lectures on Economic Growth* (Glencoe, Ill., 1959).
Lewis, W. Arthur, "World Production, Prices and Trade, 1870–1960," *The Manchester School*, XX, 2 (May, 1952).
—— and O'Leary, P. J., "Secular Swings in Production and Trade, 1870–1913," *The Manchester School*, XXIII, 2 (May, 1955).
North, D. C., "A Note on Professor Rostow's 'Take-Off' into Self-Sustained Economic Growth," *The Manchester School*, XXVI, 1 (January, 1958).
Nurkse, Ragnar, "International Investment To-Day in the Light of Nineteenth-Century Experience," *Economic Journal*, LXIV, 256 (December, 1954).
——, *Patterns of Trade and Development* (Stockholm, 1959).
Patel, Surendra J., "Rates of Industrial Growth in the Last Century, 1860–1958," *Economic Development and Cultural Change*, IX, 3 (April, 1961).
Phelps Brown, E. H., and Hopkins, S. V., "The Course of Wage Rates in Five Countries," *Oxford Economic Papers*, N.S., II, 2 (June, 1950).
Pollard, S., "Investment, Consumption and the Industrial Revolution," *Economic History Review*, 2d series, XI, 2 (December, 1958).
Rostow, W. W., *The Stages of Economic Growth* (Cambridge, Eng., 1959).
——, "The 'Take-Off' into Self-Sustained Growth," *Economic Journal*, LXVI, 261 (March, 1956).
——, "Trends in the Allocation of Resources in Secular Growth," in Leon H. Dupriez (ed.), *Economic Progress* (Louvain, 1955).

Schumpeter, Joseph A., *Business Cycles*, 2 vols. (New York, 1939).

Thomas, Brinley, *Migration and Economic Growth* (Cambridge, Eng., 1954).

Woytinsky, W. S., and Woytinsky, E. S., *World Population and Production* (New York, 1953).

Youngson, A. J., *The Possibilities of Economic Progress* (Cambridge, Eng., 1959).

PART III. THE PIONEER OF ECONOMIC GROWTH: GREAT BRITAIN

The Industrial Revolution

Ashton, T. S., *An Economic History of England: The Eighteenth Century* (London, 1955).

———, *Iron and Steel in the Industrial Revolution* (Manchester, 1924).

———, *The Industrial Revolution* (London, 1948).

———, "The Standard of Life of the Workers in England, 1790–1830," *Journal of Economic History*, Supplement IX, *Tasks of Economic History* (1949).

Berrill, K., "International Trade and the Rate of Economic Growth," *Economic History Review*, 2d series, XII, 3 (April, 1960).

Chambers, J. D., "Enclosure and Labour Supply in the Industrial Revolution," *Economic History Review*, 2d series, V, 3 (1953).

Clark, G. N., *The Idea of the Industrial Revolution* (Glasgow, 1953).

Coleman, D. C., "Industrial Growth and the Industrial Revolution," *Economica*, N.S., XXIII, 89 (1956).

Deane, P., "The Industrial Revolution and Economic Growth," *Economic Development and Cultural Change* (1957).

——— and Cole, W. A., *British Economic Growth, 1688–1959* (Cambridge, Eng., 1962), Chapters II and III.

——— and Habakkuk, H. J., "The Take-Off in Britain," to be published by the International Economic Association in a volume on the economics of the take-off, 1962.

George, M. D., *England in Transition* (London, 1931).

Griffiths, G. Talbot, *Population Problems of the Age of Malthus* (Cambridge, Eng., 1926).

Habakkuk, H. J., "The Economic History of Modern Britain" [population], *Journal of Economic History*, XVIII, 4 (December, 1958).

Hammond, J. L., "The Industrial Revolution and Discontent," *Economic History Review*, II, 2 (January, 1930).

Hartwell, R. M., "Interpretations of the Industrial Revolution in England," *Journal of Economic History*, XIX, 2 (June, 1959).

Hayek, F. A. von, (ed.), *Capitalism and the Historians* (Chicago, Ill., 1954).

Hobsbawm, E. J., "The British Standard of Living, 1790–1850," *Economic History Review*, 2d series, X, 1 (August, 1957).

Krause, J. T., "Some Neglected Factors in the English Industrial Revolution" [population], *Economic History Review*, 2d series, XIX, 4 (December, 1959).

Marshall, T. H., "The Population Problem During the Industrial Revolution," *Economic History*, Supplement to *Economic Journal* (1929).

Pressnell, L. S., *Country Banking in the Industrial Revolution* (Oxford, 1956).

—— (ed.), *Studies in the Industrial Revolution* (London, 1960).

Taylor, A. J., "Progress and Poverty in Britain, 1780–1850: A Reappraisal," *History*, XLV (1960), 16–31.

Woodruff, William, "Capitalism and the Historians," *Journal of Economic History*, XVI, 1 (March, 1956).

Youngson, A. J., *The Possibilities of Economic Progress* (Cambridge, Eng., 1959), chap. VIII on "The Acceleration of Economic Progress in Great Britain, 1750–1800."

Development and Fluctuations in the Nineteenth Century

Cairncross, A. K., *Home and Foreign Investment, 1870–1913* (Cambridge, Eng., 1953).

Chambers, J. D., *The Workshop of the World: British Economic History from 1820 to 1880* (Oxford, 1961).

Clapham, J. H., *An Economic History of Modern Britain*, 3 vols. (Cambridge, Eng., 1930, 1932, 1938).

Coppock, D. J., "The Causes of the Great Depression, 1873–96," *The Manchester School*, XXIX, 3 (September, 1961).

——, "The Climacteric of the 1890's: A Critical Note," *The Manchester School*, XXIV, 1 (January, 1956).

Court, W. H. B., *A Concise Economic History of Britain from 1750 to Recent Times* (Cambridge, Eng., 1954).

Deane, P., "Contemporary Estimates of National Income in the First Half of the Nineteenth Century," *Economic History Review*, 2d series, VIII, 3 (April, 1956).

Deane, P., and Cole, W. A., *British Economic Growth, 1688–1959* (Cambridge, Eng., 1962).

Feinstein, C. H., "Income and Investment in the United Kingdom, 1856–1914," *Economic Journal*, LXXI, 282 (June, 1961).

Gayer, A. D., Rostow, W. W., and Schwartz, A. J., *The Growth and*

Fluctuations of the British Economy, 1790–1850, 2 vols. (Oxford, 1952).

Hoffman, W., *British Industry, 1700–1950* (Oxford, 1955).

Hughes, J. R. T., *Fluctuations in Trade, Industry and Finance: A Study of British Economic Development, 1850–1860* (Oxford, 1960).

Jeffreys, J. B. and Walters, D., "National Income and Expenditure of the United Kingdom, 1870–1952," in Simon Kuznets (ed.), *Income and Wealth, Series V* (Cambridge, Eng., 1955).

Lenfant, J. H., "Great Britain's Capital Formation, 1865–1914," *Economica*, N.S., XVIII, 70 (May, 1951).

Matthews, R. C. O., *A Study in Trade Cycle History: Economic Fluctuations in Great Britain, 1833–1842* (Cambridge, Eng., 1954).

Musson, A. E., "The Great Depression in Britain, 1873–1896," *Journal of Economic History*, XIX, 2 (June, 1959).

Phelps Brown, E. H. and Weber, B., "Accumulation, Productivity and Distribution in the British Economy, 1870–1939," *Economic Journal*, LXIII, 250 (June, 1953).

Phelps Brown, E. H. and Handfield-Jones, S. J., "The Climacteric of the 1890's: A Study in the Expanding Economy," *Oxford Economic Papers*, IV (October, 1952).

Rostow, W. W., *The British Economy of the Nineteenth Century* (Oxford, 1948).

Thomas, Brinley, *Migration and Economic Growth* (Cambridge, Eng., 1954).

Ward-Perkins, C. N., "The Commercial Crisis of 1847," *Oxford Economic Papers*, II, 1 (January, 1950).

Britain and the International Economy

Cairncross, A. K., *Home and Foreign Investment, 1870–1913* (Cambridge, Eng., 1953).

Habakkuk, H. J., "Free Trade and Commercial Expansion," in *Cambridge History of the British Empire*, II (Cambridge, Eng., 1940).

Henderson, W. O., *Britain and Industrial Europe* (Liverpool, Eng., 1954).

Imlah, A. H., *The Economic Element in the Pax Britannica* (Cambridge, Mass., 1958).

Jenks, L. H., "British Experience with Foreign Investments," *Journal of Economic History*, Supplement IV, *Tasks of Economic History* (1944).

———, *The Migration of British Capital to 1875* (New York, 1938).

Kahn, A. E., *Great Britain and the World Economy* (New York, 1946).

Saul, S. B., *Studies in British Overseas Trade, 1870–1914* (Liverpool, Eng., 1960).

Schlote, W., *British Overseas Trade from 1700 to the 1930's* (Oxford, 1952).

Thomas, Brinley, *Migration and Economic Growth* (Cambridge, Eng., 1954).

PART IV. THE TRANSFORMATION OF A CONTINENT: THE UNITED STATES

Abramovitz, Moses, "Long Swings in United States Growth," *38th Annual Report* of the National Bureau of Economic Research (New York, 1958).

——, "Resource and Output Trends in the United States Since 1870," *American Economic Review*, XLVI, 2, *Papers and Proceedings* (May, 1956).

——, Statement (on long swings in economic growth) before the Joint Economic Committee, 86th Congress, 1st Session, *Employment, Growth and Price Levels*, Part 2: "Historical and Comparative Rates of Production, Productivity, and Prices" (Washington, D.C., 1959).

——, "The Nature and Significance of Kuznets Cycles," *Economic Development and Cultural Change*, IX, 3 (April, 1961).

Burns, Arthur F., *Production Trends in the United States Since 1870* (New York, 1934).

Cochran, Thomas C., "The Entrepreneur in American Capital Formation," in Universities-National Bureau Committee for Economic Research, *Capital Formation and Economic Growth* (Princeton, N.J., 1955).

Conrad, Alfred H., "Income Growth and Structural Change," in Seymour E. Harris (ed.), *American Economic History* (New York, 1961).

Creamer, Daniel, Dobrovolsky, Sergei and Borenstein, Israel, *Capital in Manufacturing and Mining* (Princeton, N.J., 1960).

Davis, Lance, Hughes, Jonathan R. T., and McDougall, Duncan M., *American Economic History, The Development of a National Economy* (Homewood, Ill., 1961).

Department of Commerce, *Historical Statistics of the United States, Colonial Times to 1957* (Washington, D.C., 1960).

Easterlin, Richard A., "Interregional Differences in Per Capita Income, Population, and Total Income, 1840–1950," National Bureau of Economic Research, *Trends in the American Economy in the Nineteenth Century* (Princeton, N.J., 1960).

Gallman, Robert E., "Commodity Output, 1839–1899," National Bureau of Economic Research, *Trends in the American Economy in the Nineteenth Century* (Princeton, N.J., 1960).

Goldsmith, Raymond W., Statement (on long-run economic growth) before the Joint Economic Committee, 86th Congress, 1st Session, *Employment, Growth and Price Levels*, Part 2: "Historical and Comparative Rates of Production, Productivity, and Prices," (Washington, D.C., 1959).

———, "The Growth of Reproducible Wealth of the U.S.A. from 1805 to 1950," in Simon Kuznets (ed.), *Income and Wealth, Series II* (Cambridge, Eng., 1952).

Goodrich, Carter, *Government Promotion of American Canals and Railroads, 1800–1890* (New York, 1960).

Harris, Seymour E. (ed.), *American Economic History* (New York, 1961).

Jenks, L. H., "Railroads as an Economic Force in American Development," *Journal of Economic History*, IV, 1 (May, 1944).

Journal of Economic History, XVI, 4 (December, 1956), articles on "The American West as an Underdeveloped Region."

Kuznets, Simon, *Capital in the American Economy: Its Formation and Financing* (Princeton, N.J., 1961).

———, "Long-Term Changes in the National Income of the United States of America Since 1870," in Simon Kuznets (ed.), *Income and Wealth, Series II* (Cambridge, Eng., 1952).

———, *National Product Since 1869* (New York, 1946).

Letwin, William (ed.), *A Documentary History of American Economic Policy Since 1789* (Garden City, N.Y., 1961).

North, Douglass C., "A Note on Professor Rostow's 'Take-Off' Into Self-Sustained Economic Growth," *The Manchester School*, XXVI, 1 (January, 1958).

———, "International Capital Flows and the Development of the American West," *Journal of Economic History*, XVI, 4 (December, 1956).

———, *The Economic Growth of the United States, 1790–1860* (Englewood Cliffs, N.J., 1961).

———, "The United States Balance of Payments, 1790–1860," in National Bureau of Economic Research, *Trends in the American Economy in the Nineteenth Century* (Princeton, N.J., 1960).

Parker, William N. and Whartenby, Franklee, "The Growth of Output Before 1840," in National Bureau of Economic Research, *Trends in the American Economy in the Nineteenth Century* (Princeton, N.J., 1960).

Sawyer, John A., "The Social Basis of the American System of Manufacturing," *Journal of Economic History*, XIV, 4 (December, 1954).

Taylor, George R., *The Transportation Revolution, 1815–1860* (New York, 1951).

Thistlethwaite, Frank, *The Great Experiment* (Cambridge, Eng., 1955).

Thomas, Brinley, *Migration and Economic Growth* (Cambridge, Eng., 1954).

Ulmer, Melville J., *Capital in Transportation, Communications and Public Utilities* (Princeton, N.J., 1960).

Weber, B. and Handfield-Jones, S. J., "Variations in the Rate of Economic Growth in the U.S.A., 1869–1939," *Oxford Economic Papers*, VI, 2 (June, 1954).

Williamson, Harold F. (ed.), *The Growth of the American Economy* (Englewood Cliffs, N.J., 1951).

Williamson, J. G., "International Trade and United States Economic Development, 1827–1843," *Journal of Economic History*, XXI, 3 (September, 1961).

PART V. INCOMPLETE DEVELOPMENT: FRANCE AND ITALY

Cameron, Rondo E., "Economic Growth and Stagnation in France, 1815–1914," *Journal of Modern History*, XXX, 1 (March, 1958).

———, *France and the Economic Development of Europe, 1800–1914* (Princeton, N.J., 1961).

Clapham, J. H., *The Economic Development of France and Germany, 1815–1914* (Cambridge, Eng., 1936).

Clough, S. B., *France: A History of National Economics, 1789–1939* (New York, 1939).

———, "Retardative Factors in French Economic Development in the Nineteenth and Twentieth Centuries," *Journal of Economic History*, Supplement IX (December, 1949).

——— and Livi, Carlo, "Economic Growth in Italy: An Analysis of Uneven Development of North and South," *Journal of Economic History*, XVI, 3 (September, 1956).

Dunham, A. L., *The Industrial Revolution in France, 1815–1848* (New York, 1955).

Eckaus, Richard S., "The North-South Differential in Italian Economic Development," *Journal of Economic History*, XXI, 3 (September, 1961).

Gerschenkron, Alexander, "Notes on the Rate of Industrial Growth in Italy, 1881–1913," *Journal of Economic History*, XV, 4 (December, 1955).

———, "Social Attitudes, Entrepreneurship, and Economic Development," *Explorations in Entrepreneurial History*, VI, 1 (October,

1953). Also see responses by David S. Landes and John E. Sawyer in subsequent numbers.

Henderson, W. O., *The Industrial Revolution on the Continent: Germany, France, Russia, 1800–1914* (London, 1961).

Hoselitz, Bert F., "Entrepreneurship and Capital Formation in France and Britain Since 1700," in Universities-National Bureau Committee on Economic Research, *Capital Formation and Economic Growth* (Princeton, N.J., 1955).

Landes, David S., "French Business and the Businessman," in *Modern France* (Princeton, N.J., 1951).

———, "French Entrepreneurship and Industrial Growth in the Nineteenth Century," *Journal of Economic History*, IX, 1 (May, 1949).

Marczewski, Jan, "Some Aspects of the Economic Growth of France, 1660–1958," *Economic Development and Cultural Change*, IX, 3 (April, 1961).

Parker, William N., "National States and National Development: A Comparison of Elements in French and German Development in the Late Nineteenth Century," in Hugh G. J. Aitken (ed.), *The State and Economic Growth* (New York, 1959).

Perroux, François, "Prise de veus sur la crossance de l'économie Française, 1780–1950," in Simon Kuznets (ed.), *Income and Wealth*, Series V (Cambridge, Eng., 1955).

Vochting, F., "Industrialization or Pre-Industrialization of Southern Italy," Banca Nazionale di Lavoro, *Quarterly Review*, 21 (1952).

PART VI. TWO LATECOMERS: JAPAN AND RUSSIA

Japan

Allen, G. C., *A Short Economic History of Modern Japan, 1867–1937* (London, 1946).

——— and Donnithorne, A. G., *Western Enterprise in Far Eastern Economic Development: China and Japan* (London, 1954).

Economic Development and Cultural Change, IX, 1, Part II (October, 1960), articles on "City and Village in Japan."

Hoselitz, Bert F., "Population Pressure, Industrialization and Social Mobility," *Population Studies*, XI, 2 (November, 1957).

Johnston, B. F., "Agricultural Productivity and Economic Development in Japan," *Journal of Political Economy*, LIX, 6 (December, 1951).

Kuznets, Simon, Moore, W. E., and Spengler, J. J. (eds.), *Economic Growth: Brazil, India, Japan* (Durham, N.C., 1955).

Levy, M. J., "Contrasting Factors in the Modernization of China and Japan," *Economic Development and Cultural Change* (1953).

Lockwood, William W., *The Economic Development of Japan: Growth and Structural Change, 1868–1938* (Princeton, N.J., 1954).

Ohkawa, K. et al., *The Growth Rate of the Japanese Economy Since 1878* (Tokyo, 1957).

Ohkawa, K. and Rosovsky, Henry, "The Role of Agriculture in Modern Japanese Economic Development," *Economic Development and Cultural Change*, IX, 1, Part II (October, 1960).

Ranis, Gustav, "Factor Proportions in Japanese Economic Development," *American Economic Review*, XLVII, 5 (September, 1957).

————, "The Financing of Japanese Economic Development," *Economic History Review*, 2d series, XI, 3 (April, 1959).

Rosovsky, Henry, *Capital Formation in Japan, 1868–1940* (Glencoe, Ill., 1961).

———— and Ohkawa, K., "The Indigenous Components in the Modern Japanese Economy," *Economic Development and Cultural Change*, IX, 3 (April, 1961).

Smith, Thomas C., "Landlords and Rural Capitalists in the Modernization of Japan," *Journal of Economic History*, XVI, 2 (June, 1956).

————, *Political Change and Industrial Development in Japan: Government Enterprise, 1868–1880* (Stanford, Calif., 1955).

————, *The Agrarian Origins of Modern Japan* (Stanford, Calif., 1959).

Tsuru, S., *Essays on the Japanese Economy* (Tokyo, 1958).

Russia

Baykov, Alexander, *The Development of the Soviet Economic System* (Cambridge, Eng., 1947).

————, "The Economic Development of Russia," *Economic History Review*, 2d series, VII, 2 (December, 1954).

Bergson, Abram, *The Real National Income of Soviet Russia Since 1928* (Cambridge, Mass., 1961).

———— (ed.), *Soviet Economic Growth* (Cambridge, Mass.,1953).

Carson, Robert, "Russia, 1890–1939," in Hugh G. J. Aitken (ed.), *The State and Economic Growth* (New York, 1939).

Dobb, M., *Soviet Economic Development* (London, 1948).

Gerschenkron, Alexander, "The Early Phases of Industrialization in Russia," to be published by the International Economic Association in a collection of articles on the economics of the take-off into sustained growth, 1962.

————, "The Problem of Economic Development in Russian Intellectual History of the Nineteenth Century," in E. Simmons (ed.), *Continuity and Change in Russian and Soviet Thought* (Cambridge, Mass., 1955).

————, "The Rate of Industrial Growth in Russia Since 1885," *Journal of Economic History*, Supplement VII (1947).

Goldsmith, Raymond A., "The Economic Growth of Tsarist Russia," *Economic Development and Cultural Change*, IX, 3 (April, 1961).

Henderson, W. O., *The Industrial Revolution on the Continent: Germany, France, Russia, 1800–1914* (London, 1961).

Hodgman, Donald, *Soviet Industrial Production, 1928–51* (Cambridge, Mass., 1954).

Jasny, Naum, *Soviet Industrialization, 1928–1952* (Chicago, Ill., 1961).

Lyashchenko, P. I., *A History of the National Economy of Russia to the 1917 Revolution* (New York, 1949).

Nutter, G. Warren, *The Growth of Industrial Production in the Soviet Union* (Princeton, N. J., 1962).

————, "Some Observations on Soviet Industrial Growth," *American Economic Review*, LXIX, 2, *Papers and Proceedings* (May, 1957).

Rimlinger, Gaston V., "The Expansion of the Labor Market in Capitalist Russia: 1861–1917," *Journal of Economic History*, XXI, 2 (June, 1961).

Rosovsky, Henry, "The Serf Entrepreneur in Russia," *Explorations in Entrepreneurial History*, VI, 4 (May, 1954).

Seton, F., "Soviet Progress in Western Perspective," *Soviet Studies*, XII, 2 (October, 1960).

Von Laue, Theodore H., "The Witte System in Russia," *Journal of Economic History*, XIII, 4 (Fall, 1953).

Index

A NOTE ON THE TYPE

This book is set in Electra, a Linotype face designed by W. A. Dwiggins. This face cannot be classified as either modern or old-style. It is not based on any historical model, nor does it echo any particular period or style. It avoids the extreme contrasts between thick and thin elements that mark most modern faces, and attempts to give a feeling of fluidity, power, and speed.